Sex Integration in Sport and Physical Culture

Scholars working in the academic field of sport studies have long debated the relationship between sport and gender. Modern sport forms, along with many related activities, have been shown to have historically supported ideals of male superiority, by largely excluding women and/or celebrating only men's athletic achievements. While the growth of women's sport throughout the twentieth and twenty-first centuries has extinguished the notion of female frailty, revealing that women can embody athletic qualities previously thought exclusive to men, the continuation of sex segregation in many settings has left something of a discursive 'back door' through which ideals of male athletic superiority can escape unscathed, retaining their influence over wider cultural belief systems. However, sex-integrated sport potentially offers a radical departure from such beliefs, as it challenges us to reject assumptions of male superiority, entertaining very different visions of sex difference and gender relations to those typically constructed through traditional models of physical culture. This comprehensive collection offers a diverse range of international case studies that reaffirm the contemporary relevance of sex integration debates, and also articulate the possibility of sport acting as a legitimate space for political struggle, resistance and change. This book was originally published as a special issue of *Sport in Society*.

Alex Channon is a Senior Lecturer in Physical Education and Sport Studies at the University of Brighton, Eastbourne, UK.

Katherine Dashper is a Senior Lecturer at Leeds Beckett University, Leeds, UK.

Thomas Fletcher is a Senior Lecturer at Leeds Beckett University, Leeds, UK.

Robert J. Lake is an Instructor in Sport Sociology at Douglas College, New Westminster, Canada.

Sport in the Global Society – Contemporary Perspectives

Series Editor: Boria Majumdar, *University of Central Lancashire, Preston, England, and Monash University, Melbourne, Australia*

The social, cultural (including media) and political study of sport is an expanding area of scholarship and related research. While this area has been well served by the *Sport in the Global Society* series, the surge in quality scholarship over the last few years has necessitated the creation of *Sport in the Global Society: Contemporary Perspectives*. The series will publish the work of leading scholars in fields as diverse as sociology, cultural studies, media studies, gender studies, cultural geography and history, political science and political economy. If the social and cultural study of sport is to receive the scholarly attention and readership it warrants, a cross-disciplinary series dedicated to taking sport beyond the narrow confines of physical education and sport science academic domains is necessary. *Sport in the Global Society: Contemporary Perspectives* will answer this need.

Gender in Physical Culture
Crossing boundaries – reconstituting cultures
Edited by Natalie Barker-Ruchti, Karin Grahn and Eva-Carin Lindgren

DIY Football
Edited by David Kennedy and Peter Kennedy

A Social and Political History of Everton and Liverpool Football Clubs
The split, 1878–1914
David Kennedy

Football Fandom in Italy and Beyond
Community through media and performance
Matthew Guschwan

Numbers and Narratives
Sport, history and economics
Wray Vamplew

Sex Integration in Sport and Physical Culture
Promises and pitfalls
Edited by Alex Channon, Katherine Dashper, Thomas Fletcher and Robert Lake

A Social and Cultural History of Sport in Ireland
Edited by David Hassan and Richard McElligott

Football and Health Improvement: an Emergent Field
Edited by Daniel Parnell and Andy Pringle

A Social and Cultural History of Sport in Ireland
Edited by Richard McElligatt and David Hassam

The Containment of Soccer in Australia
Fencing off the world game
Edited by Christopher J. Hallinan and John E. Hughson

Sex Integration in Sport and Physical Culture

Promises and Pitfalls

Edited by
Alex Channon, Katherine Dashper,
Thomas Fletcher and Robert J. Lake

Routledge
Taylor & Francis Group

First published 2017
by Routledge
2 Park Square, Milton Park, Abingdon, Oxon, OX14 4RN, UK

and by Routledge
711 Third Avenue, New York, NY 10017, USA

Routledge is an imprint of the Taylor & Francis Group, an informa business

British Library Cataloguing in Publication Data
A catalogue record for this book is available from the British Library

ISBN 13: 978-0-415-78381-1

Typeset in MinionPro
by diacriTech, Chennai

Publisher's Note
The publisher accepts responsibility for any inconsistencies that may have arisen during the conversion of this book from journal articles to book chapters, namely the possible inclusion of journal terminology.

Disclaimer
Every effort has been made to contact copyright holders for their permission to reprint material in this book. The publishers would be grateful to hear from any copyright holder who is not here acknowledged and will undertake to rectify any errors or omissions in future editions of this book.

Contents

Citation Information   xi
Notes on Contributors   xv

1   Introduction: The promises and pitfalls of sex integration in sport and
    physical culture   1
    Alex Channon, Katherine Dashper, Thomas Fletcher and Robert J. Lake

PART 1
Theorizing sex integration in sport and physical culture

2   Off the beaten path: should women compete against men?   15
    Pam R. Sailors

3   'Preserving la différence': the elusiveness of sex-segregated sport   28
    Lindsay Parks Pieper

PART 2
Integration in PE and youth sport

4   Homophobia and heterosexism: Spanish physical education
    teachers' perceptions   46
    *Joaquín Piedra, Gonzalo Ramírez-Macías, Francis Ries, Augusto Rembrandt
    Rodríguez-Sánchez and Catherine Phipps*

5   Sporting equality and gender neutrality in korfball   61
    Laura Gubby and Ian Wellard

6   Negotiations of gender discourse: experiences of co-education in a Swedish
    sports initiative for children   76
    Karin Grahn and Viveka Berggren Torell

7   Transcending gender hierarchies? Young people and floorball in Swedish
    school sport   92
    Marie Larneby

CONTENTS

PART 3
Integrated non-contact sports

8 'Guys don't whale away at the women': etiquette and gender relations in
  contemporary mixed-doubles tennis   104
  Robert J. Lake

9 Doing femininities and masculinities in a 'feminized' sporting arena:
  the case of mixed-sex cheerleading   124
  Esther Priyadharshini and Amy Pressland

10 The lived experience of sex-integrated sport and the construction of athlete
   identity within the Olympic and Paralympic equestrian disciplines   139
   Donna de Haan, Popi Sotiriadou and Ian Henry

11 Mixed-sex in sport for development: a pragmatic and symbolic device.
   The case of touch rugby for forced migrants in Rome   157
   Micol Pizzolati and Davide Sterchele

12 "We have to establish our territory": how women surfers 'carve out'
   gendered spaces within surfing   179
   Cassie Comley

PART 4
Integrated contact sports

13 Challenging the gender binary: the fictive and real world of quidditch   189
   Jeffrey O. Segrave

14 Challenging the gender binary? Male basketball practice players' views of
   female athletes and women's sports   206
   Janet S. Fink, Nicole M. LaVoi and Kristine E. Newhall

15 'They kick you because they are not able to kick the ball': normative
   conceptions of sex difference and the politics of exclusion in
   mixed-sex football   222
   Aleksandra Winiarska, Lucy Jackson, Lucy Mayblin and Gill Valentine

16 Men in a 'women only' sport? Contesting gender relations and sex integration
   in roller derby   239
   Adele Pavlidis and James Connor

17 Playing like a girl? The negotiation of gender and sexual identity among
   female ice hockey athletes on male teams   253
   Danielle DiCarlo

CONTENTS

18 Friendships worth fighting for: bonds between women and men karate
practitioners as sites for deconstructing gender inequality   264
Chloe Maclean

Index   275

Citation Information

The chapters in this book were originally published in *Sport in Society Cultures, Commerce, Media, Politics*, volume 19, issue 8–9 (October–November 2016). When citing this material, please use the original page numbering for each article, as follows:

Chapter 1
Introduction: The promises and pitfalls of sex integration in sport and physical culture
Alex Channon, Katherine Dashper, Thomas Fletcher and Robert J. Lake
Sport in Society Cultures, Commerce, Media, Politics, volume 19, issue 8–9 (October–November 2016) pp. 1111–1124

Chapter 2
Off the beaten path: should women compete against men?
Pam R. Sailors
Sport in Society Cultures, Commerce, Media, Politics, volume 19, issue 8–9 (October–November 2016) pp. 1125–1137

Chapter 3
'Preserving la difference': the elusiveness of sex-segregated sport
Lindsay Parks Pieper
Sport in Society Cultures, Commerce, Media, Politics, volume 19, issue 8–9 (October–November 2016) pp. 1138–1155

Chapter 4
Homophobia and heterosexism: Spanish physical education teachers' perceptions
Joaquín Piedra, Gonzalo Ramírez-Macías, Francis Ries, Augusto Rembrandt Rodríguez-Sánchez and Catherine Phipps
Sport in Society Cultures, Commerce, Media, Politics, volume 19, issue 8–9 (October–November 2016) pp. 1156–1170

Chapter 5
Sporting equality and gender neutrality in korfball
Laura Gubby and Ian Wellard
Sport in Society Cultures, Commerce, Media, Politics, volume 19, issue 8–9 (October–November 2016) pp. 1171–1185

Chapter 6

Negotiations of gender discourse: experiences of co-education in a Swedish sports initiative for children
Karin Grahn and Viveka Berggren Torell
Sport in Society Cultures, Commerce, Media, Politics, volume 19, issue 8–9 (October–November 2016) pp. 1186–1201

Chapter 7

Transcending gender hierarchies? Young people and floorball in Swedish school sport
Marie Larneby
Sport in Society Cultures, Commerce, Media, Politics, volume 19, issue 8–9 (October–November 2016) pp. 1202–1213

Chapter 8

'Guys don't whale away at the women': etiquette and gender relations in contemporary mixed-doubles tennis
Robert J. Lake
Sport in Society Cultures, Commerce, Media, Politics, volume 19, issue 8–9 (October–November 2016) pp. 1214–1233

Chapter 9

Doing femininities and masculinities in a 'feminized' sporting arena: the case of mixed-sex cheerleading
Esther Priyadharshini and Amy Pressland
Sport in Society Cultures, Commerce, Media, Politics, volume 19, issue 8–9 (October–November 2016) pp. 1234–1248

Chapter 10

The lived experience of sex-integrated sport and the construction of athlete identity within the Olympic and Paralympic equestrian disciplines
Donna de Haan, Popi Sotiriadou and Ian Henry
Sport in Society Cultures, Commerce, Media, Politics, volume 19, issue 8–9 (October–November 2016) pp. 1249–1266

Chapter 11

Mixed-sex in sport for development: a pragmatic and symbolic device. The case of touch rugby for forced migrants in Rome
Micol Pizzolati and Davide Sterchele
Sport in Society Cultures, Commerce, Media, Politics, volume 19, issue 8–9 (October–November 2016) pp. 1267–1288

Chapter 12

"We have to establish our territory": how women surfers 'carve out' gendered spaces within surfing
Cassie Comley

Sport in Society Cultures, Commerce, Media, Politics, volume 19, issue 8–9 (October–November 2016) pp. 1289–1298

Chapter 13
Challenging the gender binary: the fictive and real world of quidditch
Jeffrey O. Segrave
Sport in Society Cultures, Commerce, Media, Politics, volume 19, issue 8–9 (October–November 2016) pp. 1299–1315

Chapter 14
Challenging the gender binary? Male basketball practice players' views of female athletes and women's sports
Janet S. Fink, Nicole M. LaVoi and Kristine E. Newhall
Sport in Society Cultures, Commerce, Media, Politics, volume 19, issue 8–9 (October–November 2016) pp. 1316–1331

Chapter 15
'They kick you because they are not able to kick the ball': normative conceptions of sex difference and the politics of exclusion in mixed-sex football
Aleksandra Winiarska, Lucy Jackson, Lucy Mayblin and Gill Valentine
Sport in Society Cultures, Commerce, Media, Politics, volume 19, issue 8–9 (October–November 2016) pp. 1332–1348

Chapter 16
Men in a 'women only' sport? Contesting gender relations and sex integration in roller derby
Adele Pavlidis and James Connor
Sport in Society Cultures, Commerce, Media, Politics, volume 19, issue 8–9 (October–November 2016) pp. 1349–1362

Chapter 17
Playing like a girl? The negotiation of gender and sexual identity among female ice hockey athletes on male teams
Danielle DiCarlo
Sport in Society Cultures, Commerce, Media, Politics, volume 19, issue 8–9 (October–November 2016) pp. 1363–1373

Chapter 18
Friendships worth fighting for: bonds between women and men karate practitioners as sites for deconstructing gender inequality
Chloe Maclean
Sport in Society Cultures, Commerce, Media, Politics, volume 19, issue 8–9 (October–November 2016) pp. 1374–1384

For any permission-related enquiries please visit:
http://www.tandfonline.com/page/help/permissions

Notes on Contributors

Alex Channon is a Senior Lecturer in Physical Education and Sport Studies at the University of Brighton, Eastbourne, UK.

Cassie Comley is a graduate student in the Sociology Department, University of Oregon, Eugene, USA.

James Connor is based at the School of Business, University of New South Wales, Canberra, Australia.

Katherine Dashper is a Senior Lecturer at Leeds Beckett University, Leeds, UK.

Danielle DiCarlo is based at the Department of Exercise Sciences, University of Toronto, Toronto, Canada.

Donna de Haan is based at the Department of International Sports, Management and Business, Amsterdam University of Applied Sciences, Amsterdam, the Netherlands.

Janet S. Fink is based at the Mark H. McCormack Department of Sport Management, University of Massachusetts Amherst, Amherst, USA.

Thomas Fletcher is a Senior Lecturer at Leeds Beckett University, Leeds, UK.

Karin Grahn is based at the Department of Food and Nutrition, and Sport Science, University of Gothenburg, Gothenburg, Sweden.

Laura Gubby is a Lecturer in Physical Education at the School of Childhood and Education Sciences at Canterbury Christ Church University, Canterbury, UK.

Ian Henry is the Director of the Centre of Olympic Studies, Loughborough University, Loughborough, UK.

Lucy Jackson was a postdoctoral research associate at the Department of Geography, University of Sheffield, Sheffield, UK. She is now a Lecturer in Human Geography at the University of Liverpool.

Robert J. Lake is an Instructor in Sport Sociology at Douglas College, New Westminster, Canada.

Marie Larneby is a doctoral student at the Faculty of Education and Society, Malmö University, Malmö, Sweden.

NOTES ON CONTRIBUTORS

Nicole M. LaVoi is a Senior Lecturer at the Department of Kinesiology, University of Minnesota, Minneapolis, USA.

Chloe Maclean is a graduate student in the Sociology Department, University of Edinburgh, Scotland, UK.

Lucy Mayblin is a Research Fellow at the Department of Geography, University of Sheffield, Sheffield, UK.

Kristine E. Newhall is based at Smith College, Northampton, USA.

Adele Pavlidis is a Postdoctoral Fellow at the School of Humanities, Griffith University, Gold Coast, Australia.

Catherine Phipps is a full-time Vice Chancellor scholarship PhD student in the Faculty of Education and Health at the University of Greenwich, London, UK.

Joaquín Piedra is based at the Universidad de Sevilla, Educación Física y Deporte, Sevilla, Spain.

Lindsay Parks Pieper is an Assistant Professor of Sport Management, Lynchburg College, Lynchburg, USA. Her research research interests include gender and sport, sports law and Olympic history.

Micol Pizzolati is based at the Department of Economics, Management, Society and Institutions, University of Molise, Campobasso, Italy.

Amy Pressland was a Lecturer in Education at the School of Education and Lifelong Learning, University of East Anglia, Norwich, UK.

Esther Priyadharshini is a Senior Lecturer at the School of Education and Lifelong Learning, University of East Anglia, Norwich, UK.

Gonzalo Ramírez-Macías is based at the CEU San Pablo Andalucía, Centro de Estudios Profesionales, Bormujos, Spain.

Francis Ries is based at the CEU San Pablo Andalucía, Centro de Estudios Profesionales, Bormujos, Spain.

Augusto Rembrandt Rodríguez-Sánchez is based at the CEU San Pablo Andalucía, Centro de Estudios Profesionales, Bormujos, Spain.

Pam R. Sailors is a Faculty Member at the Department of Philosophy, Missouri State University Springfield, USA.

Jeffrey O. Segrave is David H. Porter Professor in the Department of Health and Exercise Sciences, Skidmore College, Saratoga Springs, USA.

Davide Sterchele is a Senior Lecturer at the School of Events, Tourism and Hospitality, Leeds Beckett University, Leeds, UK.

Popi Sotiriadou is an Associate Professor at Griffith University, Southport, Australia.

NOTES ON CONTRIBUTORS

Viveka Berggren Torell is a Senior Lecturer at the Department of Food and Nutrition, and Sport Science, University of Gothenburg, Gothenburg, Sweden.

Gill Valentine is a Professor at the Department of Geography, University of Sheffield, Sheffield, UK.

Ian Wellard is a Reader at the School of Human and Life Sciences in Canterbury Christ Church University, UK.

Aleksandra Winiarska is based at the Institute of Applied Social Sciences, University of Warsaw, Warsaw, Poland.

The promises and pitfalls of sex integration in sport and physical culture

Scholars working in the academic field of sport studies have long debated the relationship between modern sport and gender (e.g. Hargreaves 1994; Hargreaves and Anderson 2014; Lenskyj 1986; Messner 2002). Within this body of work, modern sport forms – along with a great diversity of related activities, including dance, fitness training and physical education – have consistently been shown to carry meanings relative to the structures of gender prevailing in the wider social settings within which they take place, with patterns of participation and consumption clearly mapping onto gendered ideals. However, rather than simply mirroring such social norms, research suggests that many sporting practices were invented or have been purposefully developed in order to train young men and women in socially approved gender behaviours to begin with (Cahn 1994; Hargreaves 1994; Theberge 2000). Thus, much of contemporary physical culture finds its roots in the process which scholars describe as the 'social construction of gender'; in other words, doing sports and other activities in gender-differentiated ways has long been a means of producing and maintaining difference in the lives of men and women, girls and boys.

Considering that such gender patterns are almost always implicated in structures of power (Lenskyj 1990; Roth and Basow 2004), then this purposeful division of the sexes becomes an important topic for scholars interested in the (re)production of inequality. For instance, feminist researchers have consistently argued that the institution of competitive sport has played a key role in symbolically validating male privilege (Messner 1988; Theberge 2000). Despite the fact that not all men enjoy participating in sports, the abilities of the male athlete nevertheless lend ideological support to the notion that 'real' men are brave, competitive, disciplined and physically strong – qualities highly valued and often associated with positions of power in wider social life. Concurrently, the exclusion of women from many high-profile sporting competitions throughout much of the twentieth century preserved sport as a symbolic space for celebrating men's embodiment of these 'masculine' virtues, while the tendency to stigmatize and ridicule female athletes when they did enter the 'male' sporting arena helped prevent them from effectively challenging the legitimacy of men's symbolic ownership of sport and its requisite qualities.[1]

While this historical narrative of sport as a 'male preserve' (Dunning 1986) has appeared widely throughout the vast body of scholarship on gender and physical culture, so too has there been a consistent fascination with the possibility for challenging or subverting male privilege within these exact same sites where it is otherwise seen to be produced and maintained. Principally, these arguments arise from research on women's participation in a range of sports and related activities. Here, there is compelling evidence of the potential for individual women to feel 'empowered' through the embodied experiences sport provides, as they learn to resist restrictive norms of femininity typically regulating the female body (e.g. Dowling 2000). Meanwhile, other work has argued for the possibility of wider cultural change driven by women's sport, as the symbolic value of iconic female athletes challenges ideological beliefs about inherent male superiority (e.g. Heywood and Dworkin 2003). This argument typically suggests that if women's and men's sporting accomplishments are equally valued, and women recognized as being equally capable of embodying the highly prized qualities associated with (particularly) competitive sports, then perhaps their example might have a progressive, transformative impact on wider culture. In essence, such women overtly challenge the notion that it is only men who can be brave, competitive, or strong.[2]

By the second decade of the twenty-first century, physical cultural practices in many parts of the Western world have undergone significant changes compared to their historical forebears, undoubtedly shifting ideals of gender constructed within and through them in the process. With particular respect to competitive sports, male and female athletes attend major global sports events such as the Olympic and Paralympic Games in almost equal numbers (Donnelly and Donnelly 2013); women increasingly participate in sports thought of as the most 'masculine' of all, including full-contact team games like rugby and ice hockey, or combat sports like boxing and mixed martial arts (Channon and Matthews 2015; Finkel 2014; Woodward 2014); and a host of elite-level female athletes such as Hailey Wickenheiser (ice hockey), Ronda Rousey (mixed martial arts) and Serena Williams (tennis) have become well known internationally. Yet in spite of women's increasing prominence in these (and other) respects, their propensity to challenge traditional gender ideology remains stunted by the institutionalized segregation of men's and women's sport (McDonagh and Pappano 2008). If the growth of women's sport has put the lie to ideals of female frailty (Dowling 2000) and revealed that women can indeed embody athletic qualities previously thought exclusive to men, then the continuation of sex segregation has left something of a discursive 'back door' through which ideals of male athletic superiority can escape unscathed, retaining their influence over wider cultural belief systems. While allowing for the admission that women can be strong, competitive, resilient, etc., the culture of segregated sport continues to insist that they will never be able to be these things in ways which compare favourably to men. In other words, men remain positioned as the superior sex group by virtue of their assumed prowess in essentially often hypothetical, mixed-sex sporting competitions.

In this context, sex-integrated sport potentially offers a radical departure from such beliefs. In its simplest form, the fundamental 'promise' of sex integration lies in the fact that it challenges us to reject a priori assumptions of male superiority and to entertain a very different vision of sex difference and gender relations to those typically constructed through traditional models of gendered physical culture. When women and men face each other as ostensible equals in athletic contests, when they train with one another in ways which are taken to be mutually beneficial, or when they must rely on one another's athletic prowess for the sake of team success, the usual gendered logic stressing inevitable male predominance stands to be challenged. While sex integration in sport and physical cultural settings can take many forms, and not all of these are equally radical in their relationship to the normative gendered culture of sport, the possibilities that these practices present for challenging the traditional sexual hierarchies embedded within sporting practices make this a fascinating area of research for sport scholars.

The question of sex integration in physical education has been debated by physical educationists (in the UK) for some time, as changes in government policies regarding co-educational classes drove academic interest since at least the 1980s (e.g. Evans et al. 1987; Hills and Crosston 2012; Lines and Stidder 2003). Yet in relation to sports, relatively little attention has been paid to sex integration, and despite the prominence of gender research in sport sociology since the 1970s, research on sex integration in sports only began to gather pace from the mid-1990s (e.g. Henry and Comeaux 1999; Snyder and Ammons 1993). Today, such enquiry features as a more prominent aspect of scholarship on sport and gender, with research publications since the mid-2000s proliferating across various national and sporting contexts. With reference to a selected number of publications from this emerging body of work, we now briefly address what we perceive to be some central issues regarding both the promise and pitfalls of sex integration, before introducing the works comprising the rest of this collection.

'The promise': anti-sexism, hetero-sociality and wider inclusivity through sex-integrated sport

One of the most problematic aspects of sex segregation in sport is that it reinforces the incorrect notion that *all* men and women are categorically different from each other with respect to specific dimensions of athletic performance. Sex segregation occurs in most (adult) sports, regardless of the actual ability of individual participants, based on the belief that for most such sports, men are 'naturally', and thus inevitably, superior athletes to women.[3] Yet the premise of sex-integrated sports challenges this belief, instead assuming a broad overlap between *individual* men and women in many dimensions of athletic ability. Thus, when men and women compete against each other on equal terms, as happens in equestrian sport at all levels (Dashper 2012a; de Haan Sotiriadou and Henry 2015, inthis volume), it becomes apparent that specific aspects of athletic performance are not fundamentally rooted in sex difference. Moreover, when women demonstrate an ability to compete with, or even defeat male opposition in sports which are typically not integrated, they stimulate reflection on otherwise entrenched beliefs about bodily capabilities, potentially inviting challenges to the sexist assumptions that all women are always athletically inferior to all men (McDonagh and Pappano 2008; Wachs 2005). Further still, when men and women face each other in traditionally male-dominated and deeply masculinized contexts, such as combat sports (Channon 2014; Fields 2005; Maclean 2015, in this volume; McNaughton 2012), ideas that all women are 'weak' and in need of protection from men's inevitably superior strength and power can be radically debunked. And if, as outlined above, we accept that notions of male athletic superiority often help underpin wider social constructions of male hegemony, then such challenges to these assumptions take on a clear symbolic importance (McDonagh and Pappano 2008).

Beside this political argument though, sex integration also has other benefits in relation to reworking gender relations within sport, principally regarding the establishment of positive, heterosocial relationships and greater inclusivity of non-binary people. Regarding this first point, Anderson's (2008) study of mixed-sex cheerleading illustrated how integration had transformed certain men's views of women's athleticism, leading to greater respect for female ability and leadership, ultimately helping them to befriend women and view them in more humanized ways than during their participation in male-only sports teams. Maclean's study of karate training revealed similar phenomena within mixed-sex clubs, wherein female karateka were accorded equal respect as their male counterparts (2015a; see also 2015b this volume). Indeed, some research showcased in this collection suggests that when men and women play together in a variety of team sports, as is the case in mixed-doubles tennis, korfball, floorball and quidditch (see Lake 2015; Gubby and Wellard 2015; Larneby, 2015 and Segrave 2015, respectively – all this volume), collaboration and teamwork can become more important than policing gender divisions and broadly help to establish positive, supportive, mutually respectful relationships between men and women.

Regarding the wider inclusivity embedded within sex-integrated sport, Dashper's (2012b) study of the experiences of gay men within equestrian sport suggests that sex integration can reduce tension and make for a more welcoming and accepting environment for gay men than is often seen within other competitive sporting contexts. Meanwhile, sex-integrated sports may also provide spaces for those who are otherwise excluded by the binary sex classifications of 'male' and 'female' upon which almost all of modern sport is built – particularly intersex, transgender or otherwise non-binary individuals (Buzuvis 2011; see also NUS 2012). By not requiring people to classify themselves within one of only two distinct sex categories, integrated sports have the potential to offer inclusive spaces for such athletes. Debates over the possibility of such inclusion are evidenced by Tagg's research on mixed netball (2012, 2014), Travers' discussion of softball and baseball (2013; see also Travers and Deri 2011) and Pavlidis and Connor's (2015) account of the controversies over inclusion policies in roller derby (in this volume).

'The pitfalls': resilient paternalism, male predominance and problematic implementation of sex-integrated sport

While sex integration has the potential to challenge some aspects of 'gender injustice' in sport (Travers 2008), it should not be considered a panacea to the deep-rooted patterns of gender inequality that characterize sport and sporting practices. Firstly, in many contexts, the potential for transformative experiences in sex-integrated sports is thwarted or at least slowed by the persistence of deep, historically rooted and often taken-for-granted practices which marginalize women, rationalize the ascendency of men into positions of authority and normalize the unspoken behavioural etiquette associated with the wider societal expectation that 'boys don't hit girls' (Channon and Jennings 2013; Sailors 2015, in this volume; Snyder and Ammons 1993; Wachs 2002). Indeed, the reluctance of many men to engage meaningfully with women in mixed competition regularly sees the proposition framed as a 'lose-lose' situation, where defeating a woman is considered dishonourable while being defeated by one is emasculating (Guerandel and Mennesson 2007; McNaughton 2012). This notion rests on the continuing logic of male superiority in integrated spaces, which otherwise often manifests in different rules for men and women within matches – typically those which 'handicap' men and provide women an apparently necessary competitive advantage (e.g. Henry and Comeaux 1999). Thus, many aspects of how integrated sports are organized refuse the possibility that women might ever compete on a 'level playing field' with men. Even in those sports with a long history and widespread normalization of sex integration, behavioural norms that reinforce and support distinct gender roles – particularly those which centre on the paternalistic treatment of women by men – can be difficult to shift (e.g. Lake 2012).

Secondly, although outstanding female performances against male opposition might be thought of as potentially transformative, it is difficult to imagine that this might become a normal state of affairs across any and all integrated sports, especially at higher levels of competition. As the global talent pool for female athletes remains disproportionately shallow owing to the well-evidenced drop-out from sport of adolescent girls (e.g. Women's Sports Foundation 2012); while would-be athletic girls suffer from a lack of role models due to the near-invisibility of women's sport in the mainstream media (e.g. Cooky, Messner, and Hextrum 2013); and when the financial rewards for female athletes continue to be massively outstripped by those of their male counterparts (e.g. Women's Sports Foundation 2015), we should hardly expect competitive performance gaps between elite men and women to shrink with the speed that scholars such as sociobiologist Dyer (1982) earlier predicted. Indeed, even in many sports where (human) strength and speed are not key contributors to athletic success, such as in equestrian sports, men still tend to dominate elite levels of competition and perform disproportionately well in comparison to their female peers, almost certainly owing to a range of social, economic and cultural factors embedded in contemporary sport (Dashper 2013).

Within cultural contexts wherein athletic performance differences are most often interpreted as the expression of innate, biological limits, instances of male success in mixed competition are very likely to shore up the ideological construction of men's inevitable superiority over women. Moreover, while several scholars remain optimistic about the value of female success over male opponents in this respect, there is evidence that even these performances can be rationalized away, subsumed within dismissive or infantilizing discourse that neutralizes their subversive impact (Wachs 2005). Indeed, many sex-integrated sports that espouse the rhetoric of equality and egalitarianism, like floorball, korfball, roller derby, surfing, skydiving and snowboarding, very often in practice reproduce male dominance with respect to their organization, leadership, behavioural etiquette and differentiated styles of participation (see Booth 2002; Laurendeau and Sharara 2008; Summerfield and White 1989; Thorpe 2005; see also Comley; Larneby; Gubby and Wellard; Pavlidis and Connor – all this volume).

Additionally, while sex integration may begin to challenge male hegemony symbolically and practically within sport, it must be noted that many women value female-only sports settings. This may be for religious or cultural reasons (e.g. Dagkas, Benn, and Jawad 2011; Hylton et al. 2015) or because women simply desire separate space away from the male gaze and masculine domination which characterizes much of their everyday lives (Long et al. 2015). Several researchers who advocate sex integration as one step towards greater gender justice in sport therefore also argue for the continuation of women-only sport spaces (e.g. McDonagh and Pappano 2008; Tagg 2014; Travers 2013), making a distinction between 'coercive' and 'voluntary' segregation. Not without contention, these authors (and others) have argued for the abolition of all male-only sports contexts and competitions but suggest that women, as a subordinated group, should be able to choose between sex-integrated and sex-segregated sporting spaces. This is because 'voluntary segregation aimed at increasing group standing is an acceptable social practice for minority groups but not for dominant groups' (Travers 2008, 93). Thus, whilst sex integration within sport has potential to trouble masculine hegemony and contribute to greater gender justice, it may not be appropriate in all contexts and is not a simple solution to deeply ingrained and far-reaching sex inequality.

As is clearly evident from existing research and the essays within this collection, the goal of creating a socially inclusive sporting world that is both necessary and realistic, cannot be solely a matter of the right policy or the right time (see Priyadharshini and Pressland 2015, in this volume). If gender inequalities in all aspects of sport are to cease to be of significance, and if the promise of 'sport for all' is to be realised, then the analysis of policy needs to be related to broader relations of power in the culture of sport and society. Equal opportunities will remain unobtainable if the central tenet of the reproduction of male privilege is allowed to remain uncontested.

Important though as it is, gender equality is not the only marker of sporting inclusion. It is the way gender intersects with sexuality, 'race'/ethnicity, social class, income, disability, age, religion and other factors that shape sporting opportunities. Thus, as has been argued elsewhere, for enduring public gender equality work to be possible, the conditions for it to become embedded in the ways people really think about social justice require more subtle forms of understanding than are currently available.

Overview of the special issue

With these controversies in mind, the remainder of this special issue of *Sport in Society* attempts to shed light on contemporary manifestations of both the promises and pitfalls of sex-integrated sport and physical culture. The 18 essays which follow have been grouped into 4 broad sections: *theorizing sex integration in sport and physical culture; integration in PE and youth sport; integrated non-contact sports;* and *integrated contact sports.* These sections were constructed to mirror what we believe to be an increasing scale of incredulity shown towards the prospect of sex-integrated sport. By this, we mean that the notion of integrated play may not be altogether unsettling to sport's normative gender systems 'in theory'; once put into practice it is not so unacceptable in youth sport, before adolescence hits and individuals are increasingly segregated out along gender lines; and while sex integration in adult sports might be a highly atypical and potentially shocking prospect for many, it is most directly transgressive of gendered norms in sports which involve heavy levels of physical contact.

Thus, we intend for the arrangement of these essays to create something of an increasingly 'shocking' narrative as to the current practices of sex integration, vis-à-vis normative gender construction in sport. Assigning essays to these categories was a little difficult, and we acknowledge the dangers of compartmentalizing each contribution by recognizing that there was scope for cross-categorization in some cases. This is both a strength and weakness of the process, which was ultimately done for clarity of readership, but may underplay the interconnectedness of the issues expressed herein. As a final note on the makeup of this collection, we have included here four short, 'Research Insight' essays.[4] The purpose of these was to offer an opportunity for early career researchers to showcase their work, and due to their shorter format (4000–5000 words) provide an accessible outlet for research dissemination alongside the larger, full-length research articles comprising the other 14 contributions.

Section 1: theorizing sex integration in sport and physical culture

Section 1 begins with Pamela Sailors' essay 'Off the beaten path: Should women compete against men?'. In her essay Sailors considers three questions: Are women capable of competing against men in sporting events? If they aren't, might there be good reasons to encourage them to make the attempt anyway? If they are, might there be good reasons to prohibit such competition? Sailors proposes four possible answers to the question of whether women are capable of competing against men: (1) No, so there's no point in talking about it; (2) No, but they should make the attempt anyway; (3) Yes, so mix all the competition and get on with it; and (4) Yes, but there are good reasons not to allow it. Sailors is clear that these are meant as provocations, and ought not to be considered as sacrosanct. She warns that scholars and practitioners must not lose sight of the fact that 'equality through sex integration will require more than good intentions and a coherent theory so long as cultural ideas about male superiority persist' (2015, this volume).

Following this, in her essay '"Preserving la difference": The elusiveness of sex segregated sport' Lindsay Parks Pieper critically explores the use of medico-scientific technologies as a means of differentiating between men and women. Parks-Pieper suggests that sport authorities, when faced with the realization that girls and women were encroaching into (male) sporting spaces, and demonstrating many of the traits that previously signified 'maleness', made a number of attempts to reassert the gender order by, among other things, seeking ways to scientifically maintain a division in competition. She states that, 'Widespread social anxieties, medico-scientific ideologies, and sporting norms thereby coalesced, resulting in numerous efforts to uphold separation' (2015, this volume). Of these mechanisms, Parks Pieper traces the IAAF's and IOC's use of anatomical examinations, chromatin assessments, DNA testing and hormonal analyses in their attempt to circumscribe womanhood. She argues how, despite attempts to delineate a division of sex proving arbitrary, sport authorities have repeatedly attempted to draw a concrete line between men and women to uphold a sex-segregated sporting paradigm.

Section 2: integration in PE and youth sport

Joaqium Piedra, Gonzalo Ramírez-Macías, Francis Ries, Augusto R. Rodríguez-Sánchez and Catherine Phipps (2015) open this section with their essay 'Homophobia and heterosexism: Spanish Physical Education teachers' perceptions'. Piedra et al. note that PE is often thought of as a heteronormative environment, despite current studies highlighting the existence of positive changes in sport towards sexual diversity. Piedra et al. provide a case study of Spain, where studies into PE teachers' attitudes towards sexual minorities are rare. Their essay demonstrates that overt homophobia, especially the use of homophobic language, remains prevalent in Spanish PE lessons. They warn that this homophobia is institutionalized, with some teachers (mainly male) joining other students in expressing homophobic language:

> homosexually-themed language is still a well-used instrument in classrooms to discriminate against gays and lesbians. Some teachers are not fully aware of its effect, since many do not use inclusive language in their teaching practice, with homosexually themed language more prominent amongst male teachers. (2015, this volume)

Laura Gubby and Ian Wellard's essay 'Sporting equality and gender neutrality in korfball' also explores institutional inequality, but their focus is on deconstructing the perceived egalitarianism of korfball. Their analysis shows that while the sport is presented as sex-integrated, egalitarian and meritocratic, myths about male athletic prowess and female subordination remain entrenched within player attitudes. They argue that, while during fieldwork it was clear that male domination was rarely evident in terms of the vocal nature of the game, the physicality and competitiveness of players, or their general ability and skill, when interviewed players still constructed gender in traditional ways. The authors also witnessed a disassociation between players on and off the court. They argue that while korfball was seen to offer a space where there were possibilities for sporting equality, its influence beyond the court was less apparent.

Following this, Karin Grahn and Viveka Berggren Torell's (2015) essay 'Negotiations of gender discourse: Experiences of co-education in a Swedish sport initiative for children' explores how children perceive and construct gender in two settings: a Swedish Government-financed sports initiative and in leisure-time sports activities. Their findings identify how many of the children normalize through reproduction traditional views of boys/men as being superior at sports. However, they also uncover some instances of resistance, whereby some actively objected to this dominant discourse. They identify differences between the two settings. They suggest that there was greater potential for the children in the initiative to experience sport in less sex-segregated ways than in leisure-time sport. They attribute this to the practice of co-education, whereby girls' and boys' participation together is increasingly normalized. They conclude that,

> there was room for negotiation in the children's descriptions of leisure sports and in girls' and boys' discussions of playing together or separately … on some occasions, traditional gender patterns were (re) produced … on other occasions, there was potential for the children in the soccer project to experience soccer in less gender-segregated manners than in leisure-time soccer. (2015, this volume)

Formal vs. leisure-time sport is the focus of Marie Larneby's Research Insight essay into floorball. In 'Transcending gender hierarchies? Young people and floorball in Swedish school sport' Larneby challenges the supposition that floorball has not been masculinized in its transition from spontaneous activity to organized sport. On the contrary, Larneby argues that training in a mixed-sex group seemed to actualize a need to dichotomize and construct distinct groups of boys and girls, meaning that a 'boys are better than girls' discourse prevailed. Unlike Grahn et al. who noted a difference in attitudes towards gender difference between formal and leisure time sport settings, Larneby argues that the culture of sex segregation in leisure-time floorball diffused into formal settings. However, Larneby also presents data to suggest that as boys and girls become more accustomed to sex integrated sport settings they begin to value the contribution of each other more, thereby dispelling myths of irrefutable sex differences.

Section 3: integrated non-contact sports

Section 3 opens with Rob Lake's (2015) essay '"Guys don't whale away at the women": etiquette and gender relations in contemporary mixed-doubles tennis'. Building off historical research that examined the social constructions of male–female differences in behavioural etiquette in mixed-doubles tennis from before the Second World War, this essay examines the extent to which 'traditional' gendered norms related to court positioning, tactics and playing roles/expectations have been challenged as an outcome of post-war feminist advances and broader movements towards gender equity. Analysing instructional guides and coaching manuals published from the 1960s–1980s, alongside contemporary tennis blogs and instructional websites aimed at offering advice on mixed-doubles tactics and etiquette, Lake discovered that while a key and possibly growing demographic of advanced-level female players expected neutral and unbiased play from men – essentially, urging men to accept female teammates/opponents as equals and to *not* hold back – male players at both recreational and elite levels continued to express discomfort with doing so, despite openly acknowledging how this might be considered 'offensive' or 'insulting'. Thus, within the context of the burgeoning 'crisis of masculinity' (MacInnes 1998), men were pushed to adopt a sophisticated 'hybridized masculinity', '[blending] orthodox masculinity with more inclusive – essentially, female/gay-friendly – identities to continue asserting their social dominance', yet assuage public critiques of sexism in tennis (2015, this volume).

This is followed by Esther Priyadharshini and Amy Pressland's essay 'Doing femininities and masculinities in a "feminized" sporting arena: The case of mixed-sex cheerleading' in which they utilize personal narratives of three competitive cheerleaders in the UK to question the educative and transformative potential of mixed-sex sports. Through a critical feminist lens they question whether such promise can ever be attained and what the obstacles to its attainment may be. Their conclusions are threefold: (1) having experience of mixed-sex team membership can have a progressive influence on the gender narratives and performances of both male and female participants; (2) mixed-sex teams are not a panacea to rectify gender stereotypes and inequalities; and (3) if the implicit transformative potential of mixed-sex cheerleading is to be fully realized, then explicit organizational, promotional and structural changes to the sport itself will be needed.

Equestrian sport remains one of few sports where men and women routinely compete together. This is the focus of Donna de Haan, Popi Sotiriadou and Ian Henry's (2015) essay 'The lived experience of sex integrated sport and the construction of athlete identity within the Olympic and Paralympic Equestrian disciplines'. The essay presents data from interviews conducted with riders, performance managers and support staff of the British Equestrian Team. The authors uncover a contradiction between existing literature and their data. They acknowledge that existing research is laden with gendered references, though analysis of their data shows an 'absence of gender as an identity in the way participants see themselves and others' (2015, this volume). The authors use this to suggest that, from a participant's perspective, equestrian sport might be described as gender neutral.

Following this, in 'Mixed-sex in sport for development: A pragmatic and symbolic device. The case of touch rugby for forced migrants in Rome' Micol Pizzolati and Davide Sterchele (2016, this volume) trace the development of a touch rugby team, created by the Italian voluntary-based association Liberi Nantes, especially for female forced migrants. The authors report that, as a result of the success of a male equivalent team, Liberi Nantes wanted to create a similar space where women could come together, socialize, increase their social networks and, most importantly, feel safe. Originally established as a sex-segregated space, the authors document how the organizers took the decision to make the mixed-sex team. By drawing upon the accounts of activists and volunteers they examine the practical and symbolic reasons for the strategic use of mixed-sex sport and its implications. They highlight how its mixed-sex nature contributes to nourishing a wider rhetoric of social mixing and celebration of diversity: 'The mixed-sex dimension of touch rugby is part of this totemic representation since it contributes to this subversive symbolism of overcoming social hierarchies and boundaries by fighting segregation and favoring intersectional social mixing' (this volume).

The final contribution in this section is a Research Insight from Cassie Comley (2016, this volume). In '"We have to establish our territory": How women surfers "carve out" gendered spaces within surfing' Comley presents a case study of how female surfers in Southern California cope with and contest their marginalized status by, among other things, establishing separate spaces from men. She argues that the legitimacy of female surfers is often called into question through the male habitus of surfing. She documents accounts of how men would question the skill and legitimacy of female surfers and how these experiences have politicized the waves to the extent that women surfers felt a 'burden of representation'. Many of the women sought to separate themselves from mixed-sex environments, preferring instead to establish alternative spaces. Comley warns that separation 'may not be challenging broader cultural beliefs about women and men, but does create a space where women feel empowered and can unite over womanhood' (this volume).

Section 4: integrated contact sports

Jeffrey Segrave (2015) opens this section with 'Challenging the gender binary: the fictive and real world of quidditch' wherein he argues that dominant forms of sport are bimodal in gender classification, a construction that creates an ideology of male superiority and marginalizes women and gay, lesbian, bisexual, transgender and intersex individuals (GLBITs). One recent example of a sport that confronts traditional gendering is quidditch. The majority of readers outside the USA will think of quidditch as existing only in the fantasy world of J.K. Rowling's Harry Potter book and movie series. However, it also exists in the 'real'-world as 'muggle' quidditch and is gender inclusive. Segrave draws upon a literary analysis of Rowling's portrayal of quidditch as well as personal testimonies of muggle quidditch players to consider the ways in which both formats challenge the dominant forms of institutionalized sport and present an alternative structure for gender participation and identification. He suggests that the impact of fantasy quidditch should not be underestimated as it 'posits the assumption of gender equity in sport to a whole generation of boys and girls and men and women' whilst operating as 'incidents of resistance and emancipatory moments that demonstrate that sport, like all institutions, is not a "seamless totalitarian system"' (this volume).

In 'Challenging the gender binary? Male basketball practice players' views of female athletes and women's sports', Janet Fink, Nicole LaVoi and Kristine Newhall (2015) utilize Kane's continuum theory to examine the effects of extended sex-integrated playing experiences on male practice players' attitudes towards female athletes, female athleticism and women's sports more generally. They warn that few boys and men (or girls and women) are provided sex-integrated sport opportunities and thus, the opportunity to experience the sport continuum is rarely realized. Their findings further illuminate the complexity of gender relations in sport as the men simultaneously experienced and articulated a gender continuum while reinforcing a gender binary which kept their own power and privilege in sport intact. Thus, 'while sex-integrated sport has the potential to challenge gender ideologies, it appears the strong and pervasive patriarchy of male-centered, male run, and male dominated sport culture makes it difficult for its full positive potential to be realized' (this volume). The authors conclude that if more sex-integrated opportunities were available in youth sport settings they could provide early and consistent interruptions of the gender binary that might contribute to stronger mechanisms for feminist resistance.

In '"They kick you because they are not able to kick the ball": normative conceptions of sex difference and the politics of exclusion in mixed-sex football', Aleksandra Winiarska, Lucy Jackson, Lucy Mayblin and Gill Valentine (2015) present a case study of an anti-discrimination football tournament in Warsaw, Poland. The authors write that the tournament has a variety of anti-discriminatory aims, including anti-racism, anti-homophobia and anti-sexism, meaning that it is well placed to discuss the intersectionality of inequality. The authors ask whether initial perceptions of sex difference can be overcome via sustained sex-integrated sports involvement. They argue that, despite the tournament's aims, male perceptions of biological sex difference were unavoidable and hindered play and group integration. More specifically, they identify how perceptions of sex differences were reinforced through normative assumptions expressed by participants, which often lead to the confirmation of divisions – and also inequalities – between men and women. Over time however, they demonstrated a marked change in player attitudes. They conclude that, for the men, while participating with and against women 'at first seemed something unusual or even unthinkable … their presence became a natural and obvious fact' (this volume); a pattern that was recognized by the women who noted 'a positive experience in comparison with other social milieus, where they experienced surprise, suspicion or rejection' (this volume).

In 'Men in a "women only" sport? Contesting gender relations and sex integration in roller derby', Adele Pavlidis and James Connor note how roller derby is primarily played by women, with men having been restricted to support roles since its revival stage in the early 2000s. However, men and gender diverse skaters are increasingly playing the sport, in both mixed-sex and sex-segregated teams. This has created deep divisions within the derby community for two main reasons: (1) the legitimacy of men in a perceived women's space and (2) the playing of a full-contact sport with men against women on the track. The authors argue that the main challenge to successful sex-integrated sport is reducing, or eliminating altogether, discrimination, and this will not happen until 'one of the most obvious, visible, valorized and re-produced binaries of gender is broken – that of *sport* and *women's sport*' (this volume). They suggest that roller derby can go some way to realizing gender equality, but its contribution will likely be limited given the sport's 'deeply challenging ideas that come from trying to combine traditional conceptions of men, women and their sporting prowess to a sport that is full contact, on roller skates' (this volume).

Danielle DiCarlo's (2015) contribution 'Playing like a girl? The negotiation of gender and sexual identity among female ice hockey athletes on male teams' is the first of two Research Insights in this section. She opens her essay by suggesting that the gendering of ice hockey space is not new, but there have been numerous well-known cases of women playing on, or attempting to play on, male ice hockey teams. She documents how women have migrated into these sport spaces through the development of female teams and leagues, but also through their participation in male teams and leagues. DiCarlo's contribution is different to the majority in this collection as she presents experiences of women who have already participated in sex-integrated teams before transitioning to sex-segregated teams. She argues that the women's experiences of participating in sex-integrated environments influenced how they construct and negotiate ideas about femininity and female bodies in sex-segregated environments. She documents how the female athletes 'exhibited neither a complete adherence to nor rejection of the ideal femininity within their constructions of gender' (this volume). For these women, negotiating gender was inextricably linked to sexuality, as they 'constructed their (heterosexual) identities through comparison of self with homosexual female teammates and their narratives around heteronormativity'(this volume).

The collection comes to a close with Chloe Maclean's (2015b) Research Insight 'Friendships worth fighting for: Bonds between women and men karate practitioners as sites for deconstructing gender inequality'. Unlike many principally team sports, Maclean argues that sex-integrated karate practice not only challenges dominant expectations/interpretations of women's bodies, but can also situate women and men within mutually respectful, cherished relationships which diverge from conventional sexualized and unequal ways of 'doing gender'. Indeed, for Maclean, mixed-sex friendships in karate training offer a unique site for exploring the subversion of gender norms, ideals and hierarchies on the basis that the:

> sex-integrated practice of karate elevates the respect given to women by simultaneously disrupting both ideas of women's bodies as primarily sexual objects subordinate in ability to men … and of men and women as having, offering, and wanting distinctly different qualities in their intimate relations. (this volume)

For Maclean, unlike the vast majority of other sporting environments, in karate, 'mixed-friendships are built on mutually supportive grounds, with an embedded mutual respect for one-another as athletes and friends' (this volume).

To many critical scholars of sport and physical culture the issues raised in this collection will be familiar; resonating with a collective frustration about the unfulfilled promises of sport. The range of case studies and discussions presented here not only reaffirm the contemporary relevance of sex integration debates, but also articulate the possibility of sport acting as a legitimate space for political struggle, resistance and change, and as a modality for 'self-actualization and the reaffirmation of previously abject identities' (Carrington 2010). The collection is ambitious and covers a lot of ground, theoretically, empirically and geographically, but inevitably possesses limitations in its scope and trajectory and therefore must, as with all scholarship, be seen as part of a broader discourse. We thank the authors for their contributions and hope their essays spark interest and provoke further discussion.

Notes

1. The symbolic work done by gendered patterns of participation/exclusion (i.e. associating men with power) extend beyond the realm of competitive sport. For instance, in many forms of dance there are male and female styles or roles, which largely play upon the association of men with solidity and physical strength and women with lightness and physical beauty; fitness regimes advertized to men typically involve building muscle mass and strength, while for women they focus on toning rather than building muscle, and reducing weight and size. The consistent implication here is that men primarily ought to be larger, stronger and more capable of exerting physical power than women.
2. An alternative vision forwarded by some sports feminists suggests that, rather than trying to illustrate how some female athletes can live up to sporting ideals largely centred on attributes wherein male bodies typically outperform females (i.e. strength and speed – see Foddy and Savulescu 2011), it may be more productive to increase the cultural prestige attached to sports wherein females, on average, tend to do better than males, or where sexual differences are less pronounced (i.e. those based on flexibility and balance, or ultra-endurance events – see Chatterjee and Laudato 1996). Although this argument provides an interesting counter to that developed around women's increasing involvement in 'masculine' sport, it offers no substantial departure from binary thinking about gender which underpins sexist hierarchies supported by masculinist sports culture.
3. With the exception, of course, being those sports wherein women are thought to have a natural advantage of their own, such as specific gymnastic events, as outlined in the endnote above.
4. Research Insight essays also feature in Dashper and Fletcher (2013).

References

Anderson, E. 2008. "I Used to Think Women Were Weak: Orthodox Masculinity, Gender Segregation, and Sport." *Sociological Forum.* 23 (2): 257–280.
Booth, Douglas. 2002. "From Bikinis to Boardshorts: Wahines and the Paradoxes of the Surfing Culture." *Journal of Sport History* 28 (1): 3–22.
Buzuvis, E. 2011. "Transgender Student-athletes and Sex-segregated Sport: Developing Policies of Inclusion for Intercollegiate and Interscholastic Athletics." *Seton Hall Journal of Sports and Entertainment Law* 21 (1): 1–59.
Cahn, S. 1994. *Coming on Strong: Gender and Sexuality in Twentieth-century Women's Sport.* Boston, MA: Harvard University Press.
Carrington, B. 2010. *Race, Sport and Politics: The Sporting Black Diaspora.* London: Sage.
Channon, A. 2014. "Towards the "Undoing" of Gender in Mixed-sex Martial Arts and Combat Sports." *Societies* 4 (4): 587–605.
Channon, A., and G. Jennings. 2013. "The Rules of Engagement: Negotiating Painful and 'Intimate' Touch in Mixed-sex Martial Arts." *Sociology of Sport Journal* 30 (4): 487–503.
Channon, A., and C. R. Matthews, eds. 2015a. *Global Perspectives on Women in Combat Sports: Women Warriors around the World.* Basingstoke: Palgrave Macmillan.
Chatterjee, S., and M. Laudato. 1996. "An Analysis of World Record times of Men and Women in Running, Skating, and Swimming." *The Journal of Strength & Conditioning Research* 10 (4): 274–278.
Comley, C. 2016. "'We Have to Establish our Territory': How Women Surfers 'Carve Out' Gendered Spaces within Surfing." *Sport in Society.* Forthcoming.
Cooky, C., M. A. Messner, and R. H. Hextrum. 2013. "Women Play Sport, but Not on TV: A Longitudinal Study of Televised Sports News Media." *Communication & Sport* 1 (3): 203–230.
Dagkas, S., T. Benn, and H. Jawad. 2011. "Multiple Voices: Improving Participation of Muslim Girls in Physical Education and School Sport." *Sport, Education and Society* 16 (2): 223–239.
Dashper, K. 2012a. "Together, Yet Still Not Equal? Sex Integration in Equestrian Sport." *Asia-Pacific Journal of Health, Sport and Physical Education* 3 (3): 213–225.
Dashper, K. 2012b. "'Dressage is Full of Queens!' Masculinity, Sexuality and Equestrian Sport." *Sociology* 46 (6): 1109–1124.
Dashper, K. 2013. Beyond the Binary: Gender Integration in Equestrian Sport. In *Gender and Equestrian Sport*, edited by M. Adelman and J. Knijik. 37–53. London: Springer.
Dashper, K., and T. Fletcher. 2013. "Introduction: Diversity, Equity and Inclusion in Sport and Management." *Sport in Society* 16 (10): 1–6.

Donnelly, P., and M. K. Donnelly. 2013. *The London 2012 Olympics: A Gender Equality Audit*. Toronto: Centre for Sport Policy Studies, University of Toronto.

Dowling, C. 2000. *The Frailty Myth: Redefining the Physical Potential of Women and Girls*. New York: Random House.

Dunning, E. 1986. "Sport as a Male Preserve: Notes on the Social Sources of Masculine Identity and Its Transformations." *Theory, Culture & Society* 3 (1): 79–90.

Dyer, K. F. 1982. *Catching up the Men: Women in Sport*. London: Junction Books.

Evans, J., S. Lopez, M. Duncan, and M. Evans. 1987. "Some Thoughts on the Political and Pedagogical Implications of Mixed Sex Grouping in the Physical Education Curriculum." *British Educational Research Journal* 13 (1): 59–71.

Fields, S. K. 2005. *Female Gladiators: Gender, Law, and Contact Sport in America*. Chicago, IL: University of Illinois Press.

Fink, J. S., N. M. LaVoi, and K. E. Newhall. 2015. "Challenging the Gender Binary? Male Basketball Practice Players' Views of Female Athletes and Women's Sports." *Sport in Society*. doi:10.1080/17430437.2015.1096252.

Finkel, R. 2014. Broadcasting from a Neutral Corner? An Analysis of the Mainstream Media's Representation of Women's Boxing at the London 2012 Olympic Games. In *Sports Events, Society and Culture*, edited by K. Dashper, T. Fletcher, and N. McCullough, 85–99. London: Routledge.

Foddy, B., and J. Savulescu. 2011. "Time to Re-evaluate Gender Segregation in Athletics?" *British Journal of Sports Medicine*. 45: 1184–1188.

Grahn, K., and V. Berggren Torell. 2015. "Negotiations of Gender Discourse: Experiences of Co-education in a Swedish Sports Initiative for Children." *Sport in Society*. doi:10.1080/17430437.2015.1096262.

Gubby, L., and I. Wellard. 2015. "Sporting Equality and Gender Neutrality in Korfball." *Sport in Society*. doi:10.1080/17430437.2015.1096261.

Guerandel, C., and C. Mennesson. 2007. "Gender Construction in Judo Interactions." *International Review for the Sociology of Sport* 42 (2): 167–186.

de Haan, D., P. Sotiriadou, and I. Henry. 2015. "The Lived Experience of Sex-integrated Sport and the Construction of Athlete Identity within the Olympic and Paralympic Equestrian Disciplines." *Sport in Society*. doi:/10.1080/17430437.2015.1096259.

Hargreaves, J. 1994. *Sporting Females*. London: Routledge.

Hargreaves, J., and E. Anderson, eds. 2014. *Routledge Handbook of Sport, Gender and Sexuality*. London: Routledge.

Henry, J., and H. Comeaux. 1999. "Gender Egalitarianism in Coed Sport: A Case Study of American Soccer." *International Review for the Sociology of Sport* 34 (3): 277–290.

Heywood, L., and S. Dworkin. 2003. *Built to Win: The Female Athlete as Cultural Icon*. Minneapolis: University of Minnesota Press.

Hills, L. A., and A. Crosston. 2012. "'It Should Be Better All Together': Exploring Strategies for 'Undoing' Gender in Coeducational Physical Education." *Sport, Education & Society* 17 (5): 591–605.

Hylton, K., J. Long, T. Fletcher, and N. Ormerod. 2015. *Cricket and South Asian Communities*. Leeds: Yorkshire Cricket Board.

Lake, R. J. 2012. "Gender and Etiquette in British Lawn Tennis 1870–1939: A Case Study of 'Mixed Doubles'." *The International Journal of the History of Sport* 29 (5): 691–710.

Lake, R. J. 2015. "'Guys Don't Whale Away at the Women': Etiquette and Gender Relations in Contemporary Mixed-doubles Tennis." *Sport in Society*. doi:10.1080/17430437.2015.1067773.

Larneby, M. 2016. "Transcending Gender Hierarchies? Young People and Floorball in Swedish School Sport." *Sport in Society*. Forthcoming.

Laurendeau, Jason, and Nancy Sharara. 2008. "'Women Could Be Every Bit as Good as Guys': Reproductive and Resistant Agency in Two 'Action' Sports." *Journal of Sport and Social Issues* 32: 24–47.

Lenskyj, H. 1986. *Out of Bounds: Women, Sport and Sexuality*. Toronto: The Women's Press.

Lenskyj, H. 1990. "Power and Play: Gender and Sexuality Issues in Sport and Physical Activity." *International Review for the Sociology of Sport* 25 (3): 235–245.

Lines, G., and G. Stidder. 2003. "Reflections on the Mixed- and Single-Sex PE Debate." In *Equity and Inclusion in Physical Education*, edited by G. Stidder and S. Hayes, 65–88. London: Routledge.

Long, J., K. Dashper, T. Fletcher, and N. Ormerod. 2015. *Understanding Participation and Non-participation among BME Communities in Wales*. Leeds: Institute for Sport, Physical Activity and Leisure. http://sport.wales/media/1647168/bme_sport_in_wales_-_final.pdf.

MacInnes, J. 1998. *The End of Masculinity*. Buckingham: Open University Press.

Maclean, C. 2015a. "Beautifully Violent: The Gender Dynamic of Scottish Karate." In *Global Perspectives on Women in Combat Sports: Women Warriors around the World*, edited by A. Channon and C. R. Matthews, 155–171. Basingstoke: Palgrave Macmillan.

Maclean, C. 2015. "Friendships worth Fighting For: Bonds between Women and Men Karate Practitioners as Sites for Deconstructing Gender Inequality." *Sport in Society*. doi:10.1080/17430437.2015.1096249.

McDonagh, E., and L. Pappano. 2008. *Playing with the Boys: Why Separate is Not Equal in Sports*. New York: Oxford University Press.

McNaughton, M. J. 2012. "Insurrectionary Womanliness: Gender and the (Boxing) Ring." *The Qualitative Report* 17 (33): 1–13.

Messner, M. A. 1988. "Sports and Male Domination: The Female Athlete as Contested Ideological Terrain." *Sociology of Sport Journal* 5 (3): 197–211.

Messner, M. A. 2002. *Taking the Field: Women, Men, and Sports*. Minneapolis: University of Minnesota Press.

NUS. 2012. *Out in Sport: LGBT Students' Experiences of Sport*. London: National Union of Students.

Pavlidis, A., and J. Connor. 2015. "Men in a 'Women Only' Sport? Contesting Gender Relations and Sex Integration in Roller Derby." *Sport in Society*. doi:/10.1080/17430437.2015.1067781.

Piedra, J., G. Ramírez-Macías, F. Ries, A. R. Rodríguez-Sánchez, and C. Phipps. 2015. "Homophobia and Heterosexism: Spanish Physical Education Teachers' Perceptions." *Sport in Society*. doi:10.1080/17430437. 2015.1096257.

Pieper, L. P. 2015. "'Preserving la difference': The Elusiveness of Sex-segregated Sport." *Sport in Society*. doi:10.1080/17430437.2015.1096258.

Pizzolati, M., and D. Sterchele. 2016. "Mixed-sex in Sport for Development: A Pragmatic and Symbolic Device." *The Case of Touch Rugby for Forced Migrants in Rome*. Forthcoming.

Priyadharshini, E., and A. Pressland. 2015. "Doing Femininities and Masculinities in a 'Feminized' Sporting Arena: The Case of Mixed-Sex Cheerleading." *Sport in Society*. doi:10.1080/17430437.2015.1096253.

Roth, A., and S. A. Basow. 2004. "Femininity, Sports, and Feminism: Developing a Theory of Physical Liberation." *Journal of Sport and Social Issues* 28 (3): 245–265.

Sailors, P. R. 2015. "Off the Beaten Path: Should Women Compete against Men?." *Sport in Society*. doi:10.1080 /17430437.2015.1096255.

Seagrave, J. O. 2015. "Challenging the Gender Binary: The Fictive and Real World of Quidditch." *Sport in Society*. doi:10.1080/17430437.2015.1067783.

Snyder, Eldon E., and Ronald Ammons. 1993. "Adult Participation in Coed Softball: Relations in a Gender Integrated Sport." *Journal of Sport Behaviour* 16 (1): 3–15.

Summerfield, K., and A. White. 1989. "Korfball: A Model of Egalitarianism?" *Sociology of Sport Journal* 6 (2): 144–151.

Tagg, B. 2012. "Transgender Netballers: Ethical Issues and Lived Realities." *Sociology of Sport Journal* 29 (2): 151–167.

Tagg, B. 2014. Men's Netball or Gender-neutral Netball? *International Review for the Sociology of Sport*. Online first, doi:10.1177/1012690214524757.

Theberge, N. 2000. "Gender and Sport." In *Handbook of Sports Studies*, edited by J. Coakley and E. Dunning, 322–333. London: Sage.

Thorpe, Holly. 2005. "Jibbing the Gender Order: Females in the Snowboarding Culture." *Sport in Society* 8 (1): 76–100.

Travers, A. 2008. "The Sport Nexus and Gender Injustice." *Studies in Social Justice* 2 (1): 79–101.

Travers, A. 2013. Thinking the Unthinkable: Imagining an "Un-American," Girl-friendly, Women-and Trans-inclusive Alternative for Baseball. *Journal of Sport & Social Issues* 13 (1): 78–96.

Travers, A., and J. Deri. 2011. "Transgender Inclusion and the Changing Face of Lesbian Softball Leagues." *International Review for the Sociology of Sport* 46 (4): 488–507.

Wachs, F. L. 2002. "Leveling the Playing Field: Negotiating Gendered Rules in Coed Softball." *Journal of Sport and Social Issues* 26 (3): 300–316.

Wachs, F. L. 2005. "The Boundaries of Difference: Negotiating Gender in Recreational Sport." *Sociological Inquiry* 75 (4): 527–547.

Winiarska, A., L. Jackson, L. Mayblin, and G. Valentine. 2015. "'They Kick You because They Are Not Able to Kick the Ball': Normative Conceptions of Sex Difference and the Politics of Exclusion in Mixed-sex Football." *Sport in Society*. doi:10.1080/17430437.2015.1067778.

Women's Sports Foundation. 2012. *Do You Know the Factors Influencing Girls' Participation in Sports?* Accessed Oct 25, 2015. http://www.womenssportsfoundation.org/home/support-us/do-you-know-the-factors-influencing-girls-participation-in-sports

Women's Sports Foundation. 2015. *Pay Inequity in Athletics*. Accessed Oct 25, 2015. http://www.womenssportsfoundation.org/home/research/articles-and-reports/equity-issues/pay-inequity

Woodward, K. 2014. "Legacies of 2012: Putting Women's Boxing into Discourse." *Contemporary Social Science* 9 (2): 242–252.

Alex Channon
University of Brighton, UK

Katherine Dashper, Thomas Fletcher
Leeds Beckett University, UK

Robert J. Lake
Douglas College, Canada

Off the beaten path: should women compete against men?

Pam R. Sailors

Department of Philosophy, Missouri State University, Springfield, MO, USA

ABSTRACT

Are women capable of competing against men in sporting events? If they aren't, might there be good reasons to encourage them to make the attempt anyway? If they are, might there be good reasons to prohibit such competition? I suggest four possible answers to the question of whether women are capable of competing against men: (1) No, so there's no point in talking about it; (2) No, but they should make the attempt anyway; (3) Yes, so mix all the competition and get on with it; and (4) Yes, but there are good reasons not to allow it. I review these positions, each of which is made plausible by supporting evidence, and suggest that the arguments can be strengthened through the inclusion of four distinctions (between individual/team sports, direct/indirect competition, contact/non-contact sports and amateur/professional sports).

Introduction

Billie Jean King beat Bobby Riggs, but only after he was long past his athletic prime. Annika Sörenstam couldn't make the cut in her historic attempt at a PGA Tour event. Yet Zhang Shan won an Olympic gold medal over male competitors in skeet shooting and Danica Patrick has had at least mixed success in auto racing. Are women capable of competing against men in sporting events? If they aren't, might there be good reasons to encourage them to make the attempt anyway? If they are, might there be good reasons to prohibit such competition? Arguments regarding the issue of sex segregation in athletics have been advanced through the years. Some have focused on the legal issues raised by sex segregation (Love and Kelly 2011), particularly as related to contact sports (Fields 2005). Others have examined sex integration in actual practice in martial arts (Channon 2012, 2013, 2014), soccer (Henry and Comeaux 1999), boxing (McNaughton 2012), wrestling (Miller 2010), cheerleading (Anderson 2008, 2010), equestrian sport (Dashper 2012), softball (Wachs 2002, 2005) and judo (Guerandel and Mennesson 2007). Still, there has been little consensus about the desirability of sex segregation and little meaningful change in existing policy. As a way of exploring this issue, I suggest four possible answers to the question of whether women are capable of competing against men: (1) No, so there's no point in talking about it; (2) No, but they should make the attempt anyway; (3) Yes, so mix all the competition and get on with it; and (4) Yes, but there are good reasons not to allow it. To be clear, I don't mean to claim that these are the only possible answers, or even that these are actual answers argued for in existing academic literature. What I do want to claim is that versions of these answers are common and that this division provides a useful framework for examining the question itself. I review these positions, each of which is made plausible by supporting evidence, and suggest that the arguments can be strengthened through the inclusion of four commonly overlooked distinctions (between individual/team sports, direct/indirect competition, contact/non-contact sports and amateur/professional sports). In the end, I conclude that the discussion is both complicated and enriched by the inclusion of these distinctions and impoverished by their absence.

Before going any further, I should note that the examination and analysis here will be from a philosophical perspective as my training and experience is in philosophy. It is not at all uncommon for sociologists and philosophers to arrive at the same point, but the destination is reached by taking very different paths. Most philosophers only rarely use, and almost never gather, empirical data. In fact, those working in ethics often emphatically claim that philosophy is concerned with what *ought* to be the case, not with what *is* the case. From a sociological perspective, this might be dismissed as armchair theorizing, just as the philosopher might dismiss a description of the methodology and results of a study as a sort of dustbowl empiricism. My own view is that theory without fact is no better than fact without theory and that the kind of disciplinary boundary-setting that would beg to differ functions to the detriment of all. So, although grounded in theoretically oriented philosophy of sport, I try at least to acknowledge throughout this paper some of the fine work from empirically oriented sociology of sport bearing on the issue of sex integration.

Are women capable of competing against men?

1. *No, so there's no point in talking about it.*

According to proponents of this view, men are biologically bigger, stronger and faster than women. The average adult male is taller (by 5 inches) than the average adult female, with a greater percentage of muscle (40% vs. 23%) and lesser percentage of fat (15% vs. 25%), all of which works towards performance advantage in the major sports (Messner 2007). Because these physical traits are necessary for sporting success, women are never going to be able to compete with men in any meaningful way. In track and field, for instance, the best female performances are more than 10 percent behind those of the best males (Tucker 2010a), and 'the very best female performance in the history of sport does not even make the top 500 male performances each year' (Tucker 2010b). An advocate of this position might go on to offer specific examples of women who have attempted to compete against men and failed. In football, Mo Isom tried out as a kicker at Louisiana State University, but did not make the team – not because she couldn't kick, but because she couldn't tackle. In basketball, Ann Meyers (Drysdale) signed with the Indiana Pacers team in 1980, did three-day tryouts, but was not chosen for final team. Even in golf, a decidedly less aggressive sport, both Annika Sorenstam and Michelle Wie, given sponsor's exemptions into PGA tournaments, failed to make the cut. Women are obviously incapable of competing with men, the argument concludes, so we do nothing more than waste time by discussing it.

While this argument may be initially compelling, I don't think it's true. It is, instead, a false generalization that can be believed only by a choosing one's evidence very selectively.

Of course, there are women who have tried unsuccessfully to compete against men, but there are also (as we will see) women who have had a different outcome. The fact that some women have successfully defeated men is unlikely to convince a proponent of this argument that all women will do so. By the same token, we should refuse to accept the fact some women have failed as demonstrating that all women will share that outcome.

2. No, but they should make the attempt anyway.

While most women are currently unable to compete against men, given time perhaps women *will* be able to compete. So, for example, while Mo Isom couldn't win a placekicker slot at LSU, Katie Hnida made the team at the University of New Mexico and has the distinction of being the first woman to score in a Division I-A football game. Holley Mangold, who played on the offensive line on her high school football team, and was the first female non-kicker in Ohio Division III, didn't go on to play in college, but instead became a member of the United States Olympic weightlifting team. And while the rumours that Brittney Griner, the first NCAA basketball player ever to score 2000 points and block 500 shots, would get a tryout in the NBA never led to anything, the prevalence of the rumours and the seriousness with which people discussed them show that many took a woman playing professional basketball against men someday to be a live possibility.

Even if we assume that the day when all women can compete against men is still far in the future, we might still want to encourage some women to make the attempt now. In that way, the few women who can compete may serve as role models, sending the message that women are equal to men and should be allowed to try anything they like. If no women are allowed to complete, it sends a far different message. Philosopher Jane English wrote one of the first serious examinations of mixed competition, 'Sex Equality in Sports' (1978). In it, she points out that: 'The very need for a protected competition class suggests inferiority. The pride and self-respect gained from witnessing a woman athlete who is not only the best woman but the very best athlete is much greater' (English 1978). English did not advocate, however, that women make the attempt; in the end, she remained on the side of sex segregation, believing that women would be better served by the creation of new sports designed to reward the physical traits that are more commonly possessed by women than by men. Several feminist scholars have also taken this position, claiming that women have a unique contribution to make, 'a new vision of sport' (MacKinnon 1987) that values women's 'abilities, talents, skills, and preferences' equally to those of men (Sherwin and Schwartz 2005). Some have gone even further, claiming that the attempt to develop women's talents to the point of being able to compete effectively against men fails to respect women as persons as it makes respect contingent on physical attributes and capabilities (Giordano and Harris 2005).

To the contrary, others have pointed to the need to avoid a dangerous implicit message sent by sex segregation to undergird their support of mixed competition. Eileen McDonagh and Laura Pappano argue that disallowing mixed competition sends the message that women are too weak to compete with men, so weak, in fact, that they must be protected from them. This division of women and men into weak and strong slides into an able/disabled binary, an interpretation perpetuating the idea that (able) men are superior to (disabled) women. In a compelling parallel, McDonagh and Pappano argue:

> This mode of thinking suggests that women must be segregated from men in order to find arenas where they can compete 'at the same level' by competing only with other females, that is, with similarly disabled athletes. This way of thinking also assumes women require modified rules, which call

for them to score fewer points, run shorter distances, and otherwise lessen the challenge to make it manageable for 'disabled' athletes. Thus we can consider coercively sex-segregated sports policies as a kind of same-sex Special Olympics. Same-sex sports with same-sex rules allow 'disabled' females to learn about competition and winning, teamwork, hard work, and the thrill of participation in a manner parallel to the experience for 'able' males without suffering the inevitable defeat females would experience if they tried to compete directly with males. (McDonagh and Pappano 2008, 143)

The argument here is that sex segregation is a problem such that it should be eliminated, even if women are not currently able to compete effectively with men. Stated positively, women should be allowed to compete with men because their success, even if only by a few, sends a powerful message and model to girls and women. Stated negatively, prohibiting women from competing with men is wrong because it sends a powerful message of women's inferiority.

This position certainly seems more plausible than the first, if for no other reason than that is less dogmatic. Still, there are at least two ways in which it can be criticized. First, there may be more effective strategies to ensure that women athletes appear as role models. As mentioned, Jane English argued for the invention of alternative sports that reward the physiological characteristics, 'like balance and buoyancy', that are generally more often found in women (English 1978). This would ensure that women athletes appear as positive role models since women would be successful at these sports. Second, while it's plausible that sex segregation may establish an able/disabled binary, mixed competition might actually reinforce it. That is, since the evidence currently shows that women only rarely triumph in competitions against men, mixed competition could reinforce the attitude that women are inferior. As Angela Schneider has noted, given the nature of professional and Olympic sports, and the sorts of skills they reward, mixed competition would result in the absence of women from elite competition. And, 'excluding women from the publicity that comes from the highest levels of sporting achievement would merely serve to reinforce women's systemic subservience to men' (Schneider 2000). Unfortunately, the next position fares no better.

3. *Yes, so mix all the competition and get on with it.*

Just as with the first answer, this seems true only if we select our evidence very carefully. For example, in the 2013 Ski Jumping World Cup, men and women jumped on the same hill on the same day in the same conditions. The men, on average, were slightly better than women in distance and style, but the difference was astonishingly small, and several of the women outscored the majority of male jumpers. Triathlete Chrissie Wellington never lost a triathlon at the Ironman distance, has the four fastest times ever recorded by a woman over that distance, finished second overall at the Alpe d'Huez Triathlon, less than a minute and a half behind the first place man. At the 2009 Ironman in Hawaii, only 22 men finished faster than Wellington. In a 2010 half-ironman distance in Kansas, she finished 11th overall and, in 2011, only four men were faster than she was at the Challenge Roth Ironman. Ultrarunner Ann Trason was the women's winner in the Western States Endurance Run 14 times, second place overall twice, and third place overall three times, and was in the overall top ten 13 times. At the Leadville Trail 100, she was the women's winner four times, second overall once and third overall once. She was the first and only woman to win the National Track & Field 24-h Championship outright. And she also was the outright winner of the 1994 Silver State 50-Mile Trail Run, 1992 Quicksilver 50-Mile Trail Run, 1991 Sri Chinmoy 100 mile, 1991 Bay Area 12 h and 1989 24 h National Championship. Stories of this sort suggest that sex segregation is based on nothing more than stereotypes and discrimination.

Such stories also give credence to claims like the following, from Mary Jo Kane:

> Although, given current conditions, it is certainly the case that most elite male athletes can beat most elite female athletes in sports that privilege men, it does not automatically follow that *every* elite male can outperform *every* elite female in these same sports. Yet this is precisely what we are trained to believe because it is one of the cornerstones of the oppositional binary. And it is because of this socially constructed and rigidly maintained sport structure that females are truly at a disadvantage in sports, not because of biology. (Kane 1995, 201)

Kane goes on to argue that we should replace the male/female binary with a continuum along which individuals would fall. Similarly, Cahn (2015) points out that 'focusing on average gender differentials misses the great overlap in men's and women's skill and performance' (291). Bennett Foddy and Julian Savulescu have also suggested that gender falls along a continuum and concluded that 'once we recognize that gender is not a binary quantity, sex segregation in competitive sport must be seen as an inconsistent and unjust policy' (Foddy and Savulescu 2011). Acceptance of this position would have the additional advantage of eliminating the practice of gender verification. Contentious as this may be at first glance, not only are male and female bodies similar, they become more so at the level of elite athletes provided with equal advantages and access. Dave Zirin makes this point and extends it to suggest that changes wrought by legal action have had biological consequences: 'Title IX, the 1972 law that imposed equal funding for girls' and boys' sports in schools, has radically altered not only women's fitness and emotional well-being but their bodies as well' (Zirin 2013). It may be worth mentioning that Tamburrini and Tännsjö (2005) push this line of thought even further to argue for the use of genetic engineering to enable women to compete on the same physical level as men. Although it falls well outside the scope and focus of his paper, their view has been soundly criticized on a variety of grounds (Chadwick and Wilson 2005; Giordano and Harris 2005; Sherwin and Schwartz 2005); I mention it only to serve as an example of the radical lengths some would go to argue for sex integration. Putting genetic engineering to the side and focusing on what is currently possible, I believe that the position advocating women competing against men has strengths, but it does not avoid the weakness of potentially causing a lack of athletic female role models. One more answer remains to be evaluated.

4. *Yes, but there are good reasons not to allow it.*

As noted in an earlier section, maintaining sex segregation allows women to be the overall winners more often, thereby modelling success. When the United States women's soccer team won the World Cup in 1999, it was thought to be a momentous occasion for women's soccer and, more generally, for women's sports. The match, the most-watched soccer match in US history, was seen as significant far beyond the game itself, as it fed interest in women's sports and served as an inspiration for young girls who had not previously paid much attention to soccer, but would soon flood the country's sports fields. The desirability of role models has already been given some discussion, and I'll return to it in a later section, but I mention it again here as a justification for sex segregation.

Beyond the provision of positive role models, sex segregation can be empowering if it is chosen instead of enforced. Roller Derby, for example, provides a unique case of a women's sport that is not derived from, or a diminutive version of, a men's sport, proudly stating as its philosophy a commitment to be 'by the skaters, for the skaters', and functions as a force for reshaping ideas about women, femininity and sport (Sailors 2013). Sex segregation can be disempowering, but the women behind the rebirth of roller derby have turned it into an empowering activity because the separation is self-chosen. Susan Birrell famously made this point, arguing that we should start by looking for times and conditions when segregation might be a good thing. In doing so, what we find is that that determination depends more on how a situation came to be rather than on the situation itself. Birrell, who wants to reserve the term 'segregation' to refer to 'imposed separatism', says we should:

> examine whether separatism is chosen or dictated. When the party in power forces the under-class out of an organization arbitrary discrimination has occurred. Separatism used as an exclusionary strategy to prevent one group from meaningful participation in the benefits and rewards of society or any institution is inherently unequal. … Thus separatism based on weakness and force is far different from separatism based on strength and choice. (Birrell 1984, 26)

So, rather than forcing mixed competition, we might do better to retain segregation as a matter of choice.

What about chosen separatism for the moment, with an eye towards eventual integration? This position, advocated by Claudio Tamburrini, is derived from his belief that the provision of equal facilities and training will, over time, decrease the sporting performance disparities between men and women. In cases where women are already capable of competing with men, we would begin mixed competition immediately. In cases where women are not yet capable of competing, segregation would continue until women reach that level (Tamburrini 2000). This approach is quite similar to the position taken by the National Organization for Women (NOW) after the passage of Title IX in the United States in 1972. NOW saw the primary goal as complete integration of sports and opposed any plan for Title IX implementation that was not developed towards that end (Ware 2011). In order to reach that point, schools would create a mixed team for every sport offered. If such an arrangement resulted in a team that was, whatever the reason, almost entirely male or female, a second team would be established for the underrepresented sex. 'The team must be equal to the predominantly single-sex team in areas such as facilities, coaching, expenditures, and prestige. At the point when the non-discriminatory unitary team was no longer predominantly single-sexed, there would no longer be a need to field an additional separate team' (Ware 2011). NOW's proposal, which never reached implementation, is similar to the relatively common position that would allow mixed competition for women who are capable of competing on the same level as men, while retaining sex segregation for those who are not (e.g. see Boxill 1993 and Burke 2010). This is not, however, a plan with which Tamburrini would agree for the reason that it might result in a sort of 'athletic-flight', with the most talented females abandoning women's sports for the higher rewards of men's sport, leaving women's sports bereft of its best athletes (Tamburrini 2000). As well, it could further problematize the issue of female athletes as role models, which is exactly where the examination of this position began.

The distinctions

As I have shown, none of the four possible answers to the question of whether women should compete against men has been entirely adequate. I want to suggest that this is because the question itself seems to assume a simple yes-or-no answer in an area where only a complex and contextualized answer is possible. The variety of sports and the multitude of levels at which they are played complicate the answering of a question that seems to presuppose a homogeneity that simply does not exist. Taking the variety of sports and the levels of competition into account, then, there are four distinctions that enrich the discussion of the issue of women competing against men. Our answer should include consideration of whether we are discussing an individual sport or a team sport, whether the sport involves direct or indirect competition, whether we are discussing contact or non-contact sports, and whether the level of completion is amateur or professional. These distinctions, as I've argued in an earlier more historically oriented piece (Sailors 2014), preclude quick and easy answers, but enable a richer and more satisfying conversation. Before looking at how the distinctions work in practice, it will be useful to review just what they mean.

The first distinction is between individual and team sports. Sports that feature individuals competing against each other may require more in the way of self-sufficiency and entail more exposure to risk than sports in which teams compete against each another. Individual sports tend also to reward the stereotypically masculine virtues of independence and autonomy, while team sports place a premium on the stereotypically feminine virtue of sacrifice of the individual for the good of the whole. To the extent that this is true, it may be relevant to the discussion of whether we ought to encourage mixed competition. I say 'relevant', rather than decisive, because there are individual sports – like kayaking and rock-climbing – where dependence on and sacrifice for others is respected, and team sports – like hockey and football – where a hyper-masculine disdain for anything stereotypically feminine would make successful sex integration near impossible (Howe 2007). Further, there are instances in which independence and autonomy are crucial for success (and survival) in kayaking and rock-climbing, and times when 'taking one for the team' may constitute the highest exemplar of masculinity in hockey and football.

The second distinction is between sports that involve direct competition and those in which the competition is indirect. In direct competition, the actions of one athlete or team are designed in part to serve as an obstacle to the success of the opponent. In indirect competition, the performance of one athlete or team has no physical impact on the performance of the opponent. Basketball is an example of direct competition, since a team not only must score but must also try to prevent the other team from scoring. Field events, like high jump and discus, are examples of indirect competition, since how high one jumps or how far one throws has no bearing on the height or distance attained by one's competitors. Of course, competitors may act in ways designed to exert psychological impact on one another, but this would seem to be equally true for males or females. The stereotypical notion that women are emotionally less capable of handling this sort of pressure is refuted by plentiful examples of male athletes 'choking', for example, golfers missing easy putts and sprinters false-starting.

The third distinction, between contact and non-contact sports, overlaps to some degree with the direct/indirect competition distinction. It is likely that all contact sports also fall under the category of direct competition. But not all direct competition involves contact. So, for example, rugby is a contact sport with direct competition, while curling involves direct competition without contact. Of all the distinctions, this may be the one most relevant to the question of whether women should compete against men because it is most correlated with the inherent physical differences – the muscle gap – between male and female physiology. In another overlap, the answer to that question may also vary depending on whether the sport is individual or team, as individual sports are more weighted with moralistic concerns. So, for example, male athletes may refuse to try their hardest when competing against females in contact sports like wrestling, martial arts and boxing (Channon 2014;

Guerandel and Mennesson 2007; McNaughton 2012), adding another element of complexity to this distinction.

An additional dimension, relevant to indirect/direct completion and contact/non-contact categories, regards sports that require extra-human ingredients as integral to performance. I am thinking here of equestrian sport and automobile racing, both are sports where sex integration is already common. This dimension further complicates the larger issue, especially as there is evidence that sex integration in these sports has not made for equitable competition, with the best rides (equine and automotive) and support going to male competitors (Dashper 2012). Given that this cuts across at least a couple of the already noted distinctions, and that it raises a larger question about the efficacy of sex-integrated sport towards establishing equity, I have not chosen to separate it into an additional category. I will return to the equity problem a bit later.

Finally, the fourth distinction is between amateur and professional/elite sport. The previous distinctions are designed to take into account the wide variety of sporting activity. Focusing elsewhere, this distinction illuminates the multitude of levels of competition. The differences between 8- and 9-year-old children playing in a school soccer league, adults in a community league, and elite athletes at the World Cup are so great that it is nonsensical to believe that one policy would apply equally well in all three cases. This distinction will involve overlap with all of the preceding, as each of them will also be distinguishable into the amateur or elite/professional category.

Now that the categories have been distinguished, they can be invoked to assist us in formulating more satisfactory positions on whether women should compete against men. Returning to the first answer – 'no, so there's no point in talking about it' – the problem identified was that of a hasty generalization made possible only by a selective choice of evidence. Just as the answer here points to examples of women who have failed at mixed competition in basketball and football, a critic could point to examples of women who had success against men in football and basketball. The distinctions we might find of most use here are between contact and non-contact sports and between the amateur and elite/professional levels. Baseball and tennis may offer greater chances for successful mixed competition than rugby and football because the 'muscle gap' is less pronounced in the former sports than in the latter. Similarly, because men and women at the amateur level are likely to be closer on the continuum of sporting ability, mixed teams at the amateur level will almost certainly allow female athletes to compete more successfully with men than at the elite/professional level. As Leslie Francis has noted, mixed competition at the amateur level can 'emphasize teamwork and complementary skills – both characteristics that are arguably beneficial and useful educationally. Such teamwork opportunities might also be highly useful in acculturating women and men to work together in other contexts' (Francis 1993). Thus, the benefits may extend beyond the playing field.

The second answer – 'no, but they should make the attempt anyway' – had the strength of avoiding treating women as if they are a disabled class in need of protection, but was troubled by the issue of providing enough successful female athletes to serve as positive role models. As noted, Schneider worries that mixed competition would eliminate female athletes from contention at the elite level, which would be a problem not only for women in sport but also for women more generally. 'Seeing, and valuing, strong athletic women provides not only an example to younger women of the range of the possible for women, but it also changes our social views of what is appropriate and good for women to do' (Schneider 2000). The view is shared by Coggon, Hammond and Holm: 'If people are to identify themselves with a sex, draw role models from their particular sex and place themselves in a societal context with reference to their sex, it would indeed be regrettable if a whole sex – generally it is felt to be women – should lose sporting role models' (Coggon, Hammond, and Holm 2008). Still, as important as it is for the provision of role models that women find athletic success in sex-segregated sport, it is equally important that we see the success of female athletes who actually are capable of competing against men. '[H]ow does it help women as a group to hide the few women who are as talented as men by prohibiting qualified women from "playing with the boys"? Hiding the women who can compete with men reinforces the false assumption that no women can meet the challenge' (McDonagh and Pappano 2008). If we employ the distinction between direct and indirect competition here, we can address this apparent conundrum by suggesting that female athletes be allowed, perhaps even encouraged, to compete against men in sports where the competition is indirect. This is not historically unprecedented; women and men competed together in Olympic shooting events from 1968 until 1992, when Shan Zhang from China had a record-setting score, defeated all the men, and won the gold medal. Beginning, or resuming as the case may be, mixed competition in indirect competition sports, like shooting, has the potential to provide role models of female athletes who triumph over *all* competition, not just all female competition.

The third answer – 'yes, so mix all the competition and get on with it' – had the strength of embracing the possibility of eliminating the gender binary (and, thus, gender verification), but also involved the selective choice of evidence that leads to hasty generalization. More practically, such a move would be likely to create such a frustrating experience of failure for many female athletes that they would abandon sports entirely. This was the rationale used by the Ontario Women's Hockey Association to continue sex segregation in Ontario even though the larger Canadian Hockey Association followed the practice of mixed-gender competition. The former organization's position is 'that an organization devoted exclusively to the advancement of female hockey will better meet the needs of girls and women' (Theberge 2000). Presumably, were those needs not met, girls and women would stop playing hockey. Of course, the continued participation of females on teams in the mixed association provides evidence that this fear may be misplaced. Still, even assuming its validity, the distinction between contact and non-contact sports could be helpful here, as one could argue for the inclusion of females on male teams in non-contact positions. Since the average size and strength of men and women are closer, or equalized by, non-contact roles, we might be more willing to support girls as goalies instead of defence in hockey, or kickers instead of linebackers in football.

The fourth answer – 'yes, but there are good reasons not to allow it' – has the advantage of acknowledging the value of self-chosen separatism, but lacks, at least in this basic form, the possibility of a transition to mixed competition in the event that particularly talented female athletes wish to compete against men. While I acknowledge the empowering potential of self-chosen separatism and would not suggest that women should not be able to continue to choose all-female competition, it's important to recognize that blocking talented female athletes from competition against men is a serious impediment for those females since it stands in the way of the progression of their athletic skills. In her study of women's hockey, Nancy Theberge found that female players agreed that their abilities were not on the same level as male players, but they also believed that mixed competition could lessen the disparity by making them better players. As she describes it:

… when speaking of their experiences playing with and against men, women hockey players emphasize the significance of natural differences. At the same time, they clearly understand that the gender gap is variable. In this regard players are quick to cite the truism in sport that 'if you play against better competition, you'll get better.' While holding to the view that men are stronger and as a result 'better,' women clearly recognize that the 'muscle gap' is conditioned by social experiences. Moreover, while emphasizing the significance of the muscle gap, players also cite other aspects of the sport, such as play making and 'smarts,' where there is no gender gap. (Theberge 2000, 150)

So, allowing mixed competition in some sports, even while women are not as talented as men, makes it more likely that they will become, over time, as talented as men. The distinction we might want to use here is between team and individual sports. In team sports, mixing females and males on the same team allows the females to better their game while avoiding the frustration of being outplayed by an all-male team. At the same time, in at least most individual sports, we may want to continue the policy of sex segregation since individual females competing against males in one-on-one competition is less likely to improve skills than to lead to abandoning sport in response to failure. Of course, there will be exceptions, as in the case of females competing in wrestling or martial arts, for example, where an opportunity for genuine competition requires they compete against males. In all cases, as noted above, the choice should be *available* to female athletes rather than compelled.

Practical difficulty

I suggested early on that theory without fact is impoverished; while what ought to be the case is vitally important, what actually is the case must not be ignored. Examination of what the outcomes have been when sex integration has been put into practice shows that people don't always conform to the expectations of theory. On the positive side, Anderson (2008, 2010) has shown that sex integration in cheerleading led the male participants to think more highly of women's athletic ability and leadership qualities, and to rethink their previous sexist and misogynistic attitudes. Miller (2010) pointed to the ability of his daughter to demonstrate resistance to stereotypical notions of masculinity and femininity through wrestling against boys. Similarly, Channon argues (2012, 2013, 2014) that sex integration in martial arts can work towards 'undoing' gender by challenging sexist attitudes.

Unfortunately, the results of sex integration are not always so positive. In the fully integrated sport of equestrian, Dashper (2012) locates 'subtle discrimination and hidden barriers' (217) that work to create disadvantageous conditions for female riders and perpetuate the superiority of male riders. In co-ed soccer, Henry and Comeaux (1999) found that male players inevitably take the key positions, while women are relegated to the wings. Wachs' (2005) study of co-ed softball echoes this, noting that females end up in the positions on the field least central to the action; females are more likely to catch a ball thrown by a male who has made a play on the ball than to be in the position to instigate a play (539). The ways in which male and female performances are interpreted also reproduce ideas of gender essentialism; for example, an error by a male is interpreted as bad luck, while an error by a female is taken as proof of her inferior skill. Further, Wachs argues (2002) that the rules designed to equalize conditions actually reinforce stereotypical notions of male athletic superiority by implicitly suggesting that women are weaker athletes who would be excluded if the rules did not force inclusion. As Travers (2008) summarizes, 'where sporting spaces are currently gender integrated, many are characterized by a climate of sexism and misogyny that keeps all but the bravest and almost freakishly talented girls and women from participating' (94). Unfortunately, there is no easy legal fix to the problem, as rulings about sex segregation have often functioned to 'entrench gender inequality' by assuming an ideology of women's inferiority (Love and Kelly 2011). Thus, however we answer the question of whether men and women ought to compete together, we should bear in mind that the integration in practice has shown mixed results for gender equity and will need to be supplemented by deeper societal changes.

Conclusion

After examining four possible answers to the question of whether women athletes should compete against men, I concluded that none is completely satisfactory on its own. I suggested that this is the case, at least in part, because of a failure to recognize the complexity of sport and highlighted four distinctions to acknowledge that complexity. I then returned to the four possible answers considered earlier and applied the distinctions to show how the discussion is enriched by their inclusion. In each case, I used only one of the distinctions, but it is important to recognize that in actual practice more than one distinction should be considered in every case since the distinctions themselves overlap. It is also important not to lose sight of the fact that equality through sex integration will require more than good intentions and a coherent theory so long as cultural ideas about male superiority persist. Still, acknowledging the complexity of sport and sporting practice at least avoids the mistake of trying to answer a complicated question in a simplistic way and points us in the direction for a more fruitful conversation about sex segregation and mixed competition.

Disclosure statement

No potential conflict of interest was reported by the author.

References

Anderson, Eric. 2008. "'I Used to Think Women Were Weak': Orthodox Masculinity, Gender Segregation, and Sport." *Sociological Forum* 23 (2): 257–280.

Anderson, Eric. 2010. *Sport, Theory and Social Problems: A Critical Introduction*. New York: Routledge.

Birrell, Susan. 1984. "Separatism as an Issue in Women's Sport." *ARENA Review* 8: 21–29.

Boxill, Jan. 1993. "Title IX and Gender Equity." *Journal of the Philosophy of Sport* 20 (1): 23–31.

Burke, Michael. 2010. "A Feminist Reconstruction of Liberal Rights and Sport." *Journal of the Philosophy of Sport* 37: 11–28.

Cahn, Susan K. 2015. *Coming on Strong: Gender and Sexuality in Women's Sport*. 2nd ed. Chicago: University of Illinois Press.

Chadwick, Ruth, and Sarah Wilson. 2005. "Bio-Amazons – A Comment." In *Genetic Technology and Sport: Ethical questions*, edited by C. Tamburrini and T. Tännsjö, 205–208. New York: Routledge.

Channon, Alex. 2012. "Why Sex Segregation is Bad for Society." *On the Issues Magazine*. Accessed June 2, 2015. http://www.ontheissuesmagazine.com/2012spring/2012spring_Channon.php

Channon, Alex. 2013. "Enter the Discourse: Exploring the Discursive Roots of Inclusivity in Mixed-sex Martial Arts." *Sport in Society* 16 (10): 1293–1308.

Channon, Alex. 2014. "Towards the 'Undoing' of Gender in Mixed-sex Martial Arts and Combat Sports." *Societies* 4: 587–605.

Coggon, John, Natasha Hammond, and Soren Holm. 2008. "Transsexuals in Sport-fairness and Freedom, Regulation and Law." *Sport, Ethics and Philosophy* 2 (1): 4–17.

Dashper, Katherine. 2012. "Together, Yet Still Not Equal? Sex Integration in Equestrian Sport." *Asia-Pacific Journal of Health, Sport and Physical Education* 3 (3): 213–225.

English, Jane. 1978. "Sex Equality in Sports." *Philosophy & Public Affairs* 7 (3): 269–277.

Fields, Sarah K. 2005. *Female Gladiators: Gender, Law, and Contact Sport in America*. Chicago: University of Illinois Press.

Foddy, Benedict, and Julian Savulescu. 2011. "Time to Re-evaluate Gender Segregation in Athletics?" *British Journal of Sports Medicine* 45: 1184–1188.

Francis, Leslie P. 1993. "Title IX: Equality for Women's Sports?" *Journal of the Philosophy of Sport* 20 (1): 32–47.

Giordano, Simona, and John Harris. 2005. "What is Gender Equality in Sports?" In *Genetic Technology and Sport: Ethical Questions*, edited by C. Tamburrini and T. Tännsjö, 209–217. New York: Routledge.

Guerandel, Carine, and Christine Mennesson. 2007. "Gender Construction in Judo Interactions." *International Review for the Sociology of Sport* 42 (2): 167–186.

Henry, Jacques M., and Howard P. Comeaux. 1999. "Gender Egalitarianism in Coed Sport: A Case Study of American Soccer." *International Review for the Sociology of Sport* 34 (3): 277–290.

Howe, Leslie. 2007. "Being and Playing: Sport and the Valorization of Gender." In *Ethics in Sport*. 2nd ed, edited by William J. Morgan, 331–345. Champaign, IL: Human Kinetics.

Kane, Mary Jo. 1995. "Resistance/Transformation of the Oppositional Binary: Exposing Sport as a Continuum." *Journal of Sport & Social Issues* 19: 191–218.

Love, Adam, and Kimberly Kelly. 2011. "Equity or Essentialism? U.S. Courts and the Legitimation of Girls' Teams in High School Sport." *Gender & Society* 25 (2): 227–249.

MacKinnon, Catherine A. 1987. *Feminism Unmodified: Discourses on Life and Law*. Cambridge, MA: Harvard University Press.

McDonagh, Eileen, and Laura Pappano. 2008. *Playing with the Boys: Why Separate is Not Equal in Sports*. New York: Oxford University Press.

McNaughton, Melanie Joy. 2012. "Insurrectionary Womanliness: Gender and the (Boxing) Ring." *The Qualitative Report* 17 (article 33): 1–13.

Messner, Michael A. 2007. *Out of Play: Critical Essays on Gender and Sport*. Albany: State University of New York Press.

Miller, Shane Aaron. 2010. "Making the Boys Cry: The Performative Dimensions of Fluid Gender." *Text and Performance Quarterly* 30 (2): 163–182.

Sailors, Pam R. 2013. "Gender Roles Roll." *Sport, Ethics and Philosophy* 7 (2): 245–258.

Sailors, Pam R. 2014. "Mixed Competition and Mixed Messages." *Journal of the Philosophy of Sport* 41 (1): 65–77.

Schneider, Angela J. 2000. "On the Definition of 'woman' in the Sport Context." In *Values in Sport: Elitism, Nationalism, Gender Equality and the Scientific Manufacture of Winners*, edited by T. Tännsjö and C. Tamburrini, 123–138. New York: E & FN Spon.

Sherwin, Susan, and Meredith Schwartz. 2005. "Resisting the Emergence of Bio-Amazons." In *Genetic Technology and Sport: Ethical Questions*, edited by C. Tamburrini and T. Tännsjö, 199–204. New York: Routledge.

Tamburrini, Claudio. 2000. *The "Hand of God"? Essays in the Philosophy of Sport*. Goteborg: Acta Universitatis Gothoburgensis.

Tamburrini, Claudio, and Torbjörn Tännsjö. 2005. "The Genetic Design of a New Amazon." In *Genetic Technology and Sport: Ethical Questions*, edited by C. Tamburrini and T. Tännsjö, 181–198. New York: Routledge.

Theberge, Nancy. 2000. *Higher Goals: Women's Ice Hockey and the Politics of Gender*. Albany: State University of New York Press.

Travers, Ann. 2008. "The Sport Nexus and Gender Injustice." *Studies in Social Justice* 2 (1): 79–101.

Tucker, Ross. 2010a. "Let Male and Female Compete Together: The Abolition of Gender Categories in Sport: A Sound Argument?" Accessed June 2, 2015. http://sportsscientists.com/2010/04/let-male-and-female-compete-together/

Tucker, Ross. 2010b. "Semenya: Will Announce Her Results: And Thoughts on Natural vs Unfairadvantages." Accessed June 2, 2015. http://sportsscientists.com/2010/04/semenya-will-announce-her-results/

Wachs, Faye Linda. 2002. "Leveling the Playing Field: Negotiating Gendered Rules in Coed Softball." *Journal of Sport & Social Issues* 26 (3): 300–316.

Wachs, Faye Linda. 2005. "The Boundaries of Difference: Negotiating Gender in Recreational Sport." *Sociological Inquiry* 75 (4): 527–547.

Ware, Susan. 2011. *Game, Set, Match: Billie Jean King and the Revolution in Women's Sports.* Chapel Hill: University of North Carolina Press.

Zirin, Dave. 2013. *Game over: How Politics Has Turned the Sports World Upside Down.* New York: New Press.

'Preserving la difference': the elusiveness of sex-segregated sport

Lindsay Parks Pieper

Sport Management Department, Lynchburg College, Lynchburg, VA, USA

ABSTRACT

Sport is founded upon a belief in dimorphic sex, dichotomous gender and segregated competition. To uphold these binaries, sport authorities repeatedly relied upon medico-scientific technologies to draw a line between men and women. However, all efforts to conclusively delineate sex failed. This paper details the IAAF's and IOC's use of anatomical examinations, chromatin assessments, DNA testing and hormonal analyses in their attempt to circumscribe womanhood. The history of these efforts illustrates the elusiveness of sex determination, as well an unwavering belief in its infallibility. All four approaches proved arbitrary, reaffirmed a false system of polarized sex/gender and discriminated against individuals who fell outside society's two-sexed classification. By engaging gender, medical and sport scholarships, this paper shows how widespread social anxieties, medico-scientific ideologies and sporting norms coalesced, resulting in (unsuccessful) efforts to maintain separation. The history of sex/gender testing shows sex is indefinable, thereby suggesting sex segregation is impossible.

Introduction

An injustice jeopardized fairness in 1960s track and field. This threat also endangered the fundamental blueprint of sport. According to a 1966 *Time* magazine article, 'the incident – and what to do about them – had been bothering the International Amateur Athletic Federation (IAAF) for years'. The incident? The supposed appearance of male imposters in women's track and field events. Although no man posing as a woman had ever been discovered in sport, the IAAF acted quickly and accordingly. In 1966, the IAAF implemented a physical examination for all women 'in the interest of preserving la difference' ('Preserving la difference, 1966).

Physical contests rely upon a deeply rooted belief in dimorphic sex and dichotomous gender.[1] The development of sport therefore encompassed notions of natural sex difference and masculine superiority. Because athletic competency historically signified manhood and manliness, practitioners forged sex-segregated participation to both uphold fair play and preserve male dominion in sport (Cahn 1994; Hargreaves 1994; Messner, 1988). In other words, cultural norms dictated that, due to men's supposed natural capability – and women's supposed natural incapability – male and female athletes needed separate spaces to compete. This paradigm not only helped preserve physical contests as masculine endeavours, but also established women athletes as inferior and in need of protection.

Deeming sex segregation a necessity, and diminishing opportunities for integration in the process, sport officials sought mechanisms to separate women from men. At different historical moments, authorities implemented four innovative medico-scientific technologies to maintain sex separation in elite competition. First, as gonadal theories of sex reigned supreme in the interwar era, the IAAF and the International Olympic Committee (IOC) required that 'suspicious' female competitors undergo an anatomical investigation to verify their womanhood (Berg 2009; Cahn 1994; Heggie 2010; Tullis 2013). Next, the discovery of anatomical ambiguities and the rise of the Cold War encouraged sport officials to embrace a new sex determination technique: the buccal smear test, which checks for the presence of Barr bodies, masses typicallky seen in the X chromosome. Yet, the existence of chromosomal varieties rendered this check erroneous (Ritchie 2003; Schultz 2014; Schweinbenz and Cronk 2010; Sullivan 2011; Wiederkehr 2006). While the IAAF thusly abandoned chromatin verification in 1992, the IOC introduced a third measure. From 1992 to 1999, officials forced female Olympians to undergo DNA testing to prove their sex. Again the method failed to distinguish men from women, causing the IOC to briefly relinquish control (Pieper 2014; Serrat and García de Herreros 1996; Vignetti et al. 1996). However, the appearance of powerful female athletes in the new millennium encouraged the IAAF and IOC to reintroduce verification in 2011 (Cooky and Dworkin 2013; Nyong'o 2010; Vannini and Foernssler 2011). This fourth mechanism assessed hormonal levels (IAAF 2011; IOC 2012).

Each of these four tests not only reflected the prevailing beliefs about sex and gender in specific time periods, but they also all failed to unequivocally determine sex. As scientific writer David Epstein (2014) explains, 'Human biology does not break down into male and female as politely as sport governing bodies wish it would' (58). The ability to delineate a division of sex has historically proven arbitrary as it exists as a spectrum rather than a binary. 'Humans come in a wonderful array of types: many sizes, many abilities, and many approaches to experiencing and organizing the world', notes bioethicist Alice Domurat Dreger (1998, 3). Despite the 'truly extraordinary' variation, sport authorities repeatedly attempted to draw a concrete line between men and women to uphold a sex-segregated sporting paradigm.

This paper traces the development of sex-segregated sport and details four specific historical examples of unsuccessful medico-scientific support for the classification system. The IAAF's and IOC's use of the different technologies, which all failed to identify sex, illustrates both the elusive nature of sex determination, as well as sport officials' unwavering belief in infallible sex – despite repeated evidence to the contrary. From anatomical investigations to hormonal analyses, all four efforts to preserve 'la différence' have historically proven arbitrary, reaffirmed a false system of binary sex, upheld the belief in masculine athletic superiority, and discriminated against individuals who fell outside society's two-sexed classification system. This history also provides support for sex-integrated sport. The history of sex/gender testing shows sex is medically and scientifically indefinable, which suggests sex segregation based on medico-scientific technologies is impossible. While sex-based classifications have proven to be elusive, sex-integrated opportunities eliminate falsely constructed categories.

Sex-integrated sport has the potential to allow female athletes to demonstrate their physical prowess, unhindered by social presumptions and medico-scientific interventions.

The creation of sex-segregated sport

Physical competitions gained increased importance in the mid-nineteenth century. During this time period, many Western countries underwent massive social changes as industrialization impacted economic, familial, political and sporting norms. Increased leisure time, the rise of immigration, the trend toward urbanization and the development of the women's suffrage movement coalesced, granting sport new cultural significance (Cahn 1994; Kimmel 1997; Putney 2003). On the one hand, the middle class interpreted regimented recreations as tools to both assimilate immigrants and integrate the growing working class into the capitalist order. According to historian Cahn (1994), many viewed the 'growing numbers of poor, immigrant urban workers as an unruly mass in need of disciplined activity' (9). On the other hand, disruptions to the conventional gender pattern sparked fears of social feminization. Although many women remained bounded to domesticity by a 'separate spheres' tradition, a growing number demanded economic and political rights. The advancements in female employment and suffrage triggered a 'crisis in masculinity' at the end of the century (Kimmel 1997).

To absolve this supposed crisis, many men turned to sport as a means to demonstrate their manliness and reassert their power (Riess 1999). According to sociologist Messner (1988), 'Sport was a male-created homosocial cultural sphere that provided men with psychological separation from the perceived feminization of society while also providing dramatic symbolic proof of the "natural superiority" of men over women' (200). Or, as historian Hargreaves (1994) puts it, 'In the nineteenth century there was no question that sports were the "natural" domain of men' (43). Such ideologies proliferated and shaped women's eventual marginalized inclusion in sport.

With sport constructed as a cultural space reserved for men, and athletic prowess an attribute linked to masculinity, women's encroachment into this realm caused great social angst. As female athletes cycled, jumped, ran, swam and threw, the larger population grew anxious about the social implication. Women in sport, explains Messner (1988), 'represents a challenge to the ideological basis of male domination' (198). In other words, the appearance of the female athlete at the turn-of-the-century challenged the notion of men as inherently faster, stronger and superior to women. Therefore, to curb this threat, sport practitioners emphasized biological differences between the sexes. For example, authorities prioritized reproduction, child rearing and menstruation as moments of masculine and feminine disparity (Vertinsky, 1994). 'Biological ideas were used specifically to construct social ideas about gender and to defend inequalities between men and women in sports', argues Hargreaves (1994, 43). Men were thus characterized as naturally aggressive, competitive and powerful, whereas women were characterized as naturally passive, cooperative and weak. Consequently, sport practitioners – male and female alike – created separate activities for male and female participants. Men engaged unhindered, whereas women frequently competed in moderated activities to preserve their health and limit their exertion (Cahn 1994). The sex-segregated line was thus drawn.

Yet, with the need for a division of sex assumed – shaped by dominant gender norms – questions surfaced when female athletes demonstrated traits deemed masculine, such as aggression, muscularity, speed, strength and power. If these athletic attributes represented maleness, what did it mean when women possessed them? Because of the historical association of masculinity and sport, many viewed muscular female competitors with suspicion and derision (Cahn 1994; Ritchie 2003; Schultz 2014). Popular lore suggested that these women, those who excelled in sport by demonstrating aggression, showing strength and possessing muscles, could not be 'real' representatives of the 'weaker' sex.

Such hostile misgivings stemmed from the sex-segregated nature of elite competitions and underwrote the history of sex/gender testing. For sport to remain a bastion of masculinity, officials needed to highlight sex difference and maintain sex separation. Therefore, the IAAF and IOC implemented several medico-scientific mechanisms to continue the division between men and women. Although each measure failed, and actually illustrated the elusiveness of sex determination, officials remained dedicated to the task of separating the sexes for both the sake of sport and the larger social order.

Anatomical difference, anatomical investigations

Sport was not the first structure that sought to irrevocably divide men and women. As Dreger (1998) notes, 'many assume that if we don't keep males and females sorted, at least at some basic level, social institutions that we hold dear … will no longer be viable' (9). For example, the institutions of marriage, sexuality and sport were all built on the notion that men and women were distinct and discernible. Efforts to split the sexes therefore predated the introduction of high-stakes competition.

Anatomy and sex determination

Prior to the development of organized sport in the nineteenth century, a one-sex model held sway. The driving ideology of this paradigm was that men and women existed as two forms of the same sex. Accordingly, men and women possessed the same reproductive structure; however, male anatomy was located on the outside of the body whereas female anatomy was located on the inside (Fausto-Sterling 2000; Laqueur 1990). Put simply, women's reproductive organs were viewed as an inversion of men's (Schleiner 2000). Significantly, in the one-sex model, sex existed as a spectrum and not as a binary. For example, physicians in the Middle Ages suggested that temperatures during pregnancy sparked sex variety. Heat on the right side of the uterus created men, while coolness on the left side of the uterus created women. Foetuses in the middle became womanly men or manly women (Fisher 2011). Although the one-sex model prioritized men and maleness, the opportunity for a sex/gender continuum nevertheless existed.

The eighteenth century proved transitional as a two-sex model started to gain traction in medical circles and popular culture (Laqueur 1990). This standard characterized men and women as polar opposites, both in terms of biology and social roles. Cultural, political and scientific changes advanced this classification system. Perhaps most influentially, state and religious institutions intervened and demanded the division of sexes to bolster new gender expectations. Both the law and the church increasingly desired sexual clarity to sustain the growing authority of marriage (Cott 2000). Women's later demands for rights, as well as the lingering influences of Enlightenment thinkers, helped cement the two-sex ideology in Western society (Petersen 1998).

By the start of the nineteenth century, external anatomy took over as the preeminent feature in the labelling of dimorphic sex. Newly professionalized physicians seized control from midwives and prioritized men's and women's reproductive organs in the determination of sex (Vertinksy 1994). Importantly, anatomical theories of sex differentiation upheld the Victorian Era norms of 'separate spheres'. Measurements and assessments of male and female brain formations, reproductive organs and skull shapes supposedly explained women's domesticity, passivity and subservience. Such decisions regarding women's health and well-being stemmed more from social beliefs than scientific innovations. As historian Elizabeth Reis (2009) explains, 'medical practice cannot be understood apart from the broader culture in which it is embedded' (x). Paralleling the larger social views of women, male physicians emphasized anatomical difference. However, because of scientific innovations, experts next turned to the gonads – testes and ovaries – as the true indicators of sex.

Dreger (1998) labels the nineteenth century the 'Age of the Gonads'. Anxieties over the instability of sexual identities, angsts over the possibility of women's suffrage, fears of women's new sporting opportunities, the rise of gynaecology and the influential position of reproduction in gender roles all coalesced, pushing the gonads to the forefront of the medical literature. Medical authorities and sporting leaders alike viewed women as inferior to men, consequently shaping women's biological, social and sporting status. In terms of biology, argues Dreger (1998), physicians 'came to an agreement that every body's "true" sex was marked by one thing and one thing only: the anatomical nature of the gonadal tissue as either ovarian or testicular' (29). Because of this focus on the gonads, medical authorities did not yet consider outward appearances in the determination of sex. One could appear masculine, equipped with a beard and a penis, yet be categorized as female due to the presence of ovaries. In terms of sport, practitioners embraced the importance of gonads; however, they rejected the notion that outward appearances held no significance in the determination of sex (Ritchie 2003; Schultz 2014). Rather, sport authorities believed that outward expressions of femininity also helped indicate womanhood. Unfeminine female athletes challenged the notion of sport as a male domain; consequently, they faced scorn and disdain, particularly when competing in track and field.

Anatomy and sport

Pierre de Coubertin founded the modern Olympics in 1896 with a belief in the veracity of sex-segregated competition. Influenced by the dominant Western social norms that positioned men above women athletically, economically, legally and politically, he maintained separation by simply barring women from the first Games held in Athens. In his view (1896), female physical exertion was 'impractical, uninteresting, ungainly, and … improper', and, as a result, he infamously argued that 'the Olympic Games must be reserved for men' (542–546). Coubertin maintained his views on womanhood for the duration of his tenure as IOC president, 1896–1925; however, the expansion of the Olympics spurred the delegation of authority to local groups. The more relaxed regulations of these committees eventually permitted women's inclusion – starting immediately in the 1900 Paris Games – albeit in segregated and limited competitions (Mitchell 1977). Female Olympians competed in events deemed appropriate, such as golf and tennis, and tellingly remained prohibited from track and field, the era's most popular, masculine and gruelling sport (Cahn 1994; Hargreaves 1994). When female Olympians did finally gain access to athletics in 1928 – after years of protest from Alice Milliat and the *Fédération Sportive Féminine Internationale* – sex/gender anxieties ensued (Carpentier and Lefèvre 2006). The masculine nature of track and field concerned sport officials, medical practitioners and the public alike (Cahn 1994; Hargreaves 1994). Accordingly, female runners and throwers were too strong, too muscular and too fast to be 'real' women. Therefore, to preserve sex-segregated competition, women track and field competitors needed to prove their womanhood.

Women's track and field debuted at the 1928 Amsterdam Games; almost immediately, sport officials questioned the sex/gender of one of the runners. Silver medallist Hitomi Kinue served as Japan's first and lone female representative at the Amsterdam Games, as well as the first Japanese woman to earn an Olympic medal (Frost 2010). She was also likely the first to undergo a sex test during Olympic competition. According to US sports writer Rice (1936), prior to the 1928 Olympics, a 'case concerned a Japanese girl in Amsterdam, where the investigating committee was out two hours before it decided predominant sex'. Although a vague account, Rice's description insinuates that appearance-based suspicions encouraged the IOC to conduct an anatomical investigation to verify Hitomi's sex. In other words, because she did not outwardly present conventional notions of femininity, and instead displayed muscularity and strength, Hitomi challenged the system that reserved athleticism for men. And when questioning her gender, sport authorities turned to anatomical sex. Such checks only increased as women continued to excel in track and field.

The anxieties peaked at the 1936 Olympics. As many scholars have shown (Heggie 2010; Ritchie 2003; Schultz 2014; Sullivan 2011), the Berlin Games proved rife with accusations of male masqueraders. In the 100 m final, US runner Helen Stephens defeated world record holder Stanisława Walasiewicz, known more commonly as Stella Walsh in the United States. Because of Stephens' powerful physique, raspy voice and speedy time, some claimed the US farm girl cheated (Hanson 2004). Rumours that Stephens was actually male proliferated. According to the Polish newspaper *Kurier Poranny*, the USA had purposely entered a man into the women's event. The writer argued that (as cited in 'Polish Writer Calls') 'Miss Walasiewicz would have gained first place if she had competed only against women'. To dispel the innuendos, Berlin organizers quickly revealed that Stephens had undergone an anatomical examination prior to the Games. This inquiry marked the first widely reported sex test of the modern Olympic Movement.

Anecdotal accounts suggest that similar anatomical investigations were common practice during the interwar era to ensure only women competed in women's events. For example, when discussing Stephens' sudden publicity, US sportswriter Paul Gallico (1937) explained that the American Athletics Union 'had La Stephens frisked for sex … [and] checked her in as one hundred percent female' (234). When questioned, Stephens herself reportedly told the press to 'check the facts with the Olympic committee physician who sex-tested all athletes prior to competition' (as cited in Hanson 2004, 96). Similarly, runner-up Walsh supposedly underwent numerous examinations, likely as a result of her muscularity and speed. According to her childhood friend Casimir Bielen (as cited in Tullis 2013), Walsh 'was medically examined by hundreds of doctors' and regularly 'passed qualifying medical examinations' before competing.

The successes and appearances of track and field athletes convinced several sport organizations to implement a protective measure to ensure sex segregation continued. After resuming competitions after a brief hiatus caused by Second World War, the IAAF required that all female participants provide a physician's note verifying sex in 1946. The IOC followed suit 2 years later (Heggie 2010). Yet, fears that unscrupulous individuals might obtain fraudulent documentation convinced the IAAF to introduce compulsory anatomical investigations in 1966. As IAAF member Arne Ljungqvist (2011) later recalled, 'sport had no other means of asserting the gender of participants other than having them parade naked in front of a panel of doctors' (183). The era of obligatory sex examinations commenced.

At the 1966 British Empire & Commonwealth Games in Kingston, Jamaica, the IAAF first initiated the requisite control. British athlete Peters (1974) remembered being asked to lie down on a couch and pull her knees to her chest for the examination. She likened the process to a 'grope' and described it as the 'most crude and degrading experience I have ever known in my life' (56–57). The manual component of the inspection likely occurred as the doctors checked her gonads. As Canadian runner Abby Hoffman told the *Globe and Mail* (as cited in Jollimore 1992), 'they may have laid a hand on the genital area to make sure there were no hidden genitals'. Two weeks later, the IAAF continued the compulsory examination at the 1966 European Athletics Championship in Budapest, Hungary. This test was less intrusive as three female doctors only visually inspected the competitors' genitals. Deeming the procedure a success, the IAAF extended sex testing into the 1966 Asian Games and the 1967 Pan American Games (Ritchie 2003).

Yet, the humiliating nature of the 'nude parade', compounded by the inadequacy of anatomy as the sole determinant of sex, caused problems. Foremost, female athletes detested the procedure. As the *Times of India* reported in 1966, some women regarded the exam 'as an intolerable personal indignity', while others refused to undergo scrutiny on the basis of religious beliefs.[2] Second, the anatomical investigations did not clearly, nor easily, delineate sex. While most women have a clitoris, fallopian tubes, ovaries and a vagina, and most men have a prostate, a scrotal sac, testicles and a penis, each come in a variety of shapes and sizes, even in people considered anatomically 'normal'. Thus, the IAAF's and IOC's first attempts to scientifically uphold sex-segregated competition were erroneous.

Finally, both sport organizations relied upon gender assumptions when deciding which athletes needed verification. Because female track and field athletes most noticeably disrupted normative notions of femininity, they underwent the first round of medico-scientific testing. Upon recognizing the impossibility of determining sex with anatomical features, yet still dedicated to a sex-based classification, the IAAF and IOC next sought a more innovative technique to ensure segregated contests remained intact.

Chromosomal difference, chromatin checks

As the IAAF and IOC searched for new measures to validate women's eligibility, medico-scientific authorities continued to debate the components of sex/gender. By the middle of the twentieth century, most agreed that nuclear elements determined a person's sex at birth, which included his/her anatomy. Geneticists initially believed that chromosomes served as the most influential – and unchangeable – component. Sport authorities happily grasped onto this belief. As Richardson (2013) explains, for many 'X and Y came to represent the necessary alter ego of gender fluidity' (9). For those tasked with upholding sex segregation in sport, chromosomal composition appeared to be the easy answer.

Chromosomes and sex determination

Chromosomes exist in the nucleus of cells and are composed of tightly coiled strands of DNA. Humans usually have 46 chromosomes, arranged in 23 pairs. Of the 23, 22 pairs are labelled autosomal chromosomes and 1 pair is labelled sex chromosomes. Women characteristically possess 44 autosomal chromosomes and XX sex chromosomes (46, XX); men characteristically possess forty-four autosomal chromosomes and XY sex chromosomes (46, XY). Although many varieties of chromosomal compositions exist, XX came to indicate womanhood and XY manhood in the middle of the twentieth century. This seemingly clear-cut division increased with the discovery of sex chromatin, also known as the Barr body. The sex chromatin is a small, condensed piece of the X chromosome, located within the nucleus of cells.

The discovery of the Barr body in 1948 expanded chromosomal research. Canadian micro-anatomist Murray Barr first identified the dark material while analysing the nervous system of cats. He realized that the stains in the cells appeared to correlate with the animal's sex. Simply put, the female felines exhibited the mark and the male cats did not. Barr and his graduate student Ewart Bertram (1949) found that the appearance, or lack, of the dark spot 'is so clear … animals of both sexes may be readily sorted into two groups without prior knowledge of the sex' (676–677). They therefore reasoned that a scientist could look for the mark to identify the animal's sex. Influentially, Barr argued that 'a similar sex difference in nuclear morphology exists in the human' subject (677). With this finding, the Barr body became the main identifier of sex during the mid-twentieth century.

Scientists quickly developed the Barr body test, also known as the buccal smear test, to identify the presence or absence of the Barr body. Sport authorities, seeking a more advanced approach to sex determination, embraced the tool as a method to verify womanhood. However, chromosomal anomalies repeatedly falsified the assumption that the Barr body unequivocally indicated maleness or femaleness. For example, as McLaughlin and Donahoe (2004) demonstrate, individuals with Androgen Insensitivity Syndrome (AIS) or chromosomal mosaicism show the difficulty of dividing men and women by chromosomal constitutions. AIS occurs when a person is genetically male (46, XY) but does not respond to androgens. Individuals with AIS therefore present outwardly as female. Chromosomal mosaicism exists when a person has cell populations with different chromosomal makeups; for instance, 46, XX/XY mosaicism indicates that an individual possesses both XX and XY chromosomes. Despite the existence of such chromosomal varieties, the IAAF and IOC believed the Barr body provided irrefutable evidence to distinguish men from women in sport.

Chromosomes and sport

The IAAF first used the buccal smear screening in 1967. At the European Cup in Kiev, Soviet Union, the track and field federation replaced physical inspections with the Barr body test. Three Hungarian and three Russian physicians swabbed the cheeks of all female competitors to determine the presence or absence of sex chromatin. Polish runner Ewa Kłobukowska 'failed' the exam (Ritchie, Reynard, and Lewis 2008). Although she had previously passed the visual inspection in 1966, the European Cup control methods showed Kłobukowska possessed a 'mosaic' of chromosomes. Because the IAAF believed in the infallibility of the method, the federation swiftly deleted her records and barred her from future competition. Many detested the decision, including Polish Olympic Committee President Wlodzimierz Reczek. Reczek (1967) argued that 'there are generally no accepted criteria of sex for women athletes'. The IAAF disregarded his plea. Moreover, while the inaccuracy of the exam was seemingly apparent as the federation had previously verified Kłobukowska's sex, many other organizations followed the IAAF's chromosomal example, including the IOC.

At the 1968 Grenoble Winter Olympics, the IOC introduced chromosomal testing on an experimental basis to guarantee that only female Olympians participated in women's events. Only one-out-of-five competitors underwent the control, due to the expenses involved (Thiebault 1968). Deeming the method a success in Grenoble, the IOC required all women undergo testing at the 1968 Mexico City Summer Games. Thus for two decades, from 1968 to 1988, the IOC relied upon chromosomal testing to maintain separate contests, despite increasingly vocal opposition from endocrinologists and geneticists.

Such protests regarding the singular use of the Barr body test in elite competition surfaced in conjunction with its first use in sport. Scottish geneticist Malcolm Ferguson-Smith refused to assist the organizers of the 1970 Edinburgh Commonwealth Games with the procedure. According to the geneticist (1969), the test was inaccurate for three reasons. First, an individual's social sex – gender and/or self-identification – did not always align with his or her chromosomal constitution. Second, 7-out-of-1,000 people possessed some type of chromosomal anomaly. Third, Ferguson-Smith argued, a physical examination would better suit the IAAF's aims of uncovering male imposters. 'After serious consideration I feel I must decline your invitation to undertake the buccal smear examination'. he told the organizers. 'It is not in the best interests of the individual competitors to have this test'.

Others voiced similar sentiments. Medical doctor Elizabeth Ferris, who competed at the 1960 Olympics, argued (1979) that '*women* with rare, anomalous chromosome conditions have been the unfortunate victims of this weeding-out process' (emphasis in original). Finnish geneticist Albert de la Chapelle proved to be the most avid and persistent protestor. De la Chapelle first demonstrated wariness of the protocol in 1982 when he wrote to the IOC asking for clarification regarding its purpose. Because the buccal smear test did little to deter male masqueraders – and therefore little to ensure segregation – de la Chapelle (1982) argued that the chromatin control was a 'flagrant violation' of women's rights. 'Informing a person raised female that her chromosomes do not match her sexual identity 'is likely to create serious, if not fatal, psychological damage', he reasoned. Unfortunately, many athletes likely experienced such harm.[3]

Despite the opposition, the IOC defended the check as necessary for the preservation of fairness in sport. According to Medical Commission member Eduardo Hay (1981), 'The femininity tests were established to protect the woman athlete in competitions reserved for female competitors'. He further reasoned that the chromatin test was 'simple, valid … and follows a scientific and sportsmanlike criterion of equal opportunity for all women participating in a female competition'. Such sentiments bolstered the notion of female inferiority. Hay predicated his arguments on the assumption that 'real' female athletes needed protection from inauthentic imposters: those deemed too fast, too powerful and too strong to be women.

However, the 1985 World University Games served as an important milestone in the history of sex/gender testing. Spanish hurdler María José Martínez Patiño – who had been cleared to compete 2 years earlier at the World Track and Field Championships – forgot her 'fem card'. The IAAF and IOC granted women who 'passed' sex/gender testing femininity certificates. Without documentation, the IAAF required her to undergo the chromatin control again. This time, she failed, feigned injury and returned home (Carlson 1991a). Yet, when the team physician asked Patiño to skip the Spanish National Games the following year, she refused. Patiño excelled in the 60 m hurdles; consequently, the IAAF removed her medals, erased her records and barred her from future competition. Unlike previous women who 'failed' and quietly disappeared, Patiño protested the IAAF's ruling (Patiño 2005). Her publicity highlighted the test's inherent flaws and helped convince the IAAF to alter its criteria.

In the wake of Patiño's plight, the IAAF Medical Committee organized the 'Workshop on Approved Methods of Femininity' in 1990. Practitioners gathered to discuss the purpose, ethics and legality of the Barr body test. Arne Ljungqvist, the IAAF Medical Committee Chairman, opened the meeting with a chronological evolution of sex/gender testing in sport. He noted (1990) that 'a number of cases have occurred which support the feeling that determination of sex should not be the responsibility of sport bodies'. In contrast, Hay (1990) articulated the IOC's unwavering belief of the necessity of the exams. He explained that the Medical Commission used the buccal smear test for three reasons: it involved only minimal interference with the athlete, was completed in a short time frame and allowed for the maintenance of secrecy. 'The experiences of the past twenty years … have proven successful'. Hay argued. 'The control of femininity is necessary and well done'.

Geneticists and athletes present at the Workshop disagreed. As US professor of medical psychology Anke Erhardt (1990) explained, 'the implications of gender verification on women at large are potentially far reaching and may … lead to unintended discrimination'. Similarly, according to former US athlete Alison Carlson (1990), 'the test is discriminatory, has caused psychological harm, and does not achieve the ends designed for it'. After much conversation and debate, the participants outlined recommendations for international sport contests. Most importantly, the group suggested terminating all chromatin controls in sport, immediately. In lieu of the buccal smear test, the Workshop members suggested implementing a physical examination for all athletes, male and female, to assess health. The purpose of this check-up would be 'to determine if the athlete suffers from any condition which might lead to injury or ill-health as a result of participating in competitions' (International Athletic Foundation 1991).

Following the Workshop, the IAAF heeded the advice and instituted a 'health check' for all competitors. However, communication issues and financial concerns plagued the procedure. Moreover, many believed men did not need such an assessment, again underlining the notion that maleness and athleticism naturally go hand-in-hand. These problems led the track and field federation to abandon all forms of mandatory sex/gender testing in 1992. The IAAF Medical Committee attempted to persuade the IOC Medical Commission to do the same. However, the Medical Commission remained convinced of the need for separate competition. An unwavering desire to support conventional gender norms continued to necessitate segregated competition. Therefore, rather than abandon controls, the IOC introduced a new method to determine womanhood.

Genetic difference, polymerase chain reaction (PCR) testing

Prior to the 1992 Albertville Winter and Barcelona Summer Olympics, the IOC announced that it would start using PCR testing on women athletes. Olympic authorities embraced this third technology for it used DNA to determine sex. However, those who had previously opposed the chromatin test also found the newest technique troubling. As Myron Genel told the *Washington Post* (as cited in Anderson 1992), 'PCR is just really a more sophisticated way of looking at the same wrong thing'. As a result, discord continued until the IOC reluctantly agreed, at least on the surface, to terminate controls in 1999.

US biochemist Arthur Kornberg studied DNA replication in the 1950s. In 1957, he identified a DNA polymerase, an enzyme that synthesizes long chains of genetic material. His discovery not only earned him the Nobel Prize in Physiology or Medicine 2 years later, but also opened the door for DNA amplification. Most notably, US biochemist Kary Mullis continued Kornberg's work. Two decades after the initial discovery of the DNA polymerase, Mullis invented the PCR test, a technology that amplified a single copy of a DNA sequence. Importantly, the innovation permitted the analysis of specific genes. For this finding, Mullis earned the Nobel Prize in Chemistry in 1993.

Many medico-scientific practitioners viewed the new technique as a cost-effective tool to identify sex; the IOC latched onto this discovery. In particular, the IOC instructed scientists to use PCR testing to check female Olympians for the presence of the SRY gene and DYZ1. The SRY gene initiates male sex determination by encoding the SRY protein, also known as the sex-determining region Y protein. DYZ1 is a repetitive DNA section also located on the Y chromosome. The Medical Commission interpreted this research to mean that individuals with the SRY gene were biologically unfit to compete in the women's events.

The IOC introduced PCR testing at the 1992 Albertville Winter Games; it immediately faced opposition. As Genel lamented (1991), 'we should not end up simply substituting a dazzling but unproven technology for the outdated and discredited use of the buccal smear'. Merely substituting one test for another seemed to miss larger issues of the impossibility of sex determination through medico-scientific measures. Furthermore, as Carlson explained (1991b), scientists 'are expressing grave concerns about the use of the PCR technique, its sensitivity to contamination, and potential for false positives'. Many feared that the possibility of amplification failure, likelihood of incorrect results and the sole focus on the Y chromatin rendered PCR testing inaccurate and unethical.

Protests extended beyond those who initially voiced concerns about the Barr body test. Prior to the 1992 Opening Ceremonies, 22 French scientists denounced PCR testing on both medical and ethical grounds. The French Medical Association's ethics commission, the *Conseil de l'Ordre des Médecins*, threatened disciplinary sanctions for any French doctor who assisted with the PCR testing at the Albertville Games. 'Such mistaken and uncontrolled use of a genetic test goes against precautions taken against abuses', argued Association President Louis Rene (as cited in 'Fanfare', 1992). Similarly, six Italian paediatricians who previously assisted the IOC with sex/gender testing publicly condemned the PCR method. Vignetti et al. (1996) demanded that 'this unpleasant and counterproductive practice be abolished' immediately. Yet, the IOC continued the procedure in Barcelona, still convinced a separation device remained necessary for the sanctity of sport (Serrat and Herreros 1996).

In Spain, Spanish scientists Angels Serrat and Antonio García de Herreros conducted the exam. They oversaw the examination of 2,406 Olympians; female practitioners actually conducted the testing due to the likelihood of contamination. According to Serrat and Herreros (1996), during the first screening, the physicians amplified DYZ1, the specific repeat sequence located on the Y chromosome. Twelve samples returned positive results. Of the dozen, one proved to be a false positive, a worrisome finding for those who opposed PCR testing. The remaining 11 underwent additional analysis. In the second screening, Serrat and de Herreros amplified both the SRY and DYZ1 specific sequences. Six showed DYZ1 but not SRY; the Medical Commission thereby released them into competition. The 5 women who tested for both DYZ1 and SRY were required to undergo a physical exam prior to participation. Four did and were cleared to compete. One woman opted to skip the exam and dropped out of the Olympics rather than undergo further scrutiny. At the end of the Barcelona Olympics, Serrat and de Herreros concluded that 'Our results suggest that the use of the DYZ1 as marker of genetic sex might lead to errors in the classification of samples' (312). However, the two nevertheless recommended that SRY assessments continue in the future, due to method's overall efficiency.

Consequently, similar issues occurred at the 1996 Atlanta Olympics. Although most medical societies called for the IOC to abandon PCR testing by this time, the IOC Medical Commission continued the practice. Geneticists from Emory University conducted the PCR test on the 3,387 female athletes. Again, only women technicians interacted with the competitors due to the high probability of contamination (Elsas et al. 1997). In Atlanta, 8 Olympians produced inconclusive results and, according to the medical reports, all 8 exhibited signs of AIS. After determining that the women were not male masqueraders, the IOC permitted their inclusion. Despite the repeated inaccuracies, PCR testing occurred again at the 1998 Nagano Winter Olympics; however, minimal (reported) difficulties surfaced (Nagano Olympic Organising Committee 1998).

While innovative, PCR testing again illustrated the impossibility of scientifically determining sex. As Rupert (2011) argues, PCR testing had many inherent flaws. Foremost, it notably misclassified women with AIS. Furthermore, chromosomal anomalies can spark the inactivation or deletion of the SRY region, which would render any results inconclusive or misleading. Also a ninety-nine percent accuracy rate results in an average of 27 false positives for each Summer Olympics. Finally, and perhaps most importantly, SRY alone 'is not a definitive molecular marker of maleness' (Rupert 2011, 356).

Despite years of protest from the medical community, the IOC finally listened to the sentiments expressed by Olympians. Only when the Athletes' Commission recommended that the IOC terminate gender verification did the Executive Board agree. In 1999, the IOC dropped all mandatory controls. The reprieve lasted for only a short while.

Hormonal difference, regulations on female hyperandrogenism

Although the IAAF terminated compulsory verification measures in 1992, and the IOC followed suit in 1999, both sport organizations maintained the right to check any 'suspicious' competitors. This latent stipulation suggests the two organizations still feared the presence of individuals who blurred the lines of sex-segregated sport. Moreover, anxieties heightened in the new millennium. In the 2006 Asian Games, 25-year-old Indian runner Santhi Soundarajan finished second in the 800 m face. Based on her physical appearance,

IAAF officials required she undergo a gender verification test. Days later, when back in Tamil Nadu, her hometown, Soundarajan learned from the evening news that she had 'failed' the exam (Bhowmick and Thottam 2009). The IAAF immediately stripped her of her medals and barred her from future competition.

Three years later, South African runner Caster Semenya experienced similar scrutiny. After defeating her opponents in the 800 m final of the 2009 World Track and Field Championships, speculations about her sex stemmed from concerns about her gender (Cooky and Dworkin 2013; Nyong'o 2010; Vannini and Foernssler 2011). Semenya's muscularity, deep voice and speedy time – despite the fact that she clocked in two seconds slower than the world record – sparked doubts about her eligibility in women's events. Hostile gossip protested that she was too muscular, too powerful and too athletic to be a woman. Swayed by these social prejudices, the IAAF requested she undergo a gender verification test. Influenced by Soundarajan's and Semenya's muscularity, as well as by the suggestion of unfairness in women's track and field, the IAAF and IOC reintroduced gender verification in elite competitions. After holding a series of six workshops that discussed methods available to uphold sex-segregated sport, the two organizations introduced new regulations (International Association of Athletics Federation 2011; IOC, 2012).

Concerns about naturally produced advantages underlined this iteration of testing. This time, the IAAF and IOC targeted female athletes with higher-than-average levels of androgens. Androgenic hormones typically control muscular development; as a result, women with hyperandrogenism frequently produce a greater-than-average amount of natural testosterone. As with the anatomical investigations and the chromosomal assessments, women considered burly, physical or muscular faced derision, suspicion and exclusion. In 2011, the IOC introduced its 'Regulations on Female Hyperandrogenism', and the IAAF quickly followed with its parallel 'Regulations Governing Eligibility of Females with Hyperandrogenism to Compete in Women's Competition' (International Association of Athletics Federation 2011; IOC, 2012).

In line with previous efforts to maintain sex-segregated competition, the IOC and IAAF again focused on a singular, isolated qualification. According to scientists Francisco J. Sánchez, María José Martínez-Patiño – the Spanish runner side-lined in the 1985 World University Games – and Sanchez, Martinez-Patino, and Vilain (2013), 'there is a trait that is known to influence one's athletic performance and which happens to be sexually dimorphic: Androgens' (para. 12). Although Vilain admitted the method's imperfection, he explained that 'you have to draw a line in the sand somewhere' (as quoted in Macur 2012, para. 5). In other words, officials still demanded that sex segregation be upheld, based on normative notions of femininity, despite documented difficulties and decades of inconclusive results.

To maintain biological difference in the millennium, the IOC and IAAF also included remedies for athletes with hyperandrogenism if they wished to continue competing. Those suspected of having the 'disorder' needed to first be inspected at pre-selected reference centres. If diagnosed, she needed to undergo 'treatment' to 'normalize' her androgen levels (International Association of Athletics Federation 2011). During the 2012 London Games, officials sent 4 female Olympians to Nice and Montpellier, France, for such intervention (Littlefield 2014). The doctors completed surgeries that would 'allow [the 4 women] to continue in elite sport in the female category' (Fénichel et al. 2013). Sport authorities embraced this novel medico-scientific technique for it reaffirmed gender conventions and preserved the upper echelons of sport as a male domain. The hyperandrogenism policy, and the required medical intervention, thereby adds yet another chapter to the history of sex-segregated sport.

Conclusion

For almost an entire century, sport officials attempted to delineate sex to separate women from men in competition. With the development of organized sport, many viewed athletic prowess as a male accolade and physical contests as endeavours reserved explicitly for men. Women's encroachment into this realm thus fostered significant gender anxieties. Strong, muscular female athletes challenged the assumptions of male physicality and masculine supremacy. Simply put, women's demonstration of the traits that previously signified maleness – such as aggression, power and strength – diminished the claims of men's superiority, in both sport and society.

Consequently, to reassert the gender order, sport practitioners sought ways to scientifically maintain a division in competition. Widespread social anxieties, medico-scientific ideologies and sporting norms thereby coalesced, resulting in numerous efforts to uphold separation. The IAAF and IOC implemented anatomical examinations in the interwar era, chromosomal assessments during the Cold War, PCR screening in the 1990s and hormonal analyses in the millennium. The two organizations deployed the four technologies to verify sex segregation. All four failed to do so.

Rather than illustrate a neat categorical divide between the sexes, each method instead demonstrated a spectrum. Anatomical ambiguities, chromosomal varieties, DNA differences and hormonal variations showed that scientifically dividing women from men was an impossible feat. Each technique actually highlighted the elusive and multifaceted nature of sex, rather than showcasing its discernibility. As Rupert (2011) argues, 'There were many ways to categorise "sex", but all of them could be inconclusive and even contradictory' (347). Thus, as illustrated by the IAAF's and IOC's efforts, identifying sex has historically shown to be impossible. None of the four medico-scientific tests clearly or irrevocably split women and men.

Thus if sex separation is scientifically impossible, sex-segregated sport must be a socially created fallacy. Tellingly, this construct historically targeted women who challenged prevailing femininity prescriptions, from Hitomi Kinue in the interwar era to Caster Semenya in the millennium. Furthermore, the artifice helped preserve the notion of male supremacy and reaffirmed a belief in female inferiority. Justifications for medico-scientific interventions rendered 'real' women athletes weak and in need of protection from those castigated as too powerful, too strong or too fast.

Instead of coercively continuing the erroneous pattern of medico-scientific sex segregation, sport authorities should consider the benefits of a sex-integrated paradigm. Sex integration would diminish the incorrect assumptions of a sex binary, diminish the harmful gender assumptions prevalent in sport and allow all athletes to compete unhindered by medical or social prejudice. As McDonagh and Pappano (2008) argue, 'we should not sort athletes by what sex they are, but rather by their skill, interest, and ability' (10). Sex segregation is a harmful, outdated and biologically incorrect classification system. Sex integration, on the other hand, eliminates falsely constructed categories and allows athletes, male and female, to compete without the limitations handed down by medico-scientific assessments and social assumptions. If sex segregation is a false impossibility—as the history of sex/gender testing clearly illustrates—sport practitioners need to consider the positive potential of sex-integrated sporting practices.

Notes

1. Following a generally accepted feminist paradigm, this article uses 'sex' to indicate biology and physiology, and 'gender' to reflect socially constructed norms. Furthermore, many sport authorities regularly conflated sex and gender; therefore, 'sex/gender' is used to recognize the intertwined nature of the two ideologies.
2. Italian long jumper Maria Vittoria withdrew from competition due to the introduction of the exam. She cited religious beliefs as the reason.
3. Because the IAAF and IOC did not release the names of the women who 'failed' sex/gender testing, it is difficult to ascertain exactly how the individual athletes responded to the victimization. However, research into disorders of sex development (DSD) provides relatable insight. According to Karsten Schützmann et al. (2009), a person's quality of life typically deteriorates after he/she is labeled as having a DSD. For these individuals, self-harming behaviors and suicidal tendencies occur at rates comparable to women with histories of physical or sexual abuse.

Disclosure statement

No potential conflict of interest was reported by the author.

References

Anderson, C. 1992. "Science: Biology Tests on Athletes Can't Always Find Line between Males and Females." *Washington Post* A3, January 6.

Barr, M. L., and E. G. Bertram. 1949. "A Morphological Distinction between Neurones of the Male and Female, and the Behaviour of the Nucleolar Satellite during Accelerated Nucleoprotein Synthesis." *Nature* 163 (4148): 676–677.

Berg, S. 2009. "1936 Berlin Olympics: How Dora the Man Competed in the Women's High Jump." *Spiegel Online International*, September 15. http://www.spiegel.de/international/germany/1936-berlin-olympics-how-dora-the-man-competed-in-the-woman-s-high-jump-a-649104.html.

Bhowmick, N., and J. Thottam 2009. "Gender and Athletics: India's OWN CASTER Semenya." *Time*. http://www.time.com/time/world/article/0,8599,1919562,00.html.

Cahn, S. K. 1994. *Coming on Strong: Gender and Sexuality in Twentieth-Century Women's Sport*. Cambridge: Harvard University Press.

Carlson, A. 1990. "The Athletes View on Gender Verification. Papers Relating to the International Athletic Foundation Workshop on Approved Methods of Femininity Verification, Monte Carlo, Monaco. Papers of Malcolm Andrew Ferguson-Smith. University of Glasgow Archives, Glasgow, November.

Carlson, A. 1991a. "When is a Woman Not a Woman?" *Women's Sport and Fitness* 13 (2): 24–29.

Carlson, A. 1991b. "Letter to Arne Ljungqvist." Papers Relating to the International Athletic Foundation Workshop on Approved Methods of Femininity Verification, Monte Carlo, Monaco. Papers of Malcolm Andrew Ferguson-Smith, University of Glasgow Archives, Glasgow.

Carpentier, F., and Jean-Pierre Lefèvre. 2006. "The Modern Olympic Movement, Women's Sport and the Social Order during the Inter-War Period." *The International Journal of the History of Sport* 23 (7): 1112–1127.

Cooky, C., and S. L. Dworkin. 2013. "Policing the Boundaries of Sex: A Critical Examination of Gender Verification and the Caster Semenya Controversy." *Journal of Sex Research* 50 (2): 103–111.

Cott, N. F. 2000. *Public Vows: A History of Marriage and the Nation*. Cambridge: Harvard University Press.

Coubertin, P. 1896, 2000. "The Women at the Olympic Games." In *Pierre de Coubertin, 1863–1937—Olympism: Selected Writings*, edited by Norbert Muller, 711–713, Lausanne: International Olympic Committee.

"Current Topics: The Doubtful Sex." 1966. December 17. *Times of India*, 8.

de la Chapelle, A. 1982. Letter to De Alexandre De Mérode. Commission Medicale Correspondance, Avril 1983, Olympic Studies Centre Archives, Lausanne. August 17.

Dreger, A. D. 1998. *Hermaphrodites and the Medical Invention of Sex*. Cambridge: Harvard University Press.

Elsas, L., J. Risa, P. Hayes, and K. Muralidharan. 1997. "Gender Verification at the Centennial Olympic Games." *The Journal of the Medical Association of Georgia* 86 (1): 50–54.

Epstein, D. 2014. *The Sports Gene: Inside the Science of Extraordinary Athletic Performance*. New York: Penguin Group.

Erhardt, A. 1990, November. "Psychological Aspects of Gender Verification." Papers Relating to the International Athletic Foundation Workshop on Approved Methods of Femininity Verification, Monte Carlo, Monaco. Papers of Malcolm Andrew Ferguson-Smith. University of Glasgow Archives, Glasgow.

"Fanfare: Olympics." 1992 January 29. *Washington Post*, C2.

Fausto-Sterling, A. 2000. *Sexing the Body: Gender Politics and the Construction of Sexuality*. New York: Basic Books.

Fénichel, P., F. Paris, P. Philibert, S. Hiéronimus, L. Gaspari, J. Kurzenne, P. Chevallier, S. Bermon, N. Chevalier, and C. Sultan. 2013. "Molecular Diagnosis of 5α-Reductase Deficiency in 4 Elite Young Female Athletes through Hormonal Screening for Hyperandrogenism." *The Journal of Clinical Endocrinology & Metabolism* 98 (6): E1055–E1059.

Ferguson-Smith, M. A. 1969. Letter to James R. Owen. Correspondence regarding the Buccal Smear Examination at the 1970 Edinburgh Commonwealth Games, Nov. 6, 1969–Nov. 1969. Papers of Malcolm Andrew Ferguson-Smith. University of Glasgow Archives, Glasgow, November 21.

Ferris, E. 1979. Letter to Monique Berlioux. Commission Medicale Correspondance, Janvier-Juin 1980. Olympic Studies Centre Archives, Lausanne, December 19.

Fisher, J. A. 2011. *Gender and the Science of Difference: Cultural Politics of Contemporary Science and Medicine*. New Brunswick: Rutgers University Press.

Frost, D. 2010. *Seeing Stars: Sports Celebrity, Identity, and Body Culture in Modern Japan*. Cambridge: Harvard University Press.

Gallico, P. 1937. *Farewell to Sport*. Lincoln, NE: University of Nebraska.

Genel, M. 1991. Letter to Arne Ljungqvist. Papers Relating to the International Athletic Foundation Workshop on Approved Methods of Femininity Verification, Monte Carlo, Monaco. Papers of Malcolm Andrew Ferguson-Smith. University of Glasgow Archives, Glasgow, April 3.

Hanson, S. K. 2004. *The Life of Helen Stephens: The Fulton Flash*. Carbondale: Southern Illinois University Press.

Hargreaves, J. 1994. *Sporting Females*. London: Routledge.

Hay, E. 1981. Letter to Elizabeth Ferris. Commission Medicale Correspondance, Janvier-Avril 1981, Olympic Studies Centre Archives, Lausanne. February 22.

Hay, E. 1990. IOC Experience on Gender Verification. Papers Relating to the International Athletic Foundation Workshop on Approved Methods of Femininity Verification, Monte Carlo, Monaco. Papers of Malcolm Andrew Ferguson-Smith. University of Glasgow Archives, Glasgow, November.

Heggie, V. 2010. "Testing Sex and Gender in Sports; Reinventing, Reimagining and Reconstructing Histories." *Endeavour* 34 (4): 157–163.

International Association of Athletics Federation. 2011. IAAF Regulations Governing Eligibility with Gyperandrogenism to Compete in Women's Competition. *International Association of Athletics Federation*. http://www.iaaf.org/about-iaaf/documents/medical.

International Athletic Foundation. 1991 January. Workshop on Approved Methods of Femininity Verification. Papers Relating to the International Athletic Foundation Workshop on Approved Methods of Femininity Verification, Monte Carlo, Monaco. Papers of Malcolm Andrew Ferguson-Smith. University of Glasgow Archives, Glasgow.

International Olympic Committee Medical and Scientific Department. 2012. IOC Regulations on Female Hyperandrogenism. *International Olympic Committee*, http://www.olympic.org/Documents/Commissions_PDFfiles/Medical_commission/2012-6-22-IOC-Regulations-on-FEmale-Hyperandrogenism-eng.pdf.

Jollimore, M. June. 1992. *Gender Bender Hunt Not Necessary in the Olympics*. GAM: The Globe and Mail, June 15.

Kimmel, M. 1997. *Manhood in America: A Cultural History*. New York: The Free Press.

Laqueur, T. 1990. *Making Sex: Body and Gender from the Greeks to Freud*. Harvard University Press.

Littlefield, B. 2014. Dutee Chand: A Woman Banned from Women's Sports. *Only a Game*. http://onlyagame.wbur.org/2014/10/11/dutee-chand-banned-iaaf.

Ljungqvist, A. 1990. "Historical Perspective on Gender Verification." Papers Relating to the International Athletic Foundation Workshop on Approved Methods of Femininity Verification, Monte Carlo, Monaco. Papers of Malcolm Andrew Ferguson-Smith. University of Glasgow Archives, Glasgow, November.

Ljungqvist, A. 2011. *Doping's Nemesis*. Cheltenham: SportsBooks Limited.

Macur, J. 2012. I.O.C. Adopts Policy for Deciding Whether an Athlete Can Compete as a Woman. *New York times*. http://www.nytimes.com/2012/06/24/sports/olympics/ioc-adopts-policy-for-deciding-whether-athletes-can-compete-as-women.html.

McDonagh, E., and L. Pappano. 2008. *Playing with the Boys: Why Separate is Not Equal in Sports*. Oxford: Oxford University Press.

McLaughlin, D. T., and P. K. Donahoe. 2004. "Sex Determination and Differentiation." *New England Journal of Medicine* 350: 367–378.

Messner, M. A. 1998. "Sports and Male Domination: The Female Athlete as Contested Ideological Terrain." *Sociology of Sport Journal* 5: 197–211.

Mitchell, S. 1977. "Women's Participation in the Olympic Games, 1900–1926." *Journal of Sport History* 4 (2): 208–228.

"Move to Stop Women's Olympics." 1928. *Times of India*, 12, August 6.

Nagano Olympic Organising Committee. 1998. *The XVII Olympic Winter Games Official Report*, (Volume 2, Part 3). Nagano City: Japan.

Nyong'o, T. 2010. "The Unforgiveable Transgression of Being Caster Semenya." *Women & Performance: A Journal of Feminist Theory* 20 (1): 95–100.

Patiño, M. J. M. 2005. "Personal Account: A Woman Tried and Tested." *Lancet* 366: S38.

Peters, M. 1974. *Mary P: Autobiography*. London: Stanley Paul & Company Ltd.

Petersen, A. 1998. "Sexing the Body: Representations of Sex Difference in Gray's Anatomy, 1858 to the Present." *Body & Society* 4 (1): 1–15.

Pieper, L. P. 2014. "Sex Testing and the Maintenance of Western Femininity in International Sport." *The International Journal of the History of Sport* 31 (13): 1557–1576.

Polish Writer Calls Helen Stephens a 'Man.' 1936. *Los Angeles times*, A9, August 6.

"Preserving la Difference." 1966. *Time* 88 (12), 72, September 16.

Putney, C. 2003. *Muscular Christianity: Manhood and Sports in Protestant America, 1880–1920*. Cambridge: Harvard University Press.

Reczek, W. 1967. "Letter to Alexandre de Mérode." Commission Medicale Correspondance, 1960–1967. Olympic Studies Centre Archives, Lausanne, October 14.

Reis, E. 2009. *Bodies in Doubt: An American History of Intersex*. Baltimore, MD: John Hopkins University Press.

Rice, G. 1936. Separate Olympics for Sexes in 1940 Planned. *Los Angeles times*, A9, August 12.

Richardson, S. S. 2013. *Sex Itself*. Chicago, IL: University of Chicago Press.

Riess, Steven. 1999. *Touching Base: Professional Baseball and American Culture in the Progressive Era*. Urbana: University of Illinois.

Ritchie, I. 2003. "Sex Tested, Gender Verified: Controlling Female Sexuality in the Age of Containment." *Sport History Review* 34 (1): 80–98.

Ritchie, R., J. Reynard, and T. Lewis. 2008. "Intersex and the Olympic Games." *The Royal Society of Medicine* 101 (8): 395–399.

Rupert, J. L. 2011. "Genitals to Genes: The History and Biology of Gender Verification in the Olympics." *Canadian Bulletin of Medical History* 28 (2): 339–365.

Sánchez, F. J., Martínez-Patiño, M. J., and Vilain, E. 2013. "The New Policy on Hyperandrogenism in Elite Female Athletes is Not about 'Sex Testing.'" *Journal of Sex Research*. http://www.ncbi.nlm.nih.gov/pmc/articles/PMC3554857/.

Schleiner, W. 2000. "Early Modern Controversies about the One-Sex Model." *Renaissance Quarterly* 53: 180–191.

Schultz, J. 2014. *Qualifying times: Points of Change in U.S. Women's Sport*. Urbana: University of Illinois Press.

Schützmann, K., L. Brinkmann, M. Schacht, and H. Richter-Appelt. 2009. "Psychological Distress, Self-Harming Behavior, and Suicidal Tendencies in Adults with Disorders of Sex Development." *Archives of Sexual Behavior* 38: 16–33.

Schweinbenz, A. N, and Cronk, A. 2010. "Femininity control at the Olympic Games." *Third Space: A Journal of Feminist Theory & Culture* 9 (2). http://www.thirdspace.ca/journal/article/viewArticle/schweinbenzcronk/329.

Serrat, A., and A. García de Herreros . 1996. "Gender Verification in Sports by PCR Amplification of SRY and DYZ1 Chromosome Specific Sequences: Presence of DYZI Repeat in Female Athletes." *British Journal of Sports Medicine* 30 (4): 310–312.

Sullivan, C. 2011. "Gender Verification and Gender Policies in Elite Sport: Eligibility and 'Fair Lay.'" *Journal of Sport & Social Issues* 35 (4): 400–419.

Jacques, Thiebault. 1968. Report on the Medical Organization at the Grenoble Games. Box 89, IOC Meetings, 1968, IOC Meetings—67th Session, Mexico City. Reports by Commissions, Part II, Folder. Avery Brundage Collection. University of Illinois Archive, Urbana, July 14–17.

Tullis, M. 2013, June 27. Who Was Stella Walsh? The Story of an Intersex Olympian. *SB Nation*, http://www.sbnation.com/longform/2013/6/27/4466724/stella-walsh-profile-intersex-olympian.

Vannini, A., and Foernssler, B. 2011. 'Girl, Interrupted: Interpreting Semenya's Body, Gender Verification Testing, and Public Discourse' *Cultural Studies Critical Methodologies* 11(3): 243–257.

Vertinksy, P. A. 1994. *The Eternally Wounded Woman: Women, Doctors, and Exercise in the Late Nineteenth Century*. Illini Books Edition.

Vignetti, P., A. Rizzuti, L. Bruni, M. C. Tozzi, P. Marcozzi, and L. Tarani. 1996. "Sex Passport' Obligation for Female Athletes. Consideration and Criticisms on 364 Subjects." *International Journal of Sports Medicine* 17 (03): 239–240.

Wiederkehr, S. 2006. "We Shall Never Know the Exact Number of Men Who have Competed in the Olympics Posing as Women: Sport, Gender Verification and the Cold War." *The International Journal of the History of Sport* 23 (7): 1152–1172.

Homophobia and heterosexism: Spanish physical education teachers' perceptions

Joaquín Piedra[a], Gonzalo Ramírez-Macías[a], Francis Ries[a], Augusto Rembrandt Rodríguez-Sánchez[b] and Catherine Phipps[c]

[a]Universidad de Sevilla – Educación Física y Deporte, C/ Pirotecnia s/n, Sevilla, Spain; [b]Fundación CEU San Pablo Andalucía – Centro de Estudios Profesionales, Bormujos, Spain; [c]University of Greenwich – Secondary Education, Lifelong Learning, PE and Sport, London, UK

ABSTRACT
Physical education is traditionally a heteronormative environment, despite current studies highlighting the existence of positive changes in sport towards sexual diversity. In Spain, physical education teachers' attitudes towards sexual minorities are an under-researched area. The current study identifies physical education teachers' perceptions towards homophobia and heterosexism, raising questions as to whether societies are hostile or more tolerant in regard to gays and lesbians in sport. This research involved 170 physical education teachers from mixed schools, using a modified version of the questionnaire of homophobia and heterosexism perceptions. Results show heterosexist and homophobic behaviour is apparent in physical education lessons, with teachers aware of these behaviours. Furthermore, it is highlighted that students use homosexually themed language as an instrument to discriminate against gays and lesbians. This language use is not common amongst teachers, although when it is present, it is clearer and more frequent amongst male teachers.

Introduction

Physical education (PE) at school is an important tool for improving students' identities through their bodies. As Vidiella (2007) states, 'embodiment will be key in order to understand how people face rules or resist them'. The body and movement play a key role in the relations between students within society. PE is fundamental for education through the body, and is necessary to develop and create understanding of students' sexual identities. Nevertheless, until now PE has been fundamental in imposing objective body attributes in accordance with ethical, moral and ideological theories of the dominant classes, while failing to deal with diversity (Vicente 2010). Within PE, teachers play a key role in gender treatment (Scraton 2013), and have potential to create a safe and discrimination-free environment for all students. Spain is predominantly made up of mixed schools, with only 219 single-sex education schools among 28,064 recognized by the European Association of Single-Sex

Education in 2012 (Ministerio de Educación, Cultura y Deporte 2014). Spanish teachers can (and must) fight against discrimination in their lessons, eliminating the barriers that boys and girls face to practice PE freely and safely. Educational legislation in Spain provides these guidelines; however, PE teachers are often not motivated to accept them (Piedra et al. 2014).

The aim of our study is to identify Spanish PE teachers' perceptions towards homophobia, heterosexism and inclusion in their lessons, and increase knowledge of the problems that PE teachers find in mixed environments in regard to gay and lesbian pupils. The results of the present study, in line with previous studies undertaken in Spain (Piedra, Ramírez-Macías, and Latorre 2014; Piedra et al. 2013), allow us to make a more accurate diagnosis of the reality of heterosexism and homophobia in Spanish PE, and search for more effective solutions.

The boundaries of heteronormativity in physical education: teachers and homosexuality

The traditional patriarchal gender order has historically developed within western societies. Within this social system, there are two factors that permeate many social activities: homophobia and heterosexism. Several studies link homophobic and heteronormative behaviours with environments where traditional gender roles are maintained (Plummer 1999). Hence, the power dynamics around sexuality play an important role in building, continuing or breaking the gender order and its hierarchy (Connell 1995).

Nowadays, homosexuality is widely studied from different academic fields. For some people, homosexuality creates much controversy and fear. The fear of homosexuality, irrational in many cases, is often referred to as homophobia. Anderson (2009) also discusses the concept of homohysteria, understood as the fear of being considered homosexual. McCormack and Anderson (2014) state that 'homohysteria conceptualizes the contexts when homophobia effects (or is used to police) heterosexual men's gendered behaviors' and affirm that 'societies evolve through three periods depending on homophobia and homohysteria: from a period of homo-erasure to homohysteria and finally to a period of inclusivity'. Therefore, it is necessary to consider the social context in which research takes place, to accurately understand and explain the realities of homophobia and homohysteria.

Another pillar of a heteronormative environment is heterosexism, which is defined as the belief that everybody is heterosexual, with this sexuality considered the norm. This leaves homosexuality and other sexual orientations in a devalued and discredited position since they exceed the limits of heteronormativity (Hyde and Delamater 2006). As Herek (1996) notes, heterosexism and homophobia run in parallel to antigay feelings and feed on themselves. Heterosexism favours the idea that heterosexuality is natural and other sexual orientations are abnormal, with homophobia regarded as a direct consequence of this attitude (Dreyer 2007; Pharr 1997). Likewise, as Kian et al. (2013) point out, heterosexism forms the basis of homophobic behaviours, which are the pillars of the *don't ask, don't tell* culture, in which gay athletes' sexual identities are often not treated on par with that of heterosexual athletes. As Anderson (2002) states 'heterosexual discourse is so pervasive in sport that it subtly leads gay athletes to feel that they have no right to discuss their sexuality, despite the overflowing discussions of heterosexuality around them'. These relationships have been previously studied in the sport context (Lenskyj 2013; Nylund 2004).

Responsibility for the creation of a society free from sexual discriminations should not just be placed on social parties, but also other establishments such as families, institutions and the state itself. Among these, Blaya, Debarbieux, and Lucas (2007) emphasize the co-educative school; the role of schools is crucial in order to challenge the usual gender perspectives, and to develop a new gender culture based on respect towards differences and balanced and equal relationships among students.

Since the 1980s, there have been several studies about homosexuality and education. Within mixed schools, it is suggested PE is one of the areas which can be improved on greatly (Ayvazo and Sutherland 2009). Past research has argued the most hostile climate towards homosexuality can often be found in PE (Hemphill and Symons 2009; McCaughtry et al. 2005; O'Brien, Shovelton, and Latner 2013). Moreover, the increase in sport practice, as well as its extended presence in mass media, may mean more boys and girls are influenced and imbued by this gender order. As Ayvazo and Sutherland (2009) and Dowling (2013) state, stereotypical views of homophobia and heterosexuality, as well as of masculinity and femininity, have historically been, and continue to be, emphasized within sport contexts.

Within the field of PE, several initial studies in the 90s (Clarke 1998; Griffin 1991; Sykes 1998) show the existence of discriminatory situations, leading homosexual teachers to hide their sexualities (Devís, Fuentes, and Sparkes 2005). As Sykes (2001) indicates, they are silenced by heteronormativity. Other researchers (Brackenridge et al. 2007; Clarke 2006a; García 2011; Sykes 2004) have highlighted that the most basic (but frequent) way to oppress and bully gays and lesbians at school, and in PE lessons specifically, is the use of abusive language. Additionally, the stereotypes bound to homosexuality, such as promiscuity, have in some cases led to harassment and discrimination towards gay teachers, who may be regarded as perverted due to working with children (Lenskyj 1997; Sparkes 1994). In order to avoid this, lesbian PE teachers may aim to develop traditionally feminine attributes, in a bid to achieve what is known as hyperfemininity (Clarke 1998; Lenskyi 1994). In many cases, gay and lesbian teachers admit having more distant relationships with their students than heterosexual teachers in order to avoid suspicions (Clarke 2002). In spite of the social and legal improvements, gays and lesbians are still subject to abusive behaviour and are often victims of negative attitudes in the field of PE (White et al. 2010).

Research analysing mixed-sex schools and PE teachers' views towards homosexuality is also apparent within the literature. Morrow and Gill (2003) observed PE teachers' perceptions of homophobia, finding homophobic behaviour is common in secondary schools and colleges in the USA and that teachers, according to students (Gill et al. 2006, 2010), often do not manage to create an inclusive atmosphere in their lessons. Students emphasize the dominance of heteronormativity in PE lessons, forcing boys and girls to act in specific gendered ways which are placed within the boundaries of heterosexuality (Clarke 2002), in order to be regarded as normal (Larsson, Redelius, and Fagrell 2011). Similarly, Piedra et al. research (2013) points out, according to students, that PE teachers are often unaware of homophobia in class and that they take little action to overcome possible discriminatory situations in their lessons.

In their study about sexual sensitivity at school, American researchers McCaughtry et al. (2005), and others previously (Clarke 1998; Lenskyj 1997; Squires and Sparkes 1996), acknowledge the important role of PE teachers as implied agents in the change of sensitivity, in the acknowledgement of gays and lesbians' rights. In their review of studies regarding homophobia in PE lessons, Ayvazo and Sutherland (2009), as well as Clarke (2006b), deal with some actions to eliminate homophobia: teaching respect towards others in lessons, giving value to different sexual orientations, and showing inclusive behaviour in their classrooms. Accordingly, they suggest the need to change PE teachers' future training in order to ensure inclusive environments are fostered, in turn reducing negative attitudes in classrooms (Saraç 2012). However, many teachers prefer to ignore issues occurring at school related to homophobic discrimination in order to avoid further problems and abuse.

Finally, several studies suggest including education on homophobia within the academic curriculum, which may improve inclusivity in mixed classrooms (Toomey, McGuire, and Russell 2012). Unfortunately, there is still opposition in treating this matter openly in some areas of PE (Lenskyj 1997; Piedra, Ramírez-Macías, and Latorre 2014); some teachers argue that dealing with social issues is not part of their job in the classroom.

In recent years, there have been other studies in the Anglo-Saxon scientific sphere which contest the existence of negative attitudes towards gays and lesbians in society, mainly among the younger generation (McCormack 2012; Savin-Williams 2005). This research shows some evidence of a decline in homophobia in sport thanks to legal and social advances (Anderson 2009). In spite of the shortage of research specific to PE in Spain, recent studies elsewhere do indicate that PE is becoming more accepting of sexual diversity (Anderson 2012). In sport, athletes are less afraid to state their sexual orientation (Anderson 2011; Anderson and Bullingham 2013), teammates accept gay athletes on their teams (Adams and Anderson 2012; Margrath, Anderson, and Roberts 2013), coaches better manage the presence of gays and lesbians on their teams (Oswalt and Vargas 2013), and supporters and mass media show more signs of respect and tolerance towards gay athletes (Cashmore and Cleland 2012; Cleland 2014; Nylund 2014). Similarly, homosexually themed language that may have previously been regarded as an oppression instrument may now be perceived as non-pejorative (McCormack 2011).

Due to the scarcity of previous research, this study will be an important addition to the literature on Spanish PE, increasing current knowledge of the culture of PE for gays and lesbians. Furthermore, it will facilitate a better understanding of the levels of homohysteria and inclusivity in PE in Spain.

Materials and methods

This study used an experimental and cross-sectional descriptive design, using the survey technique (applied in the second semester of 2011–2012 academic year) in order to assess Spanish PE teachers' perceptions of homophobia and heterosexism in their lessons.

Sample

The sample was composed of 170 PE teachers from primary, secondary and pre-university education in mixed schools. The participants teach PE in different cities in the autonomous communities of Andalusia ($n = 117$) and Galicia ($n = 50$). 3 participants did not indicate their geographical background.

The sampling was non-probabilistic (incidental) as the questionnaire was only applied to those PE teachers who could be contacted. The contact procedure was completed electronically (with an online form supplied by e-mail) or in person. All the participants answered the survey on a voluntary basis, previously signing a consent form in which anonymity and data confidentiality were guaranteed. In total, 13 participants answered online and 157 using the paper version.

Regarding the participants, 106 were men and 64 women, with 49.7% working in primary education, 36.2% in compulsory secondary education and 14.1% in pre-university studies. Participants' average age was 40.6 ± 8.5-year olds. In order to avoid excessive data dispersion, they have been grouped into age ranges. Thus, the highest percentages of participants are found in the 31 to 40 and 41 to 50 age groups (42.4 and 30.6%, respectively). The rest of the participants are within the 20 to 30 (11.8%) and 51–60 age ranges (15.3%). About 45.9% have been teaching for more than 15 years, 38.8% have between 5 and 15 years of teaching experience, and 15.3% have less than 5 years. Concerning the educative teaching context, 85.1% of the teachers work in public schools, compared to 14.9% in private or semi-private schools.

Regarding the participants' sexual orientation, most of them define themselves as heterosexuals (96.4%); homosexuals stand for 2.4% and 'other sexual orientation' has the lowest value with 1.2%. Concerning sex, 97.1% of men and 95.2% of women declare being heterosexual. There are similar figures in the number of teachers declared homosexual in both sexes; 1.9% of men and 3.2% of women (two instances each), as well as 1% of men and 1.6% of women in the category 'other sexual orientations' (one instance each).

Instruments

In order to measure perceptions of homophobia and heterosexism in PE, the questionnaire created by Morrow and Gill (2003) was used. The original instrument is composed of three constructs: homophobic, heterosexist and inclusive behaviour. It consists of 16 items and the first 11 are answered on a four-point Likert scale with the last 5 items on a five-point Likert scale.

A specific section with questions regarding participants' profile (sex, age, sexual orientation and geographical location) was included. Teachers also indicated the type of school (public, semi-private or private) and the educative level they were teaching in (primary, compulsory secondary or pre-university education). Finally, they were asked about the number of years they had been teaching, and their participation in activities or tasks related to co-education.

In order to clarify concepts within the questionnaire, the following definitions were included in the initial section:

- *Heterosexist* behaviour: Behaviour that assumes all students and teachers are heterosexual, and declarations/activities that presume everyone lives in a traditional family or goes out with someone from the opposite sex.
- *Homophobic* behaviour: Abuses or physical aggressions addressed to people who are believed to be gay or lesbian, or to people or institutions who support gays and lesbians.
- *Inclusive* behaviour: This behaviour deliberately embraces everyone, including gays and lesbians.

In order to deal with questionnaire reliability and data analysis, SPSS 22.0 for Windows was used. Accordingly, the use of chi-square was considered for significance tests, as well as Cohen's *d* to calculate size effect.

Translation

In order to translate the original questionnaire, a back-translation technique (Sperber 2004) was used. Before its translation, the 16 items were analysed according to their readability, scope and comprehension. Four Spanish native speakers, all specialists in PE, translated the items from English into Spanish separately. The existing differences among the translated versions were discussed in order to get an initial version of the questionnaire in Spanish. Four English native speakers later translated this Spanish version into English. In order to reach an agreement among the translated versions, translators proof-read them again. Then, comparability and interpretation similarities (Sperber 2004) of the original text and the back-translations were discussed and the differences found were corrected. Furthermore, translated versions were given to the four bilingual PE teachers, who were not familiar with the original English version, so that they could translate the Spanish items into English. Both the original English version and the back-translated one were compared again in order to determine any significant differences.

Internal consistency of the instrument

Once the questionnaire was translated, a pilot sample was performed with 30 male and female PE teachers in Andalusia who work in mixed-sex schools. The initial reliability reached a Cronbach's α = .553. Item 16 was eliminated in the teachers' scale and the reliability increased up to Cronbach's α = .640. After final data collection, reliability was calculated again. Cronbach's alpha coefficient increased slightly up to .710. It should be noted that McMillan (2008) admits an acceptable reliability level between α = .700 and .900.

Results

The results of the responses to the 15 items that compose the questionnaire are shown in the following tables:

Response polarization among teachers was noticed when asked about perceived heterosexist behaviours amongst students. About 79.3% of the responses are found in the two highest values of Likert scale (41.4% answer 'many' and 37.9% answer 'some'). The data contrast with the data of the observation of students' heterosexist behaviours towards teachers, in which greater response dispersion is observed (Table 1).

Taking this response polarization into account, the sum of those who have witnessed more homophobic behaviours amongst students is 55.9% (adding the percentages of 'many' and 'some'), as opposed to the 44% who point out having witnessed fewer situations ('few' and 'never'). Similarly noticeable is the quantity of students' homophobic behaviours towards other students which occurs on a less regular basis (83.4% adding 'few' and 'never'), with no students reported to address homophobic behaviours towards teachers: 89.3% of teachers indicate they have never observed this behaviour from students and 91% of students have never observed this behaviour from teachers (Table 2).

Regarding the results obtained in the third construct, of relevance is the use of inclusive language where more than 60% of teachers answer with one of the two highest values. Nonetheless, very few regard gay people as role-models. The very high number of participants who answer with the two highest values (87%) when dealing with homophobic

Table 1. Relative frequencies about teachers perceptions of homophobic and heterosexist behaviours.

	A lot (%)	Some (%)	Rarely (%)	Never (%)
Item_1. As a teacher, how often have you witnessed heterosexist behaviour by students toward other students?	41.4	37.9	14.8	5.9
Item_2. As a teacher, how often have you witnessed heterosexist behaviour by students toward other teachers?	26.0	24.3	26.6	23.1
Item_3. As a teacher, how often have you witnessed homophobic behaviour by students toward other students?	11.9	44.0	36.3	7.7
Item_4. As a teacher, how often have you witnessed homophobic behaviour by students toward other teachers?	3.6	13.1	31.0	52.4
Item_5. Have you personally experienced homophobic behaviour from your students?	.0	2.4	8.3	89.3
Item_6. Have you personally experienced homophobic behaviour from your colleagues?	.0	1.2	7.8	91.0
Item_7. Have you experienced heterosexist behaviour from your colleagues	14.3	28.0	19.0	38.7
Item_8. Have you used homophobic remarks/slams/name calling?	.6	3.0	17.3	79.2
Item_9. Have you used sexist remarks in a homophobic manner (calling boys girls or girls boys)?	.0	3.1	8.0	89.0
Item_10. Have you used heterosexist comments (assuming a students are heterosexual)?	8.3	17.3	37.5	36.9
Item_11. Have you used the term normal (assuming heterosexuality is normal and anything else is not)?	4.2	7.7	21.4	66.7

behaviours is also noticeable. However, this percentage reduces to 56% when asked about the creation of safe spaces by teachers. In the second part of the results section the most relevant data obtained from the contingency analysis among the questionnaire items and the sex/sexual orientations of surveyed teachers will be explored (Tables 3 and 4).

There were differences in regard to gender concerning the frequency of actions against student's homophobia (item 5), with this number higher in men ($p = .040$, $d = -.344$). Another relevant finding is the difference ($p = .033$, $d = -.465$) found in the use of sexist remarks (item 9). Male teachers make a greater use of these remarks compared to female teachers (Tables 5 and 6).

Analysing responses regarding teachers' sexual orientation, it is necessary to observe differences ($p = .007$, $d = -.869$) noticed among heterosexual and homosexual people regarding homophobic behaviours by their classmates (item 6). The same trend is observed in item 7, concerning the existence of colleagues' heterosexist behaviours, in which there are significant differences ($p = .005$, $d = -.835$) among heterosexuals and homosexuals. The last significant item is 12, concerned with the use of inclusive language. There are significant differences in the answers given by heterosexuals and those under the term 'others' ($p = .038$, $d = -.635$) and homosexuals and others ($p = .05$, $d = .0$). Regarding these statements, it must be remembered that the reduced sample of those in the homosexual (4) and 'other sexual orientation' categories (2), compared to those declared heterosexual (149), limits the result's generalization. Nevertheless, it is necessary to point these differences out to aid further research, and provide a comprehensive review in order to later confirm or reject the results.

Table 2. Relative frequencies about teachers' use of inclusive behaviours.

	Always (%)	Offen (%)	Some (%)	Rarely (%)	Never (%)
Item_12. To what extent do you use inclusive language?	22.1	40.5	16.0	9.8	10.4
Item_13. To what extent do you use gay role models?	1.8	4.2	27.1	36.7	30.1
Item_14. To what extent do you create a safe space (hate-free zones) for all students?	23.5	33.3	17.3	11.1	14.2
Item_15. To what extent do you openly confront homophobic behaviour?	64.3	23.2	2.4	7.1	2.4

Table 3. Teachers perceptions of homophobic and heterosexist behaviours according to gender.

	A lot		Some		Rarely		Never	
	Man (%)	Woman (%)	Man (%)	Woman (%)	Man (%)	Woman (%)	Man (%)	Woman (%)
Item_1	39	45.3	39.0	35.9	17.1	10.9	4.8	7.8
Item_2	25.7	26.6	20.0	31.2	32.4	17.2	21.9	25
Item_3	10.5	14.3	41.9	47.6	40.0	30.2	7.6	7.9
Item_4	2.9	4.7	12.5	14.1	32.7	28.1	51.9	53.1
Item_5	.0	.0	2.9	1.6	12.4	1.6	84.8	96.8
Item_6	.0	.0	1.9	.0	7.7	7.9	90.4	92.1
Item_7	13.5	15.6	31.7	21.9	17.3	21.9	37.5	40.6
Item_8	.0	1.6	2.9	3.1	22.1	9.4	75	85.9
Item_9	.0	.0	5.0	.0	11	3.2	84	96.8
Item_10	12.5	1.6	16.3	18.8	37.5	37.5	33.7	42.2
Item_11	4.8	3.1	8.6	6.2	23.8	17.2	62.9	71.9

Table 4. Teachers' use of inclusive behaviours according to gender.

	Always		Offen		Some		Rarely		Never	
	Man (%)	Woman (%)	Man (%)	Woman (%)	Man (%)	Woman (%)	Man (%)	Woman (%)	Man (%)	Woman (%)
Item_12	23.0	21.3	39.0	44.3	16.0	16.4	13.0	4.9	9.0	13.1
Item_13	1.9	1.6	3.8	4.8	27.9	25.8	38.5	33.9	27.9	33.9
Item_14	23.0	24.6	34.4	33.9	16.0	19.7	12.0	9.8	16.0	11.5
Item_15	65.4	63.5	24.0	22.2	2.9	1.6	5.8	9.5	1.9	3.2

Discussion

When reviewing the literature, two lines of analysis within the area of homosexuality, sport and PE have been raised. One of the lines argues PE is a subject that emphasizes the traditional gender order most, and one in which gay men and lesbian women are consistently isolated and stigmatized. Studies by Ayvazo and Sutherland (2009), Hemphill and Symons (2009), McCaughtry et al. (2005) and O'Brien et al. (2013) highlight the hostile atmosphere for homosexuals in PE and, of course, towards other sexual orientations which differ from heterosexuality (Pérez-Samaniego et al. 2014). In Spain, studies undertaken with young students indicate that this is the current trend due to the hierarchy of the traditional gender order (Venegas 2013) which is still being reproduced. Conversely, some of the most recently published studies (Adams and Anderson 2012; Anderson 2011; Cleland 2014; Nylund 2014; Oswalt and Vargas 2013) indicate a more tolerant society, in which homophobia is decreasing among athletes, coaches and journalists within sport. Nevertheless, this social change is not described in the context of Spanish society (Piedra et al. 2013).

Table 5. Teachers perceptions of homophobic and heterosexist behaviours according to sexual orientation.

	Many times			Sometimes			Few times			Never		
	Hetero-sexual (%)	Homosexual (%)	Other (%)	Heterosexual (%)	Homosexual (%)	Other (%)	Heterosexual (%)	Homosexual (%)	Other (%)	Heterosexual (%)	Homosexual (%)	Other (%)
Item_1	41.5	50.0	50.0	37.9	50.0	50.0	15.5	.0	.0	5.6	.0	.0
Item_2	25.5	50.0	50.0	24.8	25.0	.0	26.1	25.0	50.0	23.6	.0	.0
Item_3	11.9	25.0	.0	43.8.9	50.0	100	36.9	25.0	.0	7.5	.0	.0
Item_4	3.8	.0	.0	13.1	.0	50.0	30.6	25.0	50.0	52.5	75.0	.0
Item_5	.0	.0	.0	2.5	.0	.0	7.5	25.0	50.0	90.0	75.0	50.0
Item_6	.0	.0	.0	1.3	.0	.0	6.9	50.0	.0	91.8	50.0	100
Item_7	12.5	75.0	50.0	29.4	.0	.0	20.0	.0	.0	38.1	25.0	50.0
Item_8	.6	.0	.0	3.1	.0	.0	17.5	.0	50.0	78.8	100	50.0
Item_9	.0	.0	.0	3.2	.0	.0	8.3	.0	.0	88.5	100	100
Item_10	8.8	.0	.0	18.1	.0	.0	36.3	75.0	100	36.3	25.0	.0
Item_11	4.4	.0	.0	8.1	.0	.0	20.6	25.0	100	66.9	75.0	.0

Table 6. Teachers' use of inclusive behaviours according to sexual orientation.

	Always			Often			Some			Rarely			Never		
	Hetero-sexual (%)	Homo-sexual (%)	Other (%)	Hetero-sexual (%)	Homo-sexual (%)	Other (%)	Hetero-sexual (%)	Homo-sexual (%)	Other (%)	Hetero-sexual (%)	Homo-sexual (%)	Other (%)	Hetero-sexual (%)	Homo-sexual (%)	Other (%)
Item_12	22.7	.0	.0	41.6	50.0	.0	15.6	.0	100	9.1	50.0	.0	11	.0	.0
Item_13	1.9	.0	.0	3.8	25.0	.0	27.2	25.0	.0	36.1	50.0	100	31.0	.0	.0
Item_14	24.2	.0	.0	34	25	.0	17.0	50.0	.0	11.1	.0	50.0	13.7	25.0	50.0
Item_15	65.4	50.0	.0	22.6	50.0	50.0	2.5	.0	.0	6.9	.0	50.0	2.5	.0	.0

The role of PE teachers is fundamental in creating inclusive environments. The results obtained in the present research show that male and female PE teachers in mixed schools are quite aware of the existing discrimination in their lessons. In fact, more than 75% claim having witnessed 'many' or 'some' types of heterosexist behaviour among students and also within the highest values in this scale, more than 55% have answered that they have witnessed homophobic behaviour among their students. Furthermore, most teachers claim that they face these discriminatory situations by themselves in their classrooms. However, teachers do not always take action to fight against discrimination, since there are few teachers using inclusive language and creating safe spaces in their PE lessons.

This is supported by past research by Piedra et al. (2013) who conclude that Spanish teachers are less aware of discriminatory situations and, therefore, they take little action to change this situation. Gill et al. (2010) found similar results within an American context. It is important to recognize that there are different perceptions between young people and adults about inclusion and discrimination. McCormack, Anderson, and Adams (2014) explain how the reduction of cultural homophobia and changes in the social organization of masculinity are affected by age. Nevertheless, despite the apparent contradictions between the present study and Piedra et al. (2013), it is true that both have similar results regarding homophobic and heterosexist behaviours among male and female students. Both reach similar results on the existence of homophobic and heterosexist behaviours among students (from both students' and teachers' views). Thus, in spite of students' opinions on the level of teacher awareness on homophobia and heterosexism, it is noticeable that there is a high level of concurrence among teachers and students when perceiving these kinds of behaviours. Thus, in line with Morrow and Gill (2003), this research indicates PE teachers are well aware of the existence of homophobic and heterosexist behaviours in PE. Hence, the present study, together with others undertaken in the Spanish context (Piedra et al. 2014, 2013; Pérez-Samaniego et al. 2014) suggests Spain is still deeply rooted in the heteronormative gender order, as opposed to decreasing homophobia as observed in other societies. Many countries, like the UK, Australia and the USA, have experienced social changes brought about by new legislation, public awareness campaigns, and the presence of more openly gay athletes. Spain has also started to modify its legislation; however, due to the lack of sports-specific laws and awareness campaigns, it is rare for athletes to declare their sexuality openly in public, thus contributing to the idea that homosexuality is a taboo subject in sport.

Two factors are highlighted concerning students' heterosexist and homophobic behaviours towards PE teachers. Firstly, clear differences between these behaviours are apparent, as there is a relevant dispersion in the case of heterosexist behaviours and a clear concentration of homophobic behaviours in the values 'few' and 'never'. This could be due to the idea that heterosexism may still be perceived as 'normal' and not necessarily linked to discriminatory behaviour. However, there is higher awareness on the pejorative and degrading nature of homophobic behaviour. Conversely, prudence towards homophobia may be apparent amongst teachers as most have never witnessed students' homophobic behaviours towards other teachers. This may be due to the fact that teachers are not 'equal' with students, and their position of public authority may limit their public expression.

Nonetheless, it is important to examine more deeply the apparent prudence of students' homophobic behaviours towards teachers. Heterosexuals are more aware of these kinds of behaviours; no homosexuals and only one person under 'other sexual orientation' claimed having witnessed students' homophobic behaviours towards teachers. When asked if they have been victims of students' or colleagues' homophobic behaviours, none of the gay or lesbian respondents answered that they had suffered from this behaviour 'many' or 'some' times.

It could be that these teachers aim to hide their sexual orientation, to minimize suspicion or stigmatization by other teachers and students. This hypothesis is supported by the results of several other studies such as Devís, Fuentes, and Sparkes (2005), Sykes (2001), Clarke (2002), White et al. (2010), and Saraç (2012). This would again reinforce the hypothesis that in Spain there are still high levels of homohysteria. However, the ability to generalize these results is limited by the small sample of gay and lesbian PE teachers in this research (6 people in total).

Nonetheless, significant differences among men and women were found in relation to the effects of students' homophobic behaviour (in this instance, the number of respondents is not a limiting factor due to the large sample of both sexes), with men more likely to be victims of these behaviours. These findings reinforce the connections between homophobia and the traditional gender order. The data reinforce the idea that male homosexuality is often more stigmatized than female homosexuality in the area of PE, often due to narrow definitions of masculinity and ideas that male athleticism and homosexuality are incompatible. Traditional gender roles and gender stereotyping are the basis of the established gender order; men and women are expected to behave in different ways specific to their gender, with homosexuality for men considered contradictory to a masculine athletic identity (Connell 1986). Because of this, male sport is often especially hostile to homosexuality (Anderson 2002; Roper and Halloran 2007). In contrast, women who play sport (particularly contact sports or those considered aggressive) are often considered to be unfeminine and therefore lesbian. However, in Spain, there is currently no accurate data to confirm this. Based on previous studies in other contexts, an initial hypothesis may be the lower persecution of lesbian women compared to gay men in Spanish PE.

In summary, our research indicates teachers are often aware of the existing problems related to homophobia and heterosexism in their PE lessons. Furthermore, they are often conscious that these problems can affect themselves as well as their students. Taking this into consideration, a question arises: what can they do? In regard to homosexually themed language, often the main source of heteronormativity, surveyed teachers indicated they mostly did not use homophobic or sexist remarks and aimed to use politically correct language. Moreover, most indicated they did not automatically consider heterosexuality the norm. As stated, there are also significant differences among men and women, with the use of sexist and homophobic remarks more frequent for male than female teachers. It could be argued men are more likely to authorize traditional notions of gender, and displays of homophobia may be regarded as a means to express masculine values to ensure they remain dominant.

Ultimately, the main instrument for stigmatization against gays and lesbians in societies with high levels of homohysteria is language. Teachers in this study indicate their language is mostly free from any heteronormative influence. In itself, this is fundamental to create an inclusive atmosphere in PE lessons. Nevertheless, Piedra et al. (2013) and Gill et al. (2010) suggest that, according to students, PE teachers do not fully achieve a safe and inclusive space in their lessons. Teachers in our research stated that they are careful regarding their use of language, but there are limitations to this questionnaire data, including the fact participants may have answered in a 'politically correct' way. Is it possible that we are in a society with high levels of homohysteria but some factors, such as use of inclusive language, indicate a shift towards a more gay-friendly culture? This remarkable divergence between students' and teachers' views requires more research using a variety of different data collection methods. This would allow a clearer definition of how homophobia and heterosexism are manifested in PE, in order to create effective solutions.

To conclude, teachers and students are aware of heterosexist and homophobic behaviours that homosexual students receive. There are still developments to be made to take efficient action so male and female students, regardless of sexuality, can feel included in PE (Larsson, Redelius, and Fagrell 2011). Moreover, further research is needed to explore homophobia and heterosexism for non-heterosexual teachers, as there is currently little awareness of the levels of homophobia and heterosexism they receive.

Conclusions and prospects

This study aimed to describe the perceptions of homophobia and heterosexism within the PE community in Spain. The research shows teachers are conscious of homophobia and heterosexism, and have witnessed these behaviours among students in their lessons. However, the research indicates teachers do not perceive these behaviours to be apparent from students towards teachers. The teachers participating in the present study claim to take action when discriminatory behaviour occurs in their lessons. However, fewer teachers claim they proactively take steps to prevent these behaviors occurring in the first place. It must be noted, however, that the scarce sample of gay and lesbian teachers in this study means these findings are not conclusive. For this reason, future studies should aim to increase the amount of gay and lesbian teachers participating.

Moreover, data show that homosexually themed language is still a well-used instrument in classrooms to discriminate against gays and lesbians. Some teachers are not fully aware of its effect, since many do not use inclusive language in their teaching practice, with homosexually themed language more prominent amongst male teachers. Future studies should consider the effect of social desirability for PE teachers; participants may not always answer truthfully with the use of questionnaires, and other methodologies that help to overcome this should be considered. Potentially, qualitative methods, such as extended observations of the PE environment may be useful. Finally, this research area could widen to include comparisons with other countries and cultures to enrich current knowledge, and consider a wide variety of initiatives and solutions to create a welcoming environment for gays and lesbians within PE.

Disclosure statement

No potential conflict of interest was reported by the authors.

References

Adams, A., and E. Anderson. 2012. "Exploring the Relationship between Homosexuality and Sport among the Teammates of a Small, Midwestern Catholic College Soccer Team." *Sport, Education and Society* 17 (3): 347–363. doi:10.1080/13573322.2011.608938.

Anderson, E. 2002. "Openly Gay Athletes. Contesting Hegemonic Masculinity in a Homophobic Environment." *Gender & Society* 16 (6): 860–877. doi:10.1177/089124302237892.

Anderson, E. 2009. *Inclusive Masculinity: The Changing Nature of Masculinities.* New York: Routledge.

Anderson, E. 2011. "Updating the Outcome. Gay Athletes, Straight Teams, and Coming out in Educationally Based Sport Teams." *Gender & Society* 25 (2): 250–268. doi:10.1177/089124310396872.

Anderson, E. 2012. "Inclusive Masculinity in a Physical Education Setting." *Thymos: Journal of Boyhood Studies* 6 (2): 151–165. doi:10.3149/thy.0602.151.

Anderson, E., and R. Bullingham. 2013. "Openly Lesbian Team Sport Athletes in an Era of Decreasing Homohysteria." *International Review for the Sociology of Sport* Online First: 1–14. doi:10.1177/1012690213490520.

Ayvazo, S., and S. Sutherland. 2009. "Uncovering the Secrets: Homophobia in Physical Education." *Action in Teacher Education* 31 (3): 56–69. doi:10.1080/01626620.2009.10463528.

Blaya, C., E. Debarbieux, and B. Lucas. 2007. "La violencia hacia las mujeres y hacia otras personas percibidas como distintas a la norma dominante: el caso de los centros educativos [Violence Towards Women and Other People Perceived as Different to the Prevailing Norm: The Case of Educational Centres]." *Revista de Educación* 342: 61–81.

Brackenridge, C., I. Rivers, B. Gough and K. Llewellyn 2007. "Driving down Participation. Homophobic Bullying as a Deterrent to Doing Sport." In *Sport & Gender Identities. Masculinities, Femininities and Sexualities* edited by C. C. Aitchison, 122–138. London: Routledge.

Cashmore, E., and J. Cleland. 2012. "Fans, Homophobia and Masculinities in Association Football: Evidence of a More Inclusive Environment." *The British Journal of Sociology* 63 (2): 370–387. doi:10.1111/j.1468-4446.2012.01414.x.

Clarke, G. 1998. "Queering the Pitch and Coming out to Play: Lesbians in Physical Education and Sport." *Sport, Education and Society* 3 (2): 145–160. doi:10.1080/1357332980030202.

Clarke, G. 2002. "Difference Matters: Sexuality and Physical Education." In *Gender and Physical Education. Contemporary Issues and Future Directions*, edited by D. Penney, 41–56. New York: Routledge.

Clarke, G. 2006a. "There's Nothing Queer about Difference. Challenging Heterosexism and Homophobia in Physical Education." In *Equity and Inclusion in Physical Education and Sport*, edited by S. Hayes and G. Stidder, 91–104. London: Routledge.

Clarke, G. 2006b. "Sexuality and Physical Education." In *Handbook of Physical Education*, edited by D. Kirk, D. MacDonald, and M. O'Sullivan, 723–739. London: Sage.

Cleland, J. 2014. "Racism, Football Fans, and Online Message Boards: How Social Media Has Added a New Dimension to Racist Discourse in English Football." *Journal of Sport & Social Issues* 38 (5): 415–431. doi:10.1080/02614367.2010.541481.

Connell, R. W. 1986. "Theorising Gender." *Sociology* 19 (2): 260–272. doi:10.1177/0038038585019002008.

Connell, R. W. 1995. *Masculinities.* Cambridge: Polity Press.

Devís, J., J. Fuentes, and A. C. Sparkes. 2005. "¿Qué permanece oculto del currículum oculto? Las identidades de género y de sexualidad en la educación física [What Remains Hidden from Hidden Curriculum? Gender Identities and Sexuality in Physical Education]." *Revista Iberoamericana de Educación* 39: 73–90.

Dowling, F. 2013. "Teacher Educators' Gendered Workplace Tales." In *Gender and Sport. Changes and Challenges*, edited by G. Pfister and M. K. Sisjord, 217–231. Münster: Waxmann.

Dreyer, Y. 2007. "Hegemony and the Internalization of Homophobia Caused by Heteronormativity." *HTS Theological Studies* 63 (1): 1–18. doi:10.4102/hts.v63i1.197.

García, C. 2011. "Gender Expression and Homophobia: A Motor Development and Learning Perspective." *Journal of Physical Education, Recreation & Dance* 82 (8): 47–49. doi:10.1080/07303084.2011.10598678.

Gill, D. L., R. G. Morrow, K. E. Collins, A. B. Lucey, and A. M. Scultz. 2006. "Attitudes and Sexual Prejudice in Sport and Physical Activity." *Journal of Sport Management* 20: 554–564.

Gill, D. L., R. G. Morrow, K. E. Collins, A. B. Lucey, and A. M. Schultz. 2010. "Perceived Climate in Physical Activity Settings." *Journal of Homosexuality* 57 (7): 895–913. doi:10.1080/00918369.2010.493431.

Griffin, P. 1991. "Identity Management Strategies among Lesbian and Gay Educators." *International Journal of Qualitative Studies in Education* 4 (3): 189–202. doi:10.1080/0951839910040301.

Hemphill, D., and C. Symons. 2009. "Sexuality Matters in Physical Education and Sport Studies." *Quest* 61 (4): 397–417. doi:10.1080/00336297.2009.10483623.

Herek, G. M. 1996. "Heterosexism and Homophobia." In *Textbook of Homosexuality and Mental Health*, edited by R. Cabaj and T. Stein, 101–113. Arlington, VA: American Psychiatric Association.

Hyde, S., and I. D. Delamater. 2006. *Understanding Human Sexuality*. 9th ed. Boston, MA: McGraw-Hill.

Kian, E. M., E. Anderson, J. Vincent, and R. Murray. 2013. "Sport Journalists' Views on Gay Men in Sport, Society, and within Sport Media." *International Review for the Sociology of Sport*. Online First: 1–17. doi:10.1177/1012690213504101.

Larsson, H., K. Redelius, and B. Fagrell. 2011. "Moving (in) the Heterosexual Matrix. on Heteronormativity in Secondary School Physical Education." *Physical Education and Sport Pedagogy* 16 (1): 67–81. doi:10.1080/17408989.2010.491819.

Lenskyi, H. J. 1994. "Sexuality and Femininity in Sport Contexts: Issues and Alternatives." *Journal of Sport and Social Issues* 18 (4): 356–376. doi:10.1177/019372394018004005.

Lenskyj, H. J. 1997. "No Fear? Lesbians in Sport and Physical Education." *Women in Sport and Physical Activity Journal* 6: 7–22.

Lenskyj, H. J. 2013. "Reflections on Communication and Sport: On Heteronormativity and Gender Identities." *Sport & Communication* 1 (1/2): 138–150. doi:10.1177/2167479512467327.

Margrath, R., E. Anderson and S. Roberts. 2013. "On the Door-step of Equality: Attitudes toward Gay Athletes among Academy-level Footballers". *International Review for the Sociology of Sport*, Online First, 1–18. doi:10.1177/1012690213495747.

McMillan, J. H. 2008. *Assessment Essentials for Standards-based Education*. New York: Corwin Press.

McCaughtry, N., S. R. Dillon, E. Jones, and S. Smigell. 2005. "Sexuality Sensitive Schooling." *Quest* 57 (4): 426–443. doi:10.1080/00336297.2005.10491865.

McCormack, M. 2011. "Mapping the Terrain of Homosexually-themed Language." *Journal of Homosexuality* 58 (5): 664–679. doi:10.1080/00918369.2011.563665.

McCormack, M. 2012. *The Declining Significance of Homophobia. How Teenage Boys are Redefining Masculinity and Heterosexuality*. Oxford: Oxford University Press.

McCormack, M., and E. Anderson. 2014. "Homohysteria: Definitions, Context and Intersectionality." *Sex Roles* 71: 152–158. doi:10.1007/s11199-014-0401-9.

McCormack, M., E. Anderson, and A. Adams. 2014. "Cohort Effect on the Coming out Experiences of Bisexual Men." *Sociology* 48 (6): 1207–1223. doi:10.1177/0038038513518851.

Ministerio de Educación, Cultura y Deporte. 2014. "El ministro de Educación, Cultura y Deporte, José Ignacio Wert, presenta el informe 'Datos y cifras. Curso escolar 2014–2015.'" *Ministerio de Educación, Cultura y Deporte*, September 15. http://www.mecd.gob.es/prensa-mecd/actualidad/2014/09/20140915-datos.html.

Morrow, R. G., and D. L. Gill. 2003. "Perceptions of Homophobia and Heterosexism in Physical Education." *Research Quarterly for Exercise and Sport* 74 (2): 205–214. doi:10.1080/02701367.2003.10609082.

Nylund, D. 2004. "When in Rome: Heterosexism, Homophobia, and Sports Talk Radio." *Journal of Sport & Social Issues* 28 (2): 136–168. doi:10.1177/0193723504264409.

Nylund, D. 2014. "Transmitting Softer Masculinity. Sports Talk Radio and Masculinity" In *Routledge Handbook of Sport, Gender and Sexuality*, edited by J. Hargreaves and E. Anderson, 453–460. London: Routledge.

O'Brien, K. S., H. Shovelton, and J. D. Latner. 2013. "Homophobia in Physical Education and Sport: The Role of Physical/Sporting Identity and Attributes, Authoritarian Aggression, and Social Dominance Orientation." *International Journal of Psychology* 48 (5): 891–899. doi:10.1080/00207594.2012.713107.

Oswalt, S. B., and T. M. Vargas. 2013. "How Safe is the Playing Field? Collegiate Coaches' Attitudes towards Gay, Lesbian, and Bisexual Individuals." *Sport in Society* 16 (1): 120–132. doi:10.1080/17430437.2012.690407.

Pérez-Samaniego, V., J. S. Fuentes-Miguel, S. Pereira, and J. Devís. 2014. "Abjection and Alterity in the Imagining of Transgender in Physical Education and Sport: A Pedagogical Approach in Higher Education." *Sport, Education and Society*. doi:10.1080/13573322.2014.981253.

Pharr, S. 1997. *Homophobia: A Weapon of Sexism*. Inverness, CA: Chardon Press.

Piedra, J., R. García-Pérez, E. Fernández-García, and M. A. Rebollo. 2014. "Gender Gap in Physical Education: Teachers' Attitudes Towards Equality." *Revista Internacional de Medicina y Ciencias de la Actividad Física y el Deporte* 14 (53): 1–21.

Piedra, J., G. Ramírez-Macías, and A. Latorre. 2014. "Visibilizando lo invisible: Estudio de casos de las creencias del profesorado de educación física sobre homofobia y masculinidades [Making Visible the Invisible: Physical Education Teachers' Believes about Homophobia and Masculinities]." *Retos Nuevas Tendencias en Educación Física, Deporte y Recreación* 25: 36–42.

Piedra, J., A. R. Rodríguez-Sánchez, F. Ries and G. Ramírez-Macías. 2013. "Homofobia, heterosexismo y educación física: percepciones del alumnado [Homophobia, Heterosexism and Physical Education: Students' Perception]." *Profesorado. Revista de Currículum y Formación del Profesorado* 17 (1): 325–338.

Plummer, D. 1999. *One of the Boys: Masculinity, Homophobia and Modern Manhood*. New York: Harrington Park Press.

Roper, E., and E. Halloran. 2007. "Attitudes toward Gay Men and Lesbians among Heterosexual Male and Female Student-Athletes." *Sex Roles* 57 (11–12): 919–928. doi:10.1007/s11199-007-9323-0.

Saraç, L. 2012. "Attitudes of Future Physical Education Teachers in Turkey toward Lesbians and Gay Men." *Psychological Reports* 111: 765–775. doi:10.2466/11.06.21.PR0.111.6.765-775.

Savin-Williams, R. C. 2005. *The New Gay Teenager*. Cambridge, MA: Harvard University Press.

Scraton, S. 2013. "Feminism and Physical Education: Does Gender Still Matter?" In *Gender and Sport. Changes and Challenges*, edited by G. Pfister and M. K. Sisjord, 199–216. Münster: Waxmann.

Sparkes, A. C. 1994. "Self, Silence and Invisibility as a Beginning Teacher: A Life History of Lesbian Experience." *British Journal of Sociology of Education* 15: 93–118. doi:10.1080/0142569940150106.

Sperber, A. D. 2004. "Translation and Validation of Study Instruments for Cross-cultural Research." *Gastroenterology* 126: S124–S128. doi:10.1053/j.gastro.2003.10.016.

Squires, S. I., and A. C. Sparkes. 1996. "Circles of Silence: Sexual Identity in Physical Education and Sport." *Sport, Education and Society* 1: 77–101. doi:10.1080/1357332960010105.

Sykes, H. 1998. "Turning the Closets inside/out: Towards a Queer-feminist Theory in Women's Physical Education." *Sociology of Sport Journal* 15: 154–173.

Sykes, H. 2001. "Understanding and Overstanding: Feminist-poststructural Life Histories of Physical Education Teachers." *International Journal of Qualitative Studies in Education* 14 (1): 13–31. doi:10.1080/0269172001009744.

Sykes, H. 2004. "Pedagogies of Censorship, Injury, and Masochism: Teacher Responses to Homophobic Speech in Physical Education." *Journal of Curriculum Studies* 36: 75–99. doi:10.1080/002202703 2000148306.

Toomey, R. B., J. K. McGuire, and S. T. Russell. 2012. "Heteronormativity, School Climates, and Perceived Safety for Gender Nonconforming Peers." *Journal of Adolescence* 35: 187–196. doi:10.1016/j.adolescence.2011.03.001.

Venegas, M. 2013. "Sex and Relationships Education and Gender Equality: Recent Experiences from Andalusia (Spain)." *Sex Education* 13 (5): 573–584.

Vicente, M. 2010. "Educación física e ideología. Creencias pedagógicas y dominación cultural en las enseñanzas culturales del cuerpo [Physical Education and Ideology. Pedagogical Beliefs and Cultural Domination in the School Education of the Body]." *Retos Nuevas tendencias en Educación Física, Deporte y Recreación* 17: 76–85.

Vidiella, J. 2007. "El deporte y la actividad física como mediadores de modelos corporales: género y sexualidad en el aprendizaje de las masculinidades [Sport and Physical Activity as Mediators of Corporal Models: Gender and Sexuality in Learning of Masculinities]." *Educación Física y Ciencia* 9: 1–20.

White, C. S., S. B. Oswalt, T. J. Wyatt, and F. L. Peterson. 2010. "Out on the Playing Field: Providing Quality Physical Education and Recreational Opportunities for Lesbian, Gay, and Bisexual Youth." *Physical Educator* 67 (1): 46–56.

Sporting equality and gender neutrality in korfball

Laura Gubby and Ian Wellard

Sport Science, Canterbury Christ Church University, Canterbury, UK

ABSTRACT

This paper explores the extent to which korfball can be considered egalitarian. The intention of this research was to use ethnographic methods to discover the ways in which gender was negotiated, challenged or recreated in a junior korfball setting and examine to what extent korfball provided an opportunity to promote gender egalitarianism. Analysis of the data incorporated a broad Foucauldian lens and subsequently revealed that sex equality was visible to some degree in the junior korfball space. From observations and interviews, it was clear that male domination was rarely evident when considering the vocal nature of the game, the physicality and competitiveness of players, or their general ability and skill, yet when interviewed players still constructed gender in traditional ways. Nevertheless, korfball was seen to offer a space where there were possibilities for sporting equality although the influence that the sport had beyond the court was less apparent.

Introduction

While general opportunities for women to engage in sport have clearly improved in recent years, it would be difficult to argue that women are treated equally in all aspects of sport, whether at professional or recreational level. However, while claims that sport remains a predominantly male-dominated arena are valid, it is still misleading to assume that all men automatically experience sport positively and all women will invariably have negative experiences. Consequently, one of the central issues at the heart of the gender debate (not only in sport) is the continued approach to treating women and men as completely separate and that their experiences will always be different. What is needed is a more nuanced approach that takes into consideration the complex forms of power operating between and around those that take part in any sporting activity. A Foucauldian lens is a useful starting point when investigating complex and multiple relationships of power. Unlike the binary understandings of power relationships often recognized through hegemony (Connell 2005), Foucault (1978, 94) suggests that power is not 'a system of domination exerted by one group over another'. Subsequently, many writers exploring the field of sport have utilized Foucault to investigate the complex power relations and multiple discourses that reside within sport or physical activity. For instance, Markula and Pringle (2006) in their research into rugby in New Zealand highlight the influence of sport on the gendering of bodies where there is a presumption that the discourse of sport aids the production of contemporary gendered identities where 'masculine and feminine bodies are both docile, yet different' (Markula and Pringle 2006, 100).

By acknowledging these complex relationships of power, further insight can be made into why there remains a lack of appeal for sport by girls (and many boys). While it can be argued that there still remains a disparity between boys and girls levels of participation in sport (Bailey, Wellard, and Dismore 2004), rather than concentrate on traditional sports and offer suggestions about how girls might 'fit in' it is worthwhile to explore examples of sports that have been formulated to cater to both sexes in order to provide opportunities to look beyond simple distinctions read purely through gender. 'Traditional' sports can be seen to have a different history, one developed in the nineteenth century in the UK and heavily influenced by ideologies of Muscular Christianity (Hargreaves 1986). However, a sport such as korfball, which was created in a socially and politically different context to traditional sports, could be considered as an alternative to high-profile sports such as rugby and football. In this particular case, the example of Korfball, which was originally invented as an activity that could be played by mixed-sex teams, is explored in order to develop a more informed understanding of the complex factors that operate within the context of sports that seek to promote inclusive practices.

What is Korfball?

Korfball was developed in 1902 by a Dutch Primary School teacher (IKF 2006; Summerfield and White 1989). The main catalyst for the development of korfball was a perceived need for a competitive mixed sport that relied on cooperation, where rules were designed to encourage boys and girls to participate on a level playing field, refute violence and form an egalitarian game (Summerfield and White 1989). Within this context, Korfball offered an innovative and quite radical alternative to single-sex team sports that had been introduced to and developed in schools around the same time (IKF 2006).

Korfball is a team sport that comprises elements of basketball and netball. The aim of the game is to score goals by shooting the ball through the basket, known as the korf (Emmerik et al. undated; IKF 2006), which is situated high enough that 'dunking' is not possible (Crum 2003). To do this, players must escape from their personal opponent with skills of passing the ball and moving quickly and efficiently (IKF 2006). Winning a korfball match comes from successfully scoring goals whilst also inhibiting the other teams scoring (Crum 2003). Teams are made up of eight players, with four women and four men on each team (Crum 1988; IKF 2006). To ensure this equality and eliminate unfairness, women only mark women and men only mark men, so players are only playing directly opposite their own sex. This arguably weakens traditional sporting advantages of height, muscular strength and speed (IKF 2006). To limit probable contact, players have protected possession of the ball, meaning that whilst a player has possession no other player can take possession without the ball leaving their hands (Emmerik, et al. undated). To add to the promotion of equality and teamwork, solo play is forbidden (IKF 2006), this would include dribbling the ball and running with the ball. The concept of playing together is a key constituent and the rules make teamwork obligatory (Emmerik, et al. undated). During a korfball match, two men and two women from one team attack, whilst the other two men and women from that team defend in the opposite section (Summerfield and White 1989). In essence, due to the splitting of the playing area into two halves, a four-on-four 'duel' takes place within each rectangle (Crum 2003). As soon as two goals have been scored (by either team, or a combination of the two teams), the defenders and attackers swap ends, and in doing so they also swap roles, so attackers become defenders and vice versa (Emmerik et al. undated; IKF 2006). An important structural element of the korfball game is the need to be vocal. As players mark their opponents closely, often facing them, their teammates inform them of the play going on around them. Being vocal is embedded deeply into the *way* korfball is played, with players calling shots by opponents, and informing their teammates if opponents have a good position to feed the ball out for shots.

Gender and sports participation

Messner (1992) argues that sports have remained constant in terms of promoting accepted notions of heterosexuality and a space to emphasize masculinity, which is arguably a contributory factor to the underrepresentation of women in sport (Wachs 2003). It can still be argued that in the twenty-first century sport is still an arena predominantly for men (Wellard 2009) and continues to contribute to a situation where there are less activities made available for girls to participate in (Azzarito and Solmon 2006).

Sports can also be seen to provide a space for the demonstration of hegemonic masculinity (Connell 2005) and expected embodied masculinities (Wellard 2009), while modern day competitive sports continue to reinforce male (heterosexual) physical superiority, and simultaneously oppress women through the objectification of their physicality and sexuality (Mansfield 2006). In particular, female athletes are sexualized, infantilized, trivialized and familiarized by the media (Brookes 2002), which, in turn, plays a significant role in objectifying and sexualizing female athletes with an unspoken accent on heterosexuality, whilst underplaying women's sporting expertise (Azzarito 2010).

Fuelling the gender debate is the continued belief that biological difference is the 'fundamental reason for segregating men and women' (Foddy and Savulescu 2011, 1184). 'Sex' and the physical disparity between men and women have historically been used to rationalize the limited access that women have to sport (Mansfield 2006). Biological determinism has been used as an ideology that serves to portray men as innately possessing characteristics that conform to sporting traits, such as aggression, physical power and competitiveness, whilst assuming that women do not (Mansfield 2006). Consequently, sport serves to condone, honour and uphold the dominance of an embodied performance of heterosexual, masculinity male (Wellard 2009), while notions of femininity are interpreted through presentations of fragility, docility, elegance and a maternal caring attitude (Clark and Paechter 2007; Mansfield 2006; Woodward 2015).

However, while general theoretical debate supports the view that sport remains a predominantly male preserve, the rates of participation for women in sport have increased and opportunities are more visible than they have been historically (Hargreaves 2000; Mansfield 2006). Nevertheless, this does not mean to say that male dominance within sport will inevitably become a thing of the past (Clark and Paechter 2007). Continued maintenance and reaffirmation of a hegemonic gender structure, and the disparity between the opportunities available to women and non-heteronormative men is somewhat reliant upon the consent and complicity of those that take part. In this respect, women as well as men can be seen to maintain the status quo through engagement with more complex discourses, such as consumerism and neo-liberalism, operating through and beyond gender (Phipps 2014). Nevertheless, the degree to which men and women experience sports as restrictive or emancipatory is dependent upon the socially specific situation of an individual (Mansfield 2006) and their political 'visibility' (Woodward 2015). Diverse and splintered identities need to be acknowledged and factors that may influence individual experience and opportunity include race, ethnicity and religion, as well as age, economic status, political climate and level of physical (dis)ability (Wellard 2007).

Where gender separation normally exists within sports, male versions of sport are often the main focus and have a larger cultural following (Tolvhed 2013). However, there is a common problem when comparing the sporting performances of men and women, because of the way that gender segregation is normalized, and that there are relatively few opportunities for men and women to play directly against each other. Consequently, general comparisons are made when considering directly measurable units, such as time and distance, where men often perform better than women (Chalabaev et al. 2013). The idea of a 'natural' superiority of the male physique fails to be challenged on a regular basis, in part because of the limited opportunities women have had historically to perform directly against men. Equality in sport has all too often concentrated on giving women equal opportunities whilst keeping them separate from men. Perceived disparity between the sexes has meant that different sports are more readily accessible to different sexes, and rules and equipment difference are reflected in sex-specific formulations of games (Cahn 1994; Wachs 2002). Nonetheless, Azzarito (2010) describes how female athletes do portray strong athletic identities, something she recognizes as 'alpha femininities' and suggests that girls can develop fit identities focused on success and physical accomplishments. Additionally, it could be claimed that women who participate in sport are able to contest essentialist ideas which associate women with weakness and submissiveness and further challenge taken for granted 'natural' gender differences (Butler 1998).

While Foucault did not look specifically at either gender or sport, his ideas are nevertheless important when applied to sporting contexts, especially when considering gendered relationships of power. A Foucauldian analysis not only allows us to research bodies and power within sport, but it also allows us to investigate connections between sport and other power networks (Smith Maguire 2002), for example, masculinities and femininities.

One useful disciplinary technique to consider is Foucault's (1979) concept of normalization and normalizing judgement, which aims to homogenize individuals through the acknowledgement of hierarchized difference. Drury (2011) applies this concept to explain how particular spaces, specifically sporting spaces, provide the opportunity for normalization of identities that are not normalized within wider society. Drury's (2011) research findings from a study into women's football demonstrated how there were 'greater opportunities for the discursive subversion of normative sexuality than those available in mainstream football. Indeed, many players referred to the importance of being able to socialise with other non-heterosexual women in a context in which lesbian sexuality was normalised' (2011, 431). This demonstrates how normalization occurs through the influence of discourses relevant to specific times and places.

A number of studies into gender and sport have utilized Foucault's explanations and applications of discourse in order to explain relationships of power. For example, Pringle and Markula (2005) demonstrate how discourses of masculinities are unified systems of thought that recognize specific bodies as male and specific practices as masculine, and 'in the process, help constitute multiple and fragmented masculine subjectivities' (Pringle and Markula 2005, 477). Discourses have also been seen to marginalize 'the other' or those that do not fit the accepted norm. This was evident in Brown and Macdonald's (2007) study into physical recreation where they suggested that physical recreation students used homophobic discourses, and various discourses of masculinity to understand situations within a physical recreation setting. Sexist and homophobic discourses allowed students to ridicule each other in order to 'exclude and marginalise female students and less stereotypically athletic male students' (2007, 33). Consequently, discourses within sport, like any discourses, can be viewed as unwritten rules that form specific practices and gender relations in particular times and places (Markula and Pringle 2006). For example, Light and Kirk (2010) explained how hegemonic masculinity helped maintain and reproduce rugby training at a school they were researching, they explained how 'practice was surrounded by a discourse of domination, aggression, ruthless competitiveness and giving all for the school' (2010, 167). These forms of knowledge were reproduced from generation to the next through coaches and teachers, Old Boys and family members who had previously attended the school.

Foucault's acknowledgement of the influence of surveillance has also been applied in research seeking to explain power within physical activity and gender. For instance, Azzarito (2009) in her exploration of physical education in the USA demonstrated how girls within the physical education environment projected a gaze and classified other girls' bodies within the boundaries as broader social gendered discourse. For instance, through self-surveillance, 'the gendered discourse of the body prevents the development of conceptions of muscularity as an "attractive" trait for females' (Azzarito 2009, 29).

Methods

The material for this paper was taken from a larger PhD study exploring the history of korfball and the experiences of young people taking part in the sport. Ethnographic fieldwork was incorporated, including interviews and observation, conducted within a korfball team based in South East England. Data were collected by the first author who participated as a 'helper' for the under 13s team (which had players ranging from 11 to 13 years old) and also a senior player within the same club. This 'insider' role allowed for a greater access to the other participants and provided opportunities to observe, engage in informal conversations as well as conduct interviews with individuals and groups (Kvale 2007; Thorpe 2012). Active participation enabled the researcher to gain a greater understanding of the 'whole package' (Wellard 2013) of korfball through travelling to games and tournaments on coaches with the players, spending match and tournament time cheering the team and joining in team talks, and even dressing up in the team colours and letting the juniors paint her face in supporting colours. The researcher also had previous experience of korfball as a junior player herself which enabled a greater sense of shared understanding with the young participants. Indeed, prior knowledge as someone who had played korfball in both junior and adult capacities meant that she had a deeper understanding of the game, the rules and techniques. It could be claimed that a key to successful participant observation is to accept the paradox that one must understand the community as a participant, yet have the ability to observe the culture as a researcher (Quinn-Patton 2002; Sands 2002). The fieldwork was conducted for a full year with the junior team, thus incorporating participation through-out the korfball season as well as summer tournaments and summer training. In practical terms, participant observation was completed for 2 h per week during training and took place for approximately 2 h during the weekend when in-season games were played, and for approximately 6–16 h a weekend when summer tournaments were being played.

Informal conversations took place throughout the fieldwork and many opportunities arose during 'downtime' at summer tournaments when players were in-between games, effectively having free time and often away from the adult gaze. In addition, nine semi-struc-tured interviews were conducted, with four boys and five girls who were regular attendees of the sessions. These interviews lasted between half an hour and 45 min, and took place during the time between matches at tournaments. The questions for the semi-structured interviews were developed from questions that arose during participant observation and also from gender literature and research within the sport sociology field.

Field notes were maintained throughout the research process in the form of a diary. Interviews were recorded on a Dictaphone and then transcribed. Transcribed field notes and interviews were coded into reoccurring themes, and these main themes then became the main topics of discussion, drawing on relevant gender literature. A reflexive approach was incorporated, not only through the use of field notes and diary entries, but in conversa-tions with the second (male) author about the interpretations of the material. Consequently, reflexivity was seen as an integral part of the research in that it incorporated awareness of practical methodological considerations (Bourdieu and Wacquant 1992; Hammersley and Atkinson 1995) as well as the personal and emotional elements of 'doing' research in the field (Burkitt 2012). For the purpose of this paper, the discussion concentrates on interview data, although, as with any ethnographic study, experiences within the field have influenced the way that the data have been analysed.

Consent was obtained from all participants and steps were taken to protect confidenti-ality including assigning both places and people's names with pseudonyms (Fontana and Frey 2008). As minors were involved, parents or legal guardians were provided with written consent for the junior players to take part in the research project.

Performances of gender on the korfball court

The discussion that follows focuses upon the presentation of the gendered body in korfball, in particular the young player's considerations of how korfball players should look, how masculinity and femininity should be enacted, and the significance of physical differences. Consequently, the focus of the discussion in this paper is to assess the extent to which gender, within the context of korfball, is considered an issue or not. The relevance of gender will be assessed alongside other issues that arose during the research which relate to sporting ability and performance, and the influence of broader, external gendered expectations. Despite it being clear from observations and interviews that male domination was rarely evident when considering the vocal nature of the game, the physicality and competitiveness of players, or their general ability and skill, notions of gender norms or understandings frequently occurred in interview data, and the way in which players used their gendered bodies was also sometimes apparent during observation. When interviewed, the junior korfball players demonstrated conflicting perceptions of masculinity and femininity, and often used their bodies in ways which would conform with, or resist, gender norms.

Skorts and shorts

At the start of the research, it was apparent that the korfball uniform played a significant part, not only in creating a korfball 'identity' but as a marker of gender. Consequently, from the outset, wearing the designated korfball kit presented a clear indicator of gendered roles. The korfball uniform separated players' sex by having boys wear shorts, whilst girls wore skorts (a one-piece skirt-shorts combination with shorts sewn in underneath a skirt which is the outward facing component).

Despite several male and female players explaining that they did not even consider how they looked when they played korfball, they still described the importance of everyone having a specific kit to wear during matches and that standard fitness clothing was worn by all during training. However, some of the other female players did demonstrate more conscious concern for how they looked when they played korfball. Louise explained how she tried to make sure her hair looked nice, and even made efforts to put it right again immediately after a match,

> Yeah, I sort of make it look nice, I get a comb, start brushing it and make it all nice and thick … I always try and make my hair look nice so it's just a natural thing … but my hair don't look nice now because I was just in the middle of a game, I'll have a chance to sort it out in a minute. (Louise)

Louise clearly cared how she looked when playing korfball and found it important to look a certain way within korfball spaces. She went on to explain how she took time to look at herself in a mirror and assess how she looked,

> I like the clothes we wear, and before a game I'll go in to a mirror and do my hair and everything. I don't normally put on make- up for korfball unless it's stayed on from like the night before or something. Erm, but I don't usually put on make-up at all. (Louise)

Boys were also aware of the significance of gendered dress and Chris explained that girls wore skorts because they were more feminine, and that girls that wore boy's clothing and boys that wear girl's clothing were susceptible to being teased.

> Erm I think it's because, really it wouldn't be right if the girls were just wearing shorts because it's not really feminine, kind of thing, for a girl to wear shorts … erm, well kind of, it wouldn't seem right if a girl walked in, and then like they were wearing shorts and all boys stuff, and then the girls, and then a boy walks in to a room wearing all girls stuff, wearing girls perfume and looking like a girl [laughs], wearing makeup … I don't know I think just people would like start taking the Mickey out of them. (Chris)

Chris explained how gender transgression 'wouldn't be right', which suggested evidence of judgement when individuals transgress from social norms (Foucault 1978). In doing so, Chris gives the impression of the abnormal being individualized (Foucault 1988) while, at the same time, presenting himself as an actor in the reinforcement of gender norms. Scott ventured that girls look better in skorts, by suggesting that they looked 'gorgeous' in skorts rather than shorts, and that people could see their legs. Although this observation could be interpreted as a sexualized view coming from a male player, in a subsequent group discussion, Georgie joked that one of the reasons she wore a skort was 'to show off my legs, my tanned legs'. To which a number of other girls either agreed or disagreed, and the conversation developed into light-hearted banter about the paleness of some girls' legs, demonstrating that the influence of wider youth cultural discourses relating to body image, in this case having tanned legs. This demonstrated how the girls were both subjects and objects of power (Foucault 1994), complying with social accepted gender norms themselves, and also judging others who did not comply.

Georgie and Daniel described the way in which it did not matter if the boys wore skorts, but both recognized that it would not be normal when they suggested that it would look 'weird' (Daniel) or 'silly' (Georgie). Consequently, whereas the young players found the wearing of the korfball uniform unproblematic, their justifications were based upon their knowledge of the rules of the game, where clear indications of the specific gendered roles were required. Players tended to demonstrate normalized views of gendered dress and actions, having seemingly internalized wider accepted gender norms (Foucault 1978, 1979).

Presenting masculinity and femininity

During discussions some players employed the terms 'masculine' or 'feminine' to explain certain bodily attributes or actions, and others inferred or subtly made reference to accepted gender norms. Despite some players giving very clear views regarding gendered stereotypes and assumptions, Sarah made it clear that her thoughts were more open to critical understanding.

> No I don't, I think it depends, like you can't say, that would be stereotypical you can't say like all the boys are really really muscley because that's not true, and all the girls have got flimsy arms because that's not true. (Sarah)

For Sarah, it could be claimed that she had not internalized societal gender norms and did not demonstrate a docile body, trained to obey bodily gender appropriateness (Foucault 1979). However, conversely, most players did deliver stereotypical gender understandings, for example:

> Yeah like girls are more delicate and then they try and like fancy themselves up, and then boys are walking around going like [makes a fist]. (Louise)

> yeah I guess because its fashion really … whereas the girls have to wear something to show their legs off, boys should have something to show that their male muscular for instance … girls always want to look beautiful and I don't blame them. (Scott)

It was apparent that the young players were attempting to make sense of the contrasting performances that they experienced on court that did not necessarily fit in with the broader discourses of gender that they were exposed to in everyday life. For example, Louise and Scott attributed muscles and aggression to boys, whilst girls were generally stereotyped with wanting to present themselves beautifully. They clearly both had understandings of gender difference related to bodies and the presentation of gendered bodies. Both Louise and Scott demonstrated normalized views regarding appropriate gendered ways for boys and girls to present their bodies, while Louise appeared to have internalized societal values (Foucault 1979). In addition to grappling with what a gendered body should look like, there were occasions when social interactions were explained as being uniquely male or female. For example, a social practice that was considered a 'girl thing' was discussed by a group of girls during a break at a tournament. They argued that girls simply cannot go to the toilet by themselves, 'because that's just not right, you can't go to the toilets on your own' (Georgie). This notion that girls only go to the toilet in pairs was clearly evident here, and when the players were questioned about boys going to the toilets in pairs, the reaction demonstrated that it was not readily accepted as Rachel retorted with, 'to the feminine loos'

(Rachel), and Georgie explained that 'yeah, some boys, if they're feminine boys then yes' (Georgie). The action of visiting the toilets in pairs was associated with girls, and boys that performed the same action were considered feminine. As a concept, the idea of feminine boys provoked laughing from female players, demonstrating that this was not an accepted norm, and instead it was a laughable notion.

In one group conversation, Georgie explained that some people had called her masculine, and Scott jumped in, seemingly to defend her, and stated, 'Georgie you're not masculine, you're not masculine' (Scott), like it was a bad thing and he wanted to reassure her. Georgie then explained that people had accused her of being masculine because of her reputation of being physically assertive, 'because loads of people at my primary school were scared of me, because I could probably take them down in like a few seconds' (Georgie). Scott agreed in this respect and invited Georgie to pinch him to prove his point, 'No look at her pinch, her pinch is like so deadly, look … I'm used to it now' (Scott). Scott let Georgie pinch her until his skin was quite badly marked, but he did not noticeably react, which could, in itself, be interpreted as a performance of masculinity in that he was able to demonstrate his ability to withstand pain in front of the girls and was not hurt by a girl. A competition then broke out between the girls, where they described how physically capable they were of hurting others, which might suggest not only the adoption of heteronormative 'masculine' behaviours but also more complex forms of relationships of power that are not necessarily based upon the dominance of one group over another (Foucault 1985). Rachel asserted, 'But I know where all the pressure points on someone's body' (Rachel), and Georgie retorted, 'give me a second, because my uncles in the army' (Georgie). Again, Scott 'defended' the girls and asserted that 'they're not masculine but they've got masculine things' (Scott), such as not being worried about getting dirty. At the point that Scott suggested the girls had some masculine attributes, Rachel responded with 'like a willy!' which, by using both humour and references to the biological reaffirmed the notion of difference between the sexes.

A specific term that also came into conversation when interviewing the junior players was the 'tomboy'. Although it was not as significant in this research as other issues, such as physicality, it is worth considering the understanding and judgement of the term when used. A number of the female players discussed 'tomboys', either referring to themselves as tomboys, or talking about tomboys in a more negative or undesirable sense. Sarah described herself quite positively as a tomboy, 'Yeah like I'm a tomboy so, and I didn't want to play, and I like football but I didn't want to play for the boys' team and I didn't want to play for the girls' team' (Sarah). When asked for some further explanation regarding why she considered herself to be a tomboy, she argued, 'I don't like to do girl things, yeah sports, and I don't like going to like beauty pageants [laughs]' (Sarah). Players also labelled others as tomboys, for example, Georgie described Jess as a tomboy in a rather indifferent way,

> I don't think it matters it just like, they cos for some reason like Jessica because she's a tomboy she doesn't like wearing a skirt a skort and she wants to wear shorts. And I don't think it matters but then when Danny said oh you have to she like, I think she got a bit upset only because like she had to. (Georgie)

In this case, although Georgie was not obviously demonstrating evidence of normalizing judgement, or evidence of repression due to transgression (Foucault 1988) she did, however acknowledge that Jess could be considered a tomboy, and despite not seeming to cast a judgement, she did infer a difference between Jess and the other female korfball players. Georgie discussed 'girly' things that Jess did not like, implying that the normal things enjoyed by girls were not enjoyed by Jess as she was a tomboy. In this instance, Jess could be seen as 'the other' (Foucault 1988), and different to the rest of the 'correctly' gendered girls.

Scott also directly referred to the term 'tomboy' but not with reference to a specific player,

> I just think it doesn't make a difference really, but I reckon, I would prefer if girls wore like skirts to shorts to show that, to show off that they're nice, good looking [laughs] … you want to show that you're, you're good at it but you're not one of those tomboys for instance, I'm not saying that's bad or anything'. (Scott)

Despite his insistence that being a tomboy was not a negative thing, he did state a preference for girls wearing skirts in order to prove that they were not tomboys. Seen in this light, tomboys were considered as 'the other' (Foucault 1988), separate and explained as different. In general, players frequently argued that male players would want to demonstrate masculine traits, and that female players would not want to be labelled as masculine, although there were often conversations around this idea that meant that players did not always think very uncritically about the terms and what they stood for, such as Scott and Rachel.

Difference

Throughout conversations with the players, the topic of 'difference' arose often, and comparisons were frequently made between the perceived physicality of boys and girls as well as the sporting experiences of boys and girls outside of korfball. Observation during participation also provided opportunities to watch and understand how the boys and girls acted differently and whether they complied with traditional gender norms or whether there were examples of resistance and contestation within korfball spaces.

Interviews demonstrated that boys and girls were perceived as being different to some players and no different to others. Scott explained that girls and boys were very similar and described how they all got on with little acknowledgement of difference, 'No I really don't see it because we have a laugh so yeah' (Scott). Despite this, when asked who the best player was, Daniel presumed his response should include both best male and female players. In doing so, Daniel demonstrated his understanding of difference, whilst at the same time also highlighted his awareness of the need to consider both sexes and display recognition for equality. Occasionally, within the training space, boys and girls were separated in practices, for example, boys on one post and girls on the other. This was only seen occasionally as, in the main, girls and boys were split evenly on the posts, or divided in relation to ability. When players were within the 'no ball' times of training they did usually seem to congregate with the same sex. Reasons for this could relate to the format of the game, whereby during training matches girls marked each other and boys marked each other, which led to easy communications with the same-sex player that they were partnered with. In general, however, after training and in water breaks, the girls tended to socialize with girls and boys with boys. This could suggest that broader gender discourses contributed to a prevailing invisible and omnipresent social surveillance which ultimately influenced the players to become principles of their own subjection through their permanent visibility (Foucault 1979) and therefore act in normalized gendered ways. Despite the division of the sexes which was not apparent all of the time, there were many times when the team were together as a whole group, or a boy and girl could be seen talking together on the bench.

Physical difference was something that players acknowledged, and Louise, Sarah, Rachel and Georgie described physical differences between girls and boys:

Erm cos like girls have got more privatey areas [laughs]. (Louise)

No because normally the boys are like taller than the girls so if the girls, if the boys marking the girls they wouldn't be able to get to shoot or stuff like that. (Sarah)

Like size and physical things because erm like, either because most boys are quite like not faster but like they are a bit stronger so like if girls were going to jump with a ball it's like quite a few times I'll get it but if it was against a boy they'll probably get it every time … and I wouldn't feel as good because normally I'll get it and it wouldn't make me feel as good. (Georgie)

Erm I think that's quite a good thing because I know some boys they are a little bit, like some boys are stronger than some girls so they might be a bit tougher on them. So I reckon it's quite a good that girls can mark girls because they're sort of like the same ability. (Georgie)

because boys have more ability of like, like being strong and thing like that but like, being in the rebound and being strong where the girls have more like skills at shooting and stuff like that. (Rachel)

Physical differences of boys and girls, which were seen to give boys an advantage included strength, height, speed and less delicate body parts. These attributes were deemed to make boys less prone to pain or injury during contact, good at defending shots, and better at collecting balls after shots. Rachel was the only player here who suggested that girls were better than boys at skilled roles such as shooting. With these different physical attributes, boys and girls were deemed to act in different ways. Girls were seen to be much less physical than boys, 'I mean like girls as they're like girls they don't really like to punch and kick each other in football and all that so they're much more gentle and yeah' (Chris). Louise agreed,

> sometimes the girls get a bit bitchy if like you don't do it right or get all stroppy whereas boys … when they get aggressive so they will like hurt you and girls don't really like pull you on the floor or anything. (Louise)

Boys were not only seen to have physical advantages such as strength, but they were assumed to be more physical than the girls, and more aggressive. There seemed to be a discretion to the norm (Foucault 1978) regarding boys and violence; it was normal and acceptable for boys to be perceived as violent or aggressive. Louise continued by explaining that it was hard playing korfball sometimes as the boys held shirts and girls did not, the boys shoved into players and girls did not, and the boys were more likely to pull players to the floor or hit. She also explained how the boys also naturally threw the ball harder than the girls, apart from Jess who was tall and therefore also threw with a lot of power. Louise discussed the boys in a general way, and then named Jess specifically as the only girl with a lot of power, and in doing so individualized the non-normal (Foucault 1979).

Traditional sports were also seen to require physical performances that were different to korfball. Sarah considered football to be 'rough', but did not see korfball in the same way. Callum also believed that korfball was 'less aggressive' than rugby and when Daniel was asked what non-players thought about korfball he described how his [male] friends 'call it a wussy sport because it's non-contact, because they do, like, football or rugby. But yeah, I think they just think it's a wussy sport but it's something I enjoy so I don't really care'. The non-contact aspect of korfball rules was a clear factor in the players' understanding of the sport to be physically less aggressive than many others. That it was considered less aggressive, and had explicit non-contact rules, could be why Louise suggested that 'boys think korfball is more girly than boy-y'. The player's perception of korfball in comparison to what they might consider as 'real sports' underlines research which asserts that korfball is perceived as a 'sissy's sport' (Crum 1988, 239). There are obviously preconceptions from 'korfball outsiders' that assume a non-contact, non-traditional, non-male-oriented sport must be 'wussy' (Lucy), suggesting that the fact it is not perceived as a masculine sport means it is perceived as a lesser sport than the likes of football or rugby.

Korfball was also regarded as different to the traditional sports that were on offer to the young players in school. Daniel commented how football and rugby dominated PE classes, despite the fact that sports such as korfball provide a great opportunity for girls and boys within PE lessons to play together. Rachel believed that korfball provided opportunities to make it easier to organize PE lessons 'so you haven't got to have, like, an all girls' lesson or only girls lesson, or only boys lesson, so you can play it throughout so both two sexes can join in'. She explained how, in her experience, PE teachers did not try to get girls equally involved in football, even though they had to play it, and they did not try to get boys equally involved in netball, even though they had to play that within PE. However, in trying to explain this further, she suggested more stereotypical gendered explanations relating to girls not liking football in the first place and that boys cannot play netball anyway 'because it is only a girls' sport'. Lucy further upheld gender stereotypes by suggesting that when girls play single-sex sport, they tend to be 'wussy', and therefore it was better to play mixed sport so that it emulated what she considered to be 'proper' sport.

It was clear from observation and interviews that a number of players had beliefs and understandings that complied with more traditional gender norms. Although not all, a number of players believed that boys had physical advantages in sport, and were likely to be more physically assertive or aggressive than girls in the same situation. Some players also problematized sports outside of korfball, or physical education classes, deeming them to be predominantly directed at boys, and discouraging girls from sport in the process. In this light, korfball was seen as a potential answer to the problem.

Conclusion

The research revealed that korfball was clearly performed and experienced in ways that were both different to and similar to traditional sports. At face value, the format of the game seemed to encourage a level of equality between the sexes on the korfball court. For the young people taking part, reflections upon their experiences of korfball highlighted the extent to which sex equality and gender neutrality were evident on or off the court. This paper has shown how the junior korfball players in this study still held understandings of gender that were often based on societal norms. It would appear that korfball, as a sport, could not eliminate these understandings within its own space, let alone within wider society. Yet, there were exceptions to a solely uncritical gendered understanding and certain players, at certain times, displayed evidence of this on various occasions. Interviews and informal conversations demonstrated both compliance to, and deviation from 'normal' gender actions at different times, with some confusion about key gender terms including masculinity, femininity and the term 'tomboy'. Players were often reluctant to think critically about accepted gender norms and on many occasions players would seem uncomfortable when prompted to explain their views, or when encouraged to consider normalized gender discourse. Yet, the findings from this study were more positive regarding equality within korfball, than previous studies displayed (Crum 1988; Summerfield and White 1989; Thompson and Finnigan 1990).

Players could also clearly be seen to be both subject and object of observation within the complex network of gazes (Foucault 1979, 1994) which exist in both the korfball spaces and wider society. Players demonstrated the use of social taboo as a judgement of transgression (Foucault 1978), for example, when Chris explained that if boys wore girls' clothes, they would be subject to teasing. However, when some players referred to a few of the girls as 'tomboys', there could be considered an individualization of the non-normal (Foucault 1979). In this case, it was apparent that the players sometimes found it difficult to align to the gender-neutral discourses that were expected from the players within the context of the korfball rules, whilst at the same time balancing their constructed understandings of gender, learnt through wider social discourse. Thus, the problematic issue of performing non-conventional gender, such as in the case of a 'tomboy' supports existing critical theory relating to the prevalence of performative gender (Butler 1990; Jackson 2006; Renold 2009). So, whereas the positive aspects of playing together were considered favourably, it was equally difficult for the young people to leave behind their restricted formulations of how to 'do gender' that had been developed in everyday social reality. At the same time, the rules of korfball could be considered equally restrictive in that they had been (historically) shaped from an initial premise of gender difference.

Nevertheless, in comparison to traditional sports, korfball could be seen to provide greater opportunities for girls and boys to play sport together. Particularly in PE lessons, where both sexes have the potential to mutually enjoy a sport that was created so that girls and boys could play in unison as a mixed-sex game within an educational setting (Broekhuysen 1949, cited in Crum 2003). Summerfield and White (1989) explain how korfball was invented as a competitive mixed sport that relied on cooperation, where rules were designed to encourage boys and girls to participate on a level playing field, refute violence and form an egalitarian game. The suggestion from this research is that, despite a lack of gender critique from players, there were more opportunities for equality between the sexes during the game of korfball, in comparison to other more popular traditional team sports, precisely because they were able to play together in the first place.

Disclosure statement

No potential conflict of interest was reported by the authors.

References

Azzarito, L. 2009. "The Panopticon of Physical Education: Pretty, Active and Ideally White." *Physical Education and Sport Pedagogy* 14 (1): 19–39.

Azzarito, L. 2010. "Future Girls, Transcendent Femininities and New Pedagogies: Toward Girls' Hybrid Bodies?" *Sport, Education and Society* 15 (3): 261–275.

Azzarito, L., and M. Solmon. 2006. "A Feminist Poststructuralist View on Student Bodies in Physical Education: Sites of Compliance, Resistance and Transformation." *Journal of Teaching in Physical Education* 25: 200–225.

Bailey, R., I. Wellard, and H. Dismore. 2004. "Girls' Participation in Physical Activities and Sports: Benefits, Patterns, Influences and Ways Forward. Technical report for the World Health Organisation. Geneva: World Health Organisation.

Bourdieu, P., and L. Wacquant. 1992. *An Invitation to Reflexive Sociology*. Cambridge: Polity Press.

Brookes, R. 2002. *Representing Sports*. London: Arnold.

Brown, S., and D. Macdonald. 2007. "Masculinities and Physical Recreation: The (Re)Production of Masculinist Discourses in Vocational Education." *Sport, Education and Society* 13 (1): 19–37.

Burkitt, I. 2012. "Emotional Reflexivity: Feeling, Emotion and Imagination in Reflexive Dialogues." *Sociology* 46 (3): 458–472.

Butler, J. 1990. *Gender Trouble: Feminism and the Subversion of Identity*. New York: Routledge.

Butler, J. 1998. "Athletic Genders: Hyperbolic Instance and/or the Overcoming of Sexual Binarism." *Stanford Humanities Review* 6 (2): 103–111.

Cahn, S. K. 1994. *Coming on Strong: Gender and Sexuality in Twentieth-century Women's Sport*. London: Harvard University Press.

Chalabaev, A., P. Sarrazin, P. Fontayne, J. Boiché, and C. Clément-Guillotin. 2013. "The Influence of Sex Stereotypes and Gender Roles on Participation and Performance in Sport and Exercise: Review and Future Directions." *Psychology of Sport and Exercise* 14: 136–144.

Clark, S., and C. Paechter. 2007. "'Why Can't Girls Play Football?' Gender Dynamics and the Playground." *Sport, Education and Society* 12 (3): 261–276.

Connell, R. W. 2005. *Masculinities*. 2nd ed. Cambridge: Polity Press.

Crum, B. 1988. "A Critical Analysis of Korfball as a "Non-Sexist Sport"." *International Review for the Sociology of Sport* 23 (3): 233–241.

Crum, B. 2003. "The Olympic Ambition of Korfball – A Critical Comment." In *'And I Went on a Voyage to Sweden' – Five Reflections on 100 Years of Korfball*, edited by F. Troost, 109–168. Utrecht: Royal Dutch Korfball Association.

Drury, S. 2011. "'It Seems Really Inclusive in Some Ways, but… Inclusive Just for People Who Identify as Lesbian': Discourses of Gender and Sexuality in a Lesbian-identified Football Club." *Soccer and Society* 12 (3): 421–442.

Emmerik, R., F. Keizer, F. Troost. undated. *Korfball an Insight*. Utrecht: Royal Dutch Korfball Association.

Foddy, B., and J. Savulescu. 2011. "Time to Re-evaluate Gender Segregation in Athletics?" *British Journal of Sports Medicine* 45: 1184–1188.

Fontana, A., and J. H. Frey. 2008. "The Interview: From Neutral Stance to Political Involvement." In *Collecting and Interpreting Qualitative Materials*, edited by N. K. Denzin and Y. S. Lincoln, 3rd ed, 115–160. Thousand Oaks, CA: Sage.

Foucault, M. 1978. *The History of Sexuality: An Introduction*. Vol. I. New York: Random House.

Foucault, M. 1979. *Discipline and Punish: The Birth of the Clinic*. London: Penguin Books.

Foucault, M. 1985. *The Archaeology of Knowledge*. London: Tavistock Publications.

Foucault, M. 1988. *Madness and Civilisation: A History of Insanity in the Age of Reason*. New York: Random House.

Foucault, M. 1994. *Birth of the Clinic: An Archaeology of Medical Perception*. London: Tavistock Publications.

Hammersley, M., and P. Atkinson. 1995. *Ethnography: Principles in Practice*. 2nd ed. London: Routledge.

Hargreaves, J. 1986. *Sport, Power and Culture*. Cambridge: Polity Press.

Hargreaves, J. 2000. *Heroines of Sport*. London: Routledge.

IKF. 2006. *Korfball in the Mixed Zone*. The Netherlands: KNKV.

Jackson, C. 2006. *Lads and Ladettes in School: Gender and a Fear of Failure*. Maidenhead: Open University Press.

Kvale, S. 2007. *Doing Interviews*. London: Sage.

Light, R., and D. Kirk. 2010. "High School Rugby, the Body and the Reproduction of Hegemonic Masculinity." *Sport, Education and Society* 5 (2): 163–176.

Mansfield, L. 2006. Gender and Sports. In *Blackwell Encyclopaedia of Sociology*, edited by G. Ritzer, 1875–1880. London: Blackwell.

Markula, P., and R. Pringle. 2006. *Foucault, Sport and Exercise: Power, Knowledge and Transforming the Self*. London: Routledge.

Messner, M. A. 1992. *Power at Play: Sports and the Problem of Masculinity*. Boston, MA: Beacon Press.

Phipps, A. 2014. *The Politics of the Body: Gender in a Neoliberal and Neoconservative Age*. Cambridge: Polity Press.

Pringle, R., and P. Markula. 2005. "No Pain is Sane after All: A Foucauldian Analysis of Masculinities and Men's Experiences in Rugby." *Sociology of Sport Journal* 22: 472–497.

Quinn-Patton, M. 2002. *Qualitative Research and Evaluation Methods*. 3rd ed. London: Sage.

Renold, E. 2009. "Tomboys and 'Female Masculinity': (Dis)Embodying Hegemonic Masculinity, Queering Gender Identities and Relations." In *The Problem with Boys: Beyond Recuperative Masculinity Politics in Boys' Education*, edited by W. Martino, M. Kehler, and M. Weaver-Hightower, 224–242. New York: Routledge.

Sands, R. R. 2002. *Sport Ethnography*. Leeds: Human Kinetics.

Smith Maguire, J. 2002. "Michel Foucault: Sport, Power, Technologies and Governmentality." In *Theory, Sport and Society*, edited by J. A. Maguire and K. Young, 293–314. Oxford: Elsevier Science.

Summerfield, K., and A. White. 1989. "Korfball: A Model of Egalitarianism." *Sociology of Sport Journal* 6: 144–151.

Thompson, S., and J. Finnigan. 1990. "Egalitarianism in Korfball is a Myth." *New Zealand Journal of Health, Physical Education and Recreation* 23 (4): 7–11.

Thorpe, H. 2012. "The Ethnographic (I)Nterview in the Sports Field: Towards a Postmodern Sensibility." In *Qualitative Research on Sport and Physical Culture*, edited by K. Young and M. Atkinson, 51–78. Bingley: Emerald Group Publishing Ltd.

Tolvhed, H. 2013. "Sex Dilemmas, Amazons and Cyborgs: Feminist Cultural Studies and Sport." *Culture Unbound: Journal of Current Cultural Research* 5: 273–289.

Wachs, F. L. 2002. "Leveling the Playing Field: Negotiating Gendered Rules in Coed Softball." *Journal of Sport and Social Issues* 26: 300–316.

Wachs, F. L. 2003. ""I Was There…": Gendered Limitations, Expectations, and Strategic Assumptions in the World of Coed Softball." In *Athletic Intruders: Ethnographic Research on Women, Culture, and Exercise*, edited by A. Bolin and J. Granskog, 177–200. Albany, NY: State University of New York Press.

Wellard, I. 2007. *Rethinking Gender and Youth Sport*. London: Routledge. pp:1–11.

Wellard, I. 2009. *Sport, Masculinities and the Body*. New York: Routledge.

Wellard, I. 2013. *Sport, Fun and Enjoyment: An Embodied Approach*. Oxon: Routledge.

Woodward, K. 2015. *The Politics of in/Visibility*. Basingstoke: Palgrave.

Negotiations of gender discourse: experiences of co-education in a Swedish sports initiative for children

Karin Grahn and Viveka Berggren Torell

Department of Food and Nutrition, and Sport Science, University of Gothenburg, Gothenburg, Sweden

ABSTRACT

The goal of this article is to explore how children perceive gender in a Swedish government-financed sports initiative and in leisure-time sports activities. We draw on group interviews with children and participant observations from two field studies of elementary school children participating in co-ed soccer and physical activity projects. A focal point of the analysis is how children negotiate their views of boys and girls participating in sports utilizing linguistic and material resources. The interviews included reproduction of traditional views of boys/men as being superior at sports but also demonstrated negotiations and objections against this perception. In addition, we present examples from participant observations regarding potential challenges to gender discourse.

Introduction

'Idrottslyftet', ('The lift for sport') is a Swedish state-funded sports initiative governed by the Swedish Sports Confederation (RF), whose goal is for children and youth to engage in physical activities and sports and to remain involved for longer periods of their lives. One manner in which to achieve this goal is for sports clubs to collaborate with schools. The clubs organize and conduct sports activities led by a sports coach during the school day. This sports initiative is particularly interesting to explore because the initiative comprises a combination of school activities and leisure activities, and this creates a new context for learning and experiencing sports, in some projects in co-educational settings. In Sweden, child and youth sports are generally organized in two separate manners: in school as physical education (PE) classes or as leisure activities in sports clubs. In leisure sports, boys are more involved in team sports such as floor ball, ice hockey and handball, whereas girls are more involved in individual sports such as dance, gymnastics and equestrian training (RF 2014). However according to RF's website (July 29 2013), soccer (association football) is the most popular sport among both girls and boys. Some individual sports such as swimming and track and field offer co-training of girls and boys although a majority of sports (particularly team sports) are organized on the principle of gender division, i.e. boys and girls who participate in the same sport are separated during training and competition. Research has shown how this shapes different social practices for girls and boys playing soccer and creates different expectations of how to be a soccer player (Eliasson 2011; cf., Messner 2002). Sports in general, particularly team sports, draw on a discourse of difference, organizing sports according to a 'binary classification model' (Coakley and Pike 2014), dividing people in one of two categories: male or female. Within this model, the male body and male participation in sports is viewed as the norm (Eliasson 2011; Theberge 2000; Williams 2003). It has been argued that this leads to sports' shaping hegemonic masculinity, excluding or 'othering', for example, female or gay athletes (Coakley and Pike 2014; Connell 2002; Theberge 2000). In contrast to the sex-divided organization of leisure sports, Swedish schools, since the 1980s, have had co-educational PE classes. The fact that Sweden has a sex-segregated organization of leisure sports and co-educational PE renders it interesting to explore what occurs when these two manners of organizing sports combine. This occurs in the sports initiative 'Idrottslyftet'. The sports initiative is of further interest from a gender perspective because the Swedish Sports Confederation has stated that the project should be based on equity and equality perspectives (RF 2009). Research is required to explore how these sports settings may influence gender discourse and children's conceptions of gender in sports. Of special interest is how these discourses are constructed within co-educational sports settings.

Previous research on mixed-sex/co-ed sports has been conducted in diverse countries (Anderson 2008; Channon 2013, 2014; Dashper 2012; Henry and Comeaux 1999; Stiebling 1999; Wachs 2005); however, mixed-sex sports are an under-researched area in Sweden. Further, except for Stiebling's study (1999), previous research has concerned adult sports. It is thus interesting to examine how children perceive and negotiate gender discourses while talking about sports and during sports participation. The aim of this article is to explore how children perceive gender in a Swedish government-financed sports initiative and in leisure sports activities. Further, this study analyses how experiences in a co-ed sports setting may engender negotiating or challenging the views of gender that children develop from leisure-time sports. The article examines (a) gender discourses in two projects in a Swedish sports initiative, (b) children's experiences and negotiations regarding gender in co-ed sports in the sports initiative, engendered by the use of linguistic and material resources, and (c) how children discuss gender in co-education in the sports initiative in relation to their views regarding and experiences with gender-divided leisure sports.

Theoretical framework

The theoretical and methodological framework is based on critical discourse analysis (CDA) (Fairclough 2001) and theories of childhood and gender (Alanen 1992; Connell 1987, 2002; James and Prout 1997; Thorne 1986, 1990).

CDA explains discourse in two manners, first as a knowledge system that represents part of the world in a particular manner. Discourses form statements about various subjects by grouping signs together (Fairclough 2003); thus, the signs can be linguistic (utterances, sentences, stretches of text) or other sounds and visual/material signs, for instance, colour (Kress and Van Leeuwen 2006). Even the cut and choice of material for a garment (Berggren Torell 2007) can be signs of communication and thus elements of discourse. Second, discourse is social practice, or more specifically, practices that are utilized while social actors are grouping certain signs and establishing them as statements with truth-claims. Discourse perceived in this manner refers to practices for excluding, emphasizing and combining signs, thereby proclaiming certain views on a subject and rendering others silent. Thus, discursive practices are about establishing positions and domination.

CDA is used to analyse the role of language in shaping experience, developing social structures, and establishing 'truths' and common knowledge while retaining the perception of people as active subjects who shape their own meaning of the world by reproducing or contesting and transforming discourses (Fairclough 1992). Fairclough (2003, 2) states that 'language is an irreducible component of social life' but also emphasizes that language is 'dialectically interconnected to other forms of social life'. Thus, when children shape their identities as a child/girl/boy, they use linguistic and oral/visual/material signs (such as the signs of clothing) available in certain contexts, such as sports. These discursive representations are embedded in power relations, which can be used to subordinate people but also to challenge or change power relations.

At an institutional level, gendered social relationships shape gender regimes (e.g. within different sports, school, family). Social practices work within an institution to shape manners of performing gender that are more or less socially accepted (Connell 1987, 2002; Mennesson 2012; Messner 2002). Within diverse gender regimes, children are active in exploring and shaping gender. Children learn 'gender competence' by adopting or distancing themselves from different gendered identities proposed by the gender regimes. Children experience opportunities and limitations in relation to gender regimes and in this process, learn diverse masculinities and femininities (Connell 2002). According to Connell and Messerschmidt (2005), there are multiple masculinities and femininities, some of which are more socially central then others and influence other masculinities and femininities (i.e. hegemonic masculinity explained as social dominant masculinity, exemplified by Connell and Messerschmidt [2005, 846] as the 'professional sports star'). However, subordinated masculinities or femininities may also influence dominant forms of masculinity (Connell and Messerschmidt 2005).

One manner in which children learn gender is to relate to masculinities and femininities in the adult world (Connell 2002). Hegemonic forms of masculinities work as 'exemplars of masculinity' or as symbols with discursive centrality (Connell and Messerschmidt 2005). How adults act, interact and express themselves influences gender relations among children. For example, if a teacher or leader acts in a manner that suggests girls and boys are different, the children will most likely act in a manner that upholds these borders between their genders (Thorne 1986, 1990). Children also learn 'gender competence' by actively involving themselves in social relationships with other children (Connell 2002). Thorne's (1986) research on gendered social relationships among school children shows how gender differs in salience in diverse contexts. Thorne suggests four manners of gendered interaction: (1) some interaction emphasizes gender differences, i.e. children shape gender borders between girls and boys; (2) children act within social relations infused with heterosexual meaning; (3) some children actively cross gender borders; and (4) children are also part of 'relaxed cross-sex interactions' (Thorne 1986, 179) in which they interact in mixed-sex groups without shaping gender borders and without explicitly performing gender differences.

Further, in sport contexts and PE, children use material resources such as clothes or colours to perform gender (Larsson, Redelius, and Fagrell 2007; Messner 2002).

Co-education in sports and physical culture

Henry and Comeaux's (1999) research on co-ed soccer showed reproduction of male domination on the field. Wachs (2005) later researched sex-integrated softball and found that gender differences were simultaneously reproduced and challenged. More recently, Dashper (2012) explored sex integration and equality in equestrian sports, and Channon (2013, 2014) examined mixed-sex training and challenges to traditional gender constructions as well as the discourses behind inclusivity in martial arts and combat sports (MACS). Channon's study (2014) shows how mixed-sex training in MACS can challenge perceptions of MACS as being an activity for men, and that women's competence as both athletes and instructors were made visible at times (cf. Wachs 2005). Simultaneously, MACS female athletes experienced that they were 'held to a lower standard than men' (594), for example, some men restrained themselves when fighting women since they were afraid of hurting them. Anderson (2008) further showed that men leaving the homosocial context of high school football for sex-integrated cheerleading developed more positive attitudes towards female athletes.

None of these studies examined children's sports. However, a former study by Stiebling (1999) explored co-ed soccer among six- to seven-year olds. Stiebling showed that when the activities were structured by the coach, frequent interaction occurred between girls and boys. In these activities, gender was not salient to the children's interactions. When activities were not structured by the coach, sex segregation appeared more frequently, and gendered behaviour was more explicit.

Research on gender in PE has more specifically studied children in the co-ed context. Swedish research showed that teaching was often conducted in a manner that separated girls from boys, even while they were co-educated (Larsson, Fagrell and Redelius 2005; Larsson, Redelius, and Fagrell 2007; Fagrell, Larsson, and Redelius 2012). Further, teachers had lower expectations of the skills or strength of girls and did not demand as much from them. By contrast, strength and athletic skills were emphasized for boys (Larsson, Redelius, and Fagrell 2007). Oliynyk's (2014) research showed similar results. Boys (but not girls) were expected to show their competence and physicality in PE. Further, children themselves were active in shaping gender by maintaining stereotypical manners of being. For example, boys behaved competitively, whereas girls were caring and helpful. These manners of acting were reinforced by the teacher. Boys acted superior to girls and took a central position in the PE lesson. However, some children challenged gender stereotypes, e.g. boys showing non-hegemonic forms of masculinity or girls performing traditionally masculine-coded actions (e.g. showing physicality and/or ball-playing skills).

Soccer – a 'male preserve?'

This article focuses on soccer because both of the investigated projects were organized by soccer clubs. Previous research has shown that soccer is perceived as a masculine activity (Clark and Paechter 2007; Eliasson 2011; Williams 2003) and that the sport promotes masculinity (Bhana 2008; Fundberg 2003; Skelton 2000).

Eliasson (2011) suggests that the organization and practice of soccer were similar for 11-year-old girls and boys in sex-divided teams although girls and boys experienced diverse social practices. In playing soccer, children learned how to 'be' a girl or a boy by acting and interacting in diverse manners. According to Eliasson, girls and boys viewed one another through a discourse of differences and often described the 'opposite sex' in negative terms. Boys described themselves as playing tougher than girls, whereas girls described themselves as having a well-developed passing play. Further, a masculine norm was constructed in soccer players' talk about girls' and boys' soccer, and boys were perceived as better soccer players (Eliasson 2011). This is consistent with previous research among children showing that boys and men are viewed as natural soccer players and that men are viewed as stronger and more suited to competitive sports (Bartholomaeus 2011; Bhana 2008; Hasbrook and Harris 1999). These results are also consistent with the study of Fagrell, Larsson, and Redelius (2012) showing that boys described girls' lack of activity during floor ball as a result of not daring to act and/or their lack of competence. Further, Clark and Paechter's (2007) ethnographic study of soccer activities during breaks in primary school showed that boys invested in masculinity by participating in soccer, which led to the exclusions of both girls and non-soccer-playing boys.

The study and methods

In this section, the two field studies of projects in the sports initiative 'Idrottslyftet' are introduced. We present the research method and discuss ethical concerns.

Field work

Collaboration between schools and sports clubs in 'Idrottslyftet' is organized in two manners: either the sports club offers activities to all children in a school, or in certain grades, or the sports club regularly offers voluntary training during the school day. In the latter situation, pupils may choose to participate as a component of their curriculum (often in lessons set aside for 'pupil's choice'). Two school-sport collaboration projects (one of each type) conducted by soccer clubs and led by soccer coaches were chosen for field studies. The first fieldwork occurred in a primary school in which physical activity (mostly different types of play and games) was offered once a week during the school day to classes in grades three, four and five (children nine to eleven years old). Participation was mandatory. The second fieldwork was conducted in a primary school in which soccer could be chosen by pupils in grades five and six (children 11–12 years old) twice a month, during the school day.

The first field study focused primarily on how child and childhood discourses were reproduced or contested in the sports initiative. The second field study focused on gender discourses (Grahn and Berggren Torell 2014). However, both gender and age were important in both field studies. Although the child is always a relational concept that situates the 'inhabitants' of childhood in relation to adults, the category of the child also relates intersectionally to other identity categories (e.g. gender), which leads to different experiences of lived childhoods, for instance, with regard to independence or power (Alanen 1992; Alanen and Mayall 2001). Thus, material gathered for interpretations of childhood discourses may also be used to discuss gender issues. By stating different skills as 'boyish' or 'girlish', gender discourses propose gendered identities for children.

For this article, field notes and filmed sequences from participant observations were analysed, and because children's views of the world are important to explore (James and Prout 1997), semi-structured group interviews were also interpreted. The purpose of the fieldwork was to explore how text (written and spoken language as well as sings such as body language or symbols) was used in the sports setting to construct local childhood and gender discourses. Because childhood and gender discourses are constructed within discursive and social practices (Fairclough 2001), we decided to use an ethnographic approach to be able to include diverse sources. The combination of CDA and ethnography has previously been suggested to be fruitful for research (Fairclough in Rogers 2004) and has been used in various research fields, including educational science (Rogers 2011).

Five group interviews with children in grade four (10-year olds) in the physical activity project and a total of six interviews in grades five and six (11–12-year olds) in the soccer project are included in the material that has been interpreted for this article. Questions were asked regarding children's perception of leisure sports in relation to gender (i.e. experiences of playing in sex-integrated or sex-segregated teams as well as their thoughts on their experiences with leisure sports). Further, the children were asked about their experiences with the sports initiative 'Idrottslyftet' and their experiences with participating in co-ed football and physical activity in the sports initiative. In addition, the article includes interpretations of field notes and filmed sequences. In the soccer project, a total of 10 participant observations, including activities filmed during six occasions, were conducted, and in the physical activity project, 11 participant observations in years 3, 4 and 5 were conducted, including filmed material from nine lessons. During participant observations, we followed the class. We sometimes stood and watched from the side and at other times moved around to be able to follow the coach and move closer to the children to observe and watch them in action. We joined the group at gatherings to follow their conversations. Field notes were gathered during each session and transcribed afterwards. Some of the activities were filmed so that we could later review communication and interactions between the coach and children and between children as well as other non-linguistic communication or signs (body language, cloths, etc.). The participant observations also enabled us to ask questions regarding what we observed. Field notes, filmed sequences and interviews were all analysed in relation to one another, rendering it possible to strengthen some interpretations while questioning other interpretations formed during observations. This led to a more holistic picture of the practices being explored as well as a more trustworthy result (Denscombe 2009).

Analysis

To analyse the interviews, we initially read the transcripts and marked interesting portions of the text, noted keywords and other comments. Relevant text (concerning experiences from leisure sports activities, experiences with co-education within the sports initiative, and perceptions of soccer/sports and gender) was analysed further. First, we explored the content of these transcripts according to language use and modality (Fairclough 2003). According to Fairclough, modality concerns commitment, attitudes and judgements. Modality refers to how people use language to state something with certainty or as common sense or, conversely, as vague or even questionable. An example ranging from high to low modality is 'certainly – probably – possibly' (Fairclough 2003). These levels of modality can be analysed by markers of modalization (Wahl 2007), i.e. verbs, adverbs, modal adjectives and other words or intonation and other aspects of how things are said, used to express the grade of certainty of a statement (Fairclough 2003). We sorted the children's statements into three levels: high, medium or low levels of modality (Fairclough 2003). When using markers of modalization (Wahl 2007) such as 'is/are', children construct a high level of modality, framing the content as true. Further, drawing on common knowledge (e.g. 'generally' or 'it is said') is considered a medium level of modality, and finally, using hypothesis or even a vague statement such as 'perhaps' suggests a low level of modality. Analysing the use of markers of modalization and sorting the statements into three levels, we noted how the children stated, negotiated or even challenged perceptions of gender inside and outside of the sports initiative. In other words, we employed modality to analyse how children used language to frame something as a certainty (i.e. something they claim to know) or as common sense or as more uncertain, with room for interpretation.

Further material from the participant observations was analysed by focusing on text broadly, understood as communication via words, body language, gestures and symbols. We began the analysis by reading field notes and watching filmed activities, taking notes and noting interesting sequences in the films. We identified activities that were significant to the construction of gender as well as material resources (clothes, colour, etc.) used to shape gender. For this article, we included examples from participant observations that are of interest in relation to what the children discuss in the interviews. Further, we have exemplified how gender discourses in some cases were challenged by how children used words, actions or material resources during the projects. This part of analysis is described by Fairclough (2010) to focus on 'positive critique', i.e. to identify possibilities for change.

Ethical concerns

Research was conducted in accordance with the ethical guidelines of the Swedish Research Council (VR). Both oral and written information regarding the aim of the research was presented to the children, and parents received all information in writing. Both children and parents filled out consent forms (VR 2015). During the observations and interviews, we have been reflective in relation to the ethical guidelines, and we were observant of signals and comments from the children (Lindsay 2000; VR 2015). Although we had consent to film the children, we did not film if it appeared that a child was bothered by being filmed (VR 2015). Children could say something or act in a manner that caused us to recognize this. For example, a boy in the physical activity project, during activities on a playground, requested that the researcher should not film him when he was playing on a toy that was meant for younger children. It appeared that he did not want his 'childishness' to be documented. We also stopped filming during the soccer project when a girl became frustrated because she could not understand the coach's instructions. Adding a camera would not have relieved her stress in this situation. Circumstances such as these were few, however. We also took more field notes in the beginning of the period of observation so that the children would become used to us being there before filming them. In addition, we attempted to render the production of research material transparent: we talked to the children about our role as observers, took notes openly and described our goal of writing a report and scientific articles mostly meant for other researchers and for sports coaches who could learn from what the children thought was good and bad about the sports initiative. We also encouraged the children to ask questions about our work at any time. Occasionally, some children asked about what we took notes on. However, most children took no notice of our presence during their activities.

In the results, we will present anonymous interview extracts. These passages were transcribed verbatim, with minor alterations made for readability.

Results

In the results, we present interpretations of interviews that show how children reproduce a discourse of differences by expressing a binary view of gender and constructing boys as superior in sports/soccer. In addition, based on interviews and material from participant observations, we discuss how children also come to negotiate these views regarding gender.

Children's experiences with gender in leisure-time sports

Many of the children in both projects were engaged in sports activities during their leisure time. During the soccer project, we asked about the children's involvement in sports and if they trained in mixed-sex or single-sex groups. Some of the children who participated in individual sports and dance had experience with mixed-sex settings; however, the majority of the children (particularly in team sports) were involved in single-sex groups.

A couple of boys who played ice hockey and one boy who played floor ball explained that they played on 'boys' teams'. However, after some consideration, they said that one or a couple of girls also played with them. One boy said, 'In floor ball, there are only boys, but we have a girl on our floor ball team because she's awesome. She's the best among the girls born -99 or -98 so she gets to play with us' (boy, year 5, soccer project). In a similar manner, a couple of boys described how some older girls played with them during ice hockey practice. The fact that girls played with the boys did not alter the discourse regarding gender differences that occurred when talking about sports. Including girls in the team practice did not make the boys reconsider defining their team as a 'boys' team'.

We further asked what the children in the soccer project thought about playing on 'girls' or boys' teams'. The interviewed children all agreed that it was good to play on sex-segregated teams. Some children (just as the boys described earlier) concluded that individual girls could play on 'boys' teams'; however, the reverse (a boy on a 'girls' team') or mixed teams were not considered. The children appeared to have normalized the sex-segregated organization of sports through their experiences with the sex-segregated gender regime of soccer (cf. Eliasson 2011; Mennesson 2012; Messner 2002). The children experienced difficulty in expressing why they thought the current organization was good: 'I think that it's good […] I don't know why, but …' (boy, year 5). Among the explanations, there were two main suggestions: (a) physical differences and (b) social differences. The first was built on arguments such as 'You can be more physical playing with the guys' (boy, year 6); 'Usually boys are tougher in their way of playing' (girl, year 6); and 'In men's soccer, and in other sports as well, they [men] play much faster than the women do, but I don't know why' (boy, year 5). The social explanation was based on friendship and familiarity: 'Boys have a great deal to talk about, and if a girl joins, maybe she will be left out' (boy, year 6); 'Situations may arise when boys pass [the ball] to boys, and girls pass to girls' (boy, year 6); and 'One might enjoy playing better when girls are with girls and boys with boys. You might feel more secure playing with girls' (girl, year 5).

According to Eliasson (2011), 11-year-old soccer players emphasized social differences between girls and boys and highlighted different styles of playing soccer, and just as in Eliasson's study, the children in the sports initiative constructed gender within a discourse of difference. However, analysis of markers of modalization (Wahl 2007) shows that there is some space for uncertainty in the children's statements because of their use of words and phrases such as 'might', 'maybe' or 'I don't know'. There were differences in the manner in which children spoke about the sex-segregated organization of team sports and why this organization was desirable. When children responded that they thought it was good to play segregated, the children used markers of modalization such as 'is/are' (Wahl 2007); however, when the participants discussed why sex segregation was the best manner in which to organize sports, the children used weaker statements, guessed and tried different 'hypotheses'. These discussions shape discursive practices (Fairclough 2001) in which different ideas, concepts and explanations are tested against one another which may lead to negotiations of previously accepted ideas. These types of discussions are further explored in the next section.

Reproduction and questioning of gendered conceptions

In both the soccer and the physical activity projects, girls and boys discussed their views on gender and sports, particularly in terms of playing together or not playing together. Negotiations were conducted regarding statements made by some children, and questioning, comments, or subtle objections to statements made by other children. In the following discussion, children in year five in the soccer project expressed their opinions regarding playing on sex-segregated teams during their leisure time.

Boy 3:   Well … yes, it is good [to play on a 'boys' team']

Children: [Laughing]

Boy 3:   Boys are a bit tougher than girls.

Girl 1:   [Clears her throat]

Children: [Giggling]

Boy 2 [in a sarcastic voice]:   Well, that was a 'good' statement.

Children: Mm … [Giggling]

In that excerpt, the statement that boys are tougher seems to evoke some resistance from a girl and a boy. The girl clears her throat exaggerated and a boy comments on the statement sarcastically.

In another grade five group in the soccer project, a similar discussion occurred:

Girl 1:   Many people say that boys have a much better ball-sense than girls. That's why they have made the setting apart [between girls' and boys' teams].

Children: [Giggling]

Girl 2:   Is one supposed to agree with that?

[Someone nearly whispers]:   Aa

The first girl makes her statement about boys having a better ball-sense by leaning on other people's statements ('Many people say …') (a moderate level of modality, Fairclough 2003; Wahl 2007). With regard to this statement, the other girl questions the accuracy of what the first girl is saying. These examples show that a discourse framing boys/men as more skilled soccer players is reproduced by some children although questioned by other children.

To become more familiar with the children's views on and experiences with co-education in the sports initiative, the children were asked about their opinions regarding dividing the co-ed group into smaller (mixed- or single-sex) groups during activities and games. When a group of children in the physical activity project were asked if it mattered if the groups were mixed or not a boy answered: 'Yes, guys are much better'. One of the girls then replied in an irritated voice, 'Thanks!' and the boy then changed the topic of the conversation. In another interview during the physical activity project, a girl and a boy got into a disagreement when asked about playing in mixed or segregated groups. A boy explained: 'I think that it is best to play girls against boys …'. When asked why a girl added, 'Guys always win'. The boy then countered, 'No, because the boys are best!' to which the girl replied, 'The girls are better!' A second boy then said that it did not matter. In the soccer project, similar expressions and discussions occurred during the interviews. Statements such as 'Boys rule!' and jokes about boys being tougher were components of the boys' modes of speaking. These examples show how children talk about boys as better or tougher within a gender discourse of male supe-riority (cf. Bartholomaeus 2011; Bhana 2008; Eliasson 2011; Hasbrook and Harris 1999). Conversely, interpretations of these conversations suggest that some children are not keen on accepting these types of statements.

Some of the girls in the physical activity project also expressed frustration with playing with boys, particularly when playing soccer. Although one girl thought it was good to mix the teams during the activities, she did not like this idea when it came to soccer: 'When we play soccer, he [the coach] usually lets us play girls against girls, because the guys do not pass [the ball]…to the girls'. Two girls took turns explaining how they experienced boys acting on the soccer field:

Girl 1: They are trying to show off much more.

Girl 2: Yes, and they sort of want to make the goals on their own. They don't pass the ball.

Girl 1: And all of a sudden, they can stop and do tricks.

The interviewer laughed and answered, 'Yes, ok', in an adult manner to inform the chil-dren that she had noted what they said; however, one of the girls apparently thought that the interviewer did not respond properly because she burst out, 'It's annoying!' The girl obviously took this type of behaviour seriously because the boys occasionally appeared to both 'steal the show' and exclude the girls. Not passing the ball to the girls can be interpreted as girls being treated as 'others' by the boys (Coakley and Pike 2014) and is in line with Channon's (2014) research showing reluctance amongst men to fight women properly in MACS. Similar expressions to those in the physical activity project were observed in a couple of interviews with the children in the soccer project: 'Some boys […] they run around thinking that they are best, and there aren't many girls doing that' (girl, year 5). Similar actions were also observed during soccer lessons in which boys (but seldom girls) 'showed off' by performing tricks and impressive moves. Some boys also placed themselves at the centre of attention, sometimes by doing things that were perceived negatively by the coach or by talking loudly or placing themselves in front of the group. Similar actions were noticed by Oliynyk (2014) and can be interpreted as boys' manner of portraying masculinity and showing superiority. This positions girls, as well as boys who do not portray hegemonic masculinity, as 'others' (Coakley and Pike 2014; Fundberg 2003; Hasbrook and Harris 1999; Oliynyk 2014).

Some children's idea of a soccer player appears to be a boy (or a man) who plays rough or shows off. This constructs a specific masculinity to which boys playing soccer are expected to adhere (cf. Bhana 2008; Eliasson 2011; Fundberg 2003; Skelton 2000). This type of action can be compared to boys portraying masculinity during PE lessons, during which they are expected to display their competence (Larsson, Redelius, and Fagrell 2007; Oliynyk 2014). However, it was also noted during observations that boys portrayed diverse masculinities (Connell and Messerschmidt 2005), and at times, some boys attempted to avoid being at the centre of attention, for example, when the group was playing 'Following John' (a game in which the children are following the movements of a leader, 'John', in a line moving around the gym hall). Some of the boys avoided being 'John' and if picked to be 'John' by the coach, kept to traditional movements (running, skipping, etc.) and led the group for as short a time as possible.

Challenges of a discourse of differences in co-educational experiences

A difference between the two projects was that in the soccer project, girls and boys played soccer together at all times, whereas in the physical activity group, girls and boys only played soccer together occasionally. In this manner, the children in the soccer project developed more experience with co-ed soccer. In the interviews, children in the soccer project expressed views similar to the views of the physical activity group regarding boys not passing the ball to the girls, particularly in the beginning of the project. However, during observations, one semester into the project for fifth graders and three semesters into the project for sixth graders, this was not noted as being an issue. Presumably, maintaining the borders between girls and boys (Thorne 1986, 1990) became less important when the children got used to playing together. This observation was also supported by the described experiences of children in one of the group interviews in sixth grade, in which a girl said, 'In the beginning when we had soccer [...], the guys passed [the ball] to other boys'. The boys in the interview agreed with this statement. The girl continued, 'But as time passed, we play more together and pass the ball and so on'. Another boy said that they had learned to work together better now. Another boy explained that the children had been practising drills that had made them understand the need to pass the ball to everyone. This is consistent with Stiebling's (1999) research showing frequent interaction between girls and boys playing soccer while being organized by the coach as well as Thorne (1986) theory of gender interaction, which suggests that girls and boys can interact in relaxed manners when participating in adult-organized activities and/or activities based on children's interests and cooperation.

When discussing the soccer project, interviewed children also made positive statements regarding playing together during school time, unlike their comments regarding playing separately during leisure time. When asked what the children thought about playing together in the soccer project, one boy in grade six responded, 'Well, I think that it is good [to play together] because then all of us can show what we can actually do. The girls are very skilled too, I think, so I think it is good that we mix'. A boy in another interview in grade six said, 'It becomes fun; it becomes more varied'. A girl in the same interview said that she liked co-education because it was more challenging to play soccer with both girls and boys.

The fact that girls and boys in grades five and six practised and played soccer together is in itself a manner of challenging a binary division of gender (Coakley and Pike 2014). The co-ed soccer project shaped a gender regime that differed from the gender regime described by the children in leisure-time soccer/sports. Playing together also challenged the discourses of difference that are produced by soccer (Eliasson 2011). The level of competence and experience varied among girls and boys. Some played with a clear focus on improving; others played solely for fun. A few of the pupils played simply to try soccer and were not involved with the sport in their spare time. Thus, the level of the players of both sexes ranged from beginners to advanced. This diversity is a challenge to soccer discourse because soccer is generally played in sex-segregated teams with all children the same age and with approximately the same skills and experience. The coach described the diverse levels of experience with the sport as a difficulty although in terms of shifting gender discourses, this diversity may be an advantage because the children may come to learn that both girls and boys can have a range of soccer skills. According to the interviewed coach, because boys and girls play together, some of the boys realize that the girls are their technical equals: 'The guys see that these girls are as good as they are, because there aren't any significant differences between them when it comes to technique'. Practising as equals is suggested by Channon (2014) to challenge conceptions of men/boys as stronger; in the case of soccer, better or tougher (cf. Wachs 2005).

During observations, it was noted that the co-ed soccer sessions frequently enabled 'relaxed cross-sex interactions' (Thorne 1986, 179) between girls and boys, i.e. interaction without the need to maintain borders between girls and boys (compare Thorne 1986, 1990) (occasions when gender-segregated patterns occurred are described in Grahn and Berggren Torell [2014]). On occasions when children participated in adult-organized drills, exercises and play, this specific sports initiative enabled children to play soccer in a context in which girls and boys were not explicitly treated as different and complementary. Thorne (1986) suggests that these relaxed interactions between girls and boys occur when children are together in gender-integrated groups because of a common interest and when they work together. This occurred in the soccer project because the children participated in the project voluntarily. Observations and filmed sequences show that when performing drills, often organized into mixed-sex groups by the coach, the children cooperated to ensure that the drill worked. On such occasions, the project had the potential to challenge a binary division of gender in this specific context. As in Stiebling's (1999) study, our observations indicate that when children's activities were not organized by the coach (between drills, before and after practice sessions, etc.), children more often chose to form single-sex groups. This indicates the importance of coaches being aware of children's 'doing of gender' (West and Zimmerman 1987) and how to avoid placing children in situations in which borders between genders are developed (Thorne 1986, 1990).

Clothes as neutralizers or as gender markers

In addition to co-education, another aspect that toned down the discourse of difference in the soccer project was clothing. In the filmed sequences, most children were dressed in soccer clothing or shorts and a t-shirt. Some of the children wore soccer socks, but most children wore regular socks. Both girls and boys had t-shirts in bright colours (none wore pink) as well as white or black. No explicit gender differences were noted between girls and boys in their manner of dressing. Previous research on PE has demonstrated that clothes are an important symbol for preferred femininity and masculinity and that certain clothing is normalized for girls and boys, whereas other clothing is viewed as taboo (Larsson, Redelius, and Fagrell 2007). Research by Berggren Torell (2010) based on interviews with adult soccer players has shown that reflections on femininity are components of considerations concerning soccer clothing. Many adult female players today wear clothes designed specifically for women and value these clothes highly. The design features that players primarily see as markers of femininity are close-fitting jerseys with curved hems on the sides and shorts that are a little shorter than men's shorts. According to observations during the soccer project, the discourse of gender differences regarding soccer attire did not appear to have reached the children; at least, it had not appeared in the children's activities in the soccer project. Both boys and girls wore loose t-shirts, and the length of the shorts varied among the children. The only difference noted was that although a few of the boys wore long, baggy shorts, none of the girls did. Only a few children wore clothing other than shorts and t-shirts, sometimes semi-long trousers (both for girls and boys) and a sports t-shirt (sometimes with tighter models for girls). In addition, all girls had long hair, often in a ponytail or loose; although most boys had short hair, some had semi-long hair. In other words, in terms of personal appearance (hair style), there were some differences; however, in clothing styles, differences were few.

The similarity of clothing in the soccer project can be compared to clothing in the physical activity project. Because this project was most often conducted in the schoolyard, the participating children did not change clothes. Sometimes it became clear that clothes were techniques of the body (Craik 2005) that constricted the children's movements or influenced their comfort and security while playing. In public debate, close-fitting girls' clothing has often been perceived as problematic from a gender perspective. One argument against girls' fashion has been that tight-cut clothes restrict body movements, allowing girls less freedom of movement than boys. However, in the physical activity project, it was observed that the most problematic garments when it came to running were loose, baggy jeans and other trousers worn by boys, often fastened with a belt but nevertheless hanging down far enough that the brand of underwear was noticeable. For example, while participating in a relay race, one boy had to stretch his arm back to hold his pants up while he was running; naturally, he did not run as fast as he otherwise might have. Another time in the middle of a game, the coach appeared irritated and shouted to a boy, 'Pull your pants up properly now!'

Observations of girls showed that they were not corrected by the coach in similar manners, rather they took responsibility for their own clothing, as if they were embarrassed to show too much of their bodies. For example, two girls who turned cartwheels during a lesson in Capoeira instantly pulled down their garments when they were back on their feet again after having been upside down. Thus, fashion for girls and boys created differences between the sexes in the physical activity project (cf. Larsson, Redelius, and Fagrell 2007). In contrast to common views on children's clothing, however, some boys were more restricted in their movements by their clothing. By contrast, in the soccer project, clothing functioned as a sports uniform (Craik 2005) and created similarity between boys and girls.

Concluding thoughts

We have argued in this article first that children discussed leisure-time soccer and soccer players within a discourse of difference (Eliasson 2011), portraying men/boys as better and tougher soccer players (cf. Bartholomaeus 2011; Bhana 2008; Eliasson 2011; Hasbrook and Harris 1999). However, these views of soccer players (primarily espoused by boys and some girls) were also challenged. There was room for negotiation in the children's descriptions of leisure sports and in girls' and boys' discussions of playing together or separately. Both girls and boys questioned statements regarding boys being better or tougher. Such challenges are consistent with Eliasson (2011) and in research on playground soccer by Clark and Paechter (2007). In the discursive practices of the interviews, gender was shaped with a certain degree of uncertainty, using a language built on markers of modalization (Wahl 2007) with a moderate level of modality (Fairclough 2003).

We further argue that the practices being observed comprised a somewhat different gender regime than what children had experienced during ball sports during leisure activities. Although the research showed that on some occasions, traditional gender patterns were (re)produced in the sports initiative (Grahn and Berggren Torell 2014), this article suggests that on other occasions, there was potential for the children in the soccer project to experience soccer in less gender-segregated manners than in leisure-time soccer. A significant difference from the practice in the soccer clubs was that girls and boys were co-educated in the soccer project. Although co-education as such does not guarantee gender equality (Channon 2014), the activities nevertheless appeared to offer a discourse somewhat different from the discourse of leisure sports. The study suggests ongoing negotiations regarding stereotypical ideas such as leisure sports being gender-segregated and boys being superior (cf. Bartholomaeus 2011; Bhana 2008; Eliasson 2011; Fagrell, Larsson, and Redelius 2012; Hasbrook and Harris 1999). New experiences and new ideas seem to have developed during the project, such as soccer as an activity that can be played together and that both girls and boys can be skilled soccer players (cf. Anderson 2008). Because there were beginners among both girls and boys, all children had to adapt to one another to make the soccer sessions work. When collaboration between the children is working well, that collaboration enables relaxed cross-sex interactions between girls and boys (Thorne 1986; Stiebling 1999).

The result of this study suggests that it is important to analyse both the use of language and other symbolic or material resources that children use to construct gender, to be able to interpret reproduction and challenges of gender discourse. A limitation of this study may be that linguistic analysis is not specifically developed to analyse the language of children. However, we have tried to be sensitive to both content and the use of language in the interpretations of the interviews, and we have combined interviews and observations to better understand the children's experiences of the sports initiative. In conclusion, we suggest that being aware of these negotiations in gender discourses occurring within the observed sports initiative, can enable teachers and coaches to further challenge children's ideas regarding gender in future practice. In the long run, this may contribute to changes in gender discourses related to sports.

Disclosure statement

No potential conflict of interest was reported by the authors.

Funding

This work was supported by the Swedish Sports Confederation [grant number 24]

References

Alanen, L. 1992. *Modern Childhood? Exploring the "Child Question" in Sociology*. Jyväskylä: Pedagogiska Forskningsinstitutet.
Alanen, L., and B. Mayall. 2001. *Conceptualizing Child–Adult Relations*. London: Routledge.
Anderson, E. 2008. "'I Used to Think Women Were Weak': Orthodox Masculinity, Gender Segregation, and Sport." *Sociological Forum* 23 (2): 257–280. doi:10.1111/j.1573-7861.2008.00058.x.

Bartholomaeus, C. 2011. "What It Means to Be 'Manly': Gender, Sport, and Primary School Students." *Outskirts* 24. http://www.outskirts.arts.uwa.edu.au/volumes/volume-24/bartholomaeus.

Berggren Torell, V. 2007. "Folkhemmets barnkläder. Diskurser om det klädda barnet under 1920–1950-Talen [Children's Clothes in the People's Home. Discourses of the Dressed Child in the. 1920s to the 1950s]." PhD diss., University of Gothenburg.

Berggren Torell, V. 2010. "It Must Be a Little More Close-fitting …'on Clothes' Contributions to Constructions of Femininity within Football." Paper for the XVII ISA World Congress of Sociology, Gothenburg, July 11–17.

Bhana, D. 2008. "'Six Packs and Big Muscles, and Stuff like That'. Primary School-aged South African Boys, Black and White, on Sport." *British Journal of Sociology of Education* 29 (1): 3–14.

Channon, A. G. 2013. "Enter the Discourse: Exploring the Discursive Roots of Inclusivity in Mixed-sex Martial Arts." *Sport in Society* 16 (10): 1293–1308. doi:10.1080/17430437.2013.790896.

Channon, A. G. 2014. "Towards the "Undoing" of Gender in Mixed-sex Martial Arts and Combat Sports." *Societies* 4: 587–605. doi:10.3390/soc4040587.

Clark, S., and C. Paechter. 2007. "'Why Can't Girls Play Football?' Gender Dynamics and the Playground." *Sport, Education and Society* 12 (3): 261–276. doi:10.1080/13573320701464085.

Coakley, J., and E. Pike. 2014. *Sports in Society*. 2nd ed. London: McGraw Hill Education.

Connell, R. 1987. *Gender and Power: Society, the Person and Sexual Politics*. Cambridge: Polity & Blackwell.

Connell, R. 2002. *Gender*. Cambridge: Polity Press.

Connell, R., and J. W. Messerschmidt. 2005. "Hegemonic Masculinity: Rethinking the Concept." *Gender and Society* 19 (6): 829–859. doi:10.1177/0891243205278639.

Craik, J. 2005. *Uniforms Exposed from Conformity to Transgression*. Oxford: Berg.

Dashper, K. 2012. "Together, Yet Still Not Equal? Sex Integration in Equestrian Sport." *Asia-Pacific Journal of Health, Sport and Physical Education* 3 (3): 13–225. doi:10.1080/18377122.2012.721727.

Denscombe, M. 2009. *Forskningshandboken -för småskaliga forskningsprojekt inom samhällsvetenskapen* [The Research Handbook -for Small Scale Reseacrh Projects within Social Science]. Lund: Studentlitteratur.

Eliasson, I. 2011. "Gendered Socialization among Girls and Boys in Children's Football Teams in Sweden." *Soccer & Society* 12 (6): 820–833. doi:10.1080/14660970.2011.609682.

Fagrell, B., H. Larsson, and K. Redelius. 2012. "The Game within the Game: Girls' Underperforming Position in Physical Education." *Gender and Education* 24 (1): 101–118. doi:10.1080/09540253.2011.582032.

Fairclough, N. 1992. *Discourse and Social Change*. Cambridge: Polity.

Fairclough, N. 2001. *Language and Power*. 2nd ed. Harlow: Longman.

Fairclough, N. 2003. *Analysing Discourse: Textual Analysis for Social Research*. New York: Routledge.

Fairclough, N. 2010. *Critical Discourse Analysis: The Critical Study of Language*. 2nd ed. Harlow: Longman.

Fundberg, J. 2003. "Kom igen, gubbar! om pojkfotboll och maskuliniteter." [Com on Guys! About Boys' Football and Masculinities.] PhD diss., Stockholm University.

Grahn, K., and V. Berggren Torell. 2014. *Barndom och genus i idrottslyftsprojekt på skoltid* [Childhood and Gender in Sports Initiatives During School Day]. Stockholm: Riksidrottsförbundet. http://www.rf.se/ImageVaultFiles/id_55344/cf_394/Barndom_och_genus_i_Idrottslyftsprojekt_p-_skoltid.PDF.

Hasbrook, C. A., and O. Harris. 1999. "Wrestling with Gender: Physicality and Masculinities among Inner-city First and Second Graders." *Men and Masculinities* 1 (3): 302–318. doi:10.1177/1097184X99001003004.

Henry, J. M., and H. P. Comeaux. 1999. "Gender Egalitarianism in Coed Sport: A Case Study of American Soccer." *International Review for the Sociology of Sport* 34 (3): 277–290.

James, A., and A.Prout. 1997. "A New Paradigm for the Sociology of Childhood? Provenance, Promise and Problems." In *Constructing and Reconstructing Childhood: Contemporary Issues in the Sociological Study of Childhood*, (2., [rev. and updated] ed.) edited by A. James and A. Prout, 7–33. London: Falmer.

Kress, G. R., and T. Van Leeuwen. 2006. *Reading Images: The Grammar of Visual Design*. 2nd ed. London: Routledge.

Larsson, H., B. Fagrell, and K. Redelius. 2005. *Kön-Idrott-Skola* [Gender-Sports-School]. http://idrottsforum.org/articles/larsson/larsson_fagrell_redelius/larsson_fagrell_redelius051214.html.

Larsson, H., K. Redelius, and B. Fagrell. 2007. "'Jag känner inte för att bli en ... kille' Om heteronormativitet i ämnet Idrott och hälsa ['I Don't Feel like Becomming a Guy'. About Heteronormativity in the Subject PE]." *Utbildning & Demokrati* 16 (2): 113–138.

Lindsay, G. 2000. "Researching Children's Perspectives: Ethical Issues." In *Researching Children's Perspective*, edited by G. Lindsay A. Lewis, 3–20. Buckingham: Open university Press.

Mennesson, C. 2012. "Gender Regimes and Habitus: An Avenue for Analyzing Gender Building in Sports Contexts." *Sociology of Sport Journal* 29: 4–21.

Messner, M. A. 2002. "Barbie Girls versus Sea Monsters: Children Constructing Gender." *Gender and Society* 14 (6): 765–784.

Oliynyk, I. 2014. "Att göra tudelning. Om att synliggöra och diskutera ämnet idrott och hälsa för de yngre åldrarna ur ett genusperspektiv [Making Dichotomy. about Making Visibly and Discussing Physical Education for the Younger Ages from a Gender Perspective]." Licentiate Theses, Malmö Universtiy.

RF (Riksidrottsförbundet/Swedish Sports Confederation). 2009. *Idrotten Vill - Idrottsrörelsens idéprogram* [Vision statement of the Sports movement]. http://www.rf.se/ImageVaultFiles/id_33077/cf_394/Idrotten_vill_-idrottens_id-program-.PDF.

RF (Riksidrottsförbundet/Swedish Sports Confederation). 2014. "Idrotten i siffror." [Sports in Figures.] http://www.rf.se/ImageVaultFiles/id_63562/cf_394/RF_i_siffror_2014.PDF.

Rogers, R. (2004, May). *[Interview with Norman Fairclough.] In Companion Website to R. Rogers. An Introduction to Critical Discourse Analysis in Education (Second Edition)*. New York: Routledge. http://cw.routledge.com/textbooks/9780415874298.

Rogers, R. 2011. "The Sounds of Silence in Educational Tracking: A Longitudinal, Ethnographic Case Study." *Critical Discourse Studies* 8 (4): 239–252. doi:10.1080/17405904.2011.601632.

Skelton, C. 2000. "'A Passion for Football': Dominant Masculinities and Primary Schooling." *Sport, Education and Society* 5 (1): 5–18. doi:10.1080/135733200114406.

Stiebling, M. T. 1999. "Practicing Gender in Youth Sports." *Visual Sociology* 14 (1): 127–144. doi:10.1080/14725869908583806.

Theberge, N. 2000. *Higher Goals: Women's Ice Hockey and the Politics of Gender*. Albany: State University of New York Press.

Thorne, B. 1986. "Girls and Boys Together ... but Mostly Apart: Gender Arrangements in Elementary Schools." In *Relationships and Development*, edited by W. W.Hartup and Z. Rubin, 167–184. London: L. Erlbaum Associates.

Thorne, B. 1990. "Children and Gender: Constructions of Difference." In *Theoretical Perspectives on Sexual Difference*, edited by L. Rhode, 100–113. York: Yale University Press.

VR (Vetenskapsrådet/Swedish Research Council). (2015). *Forskning som involverar barn* [Research Involving Children]. http://codex.vr.se/manniska1.shtml.

Wachs, F. L. 2005. "The Boundaries of Difference: Negotiating Gender in Recreational Sport." *Sociological Inquiry* 75 (4): 527–547.

Wahl, T. 2007. "Konstruktioner av kroppsfakta: Beskrivningar av barns motorik i medicinska journaler [Construction of Body Fact: Descriptions of Childrens Motor Skills in Medical Journals.]." In *Diskursanalys i praktiken* [Discourse Analysis in Practice], edited by M.Börjesson and E. Palmblad. Malmö: Liber.

West, C., and D. H. Zimmerman. 1987. "Doing Gender." *Gender & Society* 1 (2): 125–151.

Williams, J. 2003. *A Game for Rough Girls? A History of Women's Football in Britain*. London: Routledge.

Transcending gender hierarchies? Young people and floorball in Swedish school sport

Marie Larneby

Sport Sciences – Faculty of Education and Society, Malmö University, Malmö, Sweden

ABSTRACT

This research insight discusses young people's construction and display of gender in a mixed-sex floorball group in a Swedish sport school and explores in what ways gendered power relations were exercised. Observations of floorball lessons with 21 students aged 12–16 and interviews with 7 students were analysed through Lorber's concept of gender as a social institution. Findings suggested that training in a mixed-sex group seemed to actualize a need to dichotomize and construct distinct groups of boys and girls, and a 'boys are better than girls' discourse prevailed. This was explained as being a result of their experiences of playing separately in floorball clubs during leisure time. All contributed to the construction of a discourse where boys were superior and girls inferior, although they were striving towards a uniform way to play. Their attitudes and actions indicated that while gender hierarchies were not transcended, they were, to some extent, negotiated.

Introduction

Floorball is a relatively new indoor team sport. It is fast and technical, with the players passing a small ball to each other with sticks to score in the other team's goal. The Swedish Floorball Federation's website (2014-10-19) outlines that floorball developed during the 1970s as a recreational activity which took place at youth centres. Today, it is also a popular competitive team sport in Sweden, with more than 115,000 club players in 2014. There are also a range of formal competitions. The Swedish Cup was initiated for women in 1982 and 1983 for men; the International Cup was established in 1996 for men and 1997 for women. Yet, in Sweden, floorball is a men's sport in terms of members, with men constituting 74% of the players in 2014. In Swedish organized sports, boys and girls are predominantly separated due to possessing 'different physical conditions' (Swedish Sports Confederation 2009). According to Messner (2002), separation not only results in gender dichotomies, but also that boys' and girls' abilities and potential are valued differently. For Messner, sport emerged as a masculinized institution that constructs male athletes as superior. However, Ljunggren (2013) suggests that floorball does not seem to have been masculinized in its transition from spontaneous activity to organized sport, in contrast to soccer's and ice-hockey's legacy of a traditional masculine ideal and resistance towards female players. Despite the skewed distribution of male and female players, Ljunggren argues that floorball lacks the common traditional rhetoric of sports and masculinity, having 'good opportunities to be depicted in a more equal way' (2013, 10). Therefore, it is of interest to study floorball from a gender perspective.

The aim of this study was to explore and discuss the construction and display of gender in a mixed-sex floorball group at a high school with a sport profile. I ask: In what ways were gendered power relations exercised within this group?

Previous research

Traditionally, competitive sports represents an arena in which boys and men were socialized into a masculinity that emphasized aggressiveness, physical strength, heterosexuality and discontent of femininity. Anderson (2009) terms this 'orthodox masculinity', arguing this masculinity is still reproduced and culturally revered within sports, regardless of men's gender politics. Messner (2002) suggests that the world of sport is still actively constructed by and for the interests of men. Although participation rates among the majority of girls and women are increasing, and some mixed-sex sports have emerged, sports are mainly organized separately and unequally. Despite this, sports also present an arena for resistance. Anderson (2008, 2009, 2014) has studied male college and university athletes and found that many were not comfortable with this culture of orthodox masculinity. He argues that a change towards a more diverse view on men and masculinities is progressively emerging. He states, 'More egalitarian behaviors among men are likely to have *some* impact on their attitudes towards women' (Anderson 2014, 222), and mixed-sex sports may result in men viewing female athletes as worthy and competent teammates. A study of male athletes in collegiate sex-integrated cheerleading, previously playing high school football, changed their attitudes of female athletes being inferior. Anderson (2008) explains this attitude shift as being the result of a bourgeoning appreciation and respect as they became teammates.

In contrast to simply being perceived as marginalized and subordinated, women can use sports as a site of transformation; a space where they can question conventional and stereotypical images of femininity, creating new images that empower female bodies (Hargreaves 1994). However, this transformation is neither evident nor unproblematic. Steinfeldt et al. (2011) discuss that female athletes embody a paradox, in that, they strive for muscularity and athleticism (traditionally masculine traits), thus negotiating societal standards of femininity. Furthermore, Berg, Migliaccio, and Anzini-Varesio (2014) show that female American football players adhere to the masculine-defined sport ethic: playing tough, expecting pain and injuries as part of the game – 'expectations and assumptions similar to their male counterparts' (186).

When sports are discussed and debated, in media as well as in research, male athletes and male sports are sacrosanct while female athletes are frequently Othered. This is evident in an analysis of Swedish newspapers reporting from the 2012 Olympics' Equestrianism. It did not seem to matter that men and women compete as equals: although the female riders performed better results and were praised as heroic, the male riders were depicted as more competent (Hellborg and Hedenborg 2015). We can also see evidence of unequal gender socialization within youth settings. In a study of unorganized and spontaneous schoolyard soccer with 9–12-year-old children, Jonasson (2010) observed overt signs of male domination. While girls were included in the game, gender construction occurred 'in the moment' as boys differentiated themselves from girls by letting girls join only if they subordinated to boys and only possessed some roles and positions in the game, while the boys' legitimate positioning possibilities were considerably more.

Gender as a social institution

The concept of gender as a social institution explains gender as a predominant category that 'establishes patterns of expectations for individuals, orders the social processes of everyday life' (Lorber 1994, 1). Gender exists and acts prior to an individual's existence. When we are born, we enter into an already gendered structure of life, culture and society. This is why gender is often assumed to have a biological origin and why differences between women and men are perceived as natural. One paradox is that gender as a social institution continues to create and maintain socially significant differences between women and men, despite the fact that, on many levels, men and women are very similar. As Lorber (1994) notes:

> In the social construction of gender, it does not matter what men and women actually do; it does not even matter if they do exactly the same thing. The social institution of gender insists only that what they do is *perceived* as different. (26)

However, Lorber suggests that differentiation per se is not necessarily problematic, but stratifying men and women is. In a society stratified by gender, men are usually more highly valued than women, for no significant reason other than they are men. Lorber argues that since sport traditionally is a male institution, it values male and female athletes' ability and athleticism differently. Sport also rigidly divides athletes based on assumptions of biological sex difference rather than individual abilities (Lorber 1994).

Gender as a social institution offers an interesting lens through which to discuss how gender was constructed and displayed in the mixed-sex floorball group. Having in mind these students' main experience of floorball was training and competing separately in clubs during leisure time. Lorber mainly discusses the implications of differentiation and stratification for women and not so much for men since men more often are assumed to benefit from a prevailing gender order. As Anderson's (2009, 2014) research shows, this is not always the case. Therefore, it is important that we do not automatically assume that boys benefit from and girls are marginalized by a gendered structuring of sports.

Methodology

In Sweden, school sport is an optional subject and is chosen by students who often participate in sports during their leisure time. The objective is to offer more physical activity during school hours and also to improve in a specific sport. School sport has grading criteria like other subjects and differs from mandatory physical education and health, which teaches health-related practical and theoretical knowledge to enable and sustain lifelong physical activity. The content of school sport lessons in Sweden is more or less similar to the organized training during leisure time (Ferry, Meckbach, and Larsson 2013).

The present study reports on data gathered from a research project in which I undertook fieldwork with one sport school from a gender perspective. All students at this school were sport students, which is uncommon for Swedish seventh–ninth-grade schools. Usually, sport students represent a small part of the schools who offer sport profiles and they are mixed with other students. It was of interest to study this school since sport was the core of the school's practice. The study was approved by the Local Ethical Board in Lund, Sweden. One cohort of sport students was studied during their seventh–ninth grade (12–16 years), and in this study, they were in eighth grade. All students, teachers and coaches in this cohort gave consent to being observed, and several were interested in being interviewed. The school's objective was to enable athletic improvement combined with studies. By collaborating with local sport clubs to provide coaches and facilities, the students had four 90-min school sport lessons a week. Since the students also trained and competed in organized clubs during leisure time, they significantly increased the amount of training time. Seventy five to eighty students per cohort were admitted to the school through selective try-outs in specific sports, one-third girls and two-thirds boys. Most sports formed age- and gender-integrated training groups.[1]

During the fieldwork period, 21 students from seventh-ninth grades trained in floorball. With one-third girls and two-thirds boys, this group was suitable to study as a mixed-sex practice. Already having consent from the eighth-grade students, the seventh and ninth-grade floorball students approved to being observed. Observations of 10 floorball lessons (15 h) and three interviews (45–90 min in duration) were conducted during October and November 2014. This data form only one part of the major project involving the school. An ethnographic approach was used, as the students' experiences, voices, attitudes and actions were of importance to understand what it is like being a sport student in Sweden (Ennis and Chen 2012). Each observation started when the first student entered the training area and ended when the last left. All verbal and non-verbal actions and interactions that could be observed during the lessons were recorded with pen and paper or laptop as field notes. The on-pitch interactions between the students were of particular interest, as their leisure time sport was not sex integrated. All school sport floorball lessons consisted of technical and tactical exercises and ended with play. In addition, all eighth graders in the group were asked to be interviewed; five boys and two girls accepted. They wished to be interviewed as girls and boys separately, but one boy was ill and was interviewed alone. Three interviews were held in classrooms after school hours. They were digitally recorded and transcribed verbatim. Each interview started with the question: *What is it like training floorball at a sport school?* and follow-up questions related to the admission process, ambitions within floorball, experiences of the floorball group and anything else of note that emerged. The data were analysed using thematic analysis (Bryman 2012). By reading and rereading transcripts and field notes, recurring expressions, attitudes and actions displayed by the students provided insights of floorball as a mixed-sex practice. The students are given pseudonyms in the analysis and interview questions are italicized for ease of reading.

Analysis

The interviewed eighth-grade students' narratives are subjective experiences and were not considered to represent the whole group. However, analysing these narratives and observations in parallel enabled a more nuanced depiction. Having observed several floorball lessons, it was apparent that all students were skilled. As in any training group, all players were not at the exact level; in general, the ninth graders were more skilled than the seventh graders.

Differences

The first interview group discussed what training was like in school. They responded by saying:

Alice: It's good in some ways. But during last year, the boys offended us more than now …

Anna: Because we are girls and inferior compared to them.

Alice: It was kind of … 'Oh no, I got on the same team as Alice, we're going to lose'

Although an inclusive attitude within the group was most common during the observed lessons, subtle forms of subordination and exclusion frequently recurred. For instance, some boys did not pass the ball to girl team mates, despite sometimes being in a better position to score. Instead, he often lost the ball to an opponent, tried an impossible shot or passed it to a boy in a less favorable position. No girl was seen demonstratively passing only to girls. Further, there was a strong view among the girls that boys think girls are inferior, regardless of actual skills. Anna and Alice were also convinced that most boys in this group wanted to train alone. Anna said: 'Training with us made them realize that we can play floorball, too. Seeing us improve faster than them … I think it annoys them'. These views reflect Lorber's (1994) argument that it does not matter if men and women do something just as good, it is perceived as different and often stratified. Nevertheless, Anna and Alice managed this perceived subordination by improving their skills and emphasized that their improvement was due to training with boys. However, the improvement was most likely also due to training with skilled players in general, although training with boys was described as the primary factor.

The second interview group, consisting of Marcus, Gabriel, Ludvig and Fredrik, initially expressed that boys and girls should train separately. Gabriel did not think that 'boys want to train with girls, the differences are quite big'; Fredrik simply claimed that 'boys are better'. These testimonies concur with Anna's and Alice's statements and the observations discussed above. According to Lorber, 'sports illustrate the ways bodies are gendered by social practices and how the female body is socially constructed to be inferior' (1994, 41). However, when the boys discussed the integrated group, there was an attempt to contest the 'boys are better than girls' discourse:

Marcus: It's a bit cruel saying that boys often are better than girls in sports. Girls' knowledge can also be better. They need us and we need them. They can learn from us and we can learn from some of them […]. Girls have less ego. They pass the ball a little more. And our tactical understanding is better.

Although Marcus tried to nuance it, stating that boys in general, but only 'some girls' could provide competence, underpins the prevailing discourse of boys being better than girls. Furthermore, observations confirmed that several boys were egoistic on the pitch and that girls passed the ball more. The girls were actually often told by some boys to pass the ball, a fact Marcus and his friends did not reflect upon. Why the girls were less egoistic could thus be explained as a desire to be more than formally included, letting some boys set the agenda, and not an indicator of being less tactical. This relates well to the study of spontaneous schoolyard soccer, indicating that although girls were included, boys were allowed a bigger space based on an unspoken discourse of male superiority. Boys could be more egoistic with a trial-and-error approach, but girls were restricted in order to reduce mistakes (Jonasson 2010). Further, they discussed why boys were perceived as more egoistic than girls:

Ludvig: Boys maybe think they have a bigger role, because they're boys. Some believe that they … are better than girls just because you're a boy.
Why is it like that?

Gabriel: Because boys are supposed to do sports, I think that's why.

Marcus: When you were little, all boys were at the soccer field and girls sat chatting on the playground. You've grown up with it being that way.

Lorber's (1994) argument that what men do are valued higher for the sole reason of being men is clearly exemplified in this interaction. It also indicated that these boys were socialized into a homosocial sport context in which they learnt that boys are better than girls (cf. Anderson 2009; Messner 2002). It is significant that Marcus, Gabriel, Ludvig and Fredrik had a tendency to discuss boys' attitudes *in general* but never *their* attitude or what *they* did on the pitch. This tendency to speak of all boys resulted in analytical uncertainty in how they should manage this gendered discourse. They stated that 'in some ways it's like playing with lots of boys because you're used to it – you forget that you actually play with girls'. Hence, the girls' skills were acknowledged. Despite demonstrating some reflexivity, it remained the case that these four boys mainly passed the ball to each other. Seemingly, these boys were not aware of these contradictions nor how their actions and roles were complicit in constructing girls as inferior and themselves, that is boys, as superior. This ambivalence of excluding and including actions can be interpreted as a human need to conform to an established gender order, while simultaneously challenging it (Lorber 1994).

The views of these boys were not shared by all of the boys in this study. In the interview with Jack, for example, he described the group as 'quite evenly matched'. Although he talked of gender differences, he did not value boys and girls differently:

I think it's good to see that it isn't that big difference between how girls and boys play. Boys tackle more, but girls solve that by dribbling past you. It's fun playing with them too, so you know what differences there really are […]. I think that the ninth grade girls are just as good as the ninth grade boys. And Alice in eighth grade is better than some of the eighth grade boys.

In addition to this positive attitude regarding the mixed-sex setting, Jack had a more inclusive way of playing as well. In contrast to Marcus, Ludvig, Gabriel and Fredrik, it did not seem that he needed to be superior at the girls' expense. Jack appreciated differences, learning to be more flexible, which was also evident during observations. His attitude and actions correlate to the inclusive masculinity that Anderson (2009) discusses.

A recognized way to play

There were constant references to there being differences between boys and girls. This was linked specifically to their experiences of playing separately in their clubs. But the boys and girls shared motivations for participation in school sport floorball. According to Jack, rarely did students choose to attend this school merely because it was fun to play sports; their objective was to strive towards national elite level. Sharing the same ambitions seemed to unify the boys and girls, thus overcoming differences in age and gender. As interviews with the boys especially developed, it was clear that, despite initial reservations about sharing sport with girls, the boys could see the benefits of sex-integrated participation in floorball:

Marcus: I actually believe you learn different things in a mixed group. I don't think I would've had as many qualities if I didn't train here.
What are the similarities?

Marcus: All are really passionate about floorball, giving it all every lesson.
What matters most – differences or similarities?

Gabriel: Similarities!

Marcus: Similarities. Or … No, differences!

Ludvig: Why!?

Marcus: Because you learn from each other. It's better with a team with different qualities than a team with exactly the same.

Similarities, such as being passionate and ambitious, were also described as important by Jack, Anna and Alice. They explained that everyone at this school loved sport, that all shared a willingness to put time and effort into improving as athletes, which was not always the case by team mates in their sport clubs. The apparent change of heart by both the boys and girls can be attributed to a growing recognition that, gender differences aside, when participating on the same training group, they have a common objective. Differences were now discussed as positive, with their differing qualities being perceived as unique. This attitude may be a result of the mixed-sex setting, in that, as Anderson argues, 'teamsports may be uniquely effective in reducing gender stereotypes because they necessitate that men and women work together for the accomplishment of victory' (2009, 132).

To Anna and Alice, training with boys was also synonymous with improvement. They indicated that training with boys was desirable as they believed this presented the best opportunity to develop and test their skills among 'better' players:

Anna: The students here are among the best in their age in this region.

Alice: Especially the ninth grade boys are really good. And that does us good in training. You learn in a totally different way. Especially with boys, it's another speed. A different technique. Everything you learn in advance compared to others.

Anna: It's much more serious, too, everyone wants to be something. That may not be the case at home [*in the club*].

As these testimonies suggest, for Anna and Alice, the boys' way of playing was something to strive for. Indeed, although the ninth-grade girls were highly skilled in floorball, they were never mentioned as role models by either the interviewed girls or boys. On the one hand, Anna's and Alice's striving towards emulating the boys' way of playing can be interpreted as gender being an important identity marker: playing like a boy was better than playing like a girl, despite similar skill levels, based on the 'boys are better than girls' discourse. On the other hand, it can be argued that participants were ignoring the significance of gender on the basis that they were more concerned with skill development than they were supporting those who share their gender. Anna's and Alice's adopting of boys as primary role models was due to the boys playing a perceived superior form of the game, *not* because they were boys per se. However, in doing this, the boys and girls had unconsciously reinforced a dominant gender trope: boys' sport is superior and thus, hegemonic.

Indeed, adopting of the boys' 'way' was viewed as empowering by Anna and Alice who acknowledged the benefits of playing 'like' boys. For example, their improvement contributed to them being better players in their floorball team during leisure time. The explicit adopting of this way of playing did not go unnoticed by the boys. In contrast to the female athletes in Steinfeldt et al. (2011), girls adopting traditional masculine traits such as strength, toughness and aggressiveness was appreciated and neither talked of as unfeminine nor problematic, by either the girls or the boys. But adopting the boys' way of playing was a balancing act between their desire to assert their sporting identities and a passivity as they were effectively accepting that (some) boys set the agenda and girls conform (cf. Jonasson 2010). This passivity was observed in the restricted actions of the girls and not consistent with their otherwise confident play. For example, passing the ball instead of dribbling when certain boys told them to, or avoiding fighting for the ball against certain boys. According to Hargreaves, women who play male sport 'face the greatest criticism and exposure to ridicule' (1994, 171). Therefore, striving towards a homogenous (boys') way of playing might have been a strategy to avoid criticism. However, as indicated above, conformity is never unproblematic. While clearly not intended, it could be argued that, by conforming, the girls contributed to construct boys as better and girls as inferior, reinforcing gender as a stratifying factor in this group (cf. Lorber 1994).

Equally, the girls' embracing of the boys' way of playing may have reduced stratification, as the gap in skills became smaller. This was evident as Marcus, Ludvig, Gabriel and Fredrik discussed:

Ludvig: Alice, she's very strong. She plays like a boy.

Marcus: Yes … But saying 'playing like a boy'… I think it's a little patronizing! *How can you put it differently?*

Marcus: They're like a regular, good, floorball player, in my opinion. It doesn't need to be a boy or a girl.

Interestingly, Marcus's statement could be an attempt to 'un-gender' the recognized way of playing. Girls playing like boys supported a traditional sport ethic associated with male athletes (cf. Berg, Migliaccio, and Anzini-Varesio 2014), which could explain why skilled girls were acknowledged by the boys in this way. Most girls were described as individually good, strong, tactical and powerful shooters. Jack for example said that: 'Some of the girls, at least Alice… She's better than some of the eighth grade boys. She's very good'. Fredrik described the girls in the group like this: 'They're almost at the boys' level', and Gabriel said that: 'It's impossible winning against them when they form a team'.

Crucially, however, while these boys are seemingly complimenting the proficiencies of the girl players, they do so through comparing girls to boys, thus reinforcing a familiar scheme of male dominance and superiority. I would argue then that the ways we would ordinarily conceptualize 'play' and 'competition' must be reconsidered on the basis that both have been constituted in male terms, that is, the ways *boys* play and the ways *boys* compete. Although men and women do exactly the same thing, they are still perceived as different (Lorber 1994), which is obvious in this case.

This view was particularly evident in the views of Marcus, Gabriel, Ludvig and Fredrik who never discussed their way of playing. Their silence on this was as if them playing well, and in a certain way, was assumed and anticipated. Discussing the girls' way of playing implicitly described what was expected from a good floorball player, which could be any-one if s/he played 'like a boy'. In addition, the girls' skills and improvement seemed to be unexpected, with some of the boys struggling to reconcile what they were seeing and their expectations of the girls' inferiority. Whether they let the girls know this appreciation or not was never mentioned.

What we see here then is that although the gendered structure of floorball was, to some extent, renegotiated, a male structure and a 'boys are better than girls' discourse still prevailed. Hargreaves (1994) discusses that many team sports were historically described as masculine-appropriate with valued characteristics, such as strength, competitiveness, aggression and assertiveness, being defined as hegemonic. These characteristics have remained hegemonic in many sporting spaces and thus, this helps explain why these boys assumed their play was the norm. Therefore, being skilled and equal to, or even outclassing, a male opponent does not necessarily translate into sporting capital. Indeed, according to Hargreaves, these women 'threaten the concept of maleness and symbolize female empowerment' (1994, 281), which may explain why the boys in this case study were so keen to uphold the discourse.

Exercise of power

Several eighth and ninth-grade boys dominated the pitch by, among other things, never letting go of the ball, shouting loudly, hitting their sticks on the boards as a sign of frustration or demonstratively sighing when someone made a mistake. Anna and Alice said: 'the best ones dominate, mainly Samuel and Leo in ninth grade. When they attend, they don't give others any space'. It was obvious during the observed lessons that Samuel especially tried to set the agenda. It was common for him to comment on the mistakes of others, make jokes at others' expense and through generally being aggressive. He also dominated the boys' locker room:

Marcus: When Samuel isn't there, it's such a great feeling. There's nothing to say … He doesn't care …

Ludvig: It's like … We have no power over him, we can't do anything! It's almost as if the coaches can't do anything either.

Fredrik: It's not fair.

Gabriel: You just need to put up with it …

These boys showed a resignation and tolerance of this male hierarchy, which may be explained by the fact that this type of masculinity is yet culturally revered in sport (Anderson 2009). To illustrate, it was interesting to observe that when the ninth graders, Samuel included, did not attend the lessons, the four eighth-grade boys above tried to dominate the space, though not in Samuel's autocratic way. Jack reinforced these observations when he said:

It's obvious that Ludvig and Marcus dominate as if they're bosses and the best. But they don't dare when the ninth graders are here. That's my experience. [...] As soon as they get the ball they shoot … They don't *say* they're the best, but it's obvious in the way they play. And they pass only to each other.

Why do you think they act like that?

The ninth graders are like that too sometimes. And when they're not here, the others try to dominate and get respect from the seventh graders, wanting the reaction 'oh, they're really good'… I think that may be the reason.

These eighth-grade boys did not reflect upon whether their own dominating actions were as a result of having been dominated themselves by the ninth-grade boys, but it was clear to see that both the structure of team sport and the way the boys had been socialized in and through sport, that twin discourses of hegemonic masculinity and masculinity hierarchies, had a strong hold over these boys. The actions of the eighth graders contrast with Anderson's (2009) inclusive masculinity thesis that has been witnessed in educational sport settings.

Anna and Alice mainly ignored this domination by focusing on themselves, actively resisting at least the eighth-grade boys' domination. But some of the ninth-grade boys affected them in a different way:

Alice: They give us sexist comments. Right on the pitch! They comment on our bodies: 'your ass is too big' or 'your ass is too small'.

Although Anna and Alice explained the sexism as a cowardly act, they did not know how to respond. Their acknowledgement and subsequent inaction indicated an awareness of gendered power relations, which they managed by attending lessons together and striving for personal development: 'Maybe they're jealous of us in some way, since we improve more than them?' Messner's (2002) argument that when women require equal conditions in sports, they can be marginalized by men who support the taking for granted of male authority, helps explain the sexist comments. The girls said that this marginalization was more difficult to manage than their skills not being acknowledged, for example, not getting a pass, because they were powerless to effect marginalization. The ninth-grade boys were not asked to respond to these comments, but their dominating behaviour on the pitch was clearly observable, and was part of Anna's and Alice's subjective experiences.

Lorber (1994, 250) explains such overt domination on the basis that 'the intent of such harassment is to make work life so unpleasant that the woman will quit'. In contrast to being subordinated as athletes, the sexist comments objectified Anna and Alice because they were girls, as 'members of a subordinate gender may be sexually exploited' (30). Crucially, they chose not to report their views and experiences to an adult because they did not want the group to become segregated. Instead, they continued, hoping to be accepted as worthy players.

Transcending gender hierarchies?

The aim of this study was to explore and discuss the construction and display of gender in a mixed-sex floorball group at a high school with a sport profile. Referring to the formal separation of boys and girls in sports, Messner suggests that 'a more complicated process of differentiation has replaced simple exclusion' (2002, xxii). This was evident within this group and can probably be explained by considering the boys' and girls' experiences of sex-segregated sports in a club environment. A 'boys are better than girls' discourse was central in the narratives, as both boys and girls contributed to a construction of boys' superiority and girls' inferiority, though there was evidence of some (limited) contestation too. This study deliberately takes no consideration into whether boys or girls *were* the better player. The aim was not to rank player proficiency by gender, rather to discuss their focus on *perceived* differences.

The assumption that natural differences between boys and girls 'just exist' was a widespread view among the participants, and is one effect of how gender operates in the social processes of everyday life (Lorber 1994). The integration seemed to actualize a need for these students to dichotomize and construct distinct groups of male and female floorball players rather than viewing themselves as a floorball collective. According to Messner (2002), gender tends to disappear in separated contexts but becomes an organizing principle in integrated contexts. However, differentiation per se did not need to be problematic in the group, but stratifying based upon it was (cf. Lorber 1994). The experiences of the boys and girls in this study can be effectively understood through Lorber's (1994) conceptualizing of gender as a mechanism that 'establishes patterns of expectations for individuals, orders the social processes of everyday life' (1) and to a traditional gendered structure of sports. But as Lorber mainly discusses, women being marginalized from the prevailing gender order, in this case, it appeared as if the girls benefited most from training integrated, despite the dominant 'boys are better than girls' discourse. Although being objects of stratification, Anna and Alice demonstrated a view that they had been empowered through improving themselves as athletes. Perceived by the boys (and some girls) as naturally inferior, it appeared to be easier for them to improve, than for some of the interviewed boys to manage the expectations of being naturally superior and maintain this (perceived) superiority. Marcus, Gabriel, Ludvig and Fredrik showed an ambivalence in how to act and react to the mixed-sex setting. For example, they would routinely discuss how skilled girls were *in relation* to boys, but they would never discuss themselves *in relation* to the girls. Their quite negative attitude towards training with girls, and the way this manifested through stratifying actions, showed strong support for Anderson's (2009) orthodox masculinity thesis. However, they did not ignore the girls' skills completely; they realized that their preconceptions of inferiority were not necessarily applicable to this group. Being unable to tease the girls for being poor athletes, some ninth-grade boys instead turned to making sexist comments, which was the most subordinating stratification based upon gender. With reference to Anderson (2014) and the cultural reverence of 'the traditional jock' – an arrogant, aggressive and misogynistic male athlete – it may be argued that sexism was a mechanism for exercising power as these boys' presupposed athletic skills did not suffice to construct male superiority.

The students' reflections indicated an awareness that they did not *have to* conform to a prevailing gender order, though it should be stressed that they found it difficult not to. Striving towards a uniform level of skill and an ideal way of playing seemed to blur the notion of boys and girls being inconceivably different, as they actually played quite similar. Nevertheless, it was problematic for them to define this way of playing as gender neutral, as all of them defined it as a 'boys' way' of playing. The attitudes and actions of the boys and girls in this study indicated that gender hierarchies were not transcended, but they were, to some extent, negotiated.

Conclusions

Ljunggren's (2013) suggestion that floorball is not masculinized was not applicable to this group, as the boys' way of playing was presented as being hegemonic. Anderson (2008) suggests that training integrated with a common objective can reduce gender stereotypes. Whether stereotypes were reduced or not is difficult to determine in this research insight. It was assumed that boys would be better floorball players and the girls strove to emulate their male counterparts. While the boys reinforced this view by not actively discussing their own right to occupy the space, some girls were described as *equally* good as boys, though they were never credited as being *better* than boys. Therefore, while the participation of the girls and boys in a mixed-sex setting was acknowledged in a largely positive way, there was also evidence of a range of identity strategies being employed, which contributed to the reinforcement, rather than transcendence of, a masculinized discourse of contingent inclusion

Note

1. Boys and girls formed separated soccer groups, as most students were admitted in soccer. Other sports were tennis, swimming, gymnastics, floorball, ice hockey, badminton, basketball, figure skating and athletics.

Disclosure statement

No potential conflict of interest was reported by the author.

References

Anderson, E. 2008. "'I Used to Think Women Were Weak': Orthodox Masculinity, Gender Segregation, and Sport." *Sociological Forum* 23 (2): 257–280.
Anderson, E. 2009. *Inclusive Masculinities: The Changing Nature of Masculinities*. New York: Routledge.
Anderson, E. 2014. *21st Century Jock: Sporting Men and Contemporary Heterosexualities*. Basingstoke: Palegrave Macmillan.
Berg, E. C., T. A. Migliaccio, and R. Anzini-Varesio. 2014. "Female Football Players, the Sport Ethic and the Masculinity-sport Nexus." *Sport in Society* 17 (2): 176–189.
Bryman, A. 2012. *Social Research Methods*. Hong Kong: Oxford University Press.
Ennis, C., and S. Chen. 2012. "Interviews and Focus Groups." In *Research Methods in Physical Education and Youth Sport*, edited by K. Armour and D. Macdonald, 217–236 . New York: Routledge.
Ferry, M., J. Meckbach, and H. Larsson. 2013. School Sport in Sweden: What is It, and How Did It Come to Be? *Sport in Society* 16 (6): 805–818.
Hargreaves, J. 1994. *Sporting Females*. London: Routledge.
Hellborg, A. M., and S. Hedenborg. 2015. "The Rocker and the Heroine: Gendered Media Representations of Equestrian Sports at the 2012 Olympics." *Sport in Society* 18 (2): 248–261.
Jonasson, K. 2010. *Klungan och barndomens sociala rum* [The "Heap" and the Social Spaces of Childhood]. Malmö: Holmbergs.
Ljunggren, J. 2013. "Historien om det svenska innebandyundret [The History of the Swedish Floorball Miracle]." *Svensk Idrottsforskning* 4: 8–12.
Lorber, J. 1994. *Paradoxes of Gender*. New York: Yale University Press.
Messner, M. 2002. *Taking the Field: Women and Men in Sports*. Minneapolis, MN: University of Minnesota Press.
Steinfeldt, J. A., H. Carter, E. Benton, and M. C. Steinfeldt. 2011. "Muscularity Beliefs of Female College Student–Athletes." *Sex Roles* 64: 543–554.
Swedish Sports Confederation. 2009. *Idrotten Vill!* [Sport Wants!]. Stockholm: Swedish Sports Confederation.

'Guys don't whale away at the women': etiquette and gender relations in contemporary mixed-doubles tennis

Robert J. Lake

Department of Sport Science, Douglas College, New Westminster, Canada

ABSTRACT

This article examines recent developments in etiquette in contemporary mixed-doubles tennis (MDT), to position different behavioural expectations for men/women in the broader context of shifting gender relations. Content analysis of coaching guides published from the 1960–1980s revealed that historically rooted gender distinctions in terms of court positioning, tactics, and playing roles/expectations were reaffirmed, continuing to undermine and marginalize females yet privilege males based on assumed innate differences in physical attributes. Etiquette norms in this era were compared to those found in the early twenty-first century (2000–2010s), through content analysis of online forums/blogs for recreational and elite-level MDT. It was found that while gendered tactics related to court positioning and playing roles were sustained, an important shift in etiquette norms related to chivalry occurred, but was not comprehensively accepted among all players. This development was attributed to third-wave feminist challenges to male chivalry, alongside the burgeoning 'crisis of masculinity' that increasingly pushed men towards adopting a 'hybridized masculinity' to assuage public critiques of hegemonic/orthodox masculinity in sport.

Introduction

This article aims to critically examine developments in behavioural etiquette in contemporary mixed-doubles tennis (MDT) from the 1960–1980s period to today (essentially, the 2000–2010s period), and attempt to locate both changes and continuities in court positioning, tactics, and playing roles/expectations for men and women within the broader context of shifting gender relations. Of particular relevance are the second- and third-wave feminist and gay-rights movements, which collectively helped to alter social constructions of both femininity and masculinity throughout this period.

Since the 1960s, partly as a consequence of feminist advances, female players made marked advances both on the court and off, in terms of prize money, administrative power, and media coverage (Bodo 1995; Feinstein 1991; Lake 2015a; Lumpkin 1981; Mewshaw 1993; Wilson 2014), and this paper questions whether and to what extent related developments also occurred within the specific context of MDT. Mixed-doubles has been a prevalent feature of lawn tennis since the sport's inception in the 1870s. Mixed-sex participation was a salient aspect of its initial popularity among the upper-middle classes, who considered exclusive tennis clubs as suitable locations for young men and women to engage in polite courtship rituals (Lake 2015a; Wilson 2014).

Historical work by Lake (2012, 2015a) has shown how MDT etiquette for men and women in the pre-WWII (1870–1930s) period tended to reflect the dominant patriarchal structure of gender relations, whereupon men asserted their superiority through socially agreed-upon behavioural norms. While rulebooks from this period gave specific instructions to novice players on how to play the game according to strict regulations, coaching guides offered advice on tennis strokes and tactics. Those specifically related to MDT often projected gendered distinctions with respect to court positioning, shot selection/tactics and playing roles/expectations. Typically, men were instructed to adopt the more challenging backhand (left-hand) side of the court, take more of the winning or difficult shots and overhead smashes, and avoid hitting hard smashes, volleys and serves at female opponents. These expectations were predicated on a patriarchal and paternalist ideology that considered men naturally stronger and women in need of (crucially, male) protection. Most players, both male and female, voluntarily adhered to this etiquette demanding self-restraint and behavioural foresight despite associated actions sometimes limiting their competitive success. Evidently, they adjudged respecting these norms more important than winning matches. In the course of play, the ways men hit particular shots/strokes and behaved towards their female teammates/opponents revealed deeply entrenched masculine and feminine values, and the norms that governed interactions between them in the context of their middle-class backgrounds (Hargreaves 1994; Lake 2012, 2015a; McCrone 1988). This article questions the extent these behavioural expectations still prevail in twenty-first century MDT, and how any changes, particularly since the 1960–1980s period, can be accounted for.

Literature review

Particularly as an outcome of third-wave feminism, which challenged the underlying gendered meanings of male–female social interactions as oftentimes inherently prejudiced towards women, and the emergent gay-rights movement that championed more inclusive masculinities among men, the context of sport has witnessed recently the gradual erosion of orthodox masculine norms and values (Anderson 2009). Sport represents an important cultural arena where masculinity and femininity are simultaneously expressed, reproduced, negotiated and contested, but those sports that offer mixed-sex competition are particularly ripe for research into how men negotiate the 'performance' of gender when in the presence of women and vice versa (Channon 2014). While numerous team sports (e.g., basketball, football, soccer, rugby, cricket, ice hockey and baseball) have stubbornly resisted sex integration by tending to glorify and celebrate male dominance, misogyny and homophobia (Anderson 2008, 2009; McDonagh and Pappano 2008), more recently recreational co-ed leagues and competitions in these and other sports like ultimate Frisbee and softball have been created (Henry and Comeaux 1999; Miller 1995). This increase in mixed-sex/co-ed participation has been widely celebrated as an indication of progress towards gender parity, and certain mixed-sex sports, like cheerleading (Anderson 2008) and martial arts/combat sports (Channon 2014), have been credited with helping shift (crucially heterosexual) male athletes' attitudes and behaviours towards women. Men's participation with and reliance upon women in competitive sporting contexts helped 'undo' their common sexist thinking of women as sex objects and/or less-than-capable athletes and leaders. Research into extreme/alternative sports (e.g. Anderson 1999; Beal 1996; Booth 2002; Laurendeau 2004; Laurendeau and Sharara 2008; Stedman 1997; Thorpe 2005; Wheaton 2000), alongside equestrianism (Dashper 2012), has painted a more complex picture of the simultaneous deconstruction *and* reproduction of dominant feminine norms and orthodox masculinity, through structural inequalities that marginalized women's achievements and generally inhibited their progress. Other research in this area (e.g. Henry and Comeaux 1999; Snyder and Ammons 1993; Wachs 2002) identified clear differences in etiquette related to gender-role differentiation and (sometimes) rules for mixed-sex sports, which functioned to undermine women's performances.

Examining the unwritten rules of behavioural etiquette in mixed-sex sport represents a fruitful avenue to learn how gender norms are simultaneously expressed, reproduced and/or challenged, and to comprehend the often unspoken but well-understood differentiated gender roles and behavioural expectations among players. Through the outward performance of gendered behaviour in these contexts, some of the internalized ideals of masculinity and femininity can be articulated and reaffirmed. By developing an understanding of the qualitative experiences of men and women in mixed-sex sport, some of the deep-lying features of gender relations that reflect and reproduce structural and cultural inequities can be exposed and potentially challenged.

The aim of this article is to critically analyse gendered aspects of behavioural etiquette in contemporary mixed-doubles tennis (MDT), which offers considerable scope for analysis on numerous levels. Firstly, MDT is unlike many mixed-sex sports because there are no modified rules and regulations designed to neutralize *assumed* differences in playing standard, strength or physiology between men and women. This is unlike co-ed softball, where stipulations have been made on batting order, field positioning and rules for 'walks' (Snyder and Ammons 1993; Wachs 2002), and co-ed soccer, which sometimes stipulates maximum numbers of male players to eliminate the likelihood of females being marginalized, and counts goals scored by women as two (Henry and Comeaux 1999). From personal experience/knowledge, similar stipulations on player numbers and different scoring rules also exist in some university intra-mural and community recreational leagues in basketball and ice hockey in Britain and North America. Henry and Comeaux (1999) found that in such scenarios of modified point scoring, efforts are often made by males to engineer goals/points for their female teammates to enhance their chances of winning. MDT, given its two-player format and rigid point-scoring structure, does not offer such opportunities, meaning specific tactics to engineer explicit point advantages based on gender would not exist. Thus, relatively speaking, MDT etiquette presents a more honest depiction of gender relations relative to other sports.

Secondly, tennis is unique and among just a handful of sports to retain its mixed-sex competitions at the highest level, i.e. in the Grand Slam events. MDT at Wimbledon and the US, French and Australian Opens probably remains the most visible setting to view elite-level mixed-sex sporting competition, given the regular and mainstream television/newspaper coverage it attracts. Olympic organizing committees tend to offer other mixed-sex sports, like badminton and equestrianism, but of these tennis remains arguably the highest profile in terms of its media coverage and public recognition of its competitors. The MDT event at the London 2012 Olympics, for example, pulled in sell-out crowds and drew an impressively strong field, including ten former top-five singles players and seven former world-number-one doubles players; many of these including Andy Murray, Sania Mirza, Leyton Hewitt, Ana Ivanovic, and Bob and Mike Bryan are household names in their home countries. In these varied contexts, MDT represents contested terrain as far as the negotiation of gender through behavioural distinctions, particularly given marked developments during the post-1968 'open era' that witnessed players take MDT competitions more seriously in the major championships (Smith and Lutz 1975). Generally speaking, it is one of a small handful of sporting activities played at both elite and recreational levels of competition where men and women compete both with and against each other, so it represents an important context to analyse gender relations across a spectrum of sporting participation.

Thirdly, an analysis of MDT provides an important opportunity to uncover nuances in the production of masculinity and femininity within a specifically white-dominated, middle-class context, where etiquette norms including chivalry have remained a key feature. Despite efforts to expand tennis beyond its traditional playing/spectating demographic, it has retained largely its specific class and race-based cultural norms and values, where the 'policing' of working-class and non-white players bodies has remained a feature (Lake 2015a, 2015b; Schultz 2005).

This article considers the robustness of historically rooted gender ideologies by examining how MDT etiquette has developed since the 1960–1980s. A shift in behavioural norms and values has been particularly pronounced in terms of masculinity, where, particularly since the 1990s, sociologists have come to acknowledge multiple layers and nuances of different types, versions or varieties of masculinities. While what has been termed 'hegemonic' (Connell 1995) or 'orthodox' (Anderson 2009) masculinity has tended to dominate contemporary ideas about how men should behave, numerous authors have urged consideration of how masculinity is performed in increasingly 'hybridized' ways, whereby men can choose from a variety of 'masculinities' to employ in different situations (Beynon 2002; Bridges and Pascoe 2014; Demetriou 2001; Messerschmidt 2010; Messner 1993, 2007). As a consequence of the sophisticated employment of such 'hybrid' masculinities, which have tended as a consequence of feminism and the gay-rights movement to incorporate aspects of previously marginalized feminine and homosexual identities, gender and sexual inequality has remained (Bridges and Pascoe 2014). Despite the borders separating norms and values deemed 'masculine' and 'feminine' blurring, particularly as men have increasingly adopted what appears as identities, practices and belief systems that undermine orthodox masculinity – e.g. to appear more sensitive, caring, and domesticated, and willing to work in careers traditionally considered 'feminine' – key components of patriarchy in wider society and sport remain intact (Bridges and Pascoe 2014). Therefore, Messner (1993) argued, the 'softer' or more 'sensitive' masculinities more recently adopted by men have done little to emancipate women, but instead have merely reproduced traditional gender hierarchies in more subtle and sophisticated ways. Therefore, it seems that as established structures of male dominance linked to hegemonic masculinity have been eroded, they have been replaced by other structures of gender inequality, equally pervasive but often more difficult to discern.

In relation to these developments towards more sophisticated, multifarious and subtly transmitted forms of masculinity, third-wave feminism has continued to advance the gender-equality agenda by incorporating ideas from the post-modern sociological tradition, which broadly speaking sought to deconstruct messages and behaviours to reveal underlying meanings (Gilley 2005). Displays of male chivalry were increasingly targeted for critique, as products of deeply historically rooted patriarchal ideologies that reaffirmed male superiority through paternalist displays of 'gentlemanly' conduct (Viki et al. 2003). Recently, however, several writers have argued that feminism is partly to blame for the 'death of chivalry'. Sabrina Schaeffer, blogger and executive director of the *Independent Women's Forum*, argued that the freedoms previously fought for by feminists have

> too often come at the expense of all values and traditions. ... It's the modern feminist movement, which ushered away any hint of traditional chivalry. ... In years past men and women both had a better framework to determine what was acceptable behaviour and what was not (*thefederalist.com*).

Sara Chuirazzi, from the Bucknell University feminist blog, *hercampus.com*, noted that chivalry has been interpreted increasingly as a form of 'benevolent sexism', defined by Viki et al. (2003) as an ideology that favours the maintenance of traditional gender roles, but is subjectively positive in tone. Like Schaeffer, she claimed that feminism has effectively allowed women to get 'offended' if men make chivalric gestures, but equally 'disappointed that they're not treated better' when men act in non-traditional ways. Consequently, from a male-feminist perspective, Martin Daubney of *The Telegraph* (19 February 2014) described how men were now increasingly apprehensive about appearing patronizing or rude if, for example, they offered their seat to a woman on a bus. Apparently, they have become so 'baffled, dazed, confused and increasingly indignant' that they are simply 'giving up'. Despite these declarations, which are in need of further academic analysis, male chivalry and the 'benevolent sexism' that it engenders has far from vanished (Viki et al. 2003). This is due partly to the less-than-wholehearted support for the rejection of male chivalry among some men, who believe their time-honoured courteous gestures are entirely innocent and non-sexist in tone, and some women, who support what Viki et al. (2003, 534) term 'paternalistic chivalry', that is: 'extreme politeness and considerate behaviour toward women [that] also place restrictions on [their] roles'. Writer and former philosophy professor, Christina Hoff Sommers (2000), blamed what she labelled 'misguided feminism' for the 'harm' caused to young boys' self and collective masculine identities, and advocated teaching some traditional gender norms – including chivalry – so boys could learn respect for women. Despite being publically challenged, for some it seems male chivalry continues to serve important socio-cultural functions in modern, post-industrial societies.

A comparison of MDT etiquette between the 1960–1980s period and today could provide a useful barometer of change in gender norms and values in wider society. This is particularly so in relation to how men and women have grappled with the challenges of etiquette – that may or may not continue to serve practical purposes – based around historically rooted displays of 'paternalistic chivalry'. This article asks: Has MDT etiquette changed since the 1960–1980s period, and if so in what ways? What, if any, are key areas of continuity, and what can account for these developments in any case? Are there any changes noticeable in how MDT etiquette norms are reinforced and negotiated on court by male and female players? Are today's players faced with new challenges in MDT because of their participation with and against members of the opposite sex that may have developed as an outcome of recent shifting gender relations?

Methodology

The key period for commencing this analysis is the 'open era' of tennis, which commenced in 1968 when Wimbledon officials removed the amateur/professional distinction so all players could compete together in separate male and female tours. Television networks and corporate sponsors capitalized on the sport's 'boom' in popularity that came as a consequence of enhanced levels of spectatorship and media attention (Lake 2015a), and, particularly in America, the numbers of players, and the sale of rackets, balls, and tennis-related publications increased markedly (Bodo 1995; Feinstein 1991; Wilson 2014; Wind 1979).

Because of their marketability towards the burgeoning clientele of new tennis consumers, of particular popularity were coaching guides aimed at developing players and written by players/former players and/or professional coaches. These sources revealed a great deal about tennis etiquette, given their intended purposes were to influence how MDT '*ought*' to be played, often in ways that reflected the sport's gender dynamics. A total of sixteen coaching guides with sections on MDT published from the 1960–1980s were analysed, with the chief aim to investigate gendered on-court behavioural etiquette, specifically instructions related to court positioning, shot selection/tactics and playing roles/expectations. These guides were selected based on their availability to the author and, despite their random sampling, actually represent a fairly sizeable proportion of the most well-known, and likely best-selling and most widely-read, guides published during this era. Most were written by eminent male players/coaches, which is certainly a problem in the sense that women's voices were not fully represented in these discussions, yet this selection of sources still represents a true representation of the guides written and published during this period. While women represented around half of all registered/recreational players at all levels of competition, men were still over-represented as authors of coaching guides, which was likely a consequence of their assumed authority in coaching matters at this time.

In order to draw some contemporary comparisons, a content analysis of eight online forums and blogs devoted to discussions of MDT etiquette was conducted. Numerous forums and blogs were located through a simple internet search using relevant key words/phrases, related to the playing of tennis, tennis instruction and tennis etiquette. Judging by their numbers of members and views, arguably this selection represented the best known and leading forums/blogs on the subject, but of these, only those (eight) that pertained to MDT, with specific discussions/threads on the subject, were selected for this analysis. Much like the earlier guides, males were overly represented as authors of blogs, though females had a much stronger though still considerably less than equal voice in the forums. Judging by the personal information and anecdotes given, it seems the blogs tended to be authored by experienced- /advanced-level players and coaches, while the forum contributors ranged from intermediate to experienced- /advanced-level players. To provide contemporary elite-level perspectives, data from magazine articles written either by or about elite-level players and player biographies/autobiographies about former professional players/coaches were also analysed or incorporated where relevant.

Research using online sources has become recently an increasingly common and acceptable method of data collection (Hine 2005; Gibbons 2014; Gibbons and Dixon 2010; Gibbons and Nuttall 2012; Lee et al. 2008; Millward 2008). The forums and blogs analysed in this study were 'public' online environments, where content was free to view and came without requirements for registration (Sveningsson 2009). All members signed in with tag-names that concealed chosen parts of their identity. There was no intention to interact with forum members, so informed consent was not considered necessary. The forums/blogs were international in scope, with the bulk of contributors based in North America, Britain and Australia.

The key objective in analysing these forums/blogs was to identify key areas of change and continuity in MDT etiquette since the 1960–1980s and to develop a sense of why changes occurred. Overall, online forums/blogs represented ideal sources for capturing contemporary attitudes towards MDT play from men and women of different playing standards, ages and nationalities. Several key research themes were generated from the data analysis, which form the main sections of the following discussion. Overall attitudes to MDT are initially discussed, followed by an investigation into court positioning, shot selection/tactics and gender roles/expectations. Of particular interest in the latter section were recent changes for men and how representations for masculinity in MDT etiquette have changed.

Mixed-doubles as a fun and sociable diversion

Incorporated in many mixed-gender sports is the inference that men are 'playing down' by competing with and/or against women (Henry and Comeaux 1999). However, men can avoid emasculating themselves by acting in accordance with dominant masculine norms, which in MDT involves two processes: firstly, of men typically downplaying the importance of MDT competitions by maintaining they are 'just for fun'; and secondly, of men outwardly rejecting orthodox masculine values and behaviours by being chivalrous towards women, which allowed them to assert themselves in subtle but powerful ways. Bridges and Pascoe (2014) recognize this behaviour as a reaction to the increasing fluidity of masculinity, whereby men are compelled to reject hegemonic 'alpha male' masculinity without compromising their position of cultural dominance. By adopting a 'softer' masculine demeanour, they can effectively mask their intentions to remain dominant alongside any structural or social advantages that may come with doing so.

One of the sustaining and oft-repeated words used to describe MDT is 'fun'. It was reiterated constantly in both earlier guides and contemporary forums/blogs that MDT was the most 'fun' format, that 'fun' is prioritized over winning, and that 'socializing' underpins its popularity. In his coaching guide, Barnaby (1975, 196) described MDT as 'the perfect social game, ideal for mixing, fun, exercise, and play with family and friends'. Like other forum contributors, 'Gazza Wazza' from *Tennis Western Australia* (TWA) forum (*www.tenniswarehouse.com.au*) noted he played 'just for some laughs' and 'to have some fun and win some/lose some'. Male players repeatedly emphasized 'fun', which had implications for how seriously they competed compared to singles or men's doubles.

In the four major championships (Wimbledon, and US, French and Australian Opens), the MDT events have always tended to run as sideshows to the singles and single-sex doubles events that attract greater television exposure and crowds. Generally considered the lesser of the five forms of elite-level competitive play, mixed-doubles is limited to these four events, the Olympic Games and Hopman Cup, and ignored by virtually all other elite-level tournaments offering ATP/WTA/ITF ranking points and prize money.[1] In their mixed-doubles coaching guide, King and Stolle (1980, 7, 14) admitted elite-level MDT was a 'second-class citizen', and 'firmly entrenched at the bottom of the heap' for court allocations, press coverage and prize money. Just £96,000 was split by the winning pair at the 2014 Wimbledon

Championships, while both the men's and women's singles champions received a staggering £1,760,000 each. The men's and women's doubles champion teams each split £325,000.

At the recreational/club level, however, MDT is considered one of the most popular formats (Barker 1979; King and Stolle 1980; Smith and Lutz 1975), and more recent ethnographic research in tennis clubs suggests this distinction remains today (Lake 2008, 2013). The emphasis on its 'social' aspects had implications in clubs, where pressure for court-use and integrationist strategies among members pushed the doubles format generally ahead of singles (Lake 2008, 2013).

Other co-ed sports also emphasized fun and socializing, with important consequences. Henry and Comeaux (1999, 281) found in soccer: 'Most players refrained from potentially dangerous moves. … An atmosphere of relaxed, fair play generally prevailed'. In softball, men were expected to "tone down" their aggressiveness: 'This means not throwing the ball hard to a female teammate, not sliding into an opposing female infielder, and regulating their language' (Snyder and Ammons 1993, 6). In MDT, play was governed by well-understood etiquette; especially in 'social' tennis, players were expected to adjust their play to ensure fun comes before winning. 'Kenny and Coach Rick' in the *United States Tennis Association Improve Your Game* (USTAIYG) forum (*www.usta.com/improve-your-game/*) argued: 'It will be more fun for everybody in a social "hit-and-giggle" level game when you agree to keep the ball in play'. Similarly Kevin Pease in his *School of Tennis* (SOT) blog (*capecodtennislessons. blogspot.ca*) recommended: 'Be nice and remember it is fun first then winning. … I always try to create shots that make it better for my partner and fun for the other team. By fun I mean challenging'. Pease implied that male players should be responsible for ensuring a 'happy medium' was maintained; they, rather than women, were expected to adjust their play in accordance with the other players' relative abilities. Court (1975, 177) agreed that 'a woman should confess whatever weaknesses she may have right at the beginning of a match. That way, the man can adjust'. Thus, chivalry played an important role in the subtle articulation of male dominance; oftentimes, men took pride in adjusting their play to suit the overall playing standard. In their dominant positions, men were expected to act as arbiters of enjoyment and fairness.

In mixed-sex sporting environments where men are assumed to be 'playing down', women often take such competitions more seriously. Laurendeau and Sharara (2008) discovered that female snowboarders took added pleasure in demonstrating their skills to, and proving themselves against, men, while Henry and Comeaux (1999) found that instances when female soccer players dispossessed male opponents were greeted with greater appreciation from teammates and spectators than when men dispossessed women. Similarly, in MDT, there was a suggestion that men attached less importance to outcomes of MDT matches. Conversely, women were 'playing up' and revelled in the challenge of competing against male players, responding to moments of triumph with particular pleasure. '*Liz*' (TWA forum) admitted: 'Nothing beats out rallying a guy at mixed or hitting a winning volley against them! Gotta love it!'. Of course, if male players admit to 'taking it easy' then any female achievements against them are explained away. Moreover, the idea that female players should relish defeating male players regardless of their ability reinforces notions of natural and unequivocal male superiority.

Evidently, these gendered assumptions can be problematic for male as well as female players. Jimmy Connors (2013, 105) recalled feeling confused as to why Chris Evert took MDT so seriously 'compared with her success in singles', and admitted: 'Mixed-doubles just didn't matter enough in my world. ... Our different attitudes would clash on the court'. Some men mentioned feeling subdued by the extra attention and support their female opponents received. 'DeSTrOY' (TWA forum) admitted feeling 'pissed off' typically 'when I give the girl an easy put-away shot and they hit a winner, [and] everyone is cheering like she won a frickin gold medal'. Conversely, an anecdote involving John McEnroe highlights that when men take competitive MDT matches as or more seriously than their partners, they open themselves up to being embarrassed. In the 1999 Wimbledon Championships, Steffi Graf scratched last-minute from her mixed-doubles match with McEnroe at the semi-final stage to concentrate on her singles campaign. McEnroe (2002, 308) admitted blasting Graf in the locker room upon hearing the news: 'Can you believe what this [blanking] bitch did to me?'. Not only upset for having to relinquish a title challenge, McEnroe probably also felt emasculated, and made to look the fool by being 'dumped' by his female teammate.

Gender roles and the negotiation of court positioning

While the promotion of etiquette based upon safety and enjoyment in any sport are important concerns, more problematic are gendered assumptions that may underpin them: i.e. that females are necessarily weaker players that require male protection (Wachs 2002). Henry and Comeaux (1999) found that gender differences in co-ed soccer were constructed in an attempt to enact egalitarianism, by counteracting differences on the field. Similarly, Wachs (2002, 314) found in co-ed softball that rule modifications to promote 'equality' between the sexes had the overall effect of 'reifying the salience of gender difference', by conflating ability and gender, and equating 'equal' with gender rather than ability. Thus, women were afforded numerous special accommodations regardless of their skill level or other factors that might have proven stronger predictors of ability, such as height, weight, age, experience or injury status.

Similarly, in MDT, early guides reinforced patriarchal ideologies by sustaining the assumption that male players were stronger (e.g. Barker 1979; Court 1975; Cutler 1967; Douglas 1982; Graebner and Graebner 1973; Lardner 1975; Lott 1982). Accordingly, tactics related to court positioning and shot selection reflected this expectation. Lardner (1975, 47) noted how women typically lacked confidence in the 'backhand ground stroke, the backhand volley and the smash'. King and Stolle (1980, 135–136) noted the 'standard operating procedure' was to hit repeatedly to the female 'because she usually does not possess the volleying strength of her partner'.

More recently, the assumption of women's weaker play was reinforced by Matthew Cory, from the *United States Professional Tennis Association Thoughts on Tennis* (USPTATOT) blog (*usptatester.blogspot.ca*), who recommended: 'Play the skirt', by which he meant: 'Play the woman as much as possible. The most important thing in doubles ... is to play the percentages'. Similarly, the two-time mixed-doubles Grand Slam champion Wayne Black advocated: 'keep focusing on hitting at the women, ... keep drilling the weaker link'; conversely, his sister Cara Black, a five-time mixed-doubles Grand Slam champion, conceded: 'You know a lot of the time the ball is going to be coming at you, so you've got to be ready' (*Ace* May 2005, 43). 'Cruzer' from the *Talk Tennis at Tennis Warehouse* (TTTW) forum (*tt.tennis.warehouse.com*) estimated that approximately 80% of all shots in competitive matches at the recreational/club level were directed at the female.

Given the male players' limited opportunities to show his dominance, the satirist Art Hoppe (1977, 24) probably projected a half-truth when joking: 'The proper method of playing mixed-doubles [for men] is to hit the ball accidentally at the woman player as hard and as accurately as possible'. By implication, women were considered weaker and natural targets for exploiting. While some early authors of coaching guides openly questioned the etiquette of targeting the female player, by claiming it unsportsmanlike, un-gentlemanly or simply poor tactics (e.g. Barker 1979; Graebner and Graebner 1973; Lott 1982; Riessen 1975), just by acknowledging the etiquette was predicated upon assumed physical shortcomings, they reinforced rather than challenged patriarchal ideologies. Many of the behavioural guidelines for male and female players established during this earlier period have remained, and the implicit assumption that women were naturally inferior players was reflected in the primacy given routinely to physical attributes that typically advantage males, such as size and strength. In these ways, 'proper' play in MDT continues to equate to 'male' standards.

In terms of how men and women are instructed to position themselves on court, several consistent messages are given across these time periods. For example, the expectation that men should adopt the backhand (left-hand) side of the court was frequently suggested in early coaching guides (e.g. Barker 1979; Douglas 1982; Graebner and Graebner 1973; Lardner 1975; Riessen 1975). Navratilova (1983, 182) acknowledged this 'mixed-doubles rule', which she and her partner felt forced to attempt despite them each preferring the other side, claiming in hindsight: 'we'd have been much tougher the other way round'. Kevin Pease recommended similarly: 'The man should play the ad court as more points are decided there', but added 'unless the woman is the stronger player', to which he commented, flippantly: 'hey, it happens'. It has been a fairly constant strategy for men to adopt the role of main point scorer, which confirms the prevalence of 'gender stacking', defined as the disproportionate positioning of players in peripheral and/or less prestigious positions based on assumed athletic qualities accorded to sex. Similarly in co-ed soccer, men tended to adopt more central field positions, which fundamentally limited opportunities for females to participate fully (Henry and Comeaux 1999).

Connected to court positioning in MDT were expectations relating to shot selection, whereby men were supposed to take command of the winning shots, regularly 'poach' volleys, and cover drop shots, lobs and overhead smashes, while women were expected to play steady positional tennis and not make mistakes (Barker 1979; Court 1975; Graebner and Graebner, 1973; King and Stolle 1980; Navratilova 1983). In a typically paternalist tone, Cutler (1967, 103) recommended in his coaching guide: the woman should 'let the man be the aggressor. ... The only shot the lady has to hit is the serve to her'. More recently, Kevin Pease recommended that women receiving the man's service have just two simple aims: 'get into the point' and do 'not make a lot of unforced errors'. Conversely, for men, Wayne Black stated: 'At professional level, the man has to take about three-quarters of the court' (*Ace* May 2005, 43). The stated strategy is for team-mates to work together and create openings for the male player to score winning shots (Graebner and Graebner 1973; Lardner 1975; Kevin Pease [SOT blog]). For example, in the context of women both serving and returning serve, Douglas (1982, 239) recommended specific tactics to engineer opportunities 'for the man to move up court and finish the point'. Accordingly, and in tandem with earlier authors (e.g. King and Stolle 1980; Lardner 1975; Riessen 1975), Kevin Pease argued, 'holding serve' is a key expectation for men, while 'if the woman holds that is a bonus'.

Evidently, female players were expected to play more supporting, rather than leading, roles. Court (1975, 177) recommended allowing men to dictate tactics, even if this necessitated playing a more subordinate role: 'By and large, it seems to work best if the woman lets the man act as team captain. ... The man should make most of the decisions'.

Questions of shot selection and behavioural restraint

Historically speaking, the etiquette that developed to regulate MDT was predicated upon patriarchal ideals of paternalism and chivalry (Lake 2012), whereby men were expected to protect their partners and avoid exploiting their assumed weaker female opponents. Accordingly, while authors of coaching guides did not consider it inappropriate for a man to hit hard shots at his male opponent, or for a woman to do so at either her male or female opponents, men could expect admonition if they did so against the female opponent (Graebner and Graebner 1973; Smith and Lutz 1975). While tennis is a non-contact sport and provides relatively few opportunities for participants to directly physically harm or injure their opponents, the sport still exists within a culture of risk that encourages male athletes to over-conform to what Hughes and Coakley (1991) refer to as the 'sport ethic', whereby striving for distinction, seeking to overcome obstacles, ignoring or playing through pain and injury, and tolerating physical risk in the form of close-range body or head shots are normalized objectives. Snyder and Ammons (1993, 10) posit that the more competitive the sporting situation or level, 'the greater likelihood that males will dominate the interaction', taking more of the important roles/positions and greater responsibility for winning. This was the case, they argued, because achievement, alongside competitiveness, aggressiveness, toughness, courage and strength, defines masculinity. Collectively, these qualities are highly valued as markers of masculine identity and often conceived publicly as being exclusively male (Thorpe 2005). While considered necessary and expected traits for male tennis players, they are also, of course, necessary traits for successful female players, but the etiquette allows women, at the recreational/club level if not also sometimes at the elite level, to criticize their male opponents for hard serves and close-range body/head shots, whilst simultaneously be excused when hitting such shots themselves. The etiquette implies that women are not only weaker offensively (i.e. they cannot hit as hard as male players), but also that they have naturally lower pain thresholds or are more susceptible to injuries. Given the pervasive expectancy of male self-restraint in MDT, these ideas have become common sense and internalized among male and female players. Paraphrasing Lenskyj (1986), Young et al. (1994, 178) argued: 'the clearest way that health-compromising sport is consolidated as male territory is through the exclusion of women from sport on the basis that it is too risky'. Indeed, the same argument can be applied also to specific health-compromising 'moments' within a comparatively low-risk, non-contact sport like tennis.

These ideas are lent credence given evidence that suggests ideas relating to men needing to protect women from physical harm have remained in contemporary MDT etiquette among a critical mass of bloggers/forum members – which involved mostly men but, interestingly, also some women – whose attitudes seem based upon historically rooted generalizations about female frailty and male physical prowess. Like others, Matthew Cory couched his recommendations on 'safety' concerns; overhead smashes and hard, flat serves and down-the-line drives hit directly at the female opponent should be avoided because: 'men can hit the ball much harder than most women can react to it, so it is a dangerous proposition'. For smashes, he advised 'men should tell their female partner to ditch the net if ... [the male opponent] can hit a smash', and he recommended saving the 'cannon-ball' serve and 'side-line drives at close range' for the male opponent; instead: 'try a lob, go crosscourt, or take something off the ball. ... If you can demonstrate you have control, you should be able to get the ball by her down the alley with no fear of decapitating her'. Forum members of *both sexes* argued similarly. 'O' (TWA forum) wrote: 'Quite simply: men are built stronger than women. ... Just simply blasting the ball straight at a female opponent knowing she will be overpowered to me is bad etiquette'. Instead of hard serves, he recommended 'strong kickers and slider aces', while '*Liz*' (TTTW forum) reasoned: 'I think guys shouldn't tee off as hard as they can straight at a girl. LOL But there's nothing wrong at aiming at their feet or left hip'. Given what 'Blandford' (USTAIYG forum) understood as the 'stigma' attached to hard play towards female opponents, 'mixing it up' was generally recommended.

It was evident that context was important, in that different etiquette directed 'social' and competitive MDT. 'Geezer Guy' (TTTW forum) compared a 'social' tournament to more competitive tennis:

> This is NOT the time for you to fire up your cannon serves against the little old lady that plays once a week. This is NOT the time for you to blast returns of weak serves at the opposing net person. This is the time for you to play graciously and politely.

Male players seemed not to object to tempering their play if they felt the situation 'demanded it'. Not only were opportunities afforded to assert their masculine dominance through 'paternalistic chivalry' – i.e. exhibiting restrained behaviour – but also to acceptably excuse themselves from defeat if they lost the match. Even in more competitive situations, however, the recommendation that came chiefly from male players was to avoid hitting 'at' the female opponent. Both 'Anthony' and 'Verlin' (TWA forum) recommended hitting 'past' the female opponent but not at the body. Employing 'common sense limits to aggression', 'Eric' (USTAIYG forum) advised: 'hit to the feet only or to the open kill zones'. These comments seem to represent an emphatic acceptance of chivalric gestures in MDT, and thus the wholesale rejection of egalitarian principles of gender equality.

Not only were men expected to take responsibility for protecting women, but also everyone's safety and enjoyment overall. Female players had fewer duties or constraints. The factors that male players likely considered subconsciously when deciding on a particular shot/stroke or tactic included: the type or status of match being played, the context of the particular point, and the relative physical strength and playing ability of the female opponent. Unsurprisingly, numerous male bloggers/forum members felt these mitigating circumstances made it 'difficult' or 'tough' for men to make the 'right' decisions. As his default position, 'dennis1188' (TTTW forum) recommended always trying to play 'without any distractions', by which he alluded to the difficult (and sometimes split-second) decisions regarding the 'correct' shot to play. Mark Hodgkinson in *The Tennis Space* (TTS) blog (*www.thetennisspace.com*) admitted: 'The etiquette can be so difficult for a man ... as he must make up his own mind whether it is right to drill the ball at his female opponent'. Similarly, Wayne Black (*Ace* May 2005, 43) argued male players must gauge 'how strong your opponents are and what the score is. It's a fine line between actually going for her and just trying to make her miss'. Kevin Pease called the expected adjustments for men 'very frustrating' and 'the most difficult part about playing mixed'; he advised: 'Be respective of the levels on the court. ... The key is to play your best without hurting anyone physically or emotionally'.

Implicit within this etiquette that has sustained over the years was another expectation that the male player should seek retribution if/when his male counterpart hits 'at' his female partner. In their MDT coaching guide, Clark Graebner and Carole Graebner (1973, 23) recommended not to 'pick on' the female opponent, or else 'you'll incur the immediate wrath of the male opponent'. More recently, 'tarheelbornjohn' (TTTW forum) described the man's responsibility as 'enforcer':

> Remember, you have a lady on your side too. ... Drill [their] partner with a sitter or even play shots at their head to shake them up and you then have a very hard time saying anything when they do it.

Emphasizing the support this etiquette norm received from some female players, 'Cindysphinx' (TTTW forum) agreed: 'In league play, the etiquette seems to be that the men don't try to drill the lady unless the other guy drills his partner first'.

The expression of attitudes towards gender roles, court position, shot selection and behavioural restraint as examined here has worked to assert gender distinctions by normalizing ideas about female frailty and male physical prowess. In these areas, contemporary MDT etiquette seems deeply historically rooted, but in other areas, different narratives are being written, as both women and men have come to reject some features of etiquette considered outdated, unfair or impractical. It is posited that recent feminist advances have helped alter the cultural environment for MDT players. Yet, it seems men have sustained their dominance subtly by adopting more inclusive masculine values that have worked covertly to undermine and marginalize female players. It is apparent that etiquette norms have progressed into unknown territory where men are faced with conflicting instructions about how to behave, which could be considered an outcome of the 'crisis of masculinity' that emerged as a public debate in the 1990s. Here, a distinct break with etiquette from the 1960–1980s is apparent.

Conflicting etiquette for men and the 'crisis of masculinity'

Comparing the two historical periods, several key areas of change and conflict were identified. During the 1960–1980s, most authors continued to recommend that men 'ease off' their female opponents when serving or close-range hitting (e.g. Graebner and Graebner 1973; Smith and Lutz 1975), but conflated with elite-level player testimonies, there were signs of developing tensions. Connors (2013, 105) recalled some difficulties playing MDT with Chris Evert:

> I've always refused to blast the ball at my female opponent, even if the other guy is aiming at my partner. ... I'd give the guy some shit, but I would never take my anger out on his teammate. Chrissie wasn't particularly happy about that and said she thought I should go ahead and bury the other woman.

Similarly, Boris Becker (as quoted in Hodgkinson, TTS blog) admitted that conflicting etiquette norms adversely affected his game:

> I couldn't hit the woman when she was at the net. The woman would always hit the ball hard at me, though. My partner would say, "Go on Boris, hit it, hit the ball at the woman", but I just couldn't do it. ... I was usually the worst player on the court.

Also somewhat a traditionalist in this respect, McEnroe (2002, 71) believed it was an 'unspoken code' in MDT that 'guys don't whale away at the women'. However, he recalled an incident during the 1977 Wimbledon quarter-final when at 8–8 in the final set Dennis Ralston smashed a ball right at McEnroe's partner Mary Carillo:

To this day, I don't forgive Ralston, because he could have put that overhead anywhere. ... [Mary had] tears streaming down her face. I felt like killing the guy. ... That was the beginning of the end for me and mixed-doubles.

These testimonies signal shifting etiquette for both men and women, and the concomitant struggles to define appropriate behaviour. Considered progressive for its time, Smith and Lutz (1975, 15) acknowledged how 'money has brought out the killer instinct in both sexes', and accordingly: 'men are overcoming their hang-ups about banging balls at women playing net'. They elaborated: 'If the woman is equal of the man, targeting her may be justified at times – and many women today would not have it otherwise' (32). Indeed, Barker (1979, 110) agreed that 'easing up' when serving or hitting to a woman was recommended in 'club tennis', but in a more competitive setting, admitted: 'I would feel a little bit insulted if anyone did it against me'. Lott (1982, 33) warned that a female 'may surprise you with her return [of serve], and you also don't want to embarrass her'. Moving onward into the twenty-first century, with rising relative playing standards, strengths and fitness levels of female players, alongside third-wave feminist advances that stressed a critical re-evaluation of chivalry and its underlying meanings and values, it is perhaps unsurprising that numerous female forum members demanded that men play unrestrained MDT. 'Rene' (USTAIYG forum) argued: 'your best level of play is fair game. ... If an opponent feels like they can't handle your serve, that person shouldn't be playing at that level'. This preference reflected a strong expectation that everyone 'play to win'; women were 'insulted' and found it 'offensive', 'very patronizing' and 'annoying' when men intentionally weakened their serves or did not play 'their' game. 'MariaS' (TTTW forum) complained of being made to 'look like a wimp' when a man '[took] some pace off his serve'; 'Kristi', overall, advised men: 'bring whatever you have to the table'. In this regard, women have become more influential on court; instead of being passive observers and recipients of chivalry, they are now actively determining the unwritten rules of conduct for their male opponents by voicing their preference for defer-ential conduct ('paternalistic chivalry') or demanding equal treatment.

To the latter request, some men responded accordingly. Wayne Black contended: 'When it's tight at pro level, etiquette goes out of the window' (*Ace* May 2005, 43). Some forum members agreed that in high-level competitions where considerable prestige and prize money were at stake, there was less inclination or expectation for men to restrain themselves. 'R. Jayakrishnan' from the *Steve G Tennis* (SGT) forum (*www.stevegtennis.com*) rejected the notion of male chivalry: 'If he deliberately cuts down on his speed, then he is being patronizing to women'. Others rationalized *not* restraining themselves out of respect for their partners, who expected them to play their best regardless of their opponent's sex, but also, interestingly, still adopt the 'enforcer' role. 'Bernie' (USTAIYG forum) remarked: 'If you're playing in a competitive match, then it is unfair to your partner to not play your best, which includes hitting a hard serve to the women'. Similarly, 'Coach Leonard' stated: 'Remember that being polite to an opponent can be rude to your partner. Gentle serves can often result to harsh shots to your teammate at the net'.

Despite these more liberal viewpoints, numerous other male forum members expressed discomfort. When asked by 'CindySphinx'(TTTW forum) why men 'won't hit their normal serve to a woman', 'JRstriker1' answered: 'I think guys are trying to avoid looking like a jerk or bully, but ironically end up having the opposite effect'. Judged by a wide range of responses, many felt confused, and sometimes reacted negatively to, conflicts within contemporary etiquette. For some, the situation was perceived as 'lose-lose': vilified as bullies if they played too hard, yet labelled patronizing chauvinists if they played soft. This presented a unique and challenging path for male players to navigate, even in high-level competitions. 'Eric' (USTAIYG forum) described a 'grey area' that still exists with regard to the 'give-and-take of body shots', which causes some to 'draw a line and get angry'. 'FedererFed' (TWA forum) recalled an oft-experienced difficulty: 'I ease off the girl/lady, and watch in dismay as the opposition camp out vigorously on the girl on my side'. 'DeSTrOY' (TWA forum) admitted: 'I actually can't stand playing mixed unless the girl is the same or better standard than me. I feel so bad every time I hit a winner ... [and I get] dirty looks as if I committed a crime!' 'FedererFed' urged, succinctly: 'No etiquette. Smash 'em ... ☺ Are we playing or cat footing?'

It is difficult to ascertain whether such comments signalled men's collective inclinations towards gender equality in MDT, or conversely a cultural backlash against feminism, where men sought to reassert themselves as a reaction to the growing pressure for male restraint and the threat (or reality) of declining relative power. Given the tone of some comments that seem to associate the exhibition of self-restraint with (male) weakness, the latter seems quite likely. For example, when FulhamFan (SGT forum) contended that serving 140 mph to a woman was being a 'jerk', 'Dave' blasted: 'pussy'. Similarly, 'DeSTrOY' (TWA forum) was told to 'harden up' when he voiced a similar viewpoint, while 'Anthony', after admitting he did not 'feel comfortable smashing the ball at a female' was told: 'Make the girls bleed!!!!' ('Oh Yeh', TWA Forum). These and other forum members took opportunities to, by all accounts, assert orthodox, rather than inclusive, masculinity through discussing MDT etiquette. 'Oh Yeh' advised male players: 'Just smash it at the chicks, if they don't want to play then walk off the court'. 'Fedace' (TTTW forum) bragged that he always served hard 'right at the body of the girl. It works pretty well'. Forum members also ridiculed strong, powerful women who challenged gender norms through their on-court dominance. 'Oh Yeh' (TWA forum) scornfully mocked: 'You seen some of the "women" out there, they're bigger than men!' Ongoing dialogue between several male forum members demonstrated persistent sexist thinking. 'Captain Obvious' asked, with reference to etiquette: 'Isn't it supposed to be equal society these days, fellas?', to which 'GazzaWazza' directly replied: 'Women are only good for cooking eggs'.

The inconsistency of viewpoints here suggests that contemporary MDT etiquette is far from uniformly agreed-upon, enacted, or enforced among men, but challenges for them are compounded still further by two other factors. Firstly, in the recreational/club context, the establishment and sustenance of good off-court reputations was considered of critical importance. Male players are thought 'mean spirited' if they play too aggressively. Thus, winning can only bring 'real' respect if done in the 'right' spirit. 'Bernie' (USTAIYG forum) explained that if you intend to continue playing 'social' MDT, then you need to 'adjust your play' to your opponents: 'Hitting a hard serve to a weak opponent may win the point but may also lose your place on the sub list or next year's group ... and you may lose the friendship of your opponent'. Similarly, 'Linn' (USTAIYG forum) felt compelled to adjust her play because she was developing a 'reputation' for 'hitting overheads at the net player'; she admitted: 'I would rather have more friends off the court and a better reputation on the court'. From the TTTW forum, 'lostinamerica' confessed feeling so confused by the divergent etiquette norms that he quit playing MDT altogether after being repeatedly 'lectured'. He recalled a match when he 'showed no mercy to a woman' because she was repeatedly out of position, but subsequently was 'the goat among mixed-doubles and had [earned] a bad reputation as a poor sport'.

Secondly, it was suggested that some experienced female players attempted to manipulate chivalric adjustments in men's play to their tactical advantage. 'JRstriker12' (TTTW forum) reflected:

> There are little old ladies that are looking to eat you for breakfast. ... In a recent singles match with a woman, she starts the match off saying. "Don't forget to be nice to me ... [but] I won't be nice to you." And she wasn't. I barely scraped out a win.

Similarly, 'schadenfreude' (TTTW forum) recalled a match when the male opponent complained about his powerful serve: 'I adjusted and 'dialled it down' ... [but] they still picked on my opponent. ... The moral? Why should I care about looking like a bully with a big serve when the opponents prey on the weaker player, anyway?' Ethnographic research by Lake (2013) revealed how some, particularly older, female established club members used anticipated deferential treatment towards them as a clever way of asserting themselves. They asked for concessions and demanded restraint from the male players, but proceeded to play hard towards them. Not only were they successful in forcing mistakes from them, but also 'saved face' in the clubhouse, as score-lines rarely reflected true differences in ability. In situations when conflict occurred because of etiquette breaches, males were invariably labelled the antagonists while females were victims.

For sure, superior tennis players of both sexes feel pressured to adjust their play, but the expectations on shot selection and self-restraint for male and female players are negotiated in qualitatively different ways, which, as this analysis suggests, presents more challenges for men than women. Such conflicts for male MDT players can be understood as a possible outcome of what MacInnes (1998) called the 'crisis of masculinity'. Since the 1990s, increasing numbers of women began to reject men's chivalric gestures as demeaning behavioural practices that reinforced outdated conceptions of feminine frailty (see Viki et al. 2003). Consequently, Beynon (2002) argues, men entered a crisis over gender roles and expectations, which have become less clear and simple, and more dynamic and context specific. Set within a broader socio-economic context, MacInnes (1998) noted considerable male-to-female shifts in the UK and US workforces from 1960 to 1990 which, combined with deindustrialization, a decline in manufacturing jobs, and the feminist movement, effectively undermined traditional gender roles. Men found it necessary to adopt a 'hybrid' masculine identity, which blended orthodox masculinity with more inclusive – essentially, female/gay-friendly – identities, to continue asserting their social dominance (Beynon 2002; Bridges and Pascoe 2014; MacInnes 1998). Developments in MDT etiquette reflected these changes for men, not only through the ongoing conflicts of identity and behaviour as an outcome of unresolved inconsistencies in the expectations and enforcement of etiquette, but also as the behaviour of male players generally has become subject to increasing public scrutiny as an outcome of the sport's professionalization and commercialization (Lake 2015b).

Conclusion: the persistence of gender inequalities

It is apparent that MDT has recently developed to simultaneously reinforce *and* challenge dominant gender norms and values in wider society. Despite the continued aversion of some men from hitting hard at female players, which was an extension of the old-fashioned chivalric idea that 'men don't hit women', more recently some women have grown increasingly frustrated over this etiquette. It is apparent that broader feminist struggles have found their place in MDT, particularly from the third wave, as the underlying or implied messages of and meanings attached to chivalric displays of etiquette by men have increasingly been challenged on court. However, resistance to these behaviours have not been sustained or enacted in any consistent basis or even wholeheartedly supported by all or, it seems, even a majority of female players. There is a clear need for a further and deeper third-wave critique of gendered stereotypes of female players, and the underlying meanings and values attached to their perceived gender roles/expectations and the taken-for-granted approaches to shot selection, tactics and court positioning that continue to characterize MDT play at least to some extent across all playing levels.

Also, despite the softer and more inclusive masculine norms and values that male MDT players, relative to other male athletes, are expected to adopt, the persistent and multifarious demands placed upon them contributes to, rather than fundamentally challenges, gender inequality. Patriarchy is more difficult to detect in its hybridized form, as men are compelled to 'display' different masculinities at 'different times in different situations' as Beynon (2002, 6) described. Men are expected to navigate numerous on-court scenarios, make snap decisions regarding shot selection/tactics, and negotiate simultaneous roles: leader, aggressor, poacher, chief point-scorer, risk-taker, enforcer, arbiter of fun/enjoyment, but also chivalrous sportsman, supportive team-mate, and perceptive opponent. While attempting to overcome gender barriers, the belief in 'natural' female weakness is essentially reinforced also among some women, who are complicit in their adoption of different and oftentimes less demanding on-court roles, positions and shots. As in mixed-gender MMA, this gender logic has been 'extrapolated over time' and 'written into the bodies of practitioners' (Channon 2014, 597).

It is clear that MDT remains a proving ground for different masculinities, but also that its etiquette reflects class – as much as gender-based norms, from the sport's upper-middle-class roots where chivalry and self-restraint towards weaker opponents was universally demanded (Lake 2011). That 'weaker opponents' were naturally thought to be female reflected dominant gender ideology, but the fact that such decisions were made indiscriminately yet also considered in the context of the match and particular point being played is indicative of the class-based structure to which the game's etiquette emerged and developed. While it is clear that for some players, the expectations of chivalry and behavioural restraint towards women remains, there is a growing number of players who espouse a more progressive view that still differentiates and demands the enforcement of etiquette. However, this is based less on gender difference and *assumed* ability and more on *actual* ability, i.e. the etiquette of playing against a weaker novice player. Only when these two criteria, gender and ability/strength, are not conflated automatically will it be possible to move towards true gender equality in MDT.

Note

1. The Hopman Cup, named after the famous Australian coach Harry Hopman, began in 1989 as an invitational mixed-sex competition played annually between eight nations. Three rubbers are played: men's singles, women's singles and mixed-doubles.

Disclosure statement

No potential conflict of interest was reported by the author.

References

Anderson, Eric. 2008. ""I Used to Think Women Were Weak": Orthodox Masculinity, Gender Segregation, and Sport." *Sociological Forum* 23: 257–280.

Anderson, Eric. 2009. *Inclusive Masculinity: The Changing Nature of Masculinity*. Abingdon: Routledge.

Anderson, Kristin. 1999. "Snowboarding: The Construction of Gender in an Emerging Sport." *Journal of Sport and Social Issues* 23 (1): 55–79.

Barker, Sue. 1979. *Playing Tennis*. New York: Taplinger.

Barnaby, Jack. 1975. *Advantage Tennis: Racket Work, Tactics, and Logic*. Boston, MA: Allyn and Bacon.

Beal, Becky. 1996. "Alternative Masculinity and its Effects on Gender Relations in the Subculture of Skateboarding." *Journal of Sport Behaviour* 19 (3): 204–220.

Beynon, John. 2002. *Masculinities and Culture*. Buckingham: Open University Press.

Bodo, Peter. 1995. *The Courts of Babylon: Tales of Greed and Glory in the Harsh New World of Professional Tennis*. New York: Scribner.

Booth, Douglas. 2002. "From Bikinis to Boardshorts: Wahines and the Paradoxes of the Surfing Culture." *Journal of Sport History* 28 (1): 3–22.

Bridges, Tristin, and C. J. Pascoe. 2014. "Hybrid Masculinities: New Directions in the Sociology of Men and Masculinities." *Sociology Compass* 8 (3): 246–258.

Channon, Alex. 2014. "Towards the "Undoing" of Gender in Mixed-sex Martial Arts and Combat Sports." *Societies* 4: 587–605.

Connell, Robert. 1995. *Masculinities*. Berkeley: University of California Press.

Connors, Jimmy. 2013. *The Outsider: My Autobiography*. London: Bantam.

Court, Margaret. 1975. "Mixed Doubles: The Women's View." In *Tennis Strokes & Strategies*, edited by Tennis Magazine, 176–178. New York: Simon and Schuster.

Cutler, Merritt. 1967. *Basic Tennis Illustrated*. New York: Dover.

Dashper, Kate. 2012. "Together, yet still not equal? Sex integration in equestrian sport." *Asia-Pacific Journal of Health, Sport and Physical Education* 3: 213–225.

Demetriou, Demetrakis. 2001. "Connell's Concept of Hegemonic Masculinity: A Crituque." *Theory & Society* 30 (3): 337–361.

Douglas, Paul. 1982. *The Handbook of Tennis*. New York: Alfred A. Knopf.

Feinstein, John. 1991. *Hard Courts: Real Life on the Professional Tennis Tours*. New York: Villard Books.

Gibbons, Tom. 2014. *English National Identity and Football Fan Culture: Who are Ya?* Farnham: Ashgate.

Gibbons, Tom, and Kevin Dixon. 2010. "'Surf's up!': A call to take English soccer fan interactions on the Internet more seriously." *Soccer and Society* 11 (5): 599–613.

Gibbons, Tom, and Daniel Nuttall. 2012. "Using E-Surveys to Access the Views of Football Fans within Online Communities." *Sport in Society* 15 (9): 1228–1241.

Gilley, Jennifer. 2005. "Writings of the Third Wave: Young Feminists in Conversation." *Reference and Users Service Quarterly* 44 (3): 187–198.

Graebner, Clark, and Carole Graebner. 1973. *Mixed Doubles Tennis*. New York: McGraw-Hill.

Hargreaves, Jennifer. 1994. *Sporting Females*. London: Routledge.

Henry, Jacques M., and Howard P. Comeaux. 1999. "Gender Egalitarianism In Coed Sport: A Case Study of American Soccer." *International Review for the Sociology of Sport* 34: 277–290.

Hine, Christine. 2005. "Virtual Methods and the Sociology of Cyber-Social-Scientific Knowledge." Chapter 1 in Virtual Methods: Issues in *Social Research on the Internet*. 1–13. Oxford: Berg.

Hoppe, Art. 1977. *The Tiddling Tennis Theorem*. New York: Viking Press.

Hughes, Robert, and Jay Coakley. 1991. "Positive Deviance among Athletes: The Implications of Overconformity to the Sport Ethic." *Sociology of Sport Journal* 8 (4): 307–325.

King, Billie Jean, and Fred Stolle. 1980. *How to Play Mixed Doubles: The Tactics and Techniques for a Solid, Winning Partnership*. New York: Simon & Schuster.

Lake, Robert J. 2008. "Social Exclusion in British Tennis: A History of Privilege and Prejudice." PhD diss., Brunel University.

Lake, Robert J. 2011. "Social Class, Etiquette and Behavioural Restraint in British Lawn Tennis, 1870–1939." *The International Journal of the History of Sport* 28 (6): 876–894.

Lake, Robert J. 2012. "Gender and Etiquette in British Lawn Tennis 1870–1939: A Case Study of 'Mixed Doubles.'" *The International Journal of the History of Sport* 29 (5): 691–710.

Lake, Robert J. 2013. "'They treat me like I'm Scum': Social Exclusion and Established-Outsider Relations in a British Tennis Club." *International Review for the Sociology of Sport* 48 (1): 112–128.

Lake, Robert J. 2015a. *A Social History of Tennis in Britain*. London: Routledge.

Lake, Robert J. 2015b." The "Bad Boys" of Tennis: Shifting Gender and Social Class Relations in the Era of Nastase, Connors and McEnroe." *Journal of Sport History* 41 (2): 179–199.

Lardner, Rex. 1975. *Tactics in Women's Singles, Doubles and Mixed Doubles*. Garden City, NY: Doubleday & Company.

Laurendeau, Jason. 2004. "The 'Crack Choir' and the 'Cock Chorus': The Intersecton of Gender and Sexuality in Skydiving Texts." *Sociology of Sport Journal* 21 (4): 397–417.

Laurendeau, Jason, and Nancy Sharara. 2008. ""Women Could Be Every Bit As Good As Guys": Reproductive and Resistant Agency in Two "Action" Sports." *Journal of Sport and Social Issues* 32: 24–47.

Lee, Raymond, Fielding Nigel, and Grant Blank. 2008. "The Internet as a Research Medium: An Editorial Introduction to the Sage Handbook of Online Research Methods." In *The Sage Handbook of Online Research Methods*, edited by Fielding Nigel, Raymond Lee, and Grant Blank, 3–20. London: Sage.

Lenskyj, Helen. 1986. *Out of Bounds: Women, Sport and Sexuality*. Toronto: Women's Press.

Lott, David. 1982. *Pro-am Guide to Tennis*. Maplewood, NJ: Hammond.

Lumpkin, Angela. 1981. *Women's Tennis: A Historical Documentary of the Players and their Game*. New York: Whitston.

MacInnes, John. 1998. *The End of Masculinity*. Buckingham: Open University Press.

McCrone, Kathleen. 1988. *Sport and the Physical Emancipation of English Women 1870–1914*. London: Routledge.

McDonagh, Eileen, and Laura Pappano. 2008. *Playing with the Boys: Why Separate is Not Equal in Sports*. New York: Oxford University Press.

McEnroe, John. 2002. *Serious*. London: Time Warner Paperbacks.

Messerschmidt, James. 2010. *Hegemonic Masculinities and Camouflaged Politics*. Boulder, CO: Paradigm.

Messner, Michael. 1993. "'Changing Men' and Feminist Politics in the United States." *Theory and Society* 22 (5): 723–737.

Messner, Michael. 2007. "The Masculinity of the Governator." *Gender & Society* 21 (4): 461–480.

Mewshaw, Michael. 1993. *Ladies of the Court: Grace and Disgrace on the Women's Tennis Circuit*. New York: Crown.

Miller, Stuart. 1995. "When Female Athletes Compete Against Men, Does It Help or Hurt Women's Sports?" *Women's Sports and Fitness* 17 (3): 72–79.

Millward, Pete. 2008. "The Rebirth of the Football Fanzine: Using E-zines as Data Source." *Journal of Sport and Social Issues* 32 (3): 299–310.

Navratilova, Martina. 1983. *Tennis My Way*. New York: Charles Scribner's Sons.

Riessen, Marti. 1975. "Mixed Doubles: The Men's View." In *Tennis Strokes & Strategies*, edited by Tennis Magazine, 179–181. New York: Simon and Schuster.

Schultz, Jaime. 2005. "Reading the Catsuit: Serena Williams and the Production of Blackness at the 2002 U.S. Open." *Journal of Sport and Social Issues* 29 (3): 338–357.

Smith, Stan, and Bob Lutz. 1975. *Modern Tennis Doubles*. London: Angus & Robertson.

Snyder, Eldon E., and Ronald Ammons. 1993. "Adult participation in coed softball: Relations in a gender integrated sport." *Journal of Sport Behaviour* 16 (1): 3–15.

Sommers, Cristine H. 2000. *The War Against Boys: How Misguided Feminism is Harming our Young Men*. New York: Simon and Schuster.

Stedman, Leanne. 1997. "From Gidget to Gonad Man: Surfers, Feminists and Postmodernisation." *Journal of Sociology* 33 (1): 75–90.

Sveningsson, Malin. 2009. "How Do Various Notions of Privacy Influence Decisions in Qualitative Internet Research?" In *Internet Inquiry: Conversations about Method*, edited by Annette Markham and Nancy Baym, 69–87. London: Sage.

Thorpe, Holly. 2005. "Jibbing the Gender Order: Females in the Snowboarding Culture." *Sport in Society* 8 (1): 76–100.

Viki, G. Tendayi, Dominic Abrams, and Paul Hutchison. 2003. "The 'True' Romantic: Benevolent Sexism and Paternalistic Chivalry." *Sex Roles* 49 (9/10): 533–537.

Wachs, Faye L. 2002. "Leveling the Playing Field: Negotiating Gendered Rules in Coed Softball." *Journal of Sport and Social Issues* 26: 300–316.

Wheaton, Belinda. 2000. "'New Lads?': Masculinities and the 'New Sport Participant'." *Men and Masculinities* 2: 434–456.

Wilson, Elizabeth. 2014. *Love Game: A History of Tennis, from Victorian Pastime to Global Phenomenon.* London: Serpent's Tail.

Wind, Herbert W. 1979. *Game, Set and Match: The Tennis Boom of the Sixties and Seventies.* New York: C. P. Dutton.

Young, Kevin, Phil White, and William McTeer. 1994. "Body Talk: Male Athletes Reflect on Sport, Injury, and Pain." *Sociology of Sport Journal* 11: 175–194.

Doing femininities and masculinities in a 'feminized' sporting arena: the case of mixed-sex cheerleading

Esther Priyadharshini and Amy Pressland

School of Education and Lifelong Learning, University of East Anglia, Norwich, UK

ABSTRACT
This paper examines arguments that have been espoused for the educative and transformative potential of mixed-sex sports, and explores whether such promise can be attained and what the obstacles may be, in the context of the UK university-level, competitive cheerleading. Drawing on critical and feminist literature on the functioning of hegemonic masculinities, hyper-femininities and alternative, more inclusive gender performances, the paper analyses the narratives of three participants in what is often recognized as the 'feminised' activity of cheerleading. It suggests that: a) having experience of mixed-sex team membership can have a progressive influence on the gender narratives and performances of both male and female participants; b) mixed-sex teams, however, are not a panacea to rectify gender stereotypes and inequalities and c) if the implicit transformative potential of mixed-sex cheerleading is to be fully realized, then explicit organizational, promotional and structural changes to the sport itself will be needed. The paper concludes with suggestions for a new research agenda that focuses on the terms and conditions under which gender is 'learnt' and performed in a range of mixed-sex sporting contexts, and how these contexts serve to shape the 'gender pedagogies' of sports in particular ways. Such an approach will open significant new directions for research, policy and practice in the interconnected fields of gender, sport and education.

The segregation of the sexes in and through sporting activity is a ubiquitous, internationally visible phenomenon, at elite or lower level sports (Dworkin and Messner 2002). Scholars of gender in sport have articulated their concerns over such sweeping sex segregation, particularly the essentialist rationale offered for such separation, grounded in biological difference and the implications of this for the socialization of differently gendered participants (Caudwell 2003; Messner 2002; Sailors 2014). Critical, feminist and queer frameworks have been used to illustrate the ways in which major sporting activities reinforce sexual difference through rigid definitions of masculinity and femininity, and how the policing of these are central to the evolution of sport (Anderson 2008, 2005a; Messner 1988; Hargreaves 1994; Crossett 1990). The everyday elements of sports such as equipment, clothing, rules,

---

Submission to the special issue on 'Sex integration in sport and physical culture' for *Sport in Society: Cultures, Commerce, Media, Politics*.

structures and remuneration for male and female participants are constructed differently, and serve not only to keep the sexes distinct, but also shore up the belief that differences between the sexes are 'essential' or 'natural' rather than socially constructed (Theberge 1989; Cahn 1994). Sailors (2014) analysis of the 'messages' of sex segregation suggests a sort of hidden curriculum that sporting culture promotes: emphazising the able–disabled binary that positions women as 'less' than men; women as therefore not as worthy as men of sporting attention or equal reward; the spawning of a 'protectionist' attitude towards women in sporting (and social worlds); limiting the choice of sporting activity available to women. Institutionalized sex segregation also signals associated fears over 'transgression' of gender norms, ie effeminacy in men, strength/power in women and the rejection/suppression of non-heterosexualities (Adams 2005). The reproduction of a largely misogynistic and unjust sporting and thus social, culture is also facilitated through such segregative practices (Anderson 2008).

Mixed-sex sporting activity, it is hoped, may be able to stage a counter to such socially regressive gender pedagogy by providing transformative experiences that challenge traditional ideas of male superiority (McDonagh and Pappano 2008). Mixed-sex activity, it is also hoped, will offer alternative opportunities by emphasizing 'teamwork and complementary skills – both characteristics that are arguably beneficial and useful *educationally*. Such teamwork opportunities might also be highly useful in *acculturating* women and men to work together in other contexts' (Francis 1993, emphasis added). Such arguments against sex segregation and for mixed-sex teams hint at the links between sports, education (specifically learning to 'do gender' through sport) and acculturation for other social contexts. They suggest the world of sports ought to be seen as a pedagogic medium for learning about and for performing gender, one that has far reaching implications outside the world of sport. The ways in which the broad promise of mixed-sex sport plays out in different activities, contexts and cultures are bound to be different. Studying how gender is tacitly or explicitly learnt, exhibited and embodied through a range of mixed-sex sporting events can help explain how the educative and transformative potential (or pitfalls) of mixed-sex sports might work in practice. But, the relative rarity of mixed-sex sporting events has meant that they are comparatively under-researched. This paper uses the context of the UK university-level competitive cheerleading, which exists in both mixed- and single-sex formats as an entry point into these issues. Specifically, it explores how participants currently 'do' femininities and masculinities in what is seen as a 'feminised' arena, and the implications this throws up for practise, policy and future research.

Meanings of doing gender in sports

Issues of sex, gender and sexuality inevitably hold centre stage when considering mixed-sex sporting activities and their effects. The idea of 'doing' masculinities and femininities therefore needs some unpacking to understand the conditions that shape the varied meanings they hold for participants and the implications for in mixed-sex sporting activity.

Paechter (2006) notes how 'doing girl' or 'doing boy' may be commonly understood as exhibiting femininities or masculinities. But what counts as femininity or masculinity varies according to time, place and circumstance. In particular, what it means to be female or male, and performing femininities or masculinities, varies in different sporting contexts (Anderson 2005a, 2005b; Bemiller 2005; Channon 2013; Miller 2010; Paechter 2006; Tagg

2008). Femininities, for instance, are not equivalent to masculinities as they are not constructed in similar ways – femininities do not confer cultural power in the way that hegemonic masculinities (Connell 1995) do. Hegemonic masculinity can be understood as a 'sort of ideal-typical construction of what men do that may not fit what is found empirically, but does relate quite closely to collective ideas about men in any particular society' (Paecheter 2006). As Sailors (2014) and a host of others (Adams 2011; Anderson 2009; Bemiller 2005; Cahn 1994; Messner 1988) point out, sporting culture on the whole, tends to reinforce such ideas about hegemonic masculinities, ableism and heterosexuality.

Paechter (2006) asserts that distancing oneself from hegemonic masculinity is about giving up power and that, for some men, such acts could also be done in ways that are personally empowering. This helps locate the notion of inclusive masculinities (Anderson 2005a, 2005b; Jarvis 2013), which suggests that men in sports who exhibit inclusive masculinities reveal not only a greater acceptance of gay men in sports, but also of men's femininities both of which have been prone to marginalization or stigmatization. Anderson's (2009) research on men who exhibit 'inclusive masculinities' suggests that changing social mores, and working alongside women teammates, could influence some men to distance themselves from hegemonic masculinity.

However, for women, there is no equivalent to hegemonic masculinity, no 'hegemonic femininity', as hegemony is about power, 'about being able to construct the world for oneself and others so that one's power is unchallenged, taken for granted' (Paechter 2006). To be excessively feminine or hyper-feminine – the ultimate negation of the masculine – does not confer hegemonic power (Choi 2000). But renouncing femininity, for example, through tomboy or butch identification, can become an act of renouncing powerlessness, an act of claiming power. In a sporting world that valorizes the ideal of hegemonic masculinity, but which equally strictly polices acceptable gender roles to maintain sport as a 'male domain' (Dunning 1994), women who embody masculine traits can face censure, making the doing of gender as a female athlete problematic. But, as not all masculinities are masculine, and femininities, feminine, individuals could have varying relationships to the 'ideal' notions of masculinity or femininity, allowing them to perform a range of masculinities and femininities. The context of mixed-sex sports in which men and women may work individually or as a team, allows us opportunities to study how different kinds of femininities and masculinities are valued and exhibited and what they mean for all participants.

In addition, to the four useful distinctions that Sailors (2014) offers as a rubric for studying mixed-sex sports – team sport or an individual sport; direct or indirectly competitive sport; contact or non-contact sport and amateur or professional sport – there is an important fifth dimension, the gender status of a sport (Matteo 1986). This suggests that a sport that is seen as essentially a women's sport (cheerleading or rhythmic gymnastics) has different ramifications for the femininities or masculinities that its participants might be encouraged to display compared to those which are seen as embodying masculine traits, like wrestling or weightlifting. Together, these factors determine the physiognomy of a sport and the gender identities and relations that it supports.

The gender status of a sport

As different sports are in themselves microcosms of traditions, social norms and expectations, the discursive meanings they engender (Channon 2013) and therefore the acknowledged 'gender status' of a sport can differently determine the meanings of masculinities and femininities of its participants. For example, the actions of men taking part in so-called 'feminized' sports (eg. netball) and those of women taking part in those seen as traditionally 'masculine' ones (eg. weightlifting), are both gender transgressive, but have different implications for participants and for the challenging of gender hierarchies. Chimot & Louveau's study (2010) about young boys participating in rhythmic gymnastics in France illustrates how they had to contend with pressure from men and violence from boys in their peer group to combat powerful masculinist norms. Miller's (2010) work with young girl wrestlers participating in single- and mixed-sex wrestling in the US also revealed the obstacles and social pressures they needed to overcome as well as the potential the sport offered to develop fluid gendered identities that did not succumb to the double bind that one cannot do both femininity and be a successful athlete. The tradition-destabilizing potential of mixed-sex sporting encounters is therefore tied intimately to the traditions and norms that have produced that particular sport.

In addition, the particular sociocultural context in which the sport is being practised also plays its part. Tagg (2008), researching male netball players in New Zealand, charts how that particular sport was historically shaped to reinforce patriarchal ideas of passive femininity. Here, in some regional contexts, it was sometimes more acceptable for men to play social netball in mixed-sex teams than to play competitive netball in all male teams. Recreational or low-status events are therefore different from professional or high-status events in how mixing the sexes are perceived to threaten the heteronormative and hegemonic culture of sport. Nevertheless, participating in a 'feminized' sport and playing alongside women and men of different sexualities and masculinities and those from other regions of New Zealand, offered the opportunity for participants to learn and interact with each other in non-conventional ways.

The idea that certain sports carry a gender value on their own is therefore a powerful one in determining how participants are perceived by those inside and outside the sport. As the three studies mentioned above show, participants are engaged in a double battle – battling prejudices related to the gender status of their chosen sport as well as their right to display their preferred masculinities and femininities within this sport. This brings us to the relatively new, yet fast-growing and popular activity of cheerleading, and one often recognized as a 'feminised' sport, where our study is located.

The multiple discourses of C/cheerleading

An examination of cheerleading reveals it as an activity thick with multiple and contradictory discursive meanings – the diversity in its followers/participants and the huge differences between local, transnational and media-promoted versions of the activity are now well documented (Bemiller 2005; Bettis and Adams 2006; Grindstaff and West 2010; Moritz 2011). From its origins as an elite male activity, to its growth as a female activity at the sidelines of male sporting events, to its visibility more recently as a mixed-sex, competitive activity, blending sports disciplines and traditional gender identities (Moritz 2011), the mutations of cheerleading are perhaps unprecedented in any other sporting activity. Adams and Bettis (2003, 2005) have charted how the growth of radical/alternative cheerleading squads – gay, lesbian, feminist, senior citizen and anti-globalization teams – alongside more traditional ones are fracturing stereotypical notions of what cheerleading is or means. Grindstaff and

West (2010) studying US cheerleading observe the tensions between 'true believers' vs. 'technicists', the latter rejecting the more traditional, ritualized actions of make-up, eternal exuberance through winking and smiling, even selflessness and appealing display, and instead prioritize competition in a sporting field. The multiple visions and versions of cheerleading at the international, national and local levels reveal the presence of several discourses of C/cheerleading (Lamb and Priyadharshini 2013), posing a 'conundrum' to those trying to understand the particular meanings that C/cheerleading might proffer.

This proliferation of associations, meanings and interpretations has important implications for gender relations within particular squads and contexts. Bemiller's (2005) work on 'men who cheer' in a collegiate-level public university cheerleading team in the USA is an illustration of how hegemonic understandings of gender shape participant experiences. Bemiller argues that men are stigmatized and questions about their sexuality raised, when they enter a feminized arena. Work into 'saving face' is then carried out by both men and women – women help men 'do masculinity' and subordinate themselves and 'do femininity'.

Anderson's (2005b) study of male cheerleaders from collegiate sport in the US, published at the same time as Bemiller's work, throws up different kinds of findings. His investigation shows how the structure, governance and organization of cheerleading partly influences the presence of two contrasting forms of masculinity – inclusive and orthodox. Inclusive masculinity seems to be based less upon hegemonic masculinity, homophobia or anti-femininity which orthodox masculinity implicitly or explicitly subscribes to. Male cheerleaders who associate with inclusive masculinity seemed more accepting of feminine behaviour and homosexuality among their male teammates. The rules of cheerleading allowed by the more Inclusive Cheerleading Association (like throwing men in the air, awarding points for erotic dancing by male cheerleaders) no doubt facilitated the display of more inclusive masculinities. Conversely, the Orthodox Cheerleading Association's discourse promoted distinct gender roles and encouraged male cheerleaders to reinforce their heterosexuality and to embody hegemonic masculinities.

In contrast to the US context, the UK cheerleading is still nascent and there are as yet, no marked bifurcations in associations or governing bodies, signalling different rules, values or norms. Cheerleading is still referenced in media reports as an American 'import' (Barkham 2010), with often contradictory manifestations of it filtered through popular media (movies, teen musicals, televised US sporting events), popular culture, its artefacts (children's toys, interactive games) and also through its presence as a half-time filler to male sporting events (eg. Rugby). These simultaneous yet diverse associations suggest that the meanings of this activity ought to be fairly open to definition by those participating in it in conjunction with the wider sociocultural context in which it is practised.

Methodology and presentation

The context for the data used in this paper is the UK university-level competitive arena. Interview data from three cheerleaders are used to explore the gender roles and performances that are encouraged, performed and narrated and the kinds of relationships that exist between the sexes. The interviews were part of a larger data-set comprising observations, field notes and interviews collected from two universities (one English and one Welsh) and one national-level (non-university adult) competitive squads. These three particular interviews were selected for this paper as they represent between them, male and female perspectives, and a range of experiences and views about gender and cheerleading either as part of single- or mixed-sex teams. The interviews were semi-structured, in-depth ones (lasting between 30 and 45 min) conducted face-to-face or via Skype. They were transcribed and analysed for key themes and narratives before being constructed into the three anonymized portraits that are presented below.

The style of portraiture has been chosen to showcase the broader perspectives of each individual. A more traditional cross-cutting representation by themes or issues across the data-set did not seem to do justice to the embeddedness of participant utterances within specific experiences and understandings. As advocated in narrative inquiry and representational practice (Clough 2002; Smith and Sparkes 2009), the portraits are not simply verbatim extracts from interview transcripts. The portraits were designed and constructed by extracting and piecing together key quotations, and at times reordering the sequence of answers from each interview. While no new or fictional material was introduced into the participants' accounts, the crafting of the portraits – extraction, piecing together, reordering involved – makes this a thoroughly 'constructed' representation. The rationale behind this was to focus attention explicitly and specifically on the narratives around gender and gender relations. These portraits are of just three cheerleaders (2 females and 1 male) and are not meant to be representative of cheerleading experiences in the UK. Their value lies in their ability to reveal the complex positions held on gender, gendered roles in cheerleading and how these may have changed as a result of their experience in mixed-sex teams.

Participant portraits

Melinda – I love the competitive element of cheerleading and also the socializing with the squad. This is important – there should be no cliques in the team, more like a family, with a strong sense of togetherness.

The boys in our squad joined originally as part of the 'dares' they try on each other at Fresher's week – 'I'll sign you up for Cheerleading and you can sign me up for something else' kind of thing. Our coach and captain usually take them aside after the first session and show them the 'advanced' stuff. For instance like single basing – how to lift a girl high with just one hand. I suppose normal boys like to show off about these things – 'look, I can throw a girl in the air', so they really liked it and they all decided to stay on and be part of the team. There was one boy who really enjoyed it, but he ended up quitting because his rugby team-mates made too much fun of him. The other boys got a bit of like mouth from some of their friends, but then they said 'well, cheerleaders are the girls that put a lot of effort into their looks and I get to touch them and like throw them in the air and catch them!' So there's nothing gay about that!

A lot of boys struggle with the dance and 'sass' elements while girls seem to naturally like to dance and to be pretty and neat and sassy. Boys are also quite shy, I think, about doing the sassy elements. For example, we get extra points if we wink or blow kisses to the judges. So to get the boys to up their game, we've challenged them to a sort of competition amongst themselves, to project the most sassiness. That kind of eggs them on, there's a good atmosphere with everyone fooling around but also trying to do better than each other. Usually, the boys just tend to do the stronger work I think a lot of the girls feel more comfortable when they've got a boy on the ground to catch them, because they feel a boy can take their weight. There should be a good mix of boys and girls – to play up the different strengths, often you'll put the boys at the back of the dance and give them slightly simpler moves and less like sassy moves to do!

Girls get to also wear great costumes – spandex with skirts and long sleeves, but also really big, pretty bows. I used to think it was a silly girly thing, but I think now that it's like a really good sport for girls who don't want to do 'sport', because they don't want to seem that masculine. If they don't like hockey, or football, that kind of stuff. I do a lot of sports anyway, like in my first year I did football, basketball and volleyball. But then by doing just gymnastics and cheerleading this year, I noticed there were many changes in my body. I've got more muscle than I did in my first year. I've had friends of mine going, 'Wow, do you go to the gym like all the time? Like how do you do get so much muscle, like SO toned?

You get a lot of people that go, 'cheerleading's not a sport! Anyone can do it!' Then I always say to them, 'well you know, why don't you get two other people and throw someone in the air and catch her and make it look effortless?' If you show them a video, or invite them to come and watch your training, they tend to change their mind. I think there's still a big image around it just being a lot of girls that are just really into their looks, just sort of dancing around, cheering on like a basketball team. Competitive cheerleading is like a whole new sport, if you compare it to that.

Melinda's narrative emphasizes the importance of strong team spirit – no cliques or 'in groups'. This, along with the awareness that this is a feminized arena, means that everyone works to make the men feel at ease, particularly at the start. As in Bemiller's (2005) study, there is an effort by women to boost male masculinity, to help deflect queries over male sexuality and to 'save face'. Melinda offers two contrasting examples, one of the rugby player, who succumbed to the ridicule he faced from others and another, of her male teammates who stayed on, by refuting any notion of homosexuality and playing up their closeness to good-looking young women.

Melinda reiterates certain gender stereotypes by highlighting the 'natural' differences between 'normal' boys and girls – boys struggle with dance and sass, while girl fliers rely on their strength to catch them. In contrast to the literature on men in feminized spaces (Bemiller 2005) where women tended to subordinate themselves to men, here there is a hint that boys are being patronized by offering them 'safe' roles and 'putting them at the back of the dance'. This may also be a way of delineating feminine and masculine roles within the sport so that there is still a segregation of gender roles within the mixed-sex activity.

However, Melinda also highlights opportunities created by this mixed-sex team to break away from traditional norms when the girls encourage the boys to enact their less 'hetero' identities. Boys are encouraged to do 'sass' but this is managed carefully by defining it as a competition amongst the boys rather than with the girls in the team. Melinda's delight in her strength, musculature and athleticism is also similarly tempered by the reference to cheerleading women holding the reputation of being the best-looking girls. In this narrative therefore, there is some evidence of a shift away from valuing hegemonic masculinities and hyper-femininities but in careful and cautious ways that do not radically upset gender boundaries.

Melinda's narrative also highlights the different ways in which the activity is positioned by those 'inside' or 'outside' the sport. Melinda herself has moved from viewing it as a 'silly girly' activity to acknowledge it as a serious, difficult and dangerous one. The tension between her experiences in the sport compared to its reputation as a women's activity comes across when she advances it as suitable for women who do not like to appear 'sporty' even if it is physically more demanding than many other traditional sports.

Richard: I had a bit of a dare with my friend during Fresher's Week – he would do pole dancing if I did cheerleading! So I signed up for it, went to the taster sessions, and we got on well. It would have been different if we'd gone there and been put down or told we weren't good enough, but they were very welcoming.

In our team there are five guys and about 20 girls. I guess we share most of the same challenges as the girls, 'cause we're all putting in 100%. With co-eds we're meant to be able to do larger, more difficult stunts. It's the back base's job mainly to take the brunt of the weight. But there are two girls who main base because they've been doing it for years. They have the experience over the strength. But a lot of it's about getting the right timing. There's a lot of trust between single basers and fliers. As a base you do get hit in the face quite a lot. One flier is notorious for her elbows. Her base got hit in the face with her elbows and broke his nose! But he carried on. We're men! A little bit of hurt doesn't matter.

The amount of time is a factor. You have to be very dedicated because you know that if you miss sessions, then your team can't do the stunts and you can't practice a routine properly, so you (not) being there affects the whole team...it makes me worry some times.

The thing I enjoy the most about co-ed cheerleading is getting to know the girls and making some absolutely amazing friends. And having the lads there as well, just makes it even funnier. Like when we're doing the dances and you get some crazy thing that a guy just shouldn't do, but you have to do it anyway 'cause it's part of the dance, like slope dropping, when you bend forwards with your legs apart and then kind of wiggle your arse, or chest bumping. They made us do a bit of poms, which was embarrassing but fun... we were a couple of guys in the middle, throwing around poms! Of course we made it look better, but... you know, some things which a guy naturally wouldn't do. You look like a fool doing it, but it's fun anyway. And I'd rather be embarrassed than let my team down.

The guys' kit is a skin-tight top with black jogging bottoms. For the girls it's probably sparkly, they always have the shiny bows with gems on them. The girls like us to have sparkle stuff on us. Like at competitions, we're under a little bit of peer pressure by the girls...you end up with a star on your face, and you start thinking 'maybe I shouldn't do that' but as soon as it's happened it's just a laugh 'cause you're with the team. The more confident your team looks doing stunts, you get more points. That's why you always see the fliers with massive smiles – don't show you're scared, face your fears inside! But the bases have to be more focused on the stunts and getting the flier up there. So the bases don't really have to smile.

It feels like co-ed teams run a lot smoother than all-girl. No disrespect to all-girl, but when you watch them they look a lot more difficult to organise. Whereas in co-ed, things get done faster. And we do harder stunts.

There's the whole stereotype of 'Wow, you do cheerleading, you must be gay, or something' and I feel that can demoralise some people. My friends back home take the piss out of me...I don't really care. The girls are like 'just tell 'em you get to grab a girl's arse everyday!' It's a great sport to interlink boys and girls. Some girls might not enjoy it as much because they're uncomfortable with a guy having to say, grab their hips, or push up from their bottom, or something like that. Recently we caught one of the girls very awkwardly, let's say, and she was like 'don't worry, I'd rather you catch me'. She was very relaxed about it. Overall I think it's a great sport to involve both sexes together.

Richard's narrative like Melinda's, reports on the labour that goes into making men feel welcome in the feminized arena. He acknowledges the vulnerability that he and the other boys in the team felt at the beginning, echoing Melinda's view that a supportive team and management was crucial in attracting and keeping them within the activity.

Richard expresses some views that seem more aligned with hegemonic masculinity and even sexism. He looks down on all-girl teams as they appear less 'organised' to him. He also believes that co-ed teams try far riskier stunts. These views may well be a way of exhibiting a masculine identity within a mixed-sex team, a way of empowering himself even as he finds himself moving away from the power conferred by hegemonic masculinity.

Richard is vocal about the respect he holds for girls as well as boys within his team – the strength, experience, technique and hard work required from all, irrespective of gender. His understanding of the 'cheer face' is also interesting – to him, this is not just about smiling, all 'teeth and gums', as the girls are usually instructed, but about keeping a 'brave' face while pushing one's body to try risky stunts. In this, he valorizes aspects like smiling at judges as an important part of displaying courage in the face of danger, rather than associating it with a sexist performative element that has been argued as reason not to count cheerleading as a 'sport' (Sailors 2014). At the same time, he sees this (the smiling) as something that bases, and hence men, can be exempt from.

Richard's narrative highlights how he learnt to perform some less hegemonic masculinities, even while retaining some of the more hegemonic features. His forays at departing from normative masculinity are a direct result of the mixed-sex nature of the teams. He makes several references to how he has moved on to display 'unusual' behaviour like slope dropping and adding sparkles and stars to his facial make-up because there was 'peer pressure' from the women.

Echoing the literature reviewed in Bemiller (2005), Richard acknowledges the perceptions of the sport as a feminized one from the outside world and how (male) participants' sexuality can become a point of discussion. While this causes some embarrassment, he deflects it by playing up a false, sexist identity to the world outside while internally focusing on prioritizing 'the team'. His experience of less hegemonic exhibitions of masculinity starkly contrasts with his boasts of a more hegemonic, heterosexual and even sexist identity to the world outside. The strong team bonds between men and women are obvious in the 'tell them you get to grab a girl's arse everyday' advice from the women who quite clearly do not see the sport or their relationships with the men in the team in this light. Overall, there is a strong sense that there are two worlds – one within and one outside the cheerleading team – and those male cheerleaders in particular feel they need to manage their reputations with those outside in a way that bears little resemblance to the relationships between the sexes within the team. His ability to identify more strongly with his team than with the world outside – 'I'd rather be embarrassed than let down the team' – allows him to remain a member of the team against public censure or ridicule.

Richard's value as a dependable team member also comes across in his commitment to the training regime and his worries that he may be letting the team down if he cannot make training. He also suggests that the men and women in the team stay professional and trust each other to understand their roles – when there is 'awkward' touching, for example. In these examples, the ways in which he elevates 'the team' over allegiance to gender norms and hegemonic displays suggests an awareness that he has 'changed' or 'grown' in ways that those outside the team cannot comprehend.

Carrie: I wanted to try something new at uni, so I went for Cheerleading – stunt cheerleading. In terms of the difference between dance and stunt cheering, I suppose the dance team just dances and they have pompoms. And the stunt team is more the throwing-people-in-the-air-sort-of-thing. It's harder than I thought it would be, especially because I am a base and you really need strength for that. I love cheerleading for those moments when everything clicks, when the stunts work. It's more exciting than dance. It's very risky, no matter how much you practice, it may or may not gel, and with four people, even if one person does something wrong, it will fail.

I tried to be a flier for about a week but I really didn't like being up on top… didn't like putting that much trust into the bases. And as long as you build up your strength, you don't really need to be big or tall to be a base. So we do a lot of training – there's no point going to the gym and lifting weights cause it's completely different to lifting people – so just have to constantly drill the stunts and get used to the technique. It's a lot of technique as well as strength. Training's about 3 sessions per week and each lasts two hours. We tried fewer sessions last year but it wasn't enough, so we've upped it this year.

We work in groups of four – two bases, a back spot and a flier. It's currently an all girl team. Last year we did have boys but this year we decided to go it with just girls and we actually did better in the competitions. We're just competing against other university teams (this year) but last year we also entered the national division. We usually have about 90 people join in the first weeks, after a few weeks, it's about 45 who still are competing for just 25 spaces on the squad, so it's pretty intense and competitive.

It was good when we had the boys on our squad but because it isn't their 'first' sport, they weren't dedicated (enough). They were essentially footballers who were helping us out. And then we realized that they weren't actually helping that much. And only two of the American footballers came back to help out this year, so we decided it's not going to work with boys. We finally realized that actually some of the girls are just as strong if not stronger. We've even got girls who won't be fliers, but who can obviously fly and are actually really, really good. I think there are a lot of people who sort of 'flip' it – like have some of the bigger girls in the air and thinner girls basing.

At the same time, we also need to work on our 'cheer faces'. Everyone has to look like they're enjoying themselves otherwise you don't score well. Boys find this quite hard to do. Some think it's really girly and not very sporty. They just think we shake our pompoms. Once they see us perform in person, then they change their opinion. They say, 'Oh, I didn't realize that's actually what you did' – they just thought we sort of run around. Injuries are actually a big part of the sport – I've hurt my ankles, nothing major but we've had people having stitches in hospital and all sorts!

Carrie's narrative is perhaps the most progressive, feminist voice of all participants. Her realizations that cheerleading was not the *first sport* for the boys, that this made them less *dedicated*, that the boys were *not helping that much* and that *we finally realised that the girls are just as strong, if not stronger'* is a contrast to the other narratives which focus much more on the need to encourage and attract men to their teams. Perhaps the trenchant tone is a result of trying to get dependable mixed-sex teams and failing. Although she reiterates the stereotype that boys find it hard to work on their 'cheer face', she phrases this in a way that suggests that this could lead to lower scores and that therefore they are better off as an all-girl team.

Carrie's insistence that they did better in the competitions 'with just girls' is a contrast to Richard's belief that all-girl teams can look a bit disorganized. Her own experience as a slightly built person who acts as a base gives credibility to her statement that 'you don't really need to be big or tall to be a base'. By focusing on the 'strength' elements of cheerleading, Carrie is openly challenging gender and size norms – 'have some of the bigger girls in the air and the thinner girls basing'. Her idea that these roles and stereotypes can be 'flipped' goes against what might be considered gender and size legitimate behaviour. That she prefers basing when she could be a flier also flies against conventional feminine desires to be the lithe body pinging in the limelight. It is striking that this rejection of cheerleading's association with the hyper-feminine is largely possible *because* of the absence of male masculinities in the team. The idea that mixed-sex stunt-based cheerleading may actually serve to reinforce hegemonic masculinities and hyper-femininities is thus nascent in her narrative.

Perhaps this is also why Carrie is much more critical of the dance version – *'they just dance and have pompoms'*. This allows her to reinforce the 'seriousness' of stunt-based cheerleading, which is particularly pertinent as Carrie is acutely aware of the societal perception of *all* cheerleading varieties as being somewhat frivolous and 'girly'. Carrie's narrative is also slightly different in that while she believes that team work is crucial, she does not downplay the competitiveness of getting into the squad (45 competitors for 25 spaces). The theme of the squad trying hard to accommodate newcomers or behaving like a tightly knit 'family' is conspicuous by its absence.

The potential and pitfalls of mixed-sex cheerleading

The suggestion that by emphasizing 'teamwork and complementary skills' mixed-sex teams serve a beneficial and an educational purpose (Francis1993) is borne out to some modest measure in these narratives. In particular, the emergence of the team as the superseding concept, at times attracting greater allegiance than one's gender role or performance, is an interesting and encouraging finding. All three narratives dwell on the importance of team identity, reliance and interdependence between teammates irrespective of gender. Regular team practice and hard work is emphasized as essential to team success. Richard's worries about letting his team down (if he cannot make every practice session), Melinda's quote about there being no room for 'cliques' and Carrie's insistence that it is more important to have reliable teammates irrespective of gender reinforce this elevation of team roles and identification with the team. In traditional single-sex sports, the success of the team is often regarded as the single most important measure of success. It is interesting then that this concept works similarly in mixed-gender teams and emerges as a vehicle through which gender can be negotiated, challenged and at times superseded.

It also seems as if Francis (1993) hope for mixed-sex teams as an educational vehicle to learn to value/grow 'complementary' skills in the different genders is exceeded in the case of Carrie, whose experience of 'flipping' roles goes beyond gender role complementarity.

Channon notes that when gender is no longer the guiding framework for behaviour in mixed-gender sports, it '…opens opportunities for the construction of a diversity of alternative gendered practices, shaped by novel experiences of male and female bodies that do not conform to the essentialist categories productive of an immutable sexual hierarchy' (2013: 1294). It would seem that in Carrie's narrative, the novel experience of being a base gives her a new embodied understanding of herself and replaces her previous understanding of gender-appropriate roles. While an example of men and women flipping gender roles between them would be an undeniably better case of gender role transgression, Carrie's and her team's realization of the false understanding of the limits of what women can do within their sport is still a progressive outcome. And on the other hand, the dangers of reinforcing male- and female-specific roles within the team are evident in Richard's and Melinda's narratives when they insist on different tasks and roles for men and women (e.g. basing or smiling) and ensure that the boundary between the genders remains unthreatened.

It is true that there are some significant benefits from the non-segregation of genders in cheerleading – learning to break away from traditional gender norms, respecting the different roles of teammates irrespective of gender, leaning on a team ethic to combat social embarrassment or ridicule, etc. Cheerleading too, can and does offer participants the opportunity to explore fluid gender identities in mixed-gender teams and Melinda exulting in her musculature, Carrie 'flipping' gender and size norms and Richard trying slope dropping and sparkly make-up are examples of this. However, the portraits also suggest that, while there is considerable potential to challenge conventional gender roles, the mere existence of mixed-sex teams cannot be a panacea to gender inequality in sports.

It seems that, on the deeper issue of challenging heteronormativity, the picture is far more patchy. The silence over alternative sexualities for both men and women or the impact these can have on relationships between the sexes and on the sport itself, suggests that there is greater room for improvement. The observation by Anderson (2005b) that increasing inclusive masculinity amongst heterosexual male cheerleaders in the US could be attributable to their relationships with women *and* gay men as teammates is thus only partly reinforced in this study. Without the influence of men and women of non-heterosexualities, the danger of the sport to slip into endorsing essentialized roles for the genders is real. Hence, it is possible to read Carrie's experience in her team of 'flipping' size and gender norms, not as a result of having been a part of a mixed-sex team but because it failed, leading women to experiment with traditional male roles.

The portraits give a sense of the complex and varied gender positionings that the participants are both 'given' and adopt. As discourses are not 'tight boxes with neat boundaries', 'one and the same "dance" can get recognized in multiple ways, in partial ways, in contradictory ways, in disputed ways, in negotiable ways and so on and so forth …' (Gee 2008). It seems that the multiple discourses of C/cheerleading offer different and contradictory meanings of being a male or female participant in the sport and this is reflected in the portraits themselves. Participants at times conform to and at other times resist conventional notions of gender, much like Anderson's (2005b) findings. What is interesting perhaps are the ways in which mixed-gender cheerleading teams function to allow these contradictions to coexist and be justified as a way of managing the expectations of a normative world outside of cheerleading rather than as indisputable lived truths.

The awareness of the dangers of not conforming to a conservative social context seems to weigh heavily in all three portraits. The stigma and social pressures that young people experience as coming from outside the sporting field has been observed as a factor in determining participation in sports (Gorely, Holroyd, and Kirk 2003). Coaches and trainers perhaps find it easier to use such gender stereotype rather than challenge them. Efforts to increase male participation, and thus legitimize this as a sport for men ('there's nothing gay about it'), as well as using cheerleading's feminized image to promote it as a 'less masculine' sport for young women are both fraught with dangers as they fall back on heteronormative discourses that essentialize the genders while claiming to be inclusive (Lamb and Priyadharshini 2013). As long as cheerleading continues to be promoted by tying it to essentialized, gendered and heteronormative performances, by cheerleaders and coaches and PE teachers, its transformative potential cannot be realized.

As majority players in a feminized sport, female cheerleaders and the coaches seemed to labour hard to attract, support and retain male cheerleaders and boost their heterosexual identities. Richard's and Melinda's narratives point out the efforts of 'welcoming' potential male cheerleaders. While there may be advantages in this for new male participants, the benefits to women in the sport are less clear. While popular culture and media portrayals may not be particularly helpful in undoing essentialist notions of gender when it comes to cheerleading, there remains room for coaches, trainers, teachers and professional associations to address how the activity is being promoted in schools and universities. This is an issue that the main cheerleading associations as well as the UK university sports bodies need to address in an explicit manner.

There can also be greater encouragement for gender fluidity if cheerleading rules are more explicit about expectations from both genders and roles in the team. For instance, Richard's and Melinda's claims that bases do not need to smile or that the burden of showing 'sass' and 'cheer' falls mainly on the women in the team does not help. Anderson (2005b) shows how influential cheerleading associations can be in terms of encouraging particular types of gender identity and performance in the US. It seems imperative for the UK governing bodies then, to consider how they can shape the sport in socially progressive ways.

Implications and future directions

This paper used the espoused promise of mixed-sex sports, in its possible pedagogical role to counter to the lessons of segregated activities as a starting point to explore mixed-sex cheerleading in the UK university context. In the process, it has thrown up some unexpected avenues for research and intervention. The hopes pinned on mixed-sex sports to deliver socially progressive lessons for gender roles and relations seem to rest on vague assumptions that mixed-sex sport experiences ought to be transformative in nature and that the beneficial lessons of working with the opposite sex either for training or in competitive teams may then transfer to other social worlds beyond sport. These assumptions need unpicking and exploring with empirical research that explicitly focuses on sport – whether through athletic participation, audience participation, as cultural phenomenon or as media discourse – as an educational medium that imparts 'gender pedagogies', ie it functions as a teaching and learning context for 'lessons' on gender.

The questions about how far the potential of mixed-sex sporting activity to destabilize older norms and bring forth new relations between the genders can be realized, and whether this can result in positive changes for both the sport and for wider notions of gender itself can be better answered by research that looks at the terms and conditions under which gender is learnt and performed in varying contexts and activities. In the absence of such a critical educational focus, the field of gender studies in sport loses an important lever through which policy and practice can be argued to need change in socially progressive ways.

An analysis of the narratives presented here suggests that while there is potential to fulfil the promise of mixed-sex cheerleading, the practice of it is also laden with pitfalls. Mixed-sex cheerleading remains a site in which some gender norms are challenged and others reinforced. The organization and promotion of the sport and its reputation with the world external to cheerleading need to be managed more radically if its potential for gender inclusivity is to be fully met. The combination of the pressure of social perceptions of a sport, its gender status, context, history, structure and rules that define it, form formidable obstacles to the easy or quick realization of hopes for shifting traditional gender hierarchies simply by mixing the gender composition of an activity.

Disclosure statement

No potential conflict of interest was reported by the authors.

References

Adams, A. 2011. "Josh Wears Pink Cleats: Inclusive Masculinity on the Soccer Field." *Journal of Homosexuality* 58 (5): 579–596.

Adams, L. 2005. "Death to the Prancing Prince: Effeminacy." *Sport Discourses, and the Salvation of Men's Dancing', Body and Society* 11: 63–86.

Adams, N., and P. Bettis. 2003. "Commanding the Room in Short Skirts Cheering as the Embodiment of Ideal Girlhood." *Gender & Society* 17 (1): 73–91.

Adams, N. G., and P. J. Bettis. 2005. *Cheerleader! an American Icon*. New York, NY: Palgrave/ Macmillan.

Anderson, E. 2009. *Inclusive Masculinity: The Changing Nature of Masculinities*. New York, NY: Routledge.

Anderson, E. 2008. "I Used to Think Women Were Weak: Orthodox Masculinity, Gender Segregation, and Sport." *Sociological Forum* 23 (2): 257–280.

Anderson, E. 2005a. *In the Game: Gay Athletes and the Cult of Masculinity*. New York, NY: State University of New York Press.

Anderson, E. 2005b. "Orthodox and Inclusive Masculinity: Competing Masculinities among Heterosexual Men in a Feminized Terrain." *Sociological Perspectives* 48: 337–355.

Barkham, P. 2010. "Why Cheerleading is Booming in Britain's Schools." *The Guardian*. October 6. http://www.guardian.co.uk/education/2010/oct/06/cheerleading-is-boomingin-schools

Bemiller, M. 2005. "Men Who Cheer." *Sociological Focus* 38 (3): 205–222.

Bettis, P., and N. Adams. 2006. "Short Skirts and Breast Juts: Cheerleading, Eroticism and Schools." *Sex Education* 6 (2): 121–133.

Cahn, S. 1994. *Coming on Strong: Gender and Sexuality in Twentieth-century Women's Sport*. London: Harvard University Press.

Caudwell, J. 2003. "Sporting Gender: Women's Footballing Bodies as Sites/Sights for the (Re) Articulation of Sex, Gender, and Desire." *Sociology of Sport Journal* 20 (4): 371–386.

Channon, A. 2013. "Enter the Discourse: Exploring the Discursive Roots of Inclusivity in Mixed-sex Martial Arts." *Sport in Society* 16 (10): 1293–1308.

Chimot, C., and C. Louveau. 2010. "Becoming a Man While Playing a Female Sport: The Construction of Masculine Identity in Boys Doing Rhythmic Gymnastics." *International Review for the Sociology of Sport* 45 (4): 436–456.

Choi, P. 2000. *Femininity and the Physically Active Woman*. London: Routledge.

Clough, P. 2002. *Narratives and Fictions in Educational Research*. Buckingham: Open University Press.

Connell, R. 1995. *Masculinities*. Cambridge: Polity Press.

Crossett, T. 1990. "Masculinity, Sexuality, and the Development of Early Modern Sport." In *Sport, Men, and the Gender Order: Critical Feminist Perspectives*, edited by Michael A. Messner and Donald F. Sabo, 45–54. Champaign, 111: Human Kinetics Publishers.

Dunning, E. 1994. "Sport as a Male Preserve: Notes on the Social Sources of Masculine Identity and Its Transformations." In *Women, Sport and Culture*, edited by S. Birrell and C. Cole, 163–179. Human Kinetics: Leeds.

Dworkin, S., and M. Messner. 2002. "Just Do What…? Sport, Bodies and Gender." In *Gender and Sport: A Reader*, edited by S. Scraton and A. Flintoff, 17–29. London: Routledge.

Francis, L. 1993. "Title IX: Equality for Women's Sports?" *Journal of the Philosophy of Sport* 20 (1): 32–47.

Gee, J. 2008. *Ideology in Discourses*. London: Routledge.

Gorely, T., R. Holroyd, and D. Kirk. 2003. "Muscularity, the Habitus and the Social Construction of Gender: Towards a Gender-Relevant Physical Education." *British Journal of Sociology of Education* 24: 429–448.

Grindstaff, L., and E. West. 2010. "Hands on Hips, Smiles on Lips! Gender, Race, and the Performance of Spirit in Cheerleading." *Text and Performance Quarterly* 30 (2): 143–162.

Hargreaves, J. 1994. *Sport Females: Critical Issues in the History and Sociology of Women's Sports*. London: Routledge.

Jarvis, N. 2013. "The Inclusive Masculinities of Heterosexual Men within UK Gay Sport Clubs." *International Review for the Sociology of Sport*. 1–18.

Lamb, P., and E. Priyadharshini. 2013. "The Conundrum of C/Cheerleading." *Sport, Education and Society* 20 (7): 889–907. doi:10.1080/13573322.2013.852080.

Matteo, S. 1986. "The Effect of Sex and Gender-Schematic Processing on Sport Participation." *Sex Roles* 15 (7-8): 417–432.

McDonagh, E., and L. Pappano. 2008. *Playing with the Boys: Why Separate is Not Equal in Sports*. Oxford: Oxford University Press.

Messner, M. 2002. *Taking the Field: Women, Men and Sports*. Minneapolis: University of Minnesota Press.

Messner, M. 1988. "Sports and Male Domination: The Female Athlete as Contested Ideological Terrain." *Sociology of Sport Journal* 5: 197–211.

Miller, Shane Aaron 2010. "Making the Boys Cry: The Performative Dimensions of Fluid Gender." *Text and Performance Quarterly* 30 (2): 163–182.

Moritz, A. 2011. "Cheerleading: Not Just for the Sidelines Anymore." *Sport in Society* 14 (5): 660–669.

Paechter, C. 2006. "Masculine Femininities/Feminine Masculinities: Power, Identities and Gender." *Gender and Education* 18 (3): 253–263.

Sailors, P. 2014. "Mixed Competition and Mixed Messages." *Journal of the Philosophy of Sport* 41 (1): 65–77.

Smith, B., and A. Sparkes. 2009. "Narrative Inquiry in Sport and Exercise Psychology: What Can It Mean, and Why Might We Do It?" *Psychology of Sport and Exercise* 10 (1): 1–11.

Tagg, B. 2008. "Imagine, a Man Playing Netball!: Masculinities and Sport in New Zealand." *International Review for the Sociology of Sport* 43 (4): 409–430.

Theberge, N. 1989. "Women's Athletics and the Myth of Female Frailty." In *Women: A Feminist Perspective*, edited by J. Freeman, 507–522. Palo Alto, CA: Mayfield.

The lived experience of sex-integrated sport and the construction of athlete identity within the Olympic and Paralympic equestrian disciplines

Donna de Haan[a], Popi Sotiriadou[b] and Ian Henry[c]

[a]International Sports, Management and Business, Amsterdam University of Applied Sciences, Amsterdam, Netherlands; [b]Department of Tourism, Sport and Hotel Management, Griffith University, Southport, Australia; [c]Centre of Olympic Studies, Loughborough University, Loughborough, England

ABSTRACT

Equestrian sport is not subjected to the dominant binary sex segregation of most sports and therefore provides a unique opportunity to review how athlete 'identity' is constructed and framed within a sex-integrated sporting experience. This research draws on an ethnographic evaluation of the Olympic and Paralympic experience of the British Equestrian Team. A total of 28 interviews were conducted with riders, performance managers and support staff with transcripts subjected to Ethnographic Content Analysis. Results show clear constructs of identity, such as 'them and us', 'horsey' and 'discipline specific', with a noted absence of gender in the way interviewees describe themselves and others within the sport. Furthermore, in their accounts of their lives, there is a lack of salience of gender with regard to their identity as sports persons. The paper considers the implications of this phenomenon for a claim that equestrian sport might be described from a participant's perspective as gender neutral.

Introduction

Sport is increasingly acknowledged as a powerful cultural institution, strongly linked to identity and ideology, which routinely and systematically creates and reinforces the ideology of male superiority and often resists the inclusion of women (Mean 2001). The intertextuality of sport and war reinforces this male–female division, positioning the sports field as the equivalent of a battle field (Dunning 1999) in which athletes are powerful and aggressive, with bodies characterized as weapons or tools (Jansen and Sabo 1994). Indeed, Messner (2002) describes sport, especially modern sport, in its ideal form as a cultural artefact and social institution, which celebrates the supremacy of a particular culture through the representation of the ideal human as manifested in the athletic competitor engaging in ritualized combat (Messner 2002). The ideal weapon of combat with which the 'warrior' vanquishes his opponent is the athlete's body. The greater the reliance on the athlete's body for victory and the more interactive the game activity, the higher the status of the sport and its competitors. Hence, traditional 'male' contact sports, such as rugby, football or field hockey, are considered 'real' sports in ways that car racing, sailing and equine sports such as polo are not (Merlini 2004). It is interesting to note however that the terminology used to support the definition of 'real' sport, such as 'warrior', 'combat' and 'male', is indeed synonymous with military roots of equestrian sports (De Haan 2015).

The inclusion and development of equestrian sport within the modern Olympics was at the time dominated by military influences and whilst this has dissipated over time, it remains the only Olympic sport today in which athletes can compete in military attire (De Haan 2015). The historical relationship between man and horse in warfare has undoubtedly emerged from a male-dominated landscape and this is reflected in the gendered nature of some equestrian sports. Up until the 1952 Olympics in Helsinki, only male riders were permitted to compete in any Olympic equestrian discipline. In 1952, women were allowed to compete only in Dressage; in 1956, Showjumping was opened to female competitors; and in 1964, they were finally allowed to compete in the military-dominated Eventing competition (Hedenborg 2009). Men and women have however always competed against each other in Para-Equestrian Dressage, since its inclusion in the 1996 Atlanta Games.

Gender bias against the participation of women has been implicit in the history of the Olympic Movement. According to Borish (1996) the 'Olympic Games provide a rich and dense arena for understanding women's gains in autonomy and physical emancipation, as well as constraints of their quest for equality in athletic performance'. Indeed within the context of the Olympic Games today, there remains only one class of sailing and the three equestrian disciplines in which men and women can compete equally against each other. The contemporary justification for binary sex segregation of sport is based on a complex mix of factors including biological, economical and commercial arguments, combined with social norms which continue to frame sport in a male domain (Foddy and Savulescu 2011). Hargreaves (2002) explains that the historical justification for segregating sport was built around the ideas of sexual difference and the belief in the unsuitability of sport and physical activity for girls and women. Whilst mixed-gender participation can be viewed as a currency of equality, it can also be seen as a violation of social gender expectations concerning the normative gender behaviour of athletes. If masculine and athletic identities are a function of how a man 'measures up' in the eyes of other males (Messner 1995; Sabo and Runfola 1980), according to Merlini (2004), the equal 'playing field' with female athletes questions whether male athletes are 'real' men.

Bodies and physical differences are indeed at the very centre of sport since it is based on a system which systematically reveals differences and establishes a ranking based on the individual's performance (Pfister 2010). Discussions on sport and gender are often focused on the physicality or the performance aspect of sport which highlights the differences between the sexes based on the biological and socially constructed gender order in society. However, as Dashper (2012a) explains, in the context of equestrian sport, there are no sex-based biological advantages for either males or females, 'masculine sporting abilities such as speed and strength are less significant … strength of a rider plays a role, but this is limited as within the equestrian partnership the horse will always be the stronger partner'. Indeed to truly compare the gendered physicality of equestrian sport against other sports, we must define the physicality we are referring to. For example, within the Olympic discipline of Dressage, the first of the disciplines to allow female competitors or the Paralympic discipline of Para-Equestrian Dressage, scoring and hence placing are based on the quality of the horse's individual required movements. Therefore, correct training is rewarded within the scoring system and the gender of the rider is negligible, as it is the physical performance of the horse, rather than the human athlete who is judged (De Haan 2015). Equestrian sport offers an opportunity to review the phenomenon of sex integration in sport, presents a sporting arena in which normative conceptions of sex difference might be challenged, and provides an interesting lens through which the formation of athlete identity can be viewed.

Gendered discourse in equestrian sport

In Western societies, the accepted cultural perspective on gender views women and men as naturally and unequivocally defined categories of being with distinctive psychological and behavioural propensities that can be predicted from their reproductive functions (Garfinkel 1967). West and Zimmerman (1987) explain that competent adult members of these societies see differences between the genders as fundamental and enduring 'differences seemingly supported by the division of labour into women's and men's work and an often elaborate differentiation of feminine and masculine attitudes and behaviours that are prominent features of social organisations'. The traditional gendered structure of sport reflects the wider gendered social order, divisions perceived to be rooted in biology, producing in turn profound psychological, behavioural and social consequences. As Pfister (2010) explains, discussions concerning gender and sport generally cover topics on the differences between the sexes and biological aspects. Other key areas discussed include the cultural aspect of being a woman/man, which is important because 'it opened people's eyes not only to the great diversity and multiplicity of gender but also to the socially constructed gender order in our society'. This approach highlights that gender is not something we have or we are but something we present, we do.

As previously discussed the relevance of the rider's sex is unimportant in Olympic equestrian sport, as it is the physical performance of the horse, rather than the human athlete who is judged. However, this is not to say that within the context of Olympic experience the athlete's sex has not historically been seen as a differentiating factor. When Norma Matthews joined the USA Showjumping team in 1950, press coverage at the time appeared to describe a beauty pageant contestant rather than an international athlete, describing her as 'a pretty blue-eyed blonde, 5'6½", 125 pounds' (Burke 1997). Some 18 years later, Jane Bullen faced similar reference in the press when she rode for the USA Eventing team at the 1968 Olympics when she was often referred to as 'Nurse Jane Bullen'. Although she was at the time training to be a nurse, the inclusion of a typically constructed gender role emphasizes the social and dynamic aspect of role construction and enactment. As 'roles' are situated identities, assumed and relinquished as the situation demands (West and Zimmerman 1987), reference to Bullen's feminine career, one may argue, detracts from her identity as an athlete.

At the time, the riders themselves also used gendered discourse when discussing their sport. For example, Lis Hartel, twice individual Dressage silver medallist (1954, 1956), suffered from polio which affected the ligaments behind her knees, weakening and distorting the lower leg to the extent where she couldn't mount or dismount a horse without assistance. Hartel had ridden prior to the polio and was determined to continue in the sport:

> I restarted my riding in dressage competitions winning the Nordic riding games in '51. My efforts were crowned with a silver medal in 1952. It was the first time a woman had competed

equally with men in the equestrian games, and this really brought my name to the limelight worldwide, because not only was it a woman, but a handicapped woman! (Burke 1997, 67)

During the 1956 Equestrian Olympics in Stockholm, the second time Dressage had been open to female competitors, commentary was laden with masculine and feminine reference. Hedenborg (2009) explains that one Swedish newspaper at the time reported the following, 'Lis Hartel as well as Liselotte Linsenhoff showed such gentleness, grace and flexibility that they made several of their male competitors seem too strict'. Indeed the success of the female Dressage riders, who secured individual silver and bronze, with the German team, consisting of all female riders taking team silver, caused an outcry from experts and the press. The subjective scoring system present in Dressage was thought by some to favour the women because of their femininity. The Swedish gold medallist Henri St Cyr believed that the standard of women's Dressage was so high they should have their own Dressage competition (Hedenborg 2009). This statement highlights the concern at the time that mixed-gender sport was merely acceptable in the context of masculine supremacy.

Henri St Cyr comments regarding the call for women to compete separately, supports the notion of the separating principle. Indeed, Hirdman (1990) defines gender systems using either the hierarchal principle which places masculinity as the norm, or the separating principle which emphasizes that masculinity and femininity have to be kept apart. According to Hedenborg (2009), the media coverage of the 1956 Equestrian Olympics can also be explained by Hirdman's (1990) gender system's separating principle. Yet, despite this early call for separation, equestrian sport remained integrated.

Integrating men and women in physical activity settings such as competitive sports, stands against much of the traditional conception of masculinity and femininity underpinning hierarchal sex discourse (Anderson 2008). In their study reviewing gendered discourses in English flat racing, Roberts and MacLean (2012) discussed how women faced discrimination in the sport based on five main themes; a culture of sexism, including the sense that women are more nurturing; the provision and actualization of opportunities, including for women to become trainers; the impact of risk and danger; the impact of differences in body shape and strength; and finally, a sense of industry fashion and trends. Whilst in a recent analysis of gender construction in the Swedish media coverage of equestrian sport at the 2012 Olympics, Hellborg and Hedenborg (2015) concluded that many of the media narratives about male and female riders did not challenge the gender order.

As outlined so far in this paper, we have discussed how equestrian sport in the Olympic context began in a male military-dominated landscape and we have specifically looked at gendered discourse in relation to sex integration in equestrian competition. In the following section, we begin to unpack how sex integration in sport does not simply equate to participatory parity.

Sex integration and participatory parity in equestrian sport

Whilst in this study we are specifically addressing the lived experience of equestrian athletes at the elite level of Olympic and Paralympic competition, it is important to place this sporting experience within the wider gendered context of equestrian sport in general. Participatory parity in equestrian sport is essential to help understand sex integration. Fraser (2007) argued that parity necessitates 'the condition of being a peer, of being on a par with others, of interacting with them on an equal footing'. According to Dashper (2012a), equestrian

Table 1. Participation rates in equestrian events over six Olympic Games.

	Dressage			Showjumping			Eventing			Total		
	M	F	Total	M	F	Total	M	F	Total	M	F	Total
1952	20	4	24	51	0	51	59	0	59	130	4	134
1956	28	9	37	68	5	70	56	1	57	152	12	164
1960	12	5	17	68	3	71	73	0	73	153	8	161
Mean	20	6	26	62	2	64	63	0	63	145	8	153
2000	23	25	48	62	12	74	59	23	82	134	70	204
2004	24	28	52	66	11	77	52	23	75	142	62	204
2008	19	28	47	61	16	77	42	28	70	122	72	194
Mean	22	27	49	63	13	76	51	25	76	133	68	201

sport offers the conditions for equality of participation for both men and women at all levels of the sport, including the elite level. However, she suggested that 'subtle discrimination and hidden barriers combine to produce a glass ceiling effect at the top levels of the sport, denying many women participatory parity in relation to their male peers'. Sex integration does not necessarily equate to participatory parity. Therefore in this section, whilst we review gendered participation rates at an elite level, we also discuss broader changing patterns of participation at sub-elite level.

In Dumbell and de Haan's (2012) comparison of athlete profiles over 50 years of Olympic equestrian events, the authors present analysis of participation at six Olympics (Table 1).

Analysis of the gender patterns among Olympic competitors shows that on average only 5% of equestrian competitors were female in the early years compared to recent games where this figure has increased to 34% (Dumbell and de Haan 2012). At the 2008 Beijing Olympics, women made up 42% of the 11,196 athletes who competed in the games, this figure was closely mirrored in the 37% of female athletes competing in the Equestrian events.

Dumbell and de Haan (2012) outline that across all three disciplines, women were most likely to be competing in Dressage both then and now, but they now form a much greater proportion with 55% of competitors at recent games being female. Hedenborg and White (2012) highlight that it was in 1972 that the participation rate of women competing in Dressage first became higher than that of men. Showjumping, however, is still heavily dominated by male competitors with only 17% of athletes at recent games being female, although this has grown since the meagre 3% in earlier games. Finally, Eventing has seen the largest growth from no female competitors to 33% of the competing athletes now being female (Dumbell and de Haan 2012).

Hedenborg and White (2012) suggest that a likely explanation for the higher number of women in Dressage compared to the other Olympic disciplines is due to the fact that Dressage riding was more compatible with an accepted femininity. Dressage was the focus of Dashper's (2012a) ethnographic study of equestrian sport, in which she discusses notions of femininity and masculinity. Dashper (2012a) highlighted the increasing acceptance of openly gay men within the discipline of Dressage but concluded that:

> Even within equestrian sport, where men and women compete against each other on equal terms and male competitors demonstrate more inclusive forms of masculinity, those masculinities are still constructed in opposition to a devalued femininity, and this will have consequences for the relative value and status of women within the sport.

Despite the fact that to date there are no longer any explicit, formal barriers to participation for females at any level of equestrian sport (within the context of culturally specific gendered sporting access), Travers (2008) notes that this does not simply translate to equality of opportunity. One of the hidden barriers Dashper (2012b) refers to include the combination of gender and class as the following quote from a female young rider suggests:

> It's really hard to get seen, to get noticed, especially with the selectors, because they're very, well, money orientated, and also there's only a few boys and they seem to get all the attention as well. There's so many girls and everything, and the boys just really stand out, I suppose, and they're from very wealthy backgrounds, the boys are, and so they do tend to stand out more and get, you know, first choice of things. (Dashper 2012b, 217)

Dashper (2012b) also identifies and discusses the barrier of 'family'. In a sport where competing at the top doesn't necessarily have a clear retirement age, female riders face the prospect of having to take a career break to start and maintain a family. Dashper (2012b) explains that amongst the riders interviewed, on starting a family, many female riders would opt out of international competition, a requirement at the elite level of the sport, instead opting to focus on family life:

> Many riders marry other riders, and in each case of the three couples I interviewed where this was the case it was the female partner who had scaled back her competition career to concentrate on the domestic side of the horse business (training and horse care), as well as taking the lead in childcare. (Dashper 2012b, 221)

Dashper's (2012b) study focuses on equestrian sport within the UK context and highlights some of the 'hidden' barriers to participation, emphasizing the fact that sex integration doesn't necessarily equate to participatory parity. As a result of reviewing various international studies relating to participation rates in equestrian sport, Adelman and Knijnik (2013) discuss how 'feminisation' of equestrian sport 'has been identified as a world-wide tendency, but with differing degrees of intensity, affect, and effect'. Statistical evidence depicting the phenomenon in equitation is available for certain parts of the world such as France, where equestrian is top of the list of women's sport (Adelman and Knijnik 2013), Sweden, where 84% of all members of the Swedish Equestrian Federation are female (Hedenborg 2007), and the USA, where according to Rice (2003) over 80% of all those involved in field of equestrian are female, and from an international perspective, De Haan (2015) reports that 57% of the athletes represented by the Federation Equestrian International are female.

Whilst in the first part of the twentieth century, equine competition was a masculine domain associated with the military and nobility, Plymoth (2013) explains that within the Swedish context, the second half of the twentieth century saw the feminization of equestrian sport. Whilst the horse was once a status symbol related to men and masculinity, it became mainly considered as an object of female adoration. Feminization of equestrian sport in Sweden occurred around the same time as the emergence of the Swedish welfare state. Indeed, Hedenborg (2007) hypothesizes that the states involvement and hence subsequent development of public policies in relation to equestrian sport may have favoured feminization. Indeed, such is the swing from male to female participation rates in the Swedish context, that Plymoth (2013) discusses 'paths to remasculinisation' of equestrian sport.

Our narrative so far has highlighted that sex integration does not necessarily equate to participatory parity. Indeed, gender is very much present in regard to participation rates as highlighted in the studies by Dumbell and de Haan (2012) and Hedenborg and White (2012) and the associated lived experience of this as highlighted in the findings of Dashper (2012b). Plymoth (2013) describes the issue of feminization of equestrian sport as;

… undeniably interesting and also contradictory when viewed in relation to some of the physical aspects of the sport that would normally be associated with masculinity. There is no doubt that the sport is action filled. It is a matter of mastering a large animal, and there are numerous risks involved in dealing with horses … it is somewhat paradoxical that men are reluctant to ride horses when masculine characteristics such as courage, strength, leadership abilities and competition are doubtless needed on every level.

It appears therefore that the evolution of equestrian sport has provided moments in which normative conceptions of sex difference have been both reaffirmed and challenged. Even within the context of sex-integrated sport, the reference to 'masculinity' or 'feminisation' is a constant reference to a dominant gendered ideology. As Channon (2012) discusses, until we are able to conceive of male and female athletes simply as athletes, who no longer require differentiation based on their sex and who no longer hold differently gendered status, we continue to problematize the labelling of such sporting activity. The literature may suggest that sex-integrated sport remains shaped by conservative gender discourse, which highlights enduring differences between the genders but does the lived experience of participating in sex-integrated sport support this? An important part of experiencing sport is associated with the construct of athlete identity. In the following section, we move on to discuss notions and constructs of athlete identity before analysing the lived experience of this for equestrian athletes.

Notions and constructs of athlete identity

Athletic identity has been defined as 'the degree to which an individual identifies with the athlete role' (Brewer, Van Raalte, and Linder 1993), and has been researched as an extension of self-identity, which is defined as the compilation of self-referent cognitions, emotions and attitudes expressed within various aspects of life (Carver, Reynolds, and Scheier 1994).

Several 'identities' have been discussed in sport-related literature from the perspective of the individual to broader themes such as nationality, race, culture, ethnicity, gender and sexuality. Whilst sport comprises a site which provides a rich source of data about enacted identities, these often arise from intertextual links with other discourses (Lyotard 1984). As previously mentioned, sport is historically and culturally constructed as a male domain and is therefore a highly potent site for the construction of masculine identity. The dominant production of the male identity within sport therefore requires that women be positioned as the 'other'. Mean (2001) explains that positioning the 'other' serves an important sociocognitive function in defining the standard based on a hegemonic need to discriminate between categories and their membership. Social categorization is theoretically linked to many social and cognitive processes including self-concept, social perception, stereotyping and intra- and intergroup behaviours (Hogg and Abrams 1988). The place or context in which these identities are constructed is therefore also a point of discussion, influenced by factors such as sex segregation and the physicality of the sport; however the focus of research relating to sporting identity is primarily associated with the athletes' career progression, for example, from student-athlete identity through to retirement. Within this field, there is a limited amount of literature which discusses the identity of an Olympian or Paralympian or studies which discuss the construct of athlete identity within sex-integrated sports.

Whilst there are several examples of papers which focus on an individual sportsman or sportswoman who have competed in the Olympics or Paralympics, the sport/athletic identity is never the sole focus of the narrative. For example, Knight et al. (2007) and White (2008) discuss Cathy Freeman's cultural identity during the 2000 Olympics in Sydney. Canadian national identity is discussed in reference to the controversy surrounding sprinter Ben Johnson in both Jackson (2004) and Stelzl, Janes, and Seligman (2008) papers. Whilst McNeil (2009) uses the boxer Lennox Lewis as the main protagonist in a narrative wrapped up in issues of Americocentricity, Black identity and masculinity and Amir Kahn's identity as a British Asian boxer and his subsequent identity as a role model is the subject of Burdsey's (2007) paper. In Philips and Osmond's (2009) engaging paper on Australian Swimmer Dawn Fraser, numerous identities are discussed including gender, sexuality and national identity.

Even though a strong identification with the athlete role can have a positive effect on the individual (Brewer, Van Raalte, and Linder 1993), research in athletic identity and gender has produced mixed results. Brewer, Van Raalte, and Linder (1993) found that athletic identity was higher in male than in female athletes and Meyer (1990) argued that female athletes were able to commit equally to both academic and athletic commitments throughout their college career, while males tended to disassociate with their academic commitments after the first year. In contrast, other researchers have found no significant gender interactions with athletic identity (Aries et al. 2004).

It is important to note however that throughout the identified literature there is a distinct lack of an athlete voice within the discourse of athlete identity. The following two examples which also discuss identity in the context of Paralympic experience are the exception. Howe (2008), himself a Paralympian and academic, uses ethnographic data to explore the notion of body culture and the classification system experienced by athletes with disabilities. Howe's (2008) diary extract from his own classification experience at the Seoul Olympics in 1988, is evocative and insightful. He explains how the classification process not only provides parameters associated with his athletic ability, it also places his 'body' in a 'pigeonhole' and is used for non-sport-related issues such as room allocation.

Peers (2009) herself a Paralympian, critically reviews discourses which focus on Paralympic history and Paralympic empowerment, specifically critiquing two publications, 'Paralympics: where heroes come' and 'Athlete first: a history of the Paralympic movement'. In the context of identity, Peers (2009) uses several common nouns to define herself:

> I read the newspaper articles and press releases that others have written about me. I read my own grant applications, speeches and business cards. I read myself defined, in each of these, by one word: not crip, queer, athlete, activist, student, woman or lesbian, but Paralympian. I read my life story transformed into that of *The Paralympian*.

With regard to athlete identity and experience within sex-integrated sport, McDonagh and Pappano (2008) present Aaron Boss' reaction to losing to the female competitor Micheala Hutchinson in the Alaska state wrestling title in the 103 pound division, 'I don't look at it as a loss to a girl. I look at it as a loss to a wrestler'. Here, it is interesting to note the supplemented differentiating gender label with the shared identity of 'wrestler'. Anderson (2008) refers to such a response as an indication of acceptance and respect towards the female athlete and one which neutralizes the negative connotations of this specific loss within the framework of gender hierarchy and masculine identity. 'Losing to a girl' has long been seen as a sign of men's emasculation within traditional Western gender discourse and as such poses a 'powerful challenge to (male) identity' (Miller 2010). However as Channon (2012) explains, being fairly beaten by a fellow athlete is no shameful thing and it therefore stands in male athletes' best interest to accept more equitable de-gendered definitions of female competitors.

Channon (2012) examined the gender-subversive potential of mixed-sex martial arts and concluded that whilst sex-integrated sports have the potential to lead participants towards embodying and propagating such subversive gender discourses, in the context of highly masculinized sports such as combat sports, the significance of this subversion is amplified. Channon (2012) also discussed that the 'normalised' presence of women within multiple levels of participation particularly at higher levels, including coaches and competitors resulted in a shared identity as martial artists regardless of gender difference.

In this section, we have discussed notions of athlete identity, specifically focusing on the constructed identity of those athletes who have competed at an Olympic and Paralympic level and the notion of athlete identity within sex-integrated sports. We have highlighted that research in this area is limited, but we argue that it provides an insightful contribution to understanding the lived experience of these athletes.

Methodology

This study adopts a critical realist ontology and epistemology, and represents part of a wider research project which sought to identify structures in the world of Olympic and Paralympic equestrian sport, the place of this competition in the career histories of these athletes, and the process of social construction and identity formation within these structures. In this context and in regard to understanding the lived experience of these athletes, an ethnographic approach was taken with regard to data collection and analysis. As Krane and Baird explain, 'Ethnography is aimed toward understanding the culture of a particular group from the perspective of the group members. The group culture, then, will lend insight into behaviours, values, emotions, and mental states of group members' (2005, 87). This study specifically focuses on the subworld of elite competitive equestrian sport and as Crosset and Beal (1997) outline, the ethnographic approach to this type of study requires an exploration of the everyday practices, norms, interactions and relationships of those intimately involved in the social and sporting world of equestrianism. Ethnography requires access and time, the primary data collection for this study took place over a period of 18 months, from January 2008 until July 2009, during which time the primary researcher had access to numerous social and sporting situations including training camps, press conferences, quarantine holding camps and Olympic competition.

At this point, it is important to note that whilst the primary researcher has been a competitive horse rider and has worked in the horse industry, she has not competed at elite level nor has she directly worked at elite level within the context of equestrian sport, however, she is well versed in the language of equestrian competition. Whilst not therefore positioning herself as an insider, during the period of data collection the primary researcher became seen as a familiar face within the British Equestrian Team to the point where they were able to have informal conversations with members of the team and conduct participant observations. The participants were aware that the lead author was a researcher collecting data for research purposes. Further to this, the Performance Director had emailed all members of the team explaining the role of the researcher and that he and the British Equestrian Federation (BEF) supported the study and would appreciate their cooperation. This resulted in the study being positively perceived, and allowed the lead author to build rapport with the participants and engage them in interviews.

In relation to the Eliasian concept of researcher involvement–detachment as a balance, we believe the lead researcher had sufficient insider awareness/empathy to issues such as the open discourse of sexuality within the discipline of Dressage (and the absence of this within the other disciplines). However, this was combined with objectivity that allowed the lead researcher to avoid asking questions relating to sexual identity that could potentially be overt. According to Gold's (1958) typology of participant observation, we therefore place the lead researcher in the role of 'observer as participant', meaning they were mostly cast in the role of observing, but also participated in a minor social role. In the light of this cultural position, we are not claiming that this is a purely ethnographic approach to the study, but merely highlight the ethnographic nature of the data collection and analysis.

Due to the fact that the experiences of the individual athletes are not formed in isolation, the culture, community and power relations within the sport, the team and their environments, must also be considered. Therefore, interviews were conducted with members of the British Equestrian Team, including riders, performance managers and support staff, many of which work across all the disciplines (see Table 2). With regard to accessing interview participants, consent was granted by the BEF to allow the researcher access to various training and competition situations prior to, during and after the 2008 Beijing Olympic and Paralympic Games. A convenience sampling technique was applied resulting in 34 separate interviews conducted over the 18-month period, with 28 individuals, at a time and place that was convenient for the participants (see Table 2); the duration of the interview was also predominantly determined by the interviewee. Participants were asked about their career histories and their Olympic/Paralympic experience but were predominately allowed to lead the direction and pace of the interview. This facilitated a more spontaneous, free-flowing and interactive interview conducive to the ethnographic approach adopted.

All interviewees were recorded and transcribed verbatim. Altheide's approach to analysis was used *post hoc* to inform and develop the analysis. The development of the research protocol used in relation to the data coding and categorizing process did however follow Altheide's (1996) 'rules of thumb' and asked the questions 'does it generate categories that subsequently will be explored?' and 'does it allow the researcher to identify new categories?'. Primary analysis was then conducted using deductive coding, whilst simultaneously allowing space for inductive codes to emerge. A revised protocol was then developed to facilitate a systematic approach to analysis, whilst allowing the researcher to remain reflexive and move in a recursive way between concept development, coding and analysis. The constant comparison enabled the researcher to clarify themes, frames and discourse, thereby moving through stages nine and ten of Altheide's (1996) process of qualitative document analysis.

Our analysis revealed several sport-specific 'identities' for this group of participants. These range from the general equine-related identity of 'horsey', to discipline specific (both in and out of Olympic/Paralympic competition), for example, 'Dressage riders' and 'eventers', to identities specifically linked to the 'Olympics', 'Paralympics' and the wider 'Team GB'. Data analysis shows an absence of gender as an identity in the way interviewees and other participants see themselves and others. In the following section, we present the findings that specifically relate to the construct of sport-specific identities for this group of participants within a sex-integrated sport environment.

Table 2. Overview of interviewees and their Olympic experience at the point of interview.

Code	Position at point of interview	Gender	Olympic experience	Nature of Olympic experience
1	Team GB support staff	M	Two Olympic Games	Work with the Olympic riders across all three disciplines
2	Para-Equestrian Dressage rider	F	Four Paralympic Games	Rider
3	Groom	F	One Olympic Games	Groom
4	Performance Manager	M	Two Paralympic Games	Performance manager
5	Para-Equestrian Dressage rider	F	Three Paralympic Games	Rider
6	Groom	F	One Olympic Games	Rider selected but did not compete
7	Team GB support staff	M	Two Olympic and Paralympic Games	Team GB support staff – experience across all four disciplines
8	Groom	F	Two Olympic Games	Groom
9	Team GB support staff	F	Two Olympic and Paralympic Games	Provides support to all four disciplines
10	Team GB support staff	M	Two Olympic Games	Worked with the Olympic riders across all three disciplines but did not attend the games
11	Coach	M	Three Olympic Games	Coach
12	Eventing Rider	F	One Olympic Games	Selected but did not compete
13	BOA	M	One Olympic Games	Operations
14	Groom and Coach	F	Two Paralympic Games	Groom and individual coach
15	Team GB support staff	M	Two Olympic Games	Outside of the Olympics works specifically for the discipline of Eventing but during Olympic competition, works with all three disciplines
16	Groom	F	One Paralympic Games	Groom
17	British Paralympic association	F	Five Paralympic Games	Previous senior national coach and Deputy Chef d'mission Paralympics GB
18	Team GB support staff	M	One Paralympic and one Olympic Games	Para-Equestrian Dressage All three disciplines
19	Performance manager	M	Four Olympic Games	Dressage rider and team captain Dressage
20	Para-Equestrian Dressage rider	M	One Paralympic Games	Rider
21	Team GB support staff	F	Seven Olympic Games	Working with owners and supporters of Eventing
22	Para-Equestrian Dressage rider	M	One Paralympic Games	Rider
23	Para-Equestrian Dressage rider	F	Two Paralympic Games	Rider
24	Para-Equestrian Dressage rider	F	One Paralympic Games	Rider selected but did not compete
25	Coach	F	Two Olympic Games	Coach
26	Performance Director	M	Two Olympic and Paralympic Games	All four disciplines
27	Team GB support staff	F	One Olympic Games	All three disciplines
28	Performance Manager	M	Five Olympic Games	International rider Chef d'Equipe Performance Manager

Experiencing sex-integrated sport and the construction of identity

Analysis of the data highlighted several equestrian sport-specific identities. At a sport level, participants often position themselves within a 'them and us' framework, 'them' being other sports and 'us' being equestrian sport. Even within the 'us' framework, we noted that the construct of identity was often associated with the individual disciplines, as participants would refer to the differences between, for example, Showjumpers and Eventers, or Dressage and Para-Dressage riders. Through Ethnographic Content Analysis, at a personal/individual level, we noted that equestrian athletes are consistently referred to as 'riders' by fellow competitors and wider team members such as coaches and support staff. The term 'rider' not only highlights the difference between equestrian sport and other sports but also enables participants to refer to one another without a differentiating gender label instead promoting an inclusive shared identity absent of any gender reference. In the following section, we present evidence of the construct of these sport-specific identities whilst discussing the absence of gender as an element of identity in the way participants describe themselves and others within the sport.

Identity often refers to distinctive characteristics attributed to individuals or those shared by distinct groups. One such characteristic may be the common use of a language or specific terminology. Reference to the colloquial term 'horsey', as shown in the following quotes, demonstrates a distinctive 'them and us' identity:

> The sort of great saying of any publicity is good publicity is ironically quite true, but obviously we want it to be all for the good reasons, but it's just trying to sort of sell the stories and breakdown some of the barriers and the Olympics gives us the perfect opportunity, because we are on that global stage, when we have a World Equestrian Games we're on the global stage but still only to the horsey people. (Interviewee 27, Team GB support staff)

> For me, as I said, it's been my dream since I was a 6 year old and I think one of the … one of the real appeals of the Olympics is it's such a universal experience, or sporting, universal experience that, you know, if you're an Olympian, it's something that everyone can relate to, whereas, if you say 'Oh well, I've been to the World Equestrian Games', to someone who's not well versed in sort of horsey speak, there's 'Oh, that's nice'. (Interviewee 12, Eventing rider)

The use of the term 'horsey' by someone outside of the collective group could be seen as a derogatory term due to its childlike connotations and association with the 1938 children's song 'Horsey Horsey' written by Paddy Roberts. However, as these quotes demonstrate, when used by an insider, the term refers to characteristics of a collective group 'horsey people' and characteristics of a language 'horsey speak'. The way that the above two interviewees refer to the identity of 'horsey' in the context of 'them and us' shows a collective understanding of what the experience is like from within, with what could almost be described as a 'desire' to be understood by those outside. Interviewee 12 specifically differentiates between the horsey-specific experience of the World Equestrian Games and the universal experience of the Olympic Games, the latter being an experience which would be recognized/understood and implied to be more deeply valued by a wider group of people.

As with the term rider, the term horsey is again a label used to identify a group of individuals that is inclusive from a sport-specific perspective at the same time as being exclusive of gender connotations. The familiarity in which this type of phraseology is used is an indication of acceptance and respect of both male and female athletes and as with the wrestling example presented earlier, these identity associated labels neutralize the concept of gender dominance within the framework of gender hierarchy and masculine identity. Indeed, with regard to the all the interview data collected and analysed for this study, the only direct reference to gender occurred when participants were referring to the 'uniqueness' of equestrian sport in comparison to other sports as demonstrated in the example below:

> Well, when you see people that ask you about the sport compared to other sports, I mean firstly you've got males competing against females on an equal level, which is very unique. You've also

got … you could be an Olympic champion, world champion one minute, and the next week you're competing against people doing it on a part time basis and get beaten, because it's all about the horse. So it's a very levelling sport, there's no room for egos as well, because you can go on your backside very quickly and I think that's what makes it quite unique. (Interviewee 1, Team GB support staff)

It is interesting to note that instead of referring to gender as a differentiating factor, the reference to gender in this example is presented as a 'levelling' factor. Across the data, the athletes in this study are consistently referred to as riders, unless identified by a name there is no way of knowing the gender of the athlete being discussed. The absence of a gendered identity could be seen as evidence of participants placing a low importance of gender within a defined mixed-gender team. It could also mean that the generic identity of 'rider' or 'horsey' is not only void of gender or sporting 'eliteness' but it can also be used as an identity that is inclusive of both able-bodied and disabled athletes.

The comparison between 'horsey' equestrian sport and 'other sports' is again highlighted in the following quote as a member of the GB support team explains that the dynamic of the human/horse partnership results in an 'unselfish' athlete attitude in equestrian sport compared to other sports, implying that this is a unique characteristic and again illustrating the distinct identity of an equestrian athlete:

Athletes can be very frustrating to work with, because of the intensity and their selfishness sometimes, but with this lot, because they're not the most important part, the horse is the most important part, they haven't got that selfishness about them really, so they're a lot better to work with, and I enjoy this sport more than other sport. (Interviewee 1, Team GB support staff)

The ethnographic approach utilized within this study specifically left space for people to discuss what identity meant to them. This was achieved because this approach gives access to the self-understandings of the group in a variety of contexts, and allows the researcher to experience the reflexivity of group identity as well as what the identity means in practical terms (Adams 2009). It would appear that within the Olympic and Paralympic context there is recognition, at least, of the overarching collective sport-specific 'equestrian' or 'horsey' identity, which is inclusive of all the disciplines but exclusive of all other sports. However, analysis also highlighted nuances of discipline-specific identities. Some characteristics associated with discipline-specific identities have rather practical implications. The actual requirements of the horse and rider within the disciplines are very different, 'The disciplines are quite different really, all we've got is a four legged animal underneath us but it's actually bred very different, they're very different sports' (Interviewee 11, Coach).

The social interactions and behaviours of the different teams are further examined in the following sequence of quotes which are all associated with the discipline of Dressage. Here, we really start to gain an insight into the views and actions of this group of athletes. The narrative presented here not only implies specific characteristics associated with Dressage, it also acknowledges the differences between this team and the other disciplines. The first quote comes from an interview recorded in Hong Kong during the Beijing Olympics. This particular interview was recorded just prior to the start of the Dressage competition and specifically on a day when a tornado warning had meant that everything had shut down and no training could take place:

There's two things that can happen at these Games it could be quite a normal temperature, and we've already experienced that in the week that we've been out here. So then nothing will change, it'll just be like a normal World Championship, European Championship. Or, we could be facing this kind of situation, here, and what this situation will require is huge flexibility and adaptability and that's something that Dressage riders are not good at. It doesn't come into the routine, regime, discipline of Dressage. It comes into Cross Country riding, where you ride over different terrains, different weathers, no precise time, you know, or Showjumping, you don't know whether you're going to be waiting 2 h to jump or 5 min, in Dressage we know the time we ride, we know everything, everything's constant. (Interviewee 19, Performance Manager)

Not only does the interviewee recognize Dressage-specific characteristics, he also acknowledges that these are different from the other two Olympic disciplines of Eventing and Showjumping. What is interesting is the association between the requirements of the sport and the characteristics of the different riders. The nature of the Dressage competition is the completion of a pre-determined test. The riders will have completed the same test at numerous competitions; consistency is an inferred element of this sport and for these riders change is disruptive but for Showjumpers every competition is different:

When you're jumping there's nothing constant, you turn up at the show, you don't know the course plan, you don't know anything, you don't know the ring, you don't know whether it's on a hill, you don't know whether it's like this in mud. So there's no, no level playing field like we know in Dressage. So you are used to turning up to the unknown, you walk, 'Christ that's difficult, what am I going to do there', strategies, tactics, 'Shit, should have done it in 6', you know, nothing's for definite, like it is in Dressage. (Interviewee 19, Performance Manager)

In the following example, the Performance Manager refers to Dressage riders as 'private people', not as social as Showjumpers. In an Olympic competition, Dressage riders are not only competing as a team but they are also living in a team-focused environment:

As Dressage riders we're very private people, we make … we have our plan, we don't always announce it, or maybe the one we announce isn't the one we use but we have it and we do it on our own and we train on our own at home, and we don't compete like Showjumpers competing, mixing, living with each other week in, week out, we don't do that. (Interviewee 19, Performance Manager)

The discipline-specific identity of Dressage as outlined in the characteristics discussed above is not however consistent with that for Para-Equestrian Dressage. Despite the fact that the nature of the competition is the same, i.e. a pre-known Dressage test, consistently encountered at numerous competitions, Para-Equestrian Dressage riders do not come across as being private people:

Erm you know everyone wants to interact with everyone you know what I mean, we are, all the countries we've got mates with all the countries and its great for everyone to meet up again you know like we met last year at the Worlds. And yeah you do sort of get mates and you know what people are doing and you keep in touch by email to meet up so it's like a long distance friends. I mean when the actual competition day comes obviously you're very focussed with team GB and then at the same time the South African for example Philipa, I always have a laugh with her you know good luck that sort of thing you know what I mean even though she's another country she's still a mate so you want her to do well. Apparently I've been told that's quite different from the other sports, where they stay very much in their country but no, everyone just cracks on. (Interviewee 20, Para-Equestrian Dressage Rider)

Through the analysis of data presented, we have discussed how participants have described themselves and others within the sport and in comparison to other sports, therefore highlighting the sport- and discipline-specific identities of equestrian athletes. Within the context of a sex-integrated sport, the use of hierarchical gendered discourse is notably absent. The dominant male identity associated with sport, which requires the positioning of women as others, is not evident with participants choosing shared identities of 'horsey' and 'rider' over any reference to gendered labels. Even within the sub-division of discipline-specific identities, additional characteristics are used to differentiate groups but these still remain absent of any traditional discursive meanings of sex differences. We conclude that gender appears less salient in this context, given the sex integration and levelling aspects of the inclusion of the horse.

Conclusion

The aim of this study was to review the construct of athlete identity from within a sex-integrated sport. Through ethnographic analysis, which 'is generally interpretive, seeking to explicate meanings rather than make verifiable predictions' (Adams 2009), we have been able to identify the 'them' and 'us' sport-specific identity and highlight the nuances of discipline-specific identities. Whilst the majority of discourse surrounding equestrian sport as reviewed in the first part of this paper was laden with gendered reference, analysis of the current data shows an absence of gender as an identity in the way participants see themselves and others.

As we have discussed in earlier sections of this paper, sport is predominantly separated into same sex competition (unless physiological differences between men and women offer no competitive advantage or disadvantage – as is the case with equestrian sport), with male sports taking the dominant default position. However, our review of prior discourse associated with equestrian sport highlighted that sex integration does not necessarily equate to participatory parity or gender-neutral discourse. We have also noted that whilst there is a body of literature relating to discourse surrounding sex integration and sex-separated sport, there has been to date limited space given to the lived experience of athletes within the construct of sex-integrated sport. Following on from Dashper's (2012b) work on sex integration and gender equality in equestrian sport, this study sought to evaluate the lived experience of the Olympic and Paralympic Games, specifically focusing on the construct of identity for members of the British Equestrian team.

The results of this study highlight an interesting sport-specific construct of 'them and us'. 'Us' being inclusive of anyone involved in the world of horses and 'Them' being outsiders to this, which includes other sports and athletes. This in itself became most apparent when participants were referring to the multisport environment of the Olympics or Paralympics. For the participants in this study, the Olympics or Paralympics would be the only environment in which they could compete in a multisport environment. For some this presented an opportunity for them to be seen within a universally accepted sporting framework, whilst for others this simply highlighted a general lack of understanding in the wider community as to what their sport entailed.

However, within the general 'us' or 'horsey' identity, we noted discipline-specific nuances. Participants noted differences between, for example, Dressage riders and Showjumpers. A possible explanation for this is linked to the different requirements of these disciplines which may suit personal characteristics. However, regardless of the specific discipline, and the acknowledgement that different disciplines may experience diverse cultures and atmospheres which may be relevant, throughout the analysis of the data, equestrian athletes were consistently referred to as 'riders', a term devoid of gender hierarchy or Olympic or

Paralympic reference and a term that differentiated them from the generic inclusive term of 'athlete'.

In contrast to previous studies in which gender is associated with identity and the lived experience of sport, there was a distinct lack of gendered discourse present within the empirical data produced and reviewed in this study. The use of gender-neutral terminology (rider) might suggest either that gender is unimportant, or that respondents were gender-blind. We argue that our analysis shows an absence of gender with regard to the formation of equestrian athletes' identities. We conclude therefore that gender activity and behaviour expectations are not perceived as affecting the underlying reality of the performance environment of this particular sports team. This phenomenon is clearly of significance for the wider discourse on the gendered experience in sport.

Finally, we present possible considerations regarding the implication that from a participant's perspective, equestrian sport may be considered gender neutral. With regard to this phenomenon, it is worth making reference here to the recently published Olympic Agenda 2020, in which the IOC presents 40 recommendations that were discussed at the 127th IOC session and which 'lay out the strategic roadmap for the future of the Olympic Movement' (IOC 2014). The findings of this study have a direct bearing on 'Recommendation 11: Foster gender equality; sub-point 2. The IOC to encourage the inclusion of mixed-gender team events' (IOC 2014).

We are aware however, that previous studies relating to equestrian sport have in fact highlighted differences within the gendered experience of participants (Dashper 2012b; Hellborg and Hedenborg 2015) which may relate to the level of competition/participation and cultural influences. We therefore encourage additional research in this area which specifically focuses on comparative gendered experiences within sport that would inform policy direction at both elite and grassroots participation levels (e.g. Sotiriadou, Quick, and Shilbury 2006). Whilst we propose that the specificity of our study and consequent findings provide valuable insight in relationship between athlete experience and construction of identity, we believe additional research in this area that advances a more athlete-focused approach is required for a stronger representation of athlete voices.

Acknowledgements

The authors would like to acknowledge the support of the British Equestrian Federation with regard to access to participants involved in this study.

Disclosure statement

No potential conflict of interest was reported by the authors.

References

Adams, L. L. 2009. "Techniques for Measuring Identity in Ethnographic Research." In *Measuring Identity: A Guide for Social Scientists*, edited by A. I. Johnston, R. Abdelal, Y. Herrera, and R. McDemott, 316–341. New York: Cambridge University Press.

Adelman, M., and J. Knijnik, eds. 2013. *Gender and Equestrian Sport; Riding around the World*. Dordrecht: Springer.

Altheide, D. L. 1996. *Qualitative Media Analysis*. California, CA: Sage.

Anderson, E. 2008. "'I Used to Think Women Were Weak': Orthodox Masculinity, Gender Segregation, and Sport." *Sociological Forum* 23 (2): 257–280.

Aries, E., D. McCarthy, P. Salovey, and M. Banaji. 2004. "A Comparison of Athletes and Non-athletes at Highly Selective Colleges: Academic Performance and Personal Development." *Research in Higher Education* 45 (6): 577–602.

Borish, L. J. 1996. "Women at the Modern Olympic Games: An Interdisciplinary Look at American Culture." *Quest* 48: 43–56.

Brewer, B. W., J. L. Van Raalte, and D. E. Linder. 1993. "Athletic Identity: Hercules' Muscles or Achilles Heel?" *International Journal of Sport Psychology* 24: 237–254.

Burdsey, D. 2007. "Role with the Punches: The Construction and Representation of Amir Khan as a Role Model for Multiethnic Britain." *The Sociological Review* 55: 611–631.

Burke, J. C. 1997. *Equal to the Challenge: Pioneering Women of Horse Sports*. New York, NY: Howell Book House.

Carver, C. S., S. L. Reynolds, and M. F. Scheier. 1994. "The Possible Selves of Optimists and Pessimists." *Journal of Research in Personality* 28: 133–141.

Channon, A. J. 2012. "Way of the Discourse: Mixed-sex Martial Arts and the Subversion of Gender." PhD diss., Loughborough University.

Crosset, T., and B. Beal. 1997. "The Use of 'Subculture' and 'Subworld' in Ethnographic Works on Sport: A Discussion of Definitional Distinctions." *Sociology of Sport Journal* 14: 73–85.

Dashper, K. 2012a. "'Dressage is Full of Queens!' Masculinity, Sexuality and Equestrian Sport." *Sociology* 46 (6): 1109–1124.

Dashper, K. 2012b. "Together, Yet Still Not Equal? Sex Integration in Equestrian Sport." *Asia-Pacific Journal of Health, Sport and Physical Education* 3: 213–225.

De Haan, D. 2015. "Evaluating the Experience of the Olympic and Paralympic Games in the Career Histories of Elite Equestrian Athletes." PhD diss., Loughborough University.

Dumbell, L., and D. de Haan. 2012. "Has the Barrier Been Jumped? A Comparison of Athlete Profiles over 50 Years of Olympic Equestrian Events." Paper Presented at the International Convention on Science, Education and Medicine in Sport. Glasgow, Scotland.

Dunning, E. 1999. *Sport Matters: Sociological Studies of Sport, Violence and Civilization*. London: Routledge.

Foddy, B., and J. Savulescu. 2011. "Time to Re-evaluate Gender Segregation in Athletics?" *British Journal of Sports Medicine* 45: 1184–1188.

Fraser, N. 2007. "Feminist Politics in the Age of Reconstruction: A Two-dimensional Approach to Gender Justice." *Studies in Social Justice* 1 (1): 23–35.

Garfinkel, H. 1967. *Studies in Ethnomethodology*. New Jersey, NJ: Prentice-Hall.

Gold, R. L. 1958. "Roles in Sociological Field Observations." *Social Forces* 36 (3):217–223.

Hargreaves, J. 2002. *Sporting Females: Critical Issues in the History and Sociology of Women's Sport*. London: Taylor & Francis.

Hedenborg, S. 2007. "The Popular Horse: From Army to Agriculture and Leisure." http://www.idrottsforum.org/articles/hedenborg/hedenborg071121.html.

Hedenborg, S. 2009. "Unknown Soldiers and Very Pretty Ladies: Challenges to the Social Order of Sports in Post-war Sweden." *Sport in History* 29: 601–622.

Hedenborg, S., and M. H. White. 2012. "Changes and Variations in Patterns of Gender Relations in Equestrian Sports during the Second Half of the Twentieth Century." *Sport in Society* 15: 302–319.

Hellborg, A.-M., and S. Hedenborg. 2015. "The Rocker and the Heroine: Gendered Media Representations of Equestrian Sports at the 2012 Olympics." *Sport in Society* 1–14.

Hirdman, Y. 1990. *The Gender System: Theoretical Reflections on the Social Subordination of Women*. Report: Study of power and democracy in Sweden.

Hogg, M. A., and D. Abrams. 1988. *Social identifications: A social psychology of intergroup relations and group processes*. London: Routledge.

Howe, P. D. 2008. "The Tail is Wagging the Dog: Body Culture, Classification and the Paralympic Movement." *Ethnography* 9: 499–517.

IOC. 2014. *Olympic Agenda 2020; 20+20 Recommendations*. Lausanne: International Olympic Committee.

Jackson, S. J. 2004. "Exorcizing the Ghost: Donovan Bailey, Ben Johnson and the Politics of Canadian Identity." *Media, Culture & Society* 26: 121–141.

Jansen, S. C., and D. Sabo. 1994. "The Sport/War Metaphor: Hegemonic Masculinity, the Persian Gulf War, and the New World Order." *Sociology of Sport Journal* 11: 1–17.

Knight, G., N. Neverson, M. MacNeill, and P. Donnelly. 2007. "The Weight of Expectation: Cathy Freeman, Legacy, Reconciliation and the Sydney Olympics – A Canadian Perspective." *The International Journal of the History of Sport* 24: 1243–1263.

Krane, V., and S. M. Baird. 2005. "Using Ethnography in Applied Sport Psychology." *Journal of Applied Sport Psychology* 17: 87–107.

Lyotard, J.-F. 1984. "The Postmodern Condition." In *The Postmodern Turn*, edited by S. Seidman, 1994, 27–38. Cambridge: Cambridge University Press.

McDonagh, E., and L. Pappano. 2008. *Playing with the Boys: Why Separate is Not Equal in Sports*. New York, NY: Oxford University Press.

McNeil, D. 2009. "Lennox Lewis and Black Atlantic Politics: The Hard Sell." *Journal of Sport & Social Issues* 33: 25–38.

Mean, L. 2001. "Identity and Discursive Practice: Doing Gender on the Football Pitch." *Discourse & Society* 12 (6): 789–815.

Merlini, V. L. 2004. "A Case Study of the Equestrian Sport of Polo: An Integrative Approach to Issues of Structure, Function and Interaction." PhD, University of Connecticut.

Messner, M. 1995. *Power at Play: Sports and the Problem of Masculinity*. Boston, MA: Beacon Press.

Messner, M. 2002. *Taking the Field: Women, Men, and Sports*. Minnesota: University of Minnesota Press.

Meyer, B. 1990. "From Idealism to Actualization: The Academic Performance of Female Collegiate Athletes." *Sociology of Sport Journal* 7: 44–57.

Miller, S. 2010. "Making the Boys Cry: The Performative Dimensions of Fluid Gender." *Text and Performance Quarterly* 30 (2): 143–182.

Peers, D. 2009. "(Dis)Empowering Paralympic Histories: Absent Athletes and Disabling Discourses." *Disability & Society* 24: 653–665.

Pfister, G. 2010. "Women in Sport – Gender Relations and Future Perspectives1." *Sport in Society* 13 (2): 234–248.

Phillips, M. G., and G. Osmond. 2009. "Filmic Sports History: Dawn Fraser, Swimming and Australian National Identity." *The International Journal of the History of Sport* 26: 2126–2142.

Plymoth, B. 2013. "We Have to Make Horse Riding More Masculine! On the Difference between Masculine Needs and Feminine Practices in the Context of Swedish Equestrian Sports." In *Gender and Equestrian Sport Riding around the World*, edited by M. Adelman, and J. Knijnik, Chap. 9. Dordrecht: Springer.

Rice, G. 2003. "Equine Sports: A Partnership in Fitness." http://www.findarticles.com/p/articles/mi_m0675/is_2_21/ai_112982360.

Roberts, L.-J., and M. MacLean. 2012. "Women in the Weighing Room: Gendered Discourses of Exclusion in English Flat Racing." *Sport in Society: Cultures, Commerce, Media, Politics* 15 (3): 320–334.

Sabo, D., and R. Runfola. 1980. *Jock: Sports and Male Identity*. Englewood Cliffs, NJ: Prentice-Hall.

Sotiriadou, K., S. Quick, and D. Shilbury. 2006. "Sport for 'Some': Elite versus Mass Participation." *International Journal of Sport Management* 7 (1): 50–66.

Stelzl, M., L. Janes, and C. Seligman. 2008. "Champ or Chump: Strategic Utilization of Dual Social Identities of Others." *European Journal of Social Psychology* 38: 128–138.

Travers, A. 2008. "The Sport Nexus and Gender Injustice." *Studies in Social Justice* 2: 79–101.

West, C., and D. H. Zimmerman. 1987. "Doing Gender." *Gender & Society* 1 (2): 125–151.

White, L. 2008. "One Athlete, One Nation, Two Flags: Cathy Freeman and Australia's Search for Aboriginal Reconciliation." *Sporting Traditions* 25: 1–19.

Mixed-sex in sport for development: a pragmatic and symbolic device. The case of touch rugby for forced migrants in Rome

Micol Pizzolati[a] and Davide Sterchele[b]

[a]Department of Economics, Management, Society, and Institutions, University of Molise, Campobasso, Italy; [b]School of Events, Tourism and Hospitality, Carnegie Faculty, Leeds Beckett University, Leeds, UK

ABSTRACT

Following the success of its all-male refugee football team, the Italian voluntary-based association Liberi Nantes created a touch rugby team as a pilot project aimed at involving female forced migrants. Initially set up as an all-woman activity to provide a less intimidating environment, the touch rugby group was later turned into a mixed-sex team. While potentially enabling transformative experiences and generating opportunities for challenging gender stereotypes, the mixed-gender character of the touch rugby provision also served broader objectives within Liberi Nantes' mission. Focusing on the accounts of the activists and volunteers involved in the project, this paper investigates the practical and symbolic reasons for the strategic use of mixed-gender sport and its implications. Notably, by analysing the development of the touch rugby team, we highlight how its mixed-gender nature contributes to nourishing a wider rhetoric of social mixing and celebration of diversity, in which Liberi Nantes' identity is embedded.

Despite the growing consolidation of the sport-for-development sector (Giulianotti 2011), only recently have policy-makers and practitioners drawn on sport as a vehicle to foster the social inclusion specifically of males (Evers 2010) and females (Guerin et al. 2003; Palmer 2008) from refugee backgrounds (Jeanes, O'Connor, and Alfrey 2014). Sport participation has been shown to bring some benefits, although these are difficult to measure (Amara et al. 2005; Coalter 2010), such as facilitating the beneficiaries' interaction with the local environment and reducing anti-social behaviour. Nevertheless, gender boundaries and inequalities tend to remain unchallenged (Spaaij 2015) and refugee women are often excluded from participation in sports activities based on gender-related expectations that either prevent them from engaging in physical leisure activities (Evers 2010) or confine them to a spectator role. In the few cases where forced migrant women are actively involved in sport activities, this is mainly done in the context of 'typically female' sports or at least in women-only groups (Amara et al. 2005).

This sounds particularly limiting in the light of recent studies that have shown how mixed-sex sports can challenge the discourse of male dominance embedded in contemporary sport culture (Pringle 2005) by providing opportunities for unique and transformative experiences of embodied equality between male and female participants (Channon 2014).

On the basis of this, mixed-sex sport is becoming more widely-used in sport-for-development initiatives aimed at challenging normative conceptions of sex difference by trying to redefine sex boundaries and hierarchies. However, such initiatives are themselves underpinned by specific conceptions and representations of sex relations that can in turn become somehow normative or generate asymmetric relationships between sport-for-development practitioners and their beneficiaries. Moreover, mixed-sex sports provisions can sometimes play a strategic role, becoming functional in broader interventions and rhetorics.

These issues are discussed here through the exploratory study of a small sport project aimed at forced migrants in Italy, with particular focus on encouraging women's participation. In 2010, the voluntary-based sports association Liberi Nantes, which has been working with refugees and asylum-seekers in Rome since 2007, created a touch rugby[1] team that was initially composed of women only and later became a mixed-gender team.

The project – the only one in Italy that uses this method of intervention[2] – was not specifically conceived to challenge gender stereotypes and conceptions of sex differences, but was rather part of a broader effort to support the integration of refugees[3] by providing opportunities for social mixing and interaction across ethnic, sex and age boundaries.

Therefore, the aim of this paper is not to evaluate the actual impact of the project in challenging or perpetuating sex and gender stereotypes, but rather to examine the practical and symbolic reasons for, and implications of, the strategic use of mixed-gender sport. To do so, our analysis will focus on the accounts and representations of Liberi Nantes' activists and volunteers.

Women (forced) migrants and sport-for-development

Sport-based initiatives are increasingly being used to try and address a variety of social issues (Beutler 2008; Kidd 2008), although concerns have been raised about the vagueness of such claims (Black 2010; Coalter 2010; Lyras and Welty Peachey 2011), the actual contribution of many sport-for-development programmes to inclusive social change (Kelly 2011; Long and Sanderson 2001) and their potential neocolonial impact (Darnell and Hayhurst 2011).

Most research on the role of sport in helping empower marginalized groups has focused on its potential to extend social networks and increase social capital. Notably with regard to migrants' participation, mostly mainstream team sports have been studied for both their bonding effect of strengthening intra-group solidarity and cohesion, and their bridging capacity to favour inter-group relations and integration (Elling, De Knop, and Knoppers 2001; Janssens and Verweel 2014; Spaaij 2013a).

Beyond their functional potential in terms of networking, integration and acculturation (Evans 2014), sport and other leisure activities can also contribute to meeting important emotional needs of migrants (Boccagni and Baldassar 2015) and fostering a sense of identity and belonging (Ratna 2014; Walseth 2006a, 2006b) by acting as 'culturally oriented means of survival and thriving in life if engaged in a constructive and meaningful way' (Stack and Iwasaki 2009). Moreover, the very access of migrants to sport and leisure can be regarded as a right of participation and considered a matter of social justice in itself (Aitchison 2007).

Providing opportunities for meaningful engagement in sport activities becomes even more challenging in the case of refugee women, who suffer a double marginality for experiencing both gender inequalities, on the one hand, and the transient, rootless and uncertain condition of refugees, on the other. Besides coming from experiences that are 'by definition traumatic and characterized by persecution, displacement, loss, grief, and forced separation from family, home and belongings' (Olliff 2008), refugees also live a precarious existence, moving from one temporary host location to another, which makes it harder to settle and build new networks of relationships.

This clearly generates a number of limitations to their involvement in sports activities, which Olliff (2008) indicates to be structural, mediating and personal barriers. Structural barriers include the lack of funding for sustainable programmes; the tendency towards 'one size fits all' activities instead of a bespoke (tailored) provision; inconsistent referral of refugees to sport and recreation programmes by settlement services; barriers between targeted and mainstream sport and recreation options; access to transport; access to public space and facilities. Mediating barriers include: lack of inclusive and culturally sensitive practices in existing sport and recreation providers; lack of parental/guardian support in the case of young refugees; a different sport culture between the country of origin and the host country; racism and discrimination. Personal barriers include: resettlement experience, lack of time, other commitments; financial constraints; not knowing the rules of a specific sport.

Additionally, working with forced migrants in Canada, Guruge and Collins (2008) observed that 'women from countries where many refugees originate have less opportunity to engage in social and recreational activities than their male counterparts'. Ironically, being offered such opportunities in the host country does not necessarily make things easier, as they 'are expected to stay at home and care for family (not just for children but often for elders and other extended family members as well) and their fear of using social resources limits their interaction with broader society' (Guruge and Collins 2008). Studying the involvement of Somali Australian youth in community football clubs, Spaaij (2015) noted that 'while social boundaries such as clan, team and locality are porous, other boundaries of inclusion/exclusion, notably gender, ethnicity and religion, tend to be more stable and more difficult to cross' (Spaaij 2015).

While being rooted in deep cultural and social dynamics, some of these boundaries are also partly reinforced by the inner logic of mainstream traditional sports, which are based on categorization/segregation by gender, age and ability in order to ensure fair competition between equally skilled/strong/fast opponents. However, although a vast proportion of sport-for-development programmes aimed at women use football (soccer) as their main activity (Hancock, Lyras, and Ha 2013), a growing number of initiatives that aim at blurring boundaries and categorization entail either the de-sportization of traditional, mainstream sports (Sterchele 2015) or the use of alternative activities which are deemed more suitable to favour social mixing and inclusion, such as tchoukball, touch rugby, dodgeball, korfball, as well as emerging lifestyle sports (e.g. Crum 1988; Gilchrist and Wheaton 2011; Thorpe and Rinehart 2012). In either case, mixed-sex activities are organized to encourage female participation, limit male dominance and challenge gender stereotypes.

Nonetheless, researchers have highlighted the ambivalent effects of such activities by showing how segregated sport provision can offer safer spaces (Brady 2005; Jeanes, O'Connor, and Alfrey 2014; Spaaij and Schulenkorf 2014) that are more attentive to the specific gender, cultural and religious background and needs of their participants (Elling,

De Knop and Knoppers 2003; Watson, Tucker, and Drury 2013). These intersectional issues become particularly visible and have been largely explored, for instance, in the analysis of Muslim women's involvement in sports and physical activity (e.g. Ahmad 2011; Benn and Pfister 2013; Benn, Dagkas, and Jawad 2011; Dagkas, Benn, and Jawad 2011; Guerin et al. 2003; Jiwani and Rail 2010; Wray 2002; Zahidi, Syed Ali, and Nor 2012). Separated sport activities can also provide members of disempowered groups with temporary relief from the strain habitually experienced in their everyday asymmetrical interactions (Krouwel et al. 2006). Moreover, the simplistic idea that segregated sports activities only reinforce bonding social capital, whereas mixed activity generates bridging social capital, has been questioned by several studies (Elling, De Knop, and Knoppers 2001; Janssens and Verweel 2014; Spaaij 2012; Theeboom, Schaillée, and Nols 2012).

With specific reference to the sport provision for women, and particularly migrant women, the debate about the advantages and disadvantages of both mixed-sex and separated activities is still very open. However, this debate is itself partly underpinned by cultural imperialism and hegemonic representations based on a deficit model of sport participation (Toffoletti and Palmer 2015). As observed by Chawansky (2011), the fact that sport-for-development programming 'seeks to either allow for girls' sporting access in mixed-gender settings or aspires to 'empower' females in girls-only contexts' seem to imply that girls 'have gendered identities/experiences that need to be assisted, altered, or enhanced' which 'obscures an understanding of gender as a relational identity'.

The capacity of sport for breaking down gender hierarchies and divisions remains therefore a contested issue. So far, the benefits to women of involvement in mixed-sex sports have been explored only by a few studies that have investigated the 'undoing' of gender stereotypes (Channon 2014) either directly by focusing on women's empowerment or indirectly by concentrating on men's experience and the challenge to hegemonic masculinities (Channon 2013a, 2013b; Tagg 2008). The fact that several sport-for-development programmes provide mixed-sex activities despite the paucity of research and lack of evidence about their benefits suggests that such initiatives are often based on optimistic assumptions and pre-conceptions. When sports provision is proposed/imposed within the asymmetric relation between donor and beneficiaries, such underpinning assumptions can easily assume connotations of cultural imperialism. Warning of the potential neocolonial dangers of sport for development, Darnell (2007) observes that very often,

> a well-intentioned and benevolent 'mission' of training, empowering and assisting is not only based upon, but to an extent *requires*, the establishment of a dichotomy between the empowered and disempowered, the vocal and the silent, the 'knowers' and the known. [original italics]

Context and methods

Italy has only recently changed from a nation of migrants to a country of immigrants.[4] Therefore, Italian policies on migrants and notably refugees were still non-existent or largely inadequate up until the late 1990s (Korac 2001, 2003).[5] Following a series of reception projects randomly activated at the local level, a more integrated and organic system was created in the early 2000s through a network of reception centres spread around the country, enabling the hosting of 26,432 forced migrants between 2002 and 2009 (Marchetti 2014). However, such a network covers only a limited proportion of requests for admission.[6] Moreover, this system enables the government to delegate most of the burden of migrant assistance to under-resourced local authorities, which in turn tend to rely heavily on the civic sector (Alexander 2012) composed of networks of volunteer-based associations such as Liberi Nantes.

The latter is an amateur sports association created in 2007 by 10 friends, men and women, with the purpose of supporting sports participation amongst asylum-seekers and refugees in Rome,[7] where none of the few migrants' associations involved in sport activities (Granata 2013) was composed of forced migrants. Despite the formal (and occasionally financial) support received by a number of public and civic partners[8], Liberi Nantes relies heavily on the volunteer work of a small group of people who put great effort into managing to restore, through crowd-funding and other fundraising initiatives, a run-down football pitch they had been allocated by the local authorities in the Roman neighbourhood of Pietralata.

The first activity of the association was the creation of an open male football team, which from 2008 onwards has been participating 'off-table' in the lowest local level league, since the Italian Football Federation does not officially recognize all-migrants teams. Alongside the more regular players, dozens of occasional participants have been joining the training sessions on a drop-in basis, often borrowing second-hand equipment collected by the volunteers. Following the success of this initiative, which involved some 200 migrants in just two years,[9] Liberi Nantes created in early 2010 a touch rugby team with the purpose of including the further marginalized category of refugee women.[10]

With the aim of promoting this initiative and attracting participants, contact was established with one of the few reception centres for women forced migrants in Rome, namely La Casa di Giorgia (Giorgia's Home). Located quite far from Liberi Nantes' pitch, although on the same metro line, this centre has a capacity of 30–35 guests at a time and hosts around 70–90 women per year.[11] Over the three years considered by this study, about 15 migrant women overall got involved in the touch rugby project, although with very different patterns of attendance one from another.

Alongside the touch rugby provision, whose practical and symbolic implications are explored in this paper, further initiatives have been activated by Liberi Nantes, such as hiking and walking excursions and Italian language courses.

Liberi Nantes touch rugby was one of several cases investigated as part of the broader European project MIMoSA (Migrants' Inclusion Model of Sport for All) aimed at fostering migrants' inclusion/empowerment through sports by creating European networks of practitioners and policy-makers, sharing best practices, and developing models and methodologies for intervention.

As such, this case study was only funded by a small share of the overall budget and was restricted by the time framework of the wider MIMoSA project (April 2011–July 2012), which unfortunately partly overlapped with a period of several months (September 2011–January 2012) in which the pilot activities of Liberi Nantes touch rugby had to be suspended due to the lack of participants.

Moreover, the frequent turnover and the irregular patterns of the refugees' attendance, together with the 'screening' attitude adopted at times by some of our gatekeepers at Liberi Nantes (Scourfield 2012) to protect the participants and limit the research intrusiveness (Reeves 2010), further reduced the opportunities for ethnographic fieldwork and direct contact with the refugees involved in the programme.

Given these constraints, and considering the remit of the broader MIMoSA project, our purpose was not to undertake a systematic evaluation of the initiative through the voice of the refugees, which would have provided specific evidence (Banda et al. 2008; Kay 2012) of the actual contribution of the touch rugby initiative towards either the amelioration, or perpetuation, of sexual hierarchies and the inequality these involve.

Instead, our opportunistic sample (Patton 1990) focused on a small number of Liberi Nantes' activists and volunteers as information-rich cases in order to explore their experience and representations of the project, thus providing insights into the rationale and meanings underpinning the use of a mixed-gender sport activity such as touch rugby. Although all the volunteers involved in touch rugby were interviewed, theoretical saturation was not fully reached (Strauss and Corbin 2008) and further investigation is needed.

All the fieldwork was conducted by the first author. Two field visits where carried out during one-day-long touch rugby events organized by Liberi Nantes in June 2011 and March 2012. The purpose was not to undertake in-depth ethnographic investigation, but rather to get access to the field and become familiar with the context through non-participant observation, informal conversations and exploratory interviews, as well as establish contacts with some of the volunteers and arrange for formal interviews to be conducted later on via Skype (Hanna 2012).

Overall, twelve interviews were undertaken with Liberi Nantes' members and volunteers during this study: ten within the time frame of the MIMoSA project (five during the field visit in June 2011, two in November/December 2011, three in March 2012) and two follow-ups in June 2013 to gather retrospective accounts on the development of the touch rugby initiative. These involved six women directly active in the touch rugby project as players, coaches or organizers (including the president of the association, who was interviewed three times) and four men, comprising the touch rugby coach of 2012 and other Liberi Nantes' members supporting the touch rugby events but otherwise engaged in other activities of the association such as football and hiking. The duration of interviews ranged from 20 to 90 min and all the participants gave their consent for note-taking (in the field) or digital recording (via Skype). The data provided by the transcripts were also complemented by documentary material published on and off line, as well as internal project documents that Liberi Nantes kindly consented to share for this study.

In this paper, we mainly focus on data from the in-depth interviews with those female volunteers who were more directly involved in the touch rugby project.[12] A thematic analysis (Sparkes and Smith 2014) was initially developed to identify and examine those parts of the volunteers' accounts that focused on the participation of forced migrant women in the touch rugby initiative and the different outcomes of both the original women-only and the subsequent mixed-sex sports provision. However, broader meanings emerged from the subsequent sociological discourse analysis (Ruiz 2009), drawing our attention to the way the volunteers described and made sense of the birth and evolution of the touch rugby project. This partly turned our work into a narrative analysis that investigated how the stories about the touch rugby team were used by the volunteers as means to claim Liberi Nantes' identity by expressing and constructing it at the same time (Spector-Mersel 2011).

A difficult start: struggling to engage and retain refugees in a women-only team

Initially set up as a women-only activity to provide a more protective and less intimidating environment, in its first months Liberi Nantes touch rugby found it hard to recruit enough players to run regular training sessions. The pilot activities, started in early 2010, were suspended after a few months due to the lack of participants. They were resumed at the beginning of 2011, when the initiative eventually took off and a small group of 5–6 Italian female volunteers and 4 refugee women[13] managed to train twice a week for about six months, attending (as spectators) their first ever touch rugby match in April 2011 and eventually taking part in their first one-day tournament in June 2011. Contacts were thus established with a few teams in Rome and a small network of friends was gradually developed within the touch rugby community. This gave some visibility to Liberi Nantes and facilitated the involvement of the refugee women in public events.

These six months of regular training enabled the volunteers to gradually build trust and relationships with the refugees also through off-pitch convivial moments such as meals and parties:

> I've seen them change, in that at first they talked a lot among themselves and not much with us – they arrived, trained and left – while later I noticed that they really needed to open up, to talk, and to tell us their story. At the beginning it was a bit difficult, as you don't go there straight away and ask 'So where do you come from? How did you get here?' You give them time to regain their confidence, and then it is they who gradually talk about their past. Once we went for lunch together – cause at the end of the day you also have to create off-pitch moments to build a different connection – so we went together for a meal, we drew a map of Africa, and they explained to us where they came from, which route they had travelled all the way …

The initial reserve was progressively overcome, to a point where empathic relations between volunteers and refugees could even be expressed at times through emotional and physical intimacy:

> initially they came, they did this thing [the training] and then went away, full stop. Then, gradually, you became … they really saw you as a friend you can rely on and therefore they told us a little bit about their life in Italy, that eventually wasn't like the one they had expected of course, and about their problems, the fact that sometimes you noticed that they said to you 'I feel bad', 'What's the matter?', 'I feel sick, I have pain here', so we tried to figure out what the matter was so that we could maybe give advice, like 'Take an anti-inflammatory', and eventually you cuddled them a little bit and the pain was gone, it wasn't really an actual physical pain but probably something they had inside, an inner discomfort and perhaps they needed someone to give them attention, also some love …

Although only a small minority of the 30–35 refugees hosted by La Casa di Giorgia joined the touch rugby group in early 2011, this provided some of them with an alternative environment where self-expression could be encouraged, as reported by a volunteer from Liberi Nantes:

> I met a girl who last year was volunteering at La Casa di Giorgia, and so spent a lot of time with them, and she told me 'I can't understand how you girls managed to have such a special and beautiful relationship with the four girls who came [to touch rugby], who were the most complicated of all those hosted at La Casa di Giorgia at that time … for instance one of them told me that she spoke Italian with you, indeed she acted as a translator for the others as being the youngest she had learnt it the quickest, so very often it was she who translated into French for them, while at La Casa di Giorgia at one point she had stopped speaking Italian and gone back to only speaking French!'

Nonetheless, despite the encouraging results of the first half of 2011, the training sessions could not be resumed at the beginning of the new season in September because the two female volunteer coaches were not available anymore and all the refugee players had moved to other Italian or European cities following their resettlement pathway.[14]

After a few months of inactivity in autumn/winter 2011, two Liberi Nantes volunteers visited La Casa di Giorgia together with two new (male) volunteer coaches in January 2012 to try and advertise the initiative once again through a practical demonstration. As one of them recalls:

> we arrived there, they were waiting for us; actually they had understood that we would make a speech, an oral presentation of the project … and then, also, there was the problem that being January it was cold, anyway we went outside and tried to play with them, we called them, we went inside together with the social workers, then since they were at home many were wearing their pyjamas so they had to get changed, and this way we wasted time; then they slowly came out, one by one, as I say, it's cold for them … if he's a male he comes and plays, while for them that too becomes a reason for resistance, so to speak …

Similar comments, highlighting the low predisposition of refugee women to engage in outdoor physical activity in the event of bad weather, were a recurrent theme in our interviews. While many accounts tended to attribute a gendered nature to such attitude, others also referred to cultural reasons such as the lack of sporting socialization:

> the girls live far from the city centre (…) so when it's cold, having to take the metro gets complicated for them. This year we had one of the girls, Shane, who has a gorgeous one-year-old baby daughter, Nadège, so not only didn't she come when she couldn't but also when the baby was sick, therefore with the girls we suffer from this problem a little bit that they don't have a high sporting literacy, many of them have never done any sport …

Despite their benevolent intent and the acknowledgement of several other difficulties and constraints, comments of this kind partly recall the deficit model criticized by Toffoletti and Palmer (2015) and Chawansky (2011).

Notwithstanding the cold, seven migrant women still took part in the short practical demonstration at La Casa di Giorgia. Other guests of the centre preferred to stay in the dining room and watch the demonstration from the windows:

> Then the others were intrigued, they looked through the window from the dining room, although they said 'It's cold, it's cold, tell us about that here inside' (…) they clearly didn't want to get out, although we were telling them 'If you come out then you'll warm up!', which is true actually, but it is not easy to make them realise this.

Once again the volunteers seem to implicitly refer to the migrants' lack of sport experience and knowledge as the source of understandable and yet unjustified concerns, thus unintentionally confirming a representation based on a deficit model. This interpretation was often intertwined with other considerations that acknowledged and addressed the problems faced by the refugees when trying to attend the training sessions:

> in this period of January, February, March, when the days are still short, we did training around six and they were afraid of going around alone, they fear the darkness, the night more than the people, at times they didn't come also for this reason, a sprinkling of rain was enough, the fact that it was dark … on Saturday morning they would come, on Wednesday they never did … so we've cut it down to a single training session, we've made it longer, but it's on Saturday morning; during the week they also have an Italian language course, so in this way they were free from any other commitment, and then the darkness, this fear that at least some of them had, at least it was eliminated (…) they take the metro, they don't need to change, they take Line B and they are there, basically they go from one end of the line to the other, more or

less that's the route … but they're more willing to come at some times than others, it changes according to many things …

While the efforts made by the volunteers to adapt the activities to the needs of the refugees clearly demonstrate the acknowledgement of the legitimacy of such needs and the commitment to address them, expressions such as 'a sprinkling of rain was enough' still reveal a deficit-based interpretation by suggesting that these women often miss training sessions for reasons that would not be considered valid by an Italian/Western (sports)woman. Hence, bad and cold weather was often mentioned by the Italian volunteers as the main reason why the refugees did not attend very regularly:

> but then the following Saturday it was foggy, a really thick fog, I remember there was an incredible fog at my place as well, then I went to the pitch and the weather was nice, but where they live there was this fog like where I live, I'm telling you the climate factor is the first thing that keeps them away: 'it's foggy, we don't go cause the weather is dull'.

More generally, when reflecting on the difficulties of signing people up, our interviewees at Liberi Nantes tended to focus on many of the structural and practical barriers highlighted by Olliff (2008). Besides the bad weather, they often mentioned the distance to the pitch, the clash with other personal and familiar priorities, and the rapid turnover of participants due to their ongoing resettlement procedure.

While several studies highlight the importance of cultural and religious factors in influencing minority women's participation in sport (e.g. Ahmad 2011; Benn and Pfister 2013; Benn, Dagkas, and Jawad 2011; Dagkas, Benn, and Jawad 2011; Guerin et al. 2003; Jiwani and Rail 2010; Wray 2002; Zahidi, Syed Ali, and Nor 2012), the accounts of our interviewees did not focus on such aspects.

Further structural barriers (Olliff 2008) were also implicitly mentioned by some interviewees when explaining how their initial contacts with the forced migrant women was mediated and filtered by the social workers who were responsible for them at La Casa di Giorgia:

> we said that in case they were interested they could leave their names with the social workers at the Centre and we'd have liaised with them at least for the first two or three sessions, to know which people we had to wait for, who was going to come, etc.

While Liberi Nantes' volunteers clearly acknowledged and respected the role and responsibility of the social workers, they sometimes felt that their outreach potential was somewhat limited when they had the impression that some operator at La Casa di Giorgia was not particularly persistent in promoting the touch rugby activity amongst their guests:

> we are in contact with the social workers of the centre, with the supervisor and then with another girl, however I'm afraid that this girls I've been in contact with in this period … I mean, I've seen her working, more or less, and I don't feel … she doesn't show much motivation, she tries to say 'If you want to do … just go', but I don't think she motivates them that much, she doesn't …

Such a weak commitment in encouraging participation may be due to a lack of trust in the potential benefits of the sports activity, perceived as less urgent than other practical needs of the migrants such as managing the bureaucratic process related to their legal status, or completing their educational and working training programmes. Being often busy with such priorities, the social workers can act as 'screening' gatekeepers (Scourfield 2012) by protecting their guests while at the same time unintentionally limiting their opportunities.

However, although this clearly makes it harder for Liberi Nantes to recruit new players, it also guarantees that those women who join touch rugby do so out of their own free choice, rather than being pushed by their caregivers or being encouraged by linking sport participation to other transferable rewards, as happens with many sport-for-development programmes (e.g. Coalter 2010; Spaaij 2013b).

Keeping the door open: from women-only to mixed-sex

The temporary interruption of the activities due to the lack of coaches and refugee players in autumn 2011 raised serious doubts amongst the volunteers at Liberi Nantes about the efficacy of the project and the suitability of touch rugby as a tool to engage forced migrant women. However, it was also highlighted that despite the difficulties in recruiting and retaining migrant women, those (few) who got involved had clearly benefitted from the participation and therefore it was worth trying to keep this option available for other women in the future.

As a solution, in order to enlarge the pool of participants and enable the training sessions to resume, it was therefore decided to extend the participation to male players, initially by involving some members of the well-established all-male Liberi Nantes football team. Two players from the Roman team Spartaco Rugby volunteered to act as coaches, and the training sessions were eventually able to restart in winter 2011/12 with a group mixed by gender and origin. By the end of 2012, this involved 15–20 people including: Italian female volunteers from Liberi Nantes, male migrants (asylum-seekers and refugees, but also labour migrants already settled in the city), Italian young adult males interested in supporting the initiative and practising sport, and five new refugee women who gradually joined after the La Casa di Giorgia demonstration described above.

Opening up the team to male participants enabled the touch rugby activity to be advertised within the network of Reception Centres already developed by Liberi Nantes through their successful football team project and via other, more recent initiatives such as the provision of Italian language courses. Although the vast majority of the newcomers were initially more interested in playing football, the volunteers at Liberi Nantes tried to divert some of them to the touch rugby group. While this was firstly due to the practical impossibility of accommodating all the requests within the football team, the volunteers also saw it as an opportunity for the refugees to try and experience something new:

> so they went [to the football training] on Monday, they were 43, a disaster, they were so many, too much, I had told them: 'Look, keep them down to around 15', then she [the contact person at the Reception Centre] had told me '15–20 people' but it works by word of mouth amongst themselves, maybe they don't say anything to the operator and just go. So 43 of them arrived, so now we wanted to do a demonstration of touch rugby there at the Centre to try and balance the two things, cause I understand they are male and the first thing is football, however if they get to know another sport maybe they'll like it as well, I see it with some of the guys who play football with us [at Liberi Nantes], now they attend some touch rugby training cause at the end of the day it's enjoyable, it's good fun, therefore they come, if they've nothing else to do they come there as well.

According to our interviewees, the mixed-gender nature of the new touch rugby team did not seem to particularly inhibit or discourage the refugee women involved in the activity:

> I must tell you that especially this year the girls who came, let's say … apart from the initial embarrassment, which is fair enough, then they were very … I mean, they weren't ashamed to

get changed, they weren't uncomfortable (…) in fact, they connected nicely with all the guys, they didn't feel these difficulties.

However, the volunteers noted some embarrassment in the initial approach between males and females, which tended to gradually fade away with time:

every time a new person arrives you can feel this embarrassment, if a girls arrives she feels embarrassed playing with guys and vice versa, so also in the pitch there's this phase of observation and waiting, then gradually when the relationship grows and you keep playing together it's like you don't notice it anymore, so no such embarrassment anymore.

According to this interviewee, although the initial embarrassment was common to both males and females, it was more evident in the former and could be partly attributed to concerns about physical contact and potential collisions:

we noticed at the beginning the guys who arrived… the impact of finding girls playing with them too was peculiar (…) also the hesitation, because it's called 'touch' rugby, hence there is a contact, which is not violent as in rugby but yet there is a contact and therefore (…) they really seemed more reluctant about contact (…) Also this fear of hurting, I mean, it was there (…) Of course the embarrassment, why not, the embarrassment was actually visible even before they went on the pitch, meaning that once they arrived at Liberi Nantes and were welcomed by girls, you could immediately tell that the expression, the attitude, in short there was a difficulty.

Such initial discomfort tended to be expressed through mockery and ironic comments rather than explicit statements:

it was mainly as a joke, meaning that some of the guys, especially this year when that famous group of 30 guys came, they made a lot of jokes, 'we must play with girls', as if it was belittling, from a physical point of view I mean, as if it was taken for granted … that they'd win because of their physical superiority, therefore they saw it also as … also for this reason they went … 'I want to play football'.

As a strategy to cope with body-related, emotionally challenging situations (Flaming and Morse 1991), mocking comments based on gender stereotypes tended to be used as a defensive device by newly arrived, often young, male participants when they perceived mixed-gender sport as a threat to their masculine identities based on gender-segregated sporting socialization.

On the other hand, the Liberi Nantes touch rugby initiative also enabled participants to experience how it feels when players get used to a mixed-sex sporting environment and some of the initial restraints and inhibitions partly fade away. For instance, when recalling a match played against an all-men side composed of well-trained rugby players, an Italian woman volunteer observed that they did not receive any special treatment to compensate for their evident difference in physical size and strength ('which on the one hand is better, as it's a level playing field'). In her words, there seemed to be no sign of the female frustration due to males 'holding back' which is described in the studies of mixed-sex combat sports (Channon 2013a). In fact, competing against males can be slightly intimidating even in the alleged level playing field of touch rugby:

Let's say that it's very much about tactics and strategy, so non having that physically violent contact like in rugby you must try … you have to figure out where gaps can emerge to pass through, it's more about speed and tactics. Nonetheless there's also a … how can I say … the fact that you still are facing a person who is athletically formidable, you approach him in a different way (…) body size is not fundamental in touch rugby; however, since the goal is to score a try and therefore the opponent team tries to advance and push you back, if running towards you it is a physically big person it certainly has a different effect, I mean it scares you, so you tend to pull back [giggles]. If you are touched by a person who has a massive hand, it pulls you back, and since centimetres are fundamental in rugby, in touch rugby, as you have to score a try so more centimetres you move forward and the closer you get to the try, if you're touched by a big guy perhaps he pushes you out of position just with a touch. So yes, it is not important however … it has its effects, let's say (…)

These comments suggest that mixed-gender touch rugby can generate opposite dynamics compared to other practices already studied in the literature, notably mixed-sex combat sports. In fact, the latter can enable the 'undoing' of gender through participants' experiences that disconfirm sexist stereotypes within a practice which is intrinsically based on physical confrontation/collision, strength and aggression (Channon 2014). In our case, on the other hand, while touch rugby (or at least the way it is intended by Liberi Nantes' volunteers) is based on an inclusive and anti-sexist rhetoric that downplays or even denies the importance of differences in physical strength and condition, this can be disconfirmed by the actual experience of the female participants when playing against an all-male team composed of massive athletes used to physical collision. The slight ambivalence of our interviewee's account seems to evidence the cognitive dissonance generated by this contradiction.

Why touch rugby? Pragmatic reasons and symbolic meanings

The initial difficulties experienced by Liberi Nantes in the implementation of their pioneer initiative invite a reflection on both the advantages and disadvantages of using sport for social inclusion in the specific context of (women) forced migrants in Rome. Notably, this involves discussing both the rationale for, and the outcomes of, choosing touch rugby as a vehicle, as well as the implications of turning this sport provision from women-only into mixed-sex. We argue that both pragmatic and symbolic reasons and results can be highlighted.

The main pragmatic reason for using touch rugby is that being a recently established and small, volunteer-based association Liberi Nantes simply tried to offer the best that their limited resources enabled them to offer. Firstly, the choice of activities depended on the kind of competences that could be activated within the networks of volunteers. Secondly, the range of sports that could be offered to female forced migrants was restricted to those that could be played on the only available facility, i.e. Liberi Nantes' football pitch. Thirdly, the opportunity provided by touch rugby to build a mixed team by gender, age and physical condition/ability represented an important asset in a pioneering phase when the number of future participants could not be predicted and the physical condition of individuals was expected to vary. In that respect, although the activity was initially thought of as women-only, the possibility of opening it up to male participants was somehow implicit in the choice of touch rugby from the very beginning.

The practical outcomes of the project tend to be evaluated by the volunteers at two different but interrelated levels, since the specific aim of the touch rugby initiative is to engage female refugees, while the broader remit of Liberi Nantes is to provide inclusive sports opportunities for refugees in general. This leaves room for some ambiguity as the critical reflexivity about the specificity of women's involvement becomes at times merged with (and balanced by) self-encouraging considerations about the positive contribution of the touch rugby project to the broader aims of the association. For example, one interviewee illustrated how the project was providing participants with safety nets by extending their sporting and social networks even beyond the area of Rome:

> One of the Bengali guys, Shamal, who has always played with us (…) one day he came and said 'they are transferring me, I must go to Modena' so he was very sorry because he'd come to love the game, being with the group, and mostly because he was moving to a city he didn't know. So thanks to a contact we had from the Mondiali Antirazzisti, we knew there was a touch rugby team in Modena called TurtleIn (…) we called them and told them: 'there's this guy who played with us, he's moving to Modena and he needs to make new friends and keep playing touch rugby' and they adopted him.

However, it is worth noting that when trying to highlight positive outcomes of the project, many of these anecdotes referred to stories of male participants. Our interviews also seem to evidence that men were more easily attracted by Liberi Nantes' sport provision (with football generally, or at least initially, preferred to touch rugby), while women needed additional outreach efforts. On the one hand, this was due to the higher number of male refugees in the area compared to the few women-only reception centres. On the other hand, men had more freedom of movement around the city, while women seemed to be more limited by structural and mediating barriers (although cultural barriers, seldom mentioned by our interviewees, arguably play a significant role in constraining their physical and social mobility).

Yet it can be doubted whether sport and particularly mixed-sex touch rugby was an adequate tool to try and engage female forced migrants in this context. In fact, other activities organized by Liberi Nantes such as hiking and walking excursions, also mixing male and female volunteers and migrants, seemed to attract more refugee women than touch rugby. Hence, this could suggest that it is not the mixed-sex nature, but rather the type of activity that discourages refugee women from participation, since otherwise the walking tours would struggle to recruit as well as touch rugby does. More precisely, it can be reasonably argued that mixed-sex interaction generates different impacts when experienced through different activities, and (competitive team) sports can be perceived as a more challenging and intimidating environment than others.

However, turning the touch rugby provision from women-only into mixed-sex enabled Liberi Nantes to keep the initiative alive and maintain an opportunity for participation that would not have been available otherwise. It also facilitated exchange and communication between volunteers and migrants involved in the different activities of the association, with many of them moving from one activity to another or taking part in more than one at the same time.

The touch rugby team also enabled Liberi Nantes to extend their networks beyond the football field by building new friendships and establishing cooperation within the rugby community in Rome, increase the visibility of their association, recruit new volunteers, involve the neighbourhood of Pietralata and raise awareness about the condition of the refugees.

However, beyond the pragmatic reasons for, and practical outcomes of, choosing touch rugby, important symbolic factors need to be considered. For instance, a project document produced by Liberi Nantes' to advertise their initiative to the reception centres describes this sport as follows:

> rugby, as well as touch rugby, is a sport traditionally associated with the concept of fair play and because of this very characteristic it can become an instrument of mediation for those healthy and loyal relationships that are paramount for a fully-lived life. (…) the existence of

the 'third period' as an integral part of touch rugby's sports activity is an encouragement to openness and encounters between people where they see each other as human beings rather than through the labels of 'refugee' and 'Italian'.

In this vein, even ordinary aspects of the game can be magnified as representative of highly significant principles and values, as in the initial webpage of Liberi Nantes' touch rugby[15] (now replaced by a lower key description of the project):

> There is an important rule in Touch Rugby; when you are unmarked and you can receive the ball you must shout to your teammate HERE I AM, YES I'M HERE! These words embody all the strength inherent in this sport whereby the support of teammates is paramount; knowing that you are not alone on the pitch, helping the teammates who are struggling, it is funda- mental. For the guys and the girls who escape from countries where war, violence and torture are a daily occurrence, knowing that you can rely on someone is a fundamental psychological factor. They don't feel alone anymore, they are not alone anymore, they can run and play like we all do and they can take back that life, made up of simple things, which they had to give up.

The strong symbolic relevance attributed to touch rugby by Liberi Nantes plays an impor- tant role in the volunteers' attitude. This can be noted for instance when they justify their determination to pursue their goals, despite temporary difficulties and consequent doubts about the effectiveness of the project:

> touch rugby was very suitable as a sport for teaching integration, a way of living together; as I told you, despite the difficulty we had found with the women we still wanted to insist, precisely because sport is a very strong vehicle [for achieving these things], therefore we thought 'let's broaden it out and involve the boys as well and let's see if … With the girls it probably takes longer to engage them, so meanwhile let's carry on with this sport and try to keep an eye open for an opportunity to involve the girls'. And that's how it worked, I mean, this year for instance many girls came to train, also refugees.

However, this strong conviction of the inclusive value of this alternative activity risks becom- ing an unintentional expression of cultural imperialism (Darnell 2007), considering that touch rugby is a totally alien activity to the forced migrants (and to many of the volunteers as well) and thus their trust needs to be won, as if they have to be convinced of the virtues of this strange sport ('cause initially they're a bit dubious about the things that you suggest, maybe they understand them and maybe not'). Liberi Nantes' drive to promote the touch rugby initiative does not even seem to be undermined by their awareness of the evident cultural gap between this kind of sport provision and the migrants' actual expectations:

> if you present Liberi Nantes to people like Africans or … Afghans, Iranians, and you tell them about Liberi Nantes they'll come to football, none of them will ever come to touch rugby of their own free will. Maybe afterwards, when they already come to football and then you tell them: 'but why don't you go on Saturdays [to play touch rugby]?' (…) But if football is avail- able, there's no way that someone comes to play touch rugby, it's just not part of their culture. With the Asians it's been a bit easier because as soon as we arrive at the centres the Bengalis, Pakistanis and Indians ask you to play cricket as the first thing, and not having it available you tell them: 'why don't you come and try [touch rugby]?' and once they come maybe they get really keen …

As mentioned above, in the case of Liberi Nantes, the risk of unintentional cultural- imperialism is partly balanced by the absolute lack of pressure or blackmail in the way the touch rugby provision is proposed, leaving the migrants completely free to decide whether they want to take part in the activity or not (and also offering the flexibility of a drop-in format).

Besides, the volunteers' persistence in promoting touch rugby is also justified by high-lighting the importance of providing alternatives to mainstream sports and notably football, which is representative of a more general concern with the promotion of sporting pluralism as opposed to mainstream practices and homogenizing processes (Walseth and Fasting 2004). In turn, this represents the application of principles and values to the sports realm – such as the protection of minorities and biodiversity, the support to the disempowered and marginalized, the promotion of intercultural knowledge, respect and dialogue – which Liberi Nantes activists believe to be fundamental for any other area of our societies.

Therefore, the symbolic investment of Liberi Nantes in touch rugby is primarily related to its emblematic potential for social mixing. In this perspective, rather than being significant per se, the mixed-sex aspect of touch rugby is important insofar as it contributes to a broader rhetoric (and latent ideology) that celebrates any form of intersectional *mixité* and hybridity – i.e. across boundaries defined by nationality, ethnicity, class, gender, age or physical ability – as opposed to processes of classification, labelling, segregation and suppression of diversity.

To some extent, this reproduces the celebration of (super)diversity (Boccagni 2014) that characterizes the Mondiali Antirazzisti (Sterchele and Saint-Blancat 2015), the event promoted by Uisp in which Liberi Nantes were conceived.[16]

The social-mixing potential of touch rugby therefore plays a strong ritual role (Durkheim 1912; Collins 2004) as it symbolizes the core values of Liberi Nantes, the sources of their moral commitment, and ultimately Liberi Nantes themselves. This is clearly evidenced by the following quote from an internal document circulated after the first, unsuccessful attempt to start the touch rugby team:

> Touch rugby was a bet that had to be made, for many reasons. There was little energy available, though it had to be done. Conditions beyond our control (…) led to its suspension; but it has to be resumed, and quickly. A core group needs to be identified, possibly of girls, but not only, who can take this on board, since within the touch rugby experience a new rib of Liberi Nantes can form and, I dare to say, can be forged. A new experience needs to be rebuilt from scratch (…) It isn't and it won't be a joke, but it's our mission, our ultimate goal. Without this, nothing else means anything at all.

This partly explains why the mixed-sex nature of touch rugby is sometimes uncritically praised by our interviewees ('we've always seen it as a strength') and social mixing in any form tends to be magnified as a value per se as well as, or rather than, a means to an end:

> We can consider that [event] to be the inauguration of our mixed-sex touch rugby provision; 'we didn't succeed with the female-only, then let's extend it: to the men, to the nations …' [giggles], we've done it all-mixed!

Paradoxically, the mixed-sex character of Liberi Nantes touch rugby team is not a particularly distinctive feature within the touch rugby community, in fact being a common trait of a number of teams. Hence, other characteristics – such as the multi-ethnic, colourful composition of the team – become more relevant for those volunteers who consider the celebration of diversity as the main symbolic identifier of Liberi Nantes:

> we wear a fuchsia shirt and therefore the reaction is very curious cause yes it's true, the other teams have some female members as well … but we have this cross-cutting mix which is … which makes people curious anyway, and this while also bringing an activity in sport … I mean, we go and take part, we are an association while they perhaps are teams that only have a sporting objective while we bring an added value, that with sport you can also do something

else, that it is also a very powerful means to create a model of integration (…) and on this aspect we've always found very welcoming teams.

The inclusive culture of touch rugby clearly makes it easier for Liberi Nantes' social activism to be acknowledged and welcomed. However, their recognition within the Roman touch rugby community also needs to be reinforced by the gradual development of a sporting reputation:

> perhaps they expected a team that 'OK, an association that organises sport for refugees, so there's more of a human dimension to it, they won't pay attention to the sporting side'; but then the congratulations arrived for this sporting aspect too, for having been able to actually become a real team and therefore it highlighted this diversity even more.

Once the sporting reputation puts the team on the same level as their opponents, then the other distinctive features become more significant and deserve further acknowledgement. As a ritual outcome of this process, the symbolic power attached to touch rugby by Liberi Nantes' volunteers strengthens their group cohesion, gives them moral satisfaction and puts new energy into their motivations.

Conclusions

The choice of using mixed-sex touch rugby for forced migrants presented both advantages and contradictions. Given the limited resources and options available, it enabled Liberi Nantes to draw on a larger pool of male refugees to keep providing an opportunity for female participation, despite the frequent turnover and occasional lack of women participants. While extending the refugees' opportunities for social interaction, it also contributed to diversifying the range of Liberi Nantes' activities and enlarging their networks to raise further awareness of the forced migrants' cause and recruit new volunteers.

Nonetheless, female participation rates were relatively low in both the initial, women-only activities and the subsequent, mixed-sex provision. Cultural and structural barriers such as gender-role expectations, breadwinning and childcare commitments, concerns about the risks of commuting alone, and lack of sporting socialization, seem to limit forced migrant women's participation in Liberi Nantes' touch rugby regardless of the gender format of the activities. This clearly stimulates the volunteers' reflexivity, challenging them to question the appropriateness of using touch rugby specifically, and sport more generally, as a tool to engage forced migrant women in socially and personally meaningful experiences.

However, the symbolic meanings and implications of this choice appear at least as significant as (if not more significant than) its pragmatic outcomes. Touch rugby was chosen as an emblem of inclusion, equality and fair play, as well as promoted alongside/against mainstream sports like football as a symbol of sporting pluralism representing a broader commitment to celebrate diversity and support the disempowered both within and beyond the sporting field.

The mixed-sex dimension of touch rugby is part of this totemic representation since it contributes to this subversive symbolism of overcoming social hierarchies and boundaries by fighting segregation and favouring intersectional social mixing. Therefore, mixed-sex touch rugby can act as a ritual device to nourish a sense of moral purpose in Liberi Nantes' volunteers and reproduce their collective identity.

As shown by our analysis, this important identity-building power effect can be dangerous when the faith in the basic goodness of this sports provision risks overshadowing the beneficiaries' needs and expectations. At the same time, a sense of moral satisfaction is also vital to a voluntary-based association initiative to maintain group cohesion and regenerate motivations, without which Liberi Nantes – and the opportunities they provide to forced migrants women and men – would not exist.

The expectations and achievements of both the volunteers and the migrants are somehow intermingled and need to be balanced. The careful management of this balance is clearly the challenge that Liberi Nantes' activists are faced with.

Notes

1. Touch rugby is a limited-contact version of rugby in which players seek to avoid being touched, rather than tackled, while in possession of the ball.
2. A growing attention to the provision of sports opportunities for migrants in Italy is however shown by a number of initiatives run by sport-for-all organizations (e.g. Borgogni and Digennaro 2015).
3. The massive increase of asylum requests in Italy due to the very recent humanitarian emergencies in North Africa and the Middle East has increased the proliferation of legal types of partial protection, such as constitutional asylum, conventional refugee status, subsidiary protection, humanitarian protection, temporary protection (Marchetti 2010). This means that a decreasing proportion of all the asylum-seekers are actually given the full status of refugee. Hence, forced migrants, rather than refugees, would be a more appropriate term to define them all. However, for ease of reference, we will use the terms 'forced migrants' and 'refugees' interchangeably in this paper.
4. This partly consisted of labour migrants attracted by Italian economic prosperity up until the recent credit crunch (1980s–2000s) and largely of asylum-seekers and refugees following a sequence of migratory waves. Particularly from the 1990s onwards, these were generated by the terrible conflicts in Central and East Africa, the Balkans, the Middle East and more recently North Africa.
5. Moreover, most of the subsequent interventions have focused more on regulation and repression, rather than on reception and support (Ambrosini 2013).
6. For instance, in June 2010 – when Liberi Nantes' touch rugby was taking its first steps – the municipality of Rome claimed their reception centres were hosting around 2000 forced migrants but a further 3000 requests were on the waiting list (interview with the Councillor for Social Policy, available at: https://www.youtube.com/watch?v=9UIbtO7NfS4).
7. The founders were inspired by their participation in the Mondiali Antirazzisti (Antiracist World Cup), a non-competitive multi-sport and intercultural festival organized by UISP (Unione Italiana Sport Per tutti), one of the main Italian sport-for-all providers. Aiming at celebrating diversity and promoting anti-discriminatory practices, the Mondiali deliberately blur sporting categorizations and foster the creation of mixed teams by gender, age, origin, physical and technical ability (Sterchele and Saint-Blancat 2015 – both for mainstream disciplines such as football, basketball, cricket, volleyball and rugby, as well as for lesser known sports which are already inherently open to mixed-gender practice, such as tchoukball and touch rugby.
8. This network includes among others the UN High Commissioner for Refugees, Italian Council for Refugees, Jesuit Refugee Service, Diocesan Caritas of Rome, UISP-Italian Union for Sport for All, Shoot4Change and some local amateur sports clubs such as Touch Rugby Roma, Spartaco Rugby and Red&Blue Rugby, and receives limited financial support from the Lazio Region and the Province of Rome.
9. See the video-documentary by The Guardian, available at: http://www.theguardian.com/football/video/2015/oct/01/liberi-nantes-football-team-italy-refugees-video.
10. Liberi Nantes' website stated that 'in addition to persecutions, violence, torture and cruelty similar to those experienced by men, women often suffer abuse related to their gender, both

physical (e.g. rape) and social (e.g. discrimination and prohibitions or constraints on certain behaviours)'. Assuming that all this would cause 'a strong sense of helplessness, passivity, lack of self-confidence and lack of trust in other people', sport was considered as 'a useful practice to progressively re-appropriate your body, generating self-esteem and a self-awareness that facilitates the way women relate to the host society'.

11. In the first period of Liberi Nantes' touch rugby (2010–2013), examined in this paper, the guests ranged from minors to over-50s, though most of them were aged 18–30. The majority came from the Horn of Africa (notably Eritrea, Ethiopia and Somalia) and other West and Central African countries (Ivory Coast, DR Congo, Nigeria, Senegal, Guinea).
12. Since these interviewees shared similar characteristics in terms of age, social background, political orientation and level of involvement in the project, their accounts are reported in the text without attribution to each specific respondent. Instead, pseudonyms were used to anonymize any other people mentioned in the text.
13. Two of these migrant women came from English-speaking countries in the Horn of Africa, while the other two were French-speaking (one from North Africa and the other from Senegal). The linguistic divide was one of the main issues the Italian volunteers had to address in order to facilitate communication and relationships amongst the participants.
14. The difficulty or impossibility of keeping in contact with them was clearly frustrating for the volunteers as it showed how precarious and transitory the relationships can be, no matter how intense, when working with asylum-seekers and refugees.
15. http://www.liberinantes.org/touch-rugby/.
16. This is not surprising if we consider that their founders come from the same cultural and political milieu and the same networks as the Mondiali, with some of them being directly involved in both organizations.

Acknowledgements

The authors would like to thank Liberi Nantes and UISP International for their precious cooperation. They are also indebted to Mike Forshaw, Megan Chawansky, Luca Mori, Chiara Marchetti, the guest editors and the reviewers for their valuable comments and suggestions.

Disclosure statement

No potential conflict of interest was reported by the authors.

Funding

This study was funded by the European Union (Preparatory Action in the Field of Sport – EAC-2010-1325) as part of the project MIMoSA – Migrants' Inclusion Model of Sport for All (www.mimosaproject.net).

References

Ahmad, A. 2011. "British football: Where are the Muslim female footballers? Exploring the connections between gender, ethnicity and Islam". *Soccer & Society* 12 (3): 443–456. doi:10.1080/14660970.2011.568110
Aitchison, C. 2007. "Marking Difference or Making and Difference: Constructing Places, Policies and Knowledge of Inclusion, Exclusion and Social Justice in Leisure, Sport and Tourism." In *The Critical Turn in Tourism Studies*, edited by I. Ateljevic, N. Morgan and A. Pritchard, 77–90. Harlow: Elsevier.
Alexander, M. M. 2012. *Cities and Labour Immigration: Comparing Policy Responses in Amsterdam, Paris, Rome and Tel Aviv*. Ashgate. https://books.google.com/books?id=QxPbF1lNW_sC&pgis=1.

Amara, M., D. Aquilina, E. Argent, M. Betzer-Tayar, M. Green, I. Henry, F. Coalter, and J. Taylor. 2005. *The Roles of Sport and Education in the Social Inclusion of Asylum Seekers and Refugees: An Evaluation of Policy and Practice in the UK*. Loughborough: University of Loughborough and Sterling.

Ambrosini, M. 2013. "We Are against a Multi-Ethnic Society": Policies of Exclusion at the Urban Level in Italy. *Ethnic and Racial Studies* 36 (1): 136–155. doi:10.1080/01419870.2011.644312.

Banda, D., I. Lindsey, R. Jeanes, and T. Kay. 2008. *Partnerships Involving Sports-for-Development NGOs and the Fight against HIV/AIDS*. York: York St John University.

Benn, T., and G. U. Pfister. 2013. "Meeting Needs of Muslim Girls in School Sport: Case Studies Exploring Cultural and Religious Diversity." *European Journal of Sport Science* 13 (5): 567–574.

Benn, T., S. Dagkas, and H. Jawad. 2011. "Embodied Faith: Islam, Religious Freedom and Educational Practices in Physical Education." *Sport, Education and Society* 16 (1): 17–34.

Beutler, I. 2008. "Sport Serving Development and Peace: Achieving the Goals of the United Nations through Sport." *Sport in Society* 11 (4): 359–369. doi:10.1080/17430430802019227.

Black, D. R. 2010. "The Ambiguities of Development: Implications for 'Development through Sport.'" *Sport in Society* 13 (1): 121–129. doi:10.1080/17430430903377938.

Boccagni, P. 2014. "(Super)Diversity and the Migration–Social Work Nexus: A New Lens on the Field of Access and Inclusion?" *Ethnic and Racial Studies* 38 (4): 608–620. doi:10.1080/0141987 0.2015.980291.

Boccagni, P., and L. Baldassar. 2015. "Emotions on the Move: Mapping the Emergent Field of Emotion and Migration." *Emotion, Space and Society* 16: 73–80. doi:10.1016/j.emospa.2015.06.009.

Borgogni, A., and S. Digennaro. 2015. "Jugando en equipo: el rol de las organizaciones deportivas en el apoyo a la integración social de los emigrantes." [Playing Together: The Role of Sport Organisations in Supporting Migrants' Integration.] *EMPIRIA Revista de Metodología de Ciencias Sociales* 30: 109–131.

Brady, M. 2005. "Creating Safe Spaces and Building Social Assets for Young Women in the Developing World: A New Role for Sports." *Women's Studies Quarterly* 33 (1/2): 35–49. http://www.jstor.org/stable/40005500.

Channon, A. 2013a. "Do You Hit Girls?" Some Striking Moments in the Career of a Male Martial Artist. *Fighting Scholars: Habitus and Ethnographies of Martial Arts and Combat Sports* 44: 95–110. http://gala.gre.ac.uk/10197.

Channon, A. G. 2013b. "Enter the Discourse: Exploring the Discursive Roots of Inclusivity in Mixed-sex Martial Arts." *Sport in Society* 16 (10) : 1293–1308. doi:10.1080/17430437.2013.790896.

Channon, A. 2014. "Towards the "Undoing" of Gender in Mixed-sex Martial Arts and Combat Sports." *Societies* 4 (4): 587–605. doi:10.3390/soc404058.

Chawansky, M. 2011. "New Social Movements, Old Gender Games? Locating Girls in the Sport for Development and Peace Movement". In *Critical Aspects of Gender in Conflict Resolution, Peacebuilding, and Social Movements (Research in Social Movements, Conflicts and Change, Volume 32)*, edited by A.C. Snyder, S.P. Stobbe, pp.121–134. Bingley: Emerald. doi: 10.1108/S0163-786X(2011)0000032009.

Coalter, F. 2010. "The Politics of Sport-for-Development: Limited Focus Programmes and Broad Gauge Problems?" *International Review for the Sociology of Sport* 45 (3): 295–314. doi:10.1177/1012690210366791.

Collins, R.. 2004. *Interaction ritual chains*. Princeton, NJ: Princeton University Press.

Crum, B. 1988. "A Critical Analysis of Korfball as a 'Non-Sexist Sport.' *International Review for the Sociology of Sport* 23 (3): 233–241.

Dagkas, S., T. Benn, and H. Jawad. 2011. "Multiple Voices: Improving Participation of Muslim Girls in Physical Education and School Sport." *Sport, Education and Society* 16 (2): 223–239.

Darnell, S. C. 2007. "Playing with Race: Right to Play and the Production of Whiteness in 'Development through Sport." *Sport in Society* 10 (4): 560–579. doi:10.1080/17430430701388756.

Darnell, S. C., and L. M. C. Hayhurst. 2011. "Sport for Decolonization: Exploring a New Praxis of Sport-for-Development." *Progress in Development Studies* 11 (3): 183–196.

Durkheim, É. 1912. *Les formes élémentaires de la vie religieuse. Le système totémique en Australie [The elementary forms of the religious life: The totemic system in Australia]*. Paris: Alcan.

Elling, A., P. De Knop, and A. Knoppers. 2001. "The Social Integrative Meaning of Sport: A Critical and Comparative Analysis of Policy and Practice in the Netherlands." *Sociology of Sport Journal* 18 (4): 414–434.

Elling, A., P. De Knop and A. Knoppers. 2003. "Gay/lesbian Sport Clubs and Events: Places of Homo-social Bonding and Cultural Resistance?" *International Review for the Sociology of Sport* 38 (4): 441–456. doi: 10.1177/1012690203384005 6.

Evans, A. 2014. "Contesting Far Flung Fields: Sociological Studies of Migration and Acculturation through Sport." In *Acculturation: Psychology, Processes and Global Perspectives*, edited by J. Merton, 67–86. New York: Nova Science.

Evers, C. 2010. "Intimacy, Sport and Young Refugee Men." *Emotion, Space and Society* 3 (1): 56–61. doi:10.1016/j.emospa.2010.01.011.

Flaming, D., and J. M. Morse. 1991. "Minimizing Embarrassment: Boys' Experiences of Pubertal Changes." *Issues in Comprehensive Pediatric Nursing* 14 (4): 211–230. doi:10.3109/01460869109009039.

Gilchrist, P., and B. Wheaton. 2011. "Lifestyle Sport, Public Policy and Youth Engagement: Examining the Emergence of Parkour." *International Journal of Sport Policy and Politics* 3 (1): 109–131. doi:10.1080/19406940.2010.547866.

Giulianotti, R. 2011. "The Sport, Development and Peace Sector: Four Social Policy Domains." *Journal of Social Policy* 40 (4). 757–776. doi: 10.1017/S0047279410000930.

Granata, S. 2013. "Le funzioni sociali dell'associazionismo sportivo per gli immigrati in due contesti urbani europei." [The Social Functions of Amateur Sport Clubs for Migrants in Two European Urban Contexts]. *M@Gm@* 11 (1). http://www.magma.analisiqualitativa.com/1101/articolo_08.htm.

Guerin, P. B., R. O. Diiriye, C. Corrigan, and B. Guerin. 2003. "Physical Activity Programs for Refugee Somali Women: Working out in a New Country." *Women & Health* 38 (1): 83–99. doi:10.1300/J013v38n01_06.

Guruge, S., and E. Collins. 2008. *Working with Immigrant Women: Issues and Strategies for Mental Health Professionals*. Toronto: Centre for Addiction and Mental Health.

Hancock, M. G., A. Lyras, and J. Ha. 2013. "Sport for Development Programs for Girls and Women: A Global Assessment." *Journal of Sport for Development* 1 (Mar.): 15–24.

Hanna, P. 2012. "Using Internet Technologies (Such as Skype) as a Research Medium: A Research Note." *Qualitative Research* 12 (2): 239–242. doi:10.1177/1468794111426607.

Janssens, J., and P. Verweel. 2014. "The Significance of Sports Clubs within Multicultural Society. On the Accumulation of Social Capital by Migrants in Culturally "Mixed" and "Separate" Sports Clubs." *European Journal for Sport and Society* 11 (1): 35–58.

Jeanes, R., J. O'Connor, and L. Alfrey. 2014. "Sport and the Resettlement of Young People from Refugee Backgrounds in Australia." *Journal of Sport and Social Issues*. Advance online publication. doi:10.1177/0193723514558929.

Jiwani, N., and G. Rail. 2010. "Islam, Hijab and Young Shia Muslim Canadian Women's Discursive Constructions of Physical Activity." *Sociology of Sport Journal* 27 (3): 251–267.

Kay, T. 2012. "Accounting for Legacy: Monitoring and Evaluation in Sport in Development Relationships." *Sport in Society* 15 (6): 888–904. doi:10.1080/17430437.2012.708289.

Kelly, L. 2011. "'Social Inclusion' through Sports-based Interventions?" *Critical Social Policy* 31 (1): 126–150. doi:10.1177/0261018310385442.

Kidd, B. 2008. "A New Social Movement: Sport for Development and Peace." *Sport in Society* 11 (4): 370–380. doi:10.1080/17430430802019268.

Korac, M. 2001. "Cross-ethnic Networks, Self-Reception System, and Functional Integration of Refugees from Former Yugoslavia in Rome." *Journal of International Migration and Integration / Revue de l'integration et de la migration internationale* 2 (1): 1–26. doi:10.1007/s12134-001-1017-9.

Korac, M. 2003. "Integration and How We Facilitate It: A Comparative Study of Settlement Experiences of Refugees in Italy and the Netherlands." *Sociology* 37 (1): 51–68. doi:10.1177/0038038503037001387.

Krouwel, A., N. Boonstra, J. W. Duyvendak, and L. Veldboer. 2006. "A Good Sport? Research into the Capacity of Recreational Sport to Integrate Dutch Minorities." *International Review for the Sociology of Sport* 41 (2): 165–180.

Long, J., and I. Sanderson. 2001. "The Social Benefits of Sport: Where's the Proof?" In *Sport in the City: The Role of Sport in Economic and Social Regeneration*, edited by C. Gratton and I. Henry, 187–203. London: Routledge.

Lyras, A., and J. Welty Peachey. 2011. "Integrating Sport-for-Development Theory and Praxis." *Sport Management Review* 14 (4): 311–326. doi:10.1016/j.smr.2011.05.006.

Marchetti, C. 2010. "The Expanded B order. Policies and Practices of Preventive Refoulement in Italy." In *The politics of international migration management*, edited by M. Geiger and A. Pécoud, 160–183. London: Palgrave Macmillan.

Marchetti, C. 2014. "Rifugiati e migranti forzati in Italia: il pendolo tra 'emergenza' e 'sistema.'" [Refugees and forced migrants in Italy. The pendulum between 'emergency' and 'system.] *REMHU: Revista Interdisciplinar Da Mobilidade Humana* 22 (43): 53–70. doi:10.1590/1980-85852503880004304.

Olliff, L. 2008. "Playing for the Future." *Youth Studies Australia* 27 (1): 52–60.

Palmer, C. 2008. "Soccer and the Politics of Identity for Young Muslim Refugee Women in South Australia." *Soccer & Society* 10 (1): 27–38. doi:10.1080/14660970802472643.

Patton, M. 1990. *Qualitative Evaluation and Research Methods*, Newbury Park: Sage.

Pringle, R. 2005. "Masculinities, Sport, and Power: A Critical Comparison of Gramscian and Foucauldian Inspired Theoretical Tools." *Journal of Sport and Social Issues* 29 (3): 256–278. doi:10.1177/0193723505276228.

Ratna, A. 2014. "'Who Are Ya?' The National Identities and Belongings of British Asian Football Fans." *Patterns of Prejudice* 48 (3): 286–308. doi:10.1080/0031322X.2014.927603.

Reeves, C. L. 2010. "A Difficult Negotiation: Fieldwork Relations with Gatekeepers." *Qualitative Research* 10 (3): 315–331. doi:10.1177/1468794109360150.

Ruiz, J. R. 2009. "Sociological Discourse Analysis: Methods and Logic." *Forum Qualitative Sozialforschung/Forum: Qualitative Social Research*. http://www.qualitative-research.net/index.php/fqs/article/view/1298/2776.

Scourfield, P. 2012. "Defenders against Threats or Enablers of Opportunities: The Screening Role Played by Gatekeepers in Researching Older People in Care Homes." *The Qualitatibe Report* 17 (28): 1–17. http://www.nova.edu/ssss/QR/QR17/scourfield.pdf.

Spaaij, R. 2012. "Beyond the Playing Field: Experiences of Sport, Social Capital, and Integration among Somalis in Australia." *Ethnic and Racial Studies* 35(9): 1519–1538.

Spaaij, R. 2013a. "Changing People' S Lives for the Better? Social Mobility through Sport-based Intervention Programmes: Opportunities and Constraints." *European Journal for Sport and Society* 10 (1): 53–73.

Spaaij, R. 2013b. "Cultural Diversity in Community Sport: An Ethnographic Inquiry of Somali Australians' Experiences." *Sport Management Review* 16 (1): 29–40. doi:10.1016/j.smr.2012.06.003.

Spaaij, R. 2015. "Refugee Youth, Belonging and Community Sport." *Leisure Studies* 34 (3): 303–318. doi:10.1080/02614367.2014.893006.

Spaaij, R., and N. Schulenkorf. 2014. "Cultivating Safe Space: Lessons for Sport-for-Development Projects and Events." *Journal of Sport Management* 28: 633–645.

Sparkes, A. C., and B. Smith. 2014. *Qualitative Research Methods in Sport, Exercise and Health. From Process to Product*. London: Routledge.

Spector-Mersel, G. 2011. "Mechanisms of Selection in Claiming Narrative Identities: A Model for Interpreting Narratives." *Qualitative Inquiry* 17 (2): 172–185. doi:10.1177/1077800410393885.

Stack, J. A. C., and Y. Iwasaki. 2009. "The Role of Leisure Pursuits in Adaptation Processes among Afghan Refugees Who Have Immigrated to Winnipeg, Canada." *Leisure Studies* 28 (3): 239–259. doi:10.1080/02614360902951658.

Sterchele, D. 2015. "De-Sportizing Physical Activity: From Sport-for-Development to Play-for-Development." *European Journal for Sport and Society* 12 (1): 97–120.

Sterchele, D., and C. Saint-Blancat. 2015. "Keeping It Liminal: The Mondiali Antirazzisti (Anti-Racist World Cup) as a Multifocal Interaction Ritual." *Leisure Studies* 34 (2): 182–196. doi:10.1080/02614367.2013.855937.

Strauss, A., and Corbin, J. 2008. *Basics of Qualitative Research: Techniques and Procedures for Developing Grounded Theory*. Thousand Oaks: Sage. doi:10.4135/9781452230153

Tagg, B. 2008. "'Imagine, a Man Playing Netball!' Masculinities and Sport in New Zealand." *International Review for the Sociology of Sport* 43 (4): 409–430.

Theeboom, M., H. Schaillée, and Z. Nols. 2012. "Social Capital Development among Ethnic Minorities in Mixed and Separate Sport Clubs." *International Journal of Sport Policy and Politics* 4 (1): 1–21.

Thorpe, H., and R. Rinehart. 2012. "Action Sport NGOs in a Neo-Liberal Context: The Cases of Skateistan and Surf Aid International." *Journal of Sport & Social Issues* 37 (2): 115–141. doi:10.1177/0193723512455923.

Toffoletti, K., and C. Palmer. 2015. "New Approaches for Studies of Muslim Women and Sport." *International Review for the Sociology of Sport*. Advance online publication. doi:10.1177/1012690215589326.

Walseth, K. 2006a. "Sport and Belonging." *International Review for the Sociology of Sport* 41 (3–4): 447–464.

Walseth, K. 2006b. "Young Muslim Women and Sport: The Impact of Identity Work." *Leisure Studies* 25 (1): 75–94.

Walseth, K., and K. Fasting. 2004. "Sport as a Means of Integrating Minority Women." *Sport in Society* 7 (1): 109–129.

Watson, R., L. Tucker, and S. Drury. 2013. "Can We Make a Difference? Examining the Transformative Potential of Sport and Active Recreation." *Sport in Society* 16 (10): 1233–1247.

Wray, S. 2002. Connecting Ethnicity, Gender and Physicality: Muslim Pakistani Women, Physical Activity and Health. In *Gender and Sport: A Reader*, edited by S. Scraton. and A. Flintoff 124–140. London: Routledge.

Zahidi, M. A., S. K. Syed Ali, and M. R. M. Nor. 2012. "Young Muslim Women and Their Relation with Physical Education Lessons." *World Journal of Islamic History and Civilization* 2 (1): 10–18.

"We have to establish our territory": how women surfers 'carve out' gendered spaces within surfing

Cassie Comley

Sociology Department, University of Oregon, Eugene, OR, USA

ABSTRACT

This Research Insight piece examines how southern California recreational women surfers experience, cope with and contest their marginalized status within the male-dominated sport of surfing. Drawing on literature that focuses on women in alternative sports, I argue that women surfers face similar contradictions, such as developing strategies to cope with and contest their marginalized status and creating separate spaces. Surfing is a fruitful area of study because it is a recreational activity that is not bound by any formal rules or regulations that separate women and men from participating with each other, but as this study will show, surfers are constructing gender boundaries. This study builds on existing literature that examines the varying ways sporting women resist and reproduce dominant cultural understandings of gender, as well as focusing on how creating separate spaces is a source of empowerment for women in masculinized spaces.

Introduction

This study sought to understand whether women surfers face subcultural barriers within the surfing space and analyse if/how women surfers are contesting gender relations. The key to understanding lay in examining the varying ways in which women surfers navigated the surf landscape and their perceived marginalized status, which ultimately led some of them to create their own gendered spaces. Findings from this study demonstrate that women surfers do face subcultural barriers within the surfing space and tend to draw on dominant cultural understandings of gender to cope with or contest their marginalized status. Surfing is a valuable site for studying how women navigate male-dominated spaces for the following reasons: first, surfing is not an organized or traditional sport, it is a highly individualized activity and it is a mixed-sex activity (at least at the recreational level); second, it was originally a sport enjoyed by both men and women in the Polynesian Islands, but when it was introduced into the United States, it quickly became a sport dominated by men until the 1970s; third, surfing is typically gender-typed as masculine (Thorpe 2009; Stoddart 2011), even though there has been a growing number of women and girls who enter the sport's landscape (Ford and Brown 2006). Surfing is an action sport which, some scholars believe, provides a potential avenue for changing and challenging traditional cultural beliefs about gender (Beal 1996; Anderson 1999; Laurendeau 2004, 2008; Thorpe 2005).

Surfing as a gendered space

The sport of surfing provides an opportunity to explore on a deeper level how women navigate meanings of gender in an arena typically dominated by masculine gender norms. This normalization of male-centricity is well captured in this testimony from Crystal:

> If I see a guy and he isn't catching waves, well then I'll paddle over there and tell him to call me off if he has it, otherwise they're wasting it (the wave). That's how they (men) look at us. That we (women) wasted it. I'll say something to them, but they won't! They just come over and burn us. We have to establish our territory.

> Crystal, advanced-intermediate, 50 year old woman surfer

This brief but illuminating story about a woman surfer's experience of the surfing space highlights a few important themes that occur at a local surf break in southern California. First, many male surfers perceive women participants to be occupying a marginalized position within the surfing space. Women surfers in this study frequently reported being the only woman out in the line-up, feeling singled out and being treated differently by male surfers. Crystal showed her awareness of her marginalized status by adopting a more aggressive style of wave catching. Instead of waiting for the other male surfers to 'burn her' (when a surfer who doesn't have the right of way steals a wave from another surfer), she told them to let her know whether they were going for the wave or else she was going to go for it. Second, women surfers adopted a number of strategies to cope with and contest their marginalized position. Crystal adopted a strategy of being assertive and calling for waves instead of passively waiting for male surfers to 'burn' her. She had to adopt this strategy for catching waves, whereas the male surfers' strategy consisted of waiting for her to tell them to call her off or simply 'burning' her. This difference in choice of strategy further highlights the third theme; the space is male-dominated. When Crystal said 'we have to establish our territory', she emphasized the challenges and need for women to carve out gendered spaces within male-dominated environments. Instead of accepting her marginalized status within surfing, she contested her position and proved she deserved to be there and that men do not have priority over the waves. This case illustrates that some women athletes continue to face subcultural barriers within male-dominated sports, but also that they often engage in a number of strategies to cope with and contest their marginalized status.

In recreational surfing, there are no rules or formal regulations preventing women and men from surfing with each other, yet as this study shows, some men are engaging in exclusionary practices that marginalize women. Since alternative physical cultures and activities are not bound by any particular system of rules (Laurendeau and Sharara 2008), these activities are not articulated in terms of sex/gender teams or leagues (Olive, McCuaig, and Phillips 2015). Within alternative physical cultures, the marginalization or exclusion of women occurs through 'cultural understandings and expectations' of how the activities should be performed, or the assumptions about male and female performances (Olive, McCuaig, and Phillips 2015). For example, some female snowboarders believe their abilities are often compared to 'the boy's scale' (Thorpe 2005, 93) and young male skaters believe the lack of female involvement in skateboarding culture is tied to the ideology that 'girls don't like to get hurt' (Beal and Wilson 2004, 47). Some participants believe there are 'female' and 'male' appropriate ways of engaging in physical activities, so that even when women do well or show commitment to their sport, their performance is still demarcated by gender, such as they are still only 'good for a girl' (Booth 2001; Atencio, Beal, and Wilson 2009; Sisjord 2009). Exclusionary and marginalization practices are not limited to action sports; women recreational golfers reported sought out 'women-friendly' courses to avoid practices that trivialized and marginalized them as athletes (McGinnis, McQuillan, and Chapple 2005).

Exclusionary and marginalizing practices are not always contingent on gender. Within some windsurfing subcultures, women are judged not by their ability as 'a woman', but rather their level of commitment and skill (Wheaton and Tomlinson 1998). However, initial experiences with windsurfing subcultures can still be exclusionary for women. Women initially felt deterred from participating in windsurfing subcultures because of the myth of the 'macho man surfer' that feeds into the idea that there is a 'natural' association between masculinity and windsurfing (Wheaton and Tomlinson 1998). This myth can be extremely effective in marginalizing women's involvement during the early stages of their participation, but as more women challenge the association between masculinity and windsurfing, they find themselves occupying a different role within the community. Wheaton and Tomlinson (1998) found that some women's role within the subculture was dependent on their proficiency and extent of commitment to the windsurfing culture. Only women who were 'hardcore advanced windsurfers' could be seen as 'one of the lads' instead of 'a female windsurfer' (Wheaton and Tomlinson 1998, 264). Their demonstration of sporting prowess, which was an important aspect of peer approval, was still achieved in relation to other men windsurfers (Wheaton and Tomlinson 1998). Women's athletic abilities were still measured against 'the boy's scale' (Thorpe 2005, 93), but performance, not the fact that they were women, mattered more (Wheaton and Tomlinson 1998). Windsurfing provided women participants with a sense of community and collective identity, but womanhood was not a basis of unity or bonding (Wheaton and Tomlinson 1998). This is quite a different finding than I found in my own work, in which womanhood was a sense of unity and bonding for some women surfers that were not as skilled. This difference may in part be due to surfing's 'fraternal structure' of gender relations that marginalizes and excludes women surfers (Booth 2001).

When surfing was first introduced to Western cultures during the 1900s, it quickly spread between groups of men who were in the social and cultural position to participate in this new sport (Ford and Brown 2006). Since men had more freedom for leisure participation, surfing in Western culture has 'undeniably a male-dominated history' (Ford and Brown 2006, 94). It was not until the 1950s that women's surfing participation started to steadily increase. Even though surf culture in the United States currently adopts a 'fraternal structure' (Booth 2001), there were times when gender relations were less oppressive. For example, women competed against men in the International Surfing Competitions until the late 1960s when organizers thought it would be best to create different competitions for women and men (Booth 2001). There appeared to be 'fraternal tendencies' during the 1950s but the fraternal structure of surfing did not fully consolidate until the late 1970s and early 1980s (Booth 2001). According to Booth (2001), this fraternization of surf culture emerged from two shifts occurring within the culture; first, the radical shift in the surf media's representation of women in the 1980s and, second, the long struggle waged by women surfers in the 1970s and 1980s to organize their own surf competitions. Women established their own professional surfing tour because they saw the professional circuit as a way to contribute to the development of the sport and combat the fraternization of the subculture (Booth 2001). Due to these two occurring conditions, women found themselves increasingly marginalized within surf cultures (Booth 2001; see also Roy and Caudwell 2014; Olive, McCuaig, and Phillips 2015). Although there has been a 'mass movement' (Ford and Brown 2006) of women surfers, they continue to face challenges both structurally and subculturally (Booth 2001; Ford and Brown 2006; Olive, McCuaig, and Phillips 2015).

Structurally, professional women surfers earn significantly less money than male surfers (Ford and Brown 2006). For example, the male winner of a surf event earns an average of $100,000 compared to the female winner who earns about $40,000. There are more male surf events than there are female because they struggle to secure surf competitions each year (Booth 2001; Ford and Brown 2006). Even though the gender gap in participation has significantly decreased over time (Stedman 1997), male surfers still outnumber women surfers in the line-up (Roy and Caudwell 2014) and continue to dominate the covers of surfing magazines (Henderson 2001). Structural barriers are important to highlight, but as others have suggested, empirical studies examining the 'lived realities of men's and women's sporting experiences' are needed within the study of sport (Wheaton 1998; see also Hargreaves 1994). By exploring the lived experiences of women and men's sporting participation, one can further understand how these unique experiences have impacted 'the ways participants have come to understand surfing experiences and cultures' (Olive, McCuaig, and Phillips 2015, 259; see also Waitt 2008; Waitt and Warren 2008; Olive and Thorpe 2011).

In terms of subcultural barriers, women surfer's experiences of the surfing space are varied. For example, some women surfers feel patronized and differentiated by male surfers out in the line-up (Olive, McCuaig, and Phillips 2015), whereas other women surfers feel empowered and use surfing as a space to contest traditional discourses of both femininity and motherhood (Knijnik, Horton, and Cruz 2010; Spowart, Burrows, and Shaw 2010). A study examining women's surfer's experiences in a small beach town in Australia found that women felt patronized by the ways in which male surfers engaged with them (Olive, McCuaig, and Phillips 2015). Women surfers reported receiving extra levels of attention, support and encouragement from male surfers, which may seem altruistic and supportive to male surfers, but was perceived as patronizing by the female surfers. For the women, receiving additional attention and support from male surfers was more difficult to negotiate than openly discriminatory behaviour. Women surfers did not report experiencing any overtly discriminatory behaviour, but men's patronizing behaviour did make them feel as if they were not 'authentic' surfers (Olive, McCuaig, and Phillips 2015). By differentiating women in the water, male surfers reinforced and maintained the idea that they are 'women that surf' instead of 'surfers' (Olive, McCuaig, and Phillips 2015, 265). Even though women surfers felt patronized and were being differentiated they could still be agentic by refusing the advice and help they received in the line-up. By refusing to accept being differentiated, women surfers have the potential to 'carve out alternative ways of operating within the power relations that circulate in the waves' (Olive, McCuaig, and Phillips 2015, 273). This study is a reminder that it is important to understand the everyday experiences of women participants that might be overlooked at the structural level (Olive, McCuaig, and Phillips 2015; see also Roy and Caudwell 2014).

Similar to other alternative sports and sports in general, surfing can be a medium through which women can challenge dominant cultural beliefs about gender (Waitt 2008; Knijnik,

Horton, and Cruz 2010; Roy and Caudwell 2014; Olive, McCuaig, and Phillips 2015). For example, a group of professional Brazilian women surfers were both resisting and conforming to attitudes consistent with traditional ideals of the female body (Knijnik, Horton, and Cruz 2010). Most of the women surfers felt pressured to conform to traditional beauty standards and to promote their physical attractiveness, but this cohort of Brazil women are starting to 'carve out' their own space as they continue to push against normative attitudes about women's physicality. (Knijnik, Horton, and Cruz 2010). These women surfers occupied a contradictory position in the line-up because they are still 'stuck in a web of body and identity that is a central element of the dominant masculine hegemony' that is pervasive in Brazilian society (Knijnik, Horton, and Cruz 2010). The authors suggest that women in sport generally occupy a position that is both compliant with and resistant to hegemonic standards, a contradictory position that they will have to cope with at every stage of their sporting practice (Knijnik, Horton, and Cruz 2010). This case of Brazilian surfers highlights the contradictory position women surfers occupy within the surfing space and the potential for resistance.

Experiences of marginalization and exclusion are not exclusive to surfing, but rather a consistent pattern in the alternative physical culture literature. Even though non-traditional sport spaces can offer great promise for the 'realization of alternative and resistant sport forms' (Birrell and Theberge 1994, 371), women participants in non-traditional sports still face subcultural barriers. They continue to struggle with: earning respect from their male peers (Roy and Caudwell 2014), being seen as 'authentic' members of the culture (Atencio, Beal, and Wilson 2009; Olive, McCuaig, and Phillips 2015) and being viewed as 'real competitors' (Kay and Laberge 2004). Specifically within surfing, Olive, McCuaig, and Phillips (2015) argue, "The greatest barrier for women surfers is the role men play in continuing to differentiate women within male-dominated surfing cultures" (258; see also Booth 2001; Ford and Brown 2006). Even though women surfers have been a part of the subculture for centuries, they continue to face subcultural barriers, such as marginalization. The current study illustrates how women cope with and contest their perceived marginalized status.

Methods

Twenty-five (15 female and 10 male) surfers ranging from ages 18 to 50, whose surfing abilities range from beginner to advanced, were interviewed between June 2012 and September 2012 (each surfer self-reported their skill level). I spent approximately four months observing, conducting in-depth interviews and having informal conversations with surfers at a popular beach in southern California. I used in-depth interviewing because I was interested in seeking 'deep' information and knowledge from the participants (Johnson 2002). In-depth interviewing aims to explore the 'contextual boundaries' of the experience or perception; therefore, in order to understand how women surfers experience, cope with and contest their marginalized status, I needed to uncover what is usually hidden from ordinary view (Johnson 2002). The transcribed interviews were open coded, which meant I read my field notes and interviews line by line to identify and formulate any and all ideas, themes or issues suggested in the data (Berg 2007). Through open coding, I was able to analyse how women's experiences intersect with and are shaped by their marginalized gender status.

I began my field observations by hanging around the main entrance to the beach. Within a few weeks, I met two female locals who eventually helped me locate other women surfers in the region and became my 'field guides' (Berg 2007, 103). In the social world of surfing, a guide or informant would be called 'a local', which is someone most familiar with the break who has an established relationship with the region's surf community. I used this relationship with the locals to meet other surfers. At first, I was only an observer, but found it was more fruitful to get off the sand and in the water to increase my chances of making contacts. I found if I was just sitting on the beach next to my surfboard surfers were less likely to talk to me because as soon as they got out of the water, they would pack up their belongings and leave. If I got in the water and paddled amongst groups of surfers, I could strike up a conversation with surfers between sets. I used this break in the waves to generate a con- versation about the wave conditions, which in some cases, lead to making a contact. As a surfer myself, I occupied an 'insider' position within the culture. As an insider, it is assumed I understand the 'nuances of the cultural group' because I am already a member of the sport, which means I more than likely subscribe to the norms of the sporting practice (Fletcher 2014). Although being an insider may restrict a researcher's ability to be critical (Fletcher 2014), I found it to be crucial in understanding how women surfers cope with and contest their marginalized status. Based on my field observations, semi-structured interviews and conversations, I found that women's experiences, coping and contesting strategies were contextualized by their perceived marginalized gender status. In the following sections, I show how surfing continues to be perceived as a male-dominant space and how women surfers cope with and contest their status in the sport.

Findings

The Old Boys Club

I started every interview by having each surfer tell me how he or she got involved with surfing. Women surfers reported very different experiences gaining access to surfing spaces. Common themes included not being 'invited' to surf the space by male surf friends, not surfing when they were younger, getting extra attention from male surfers, feeling pressure to perform and feeling as if they had to 'represent' for all women surfers. Many male surfers interviewed reported incidents of treating women differently out in the line-up. A few male surfers reported feeling pressure to perform when they were a novice surfer, but this feeling for women never shifted with experience. All of the women, except one, said they had to take a surfing class to learn how to surf. Men reported no issues gaining access to the surfing space and none of them reported taking surf lessons. Some women even chose to surf at other beaches that were more 'women-friendly' (where they did not feel like their gender was salient), a finding similar to the experiences of female golfers (McGinnis, McQuillan, and Chapple 2005). The following quote illustrates how women experienced the surfing space differently to men:

> You have to get that first wave because everyone is watching you and waiting to see if you can perform. You have to represent, especially as a woman. You have to show them (men) that you deserve to be out there. The guys don't have to do that and we (women) know that, but we keep doing it anyway. (Katie, 44, intermediate)

Male surfers did not report having to 'represent' as a man or perform well to show they deserved to be out in the line-up. Not once did men ever mention surfing a different break because it was not 'men-friendly'. When I asked male surfers whether they ever saw women surfers being treated differently or whether they treated women differently, most of them agreed they would give a woman a wave if they thought she was having a hard time catching a wave. When I asked whether they would do this for a male surfer, they all agreed they would not. Women were aware that men treated them differently out in the line-up, which as Olive, McCuaig, and Phillips (2015) argue, suggests women surfers are not seen as 'authentic surfers' because they are treated differently from male surfers (265). Even if male surfers intend to give advice as an attempt to include and support women in the male-dominated line-up (Olive, McCuaig, and Phillips 2015), women have different interpretations of the situation. The following quote highlights how women surfers often feel conflicted about accepting a wave from a male surfer:

> You know, if you (men) want to give me this perfect A-frame wave then I am not going to complain! (laughs) Thanks! (laughs again) But by me taking it, I'm kind of going back on my beliefs. You know, a guy giving you a wave is like a slap in the face? Dude, really, we're trying to surf here. Maybe you should take us more seriously, yeah, we may not be as strong as you and that's nice of you, but really, don't do it because you feel sorry, do it because you think we need a wave because you think we are going to go crazy if we don't get one! (laughs). (Jody, 25 years old, advanced)

At first, she wants the wave, but she knows if she takes the wave, she will be conforming to dominant cultural ideologies about female physicality. In her perspective, she would be going back on her beliefs if she accepted the wave, but she was comfortable accepting the wave if the male surfer's intent was grounded in the notion that she might 'go crazy' if she did not get a wave soon. Sharing a wave with another surfer because, as a surfer, you understand the need for a wave was acceptable to Jody, but simply giving a woman a wave because she is a woman was a 'slap in the face'. Male surfers may think they are acting altruistically and not engaging in patronizing behaviours (Olive, McCuaig, and Phillips 2015), but women surfers may not see it that way. This excerpt highlights the need to further understand male surfers' intentions when they give a woman surfer a wave/extra attention. However, regardless of the intention, differentiating women in the water further marginalizing them within the community.

Understanding marginalization

Women surfers employed a number of strategies to cope with and contest their perceived marginalized status. Three coping strategies emerged from the data: women surfed at friendlier beaches, surfed the 'set waves' and/or joined all-women surf clubs. Joining an all-women surf club eventually became a way for women to contest their perceived marginalized status because surfing with a large group of women meant they could physically occupy a space. Women in the surf club reported feeling empowered over time, so even though the club started as a coping mechanism, it became a mechanism of contestation when they interacted with male surfers outside of the club. Acts of contestation varied by ability, with surfers in the advanced category individually contesting the space and surfers in the intermediate category contesting the space in groups of women. In a majority of cases, women relied on dominant cultural understandings of gender to explain why women and men experienced the space differently. For example, when some of the intermediate surfers explained why they surfed the 'set waves' (the inconsistent and less valuable waves), they typically said it was due to men 'naturally' being more aggressive:

I think guys are *a lot* harder on themselves, like they cuss at themselves and each other and I am just like, *ok*, I will just wait for the next one. It's not a big deal you know? So yeah, they are harder on themselves, we (women) are just more easy going, we're more casual, like yah know, we're just happy to be out in the water, enjoying Mother Nature. They're out there trying to catch the big bombs. We're just surfing on the set waves yah know, not waiting for the bombs. (Jenna, 49, intermediate)

Many male surfers used a similar framework for explaining gender differences. As one male surfer told me, he would rather surf with 'girls' because they 'mellow everything out'. By associating maleness with trying to catch the biggest waves and femaleness with enjoying mother nature/mellowing the vibe, male and female surfers are perpetuating the ideology that men are 'naturally' going to adopt a more aggressive style of surfing. Indeed, Waitt's (2008) study of male surfers found that men constructed their gender identity by being 'in control' of the natural environment, by paddling into dangerous surf and conquering the ocean (358). None of the male surfers challenged dominant cultural understandings of gender nor did any of them report experiences of marginalization or exclusion (except a few that reported these experiences when they were novice surfers), although many female surfers did. In order to cope with their perceived marginalized status, some women surfers often joined all-women surf groups. By surfing with an 'army of women' as one partici-pant put it, the sheer number of women in the water contested the male-dominated space. When women surf together in a surf club, it allows them to share waves with each other. Women surfers felt empowered by each other and encouraged and supported each other, which de-emphasized the competitive aspects of the sport. This finding shares similarities with other studies that found when women join all-women sports groups/clubs, they can hone their skills and increase visibility in traditionally male-dominated sports (Thorpe 2008; Stoddart 2011). As more women enter the highly masculinized space of surfing, it is pertinent to understand how their presence in the space transforms the landscape and how they 'carve' out their own spaces. Although joining all-women sport clubs may not challenge gender inequality in the sport more widely, it provides a platform for women to improve their abilities and bond over womanhood. Perhaps eventually, as was the case with female windsurfers, female surfers will be seen as 'one of the lads' or simply be judged by their commitment to the community instead of demarcated by their gender.

Conclusion: Constructing gender boundaries

This case of women surfers highlights the varying ways in which women surfers cope with and contest their marginalized status and illustrates how women surfers create separate spaces. Women surfers reported different experiences gaining access to the space and felt like they had to 'represent' for all women. Male surfers are perceived as having wave priority and differentiate women in the water, causing them to develop strategies such as surfing the 'left-over' (less valuable) waves or joining all-women surf clubs to cope with their perceived marginalized status. Joining surf clubs is an effective strategy for less-skilled women to feel empowered and challenge the highly masculinized space. Depending on a surfer's status, women directly contested the space by paddling over to groups of men and calling for waves or they surfed with an 'army of women' to physically take over the space. In some cases, women reproduced dominant cultural gender ideologies when explaining how they coped with their marginalized status.

This study shares similarities with other studies examining women's experiences in alternative sport spaces. Even though male surfers differentiated women surfers in the water, women could refuse or reject male surfers patronizing behaviours and carve out alternative ways of operating within the space (Olive, McCuaig, and Phillips 2015). Just as previous studies have shown, surfing can be a medium through which women surfers can challenge and reproduce dominant cultural understandings of gender (Waitt 2008; Knijnik, Horton, and Cruz 2010). Joining an all-women surf club or snowboarding club may not be challenging broader cultural beliefs about women and men, but does create a space where women feel empowered and can unite over womanhood. Creating more alternative spaces for women to challenge sport's masculine culture has been a strategy employed by women from a range of sports such as snowboarding (Thorpe 2005, 2009), roller derby (Finley 2010) and backcountry skiing (Stoddart 2011). For some women, this may be the only available option to contest masculinized spaces and provide a space for women to be themselves, a finding similar to Carrington's (1998) study of the Caribbean Cricket Club. Eventually, women sport participants may not need to join all-women surf clubs or snowboarding camps in order to avoid feeling marginalized, but in order for this to occur, there has to be 'deeper structural change' within surfing, as well as in the broader sport culture (Booth 2001). Examining local power relations is necessary for understanding the day-to-day experiences of sporting women because it uncovers how power is reproduced and challenged (Olive, McCuaig, and Phillips 2015). Future research could focus on the following to further understand marginalization and resistance within surf cultures: analyse how men and women's perspectives differ on matters such as giving up a wave, interview more 'hard core' members to further understand how their commitment to the sport may override gender differences and compare two surfing locations to analyse if differences are contingent on spatial location. This case of women surfers highlights the continuing need to understand the complex relationship women occupy in marginalized positions in male-dominated spaces.

Disclosure statement

No potential conflict of interest was reported by the author.

References

Anderson, K. 1999. "Snowboarding: The Construction of Gender in an Emerging Sport." *Journal of Sport & Social Issues* 23 (1): 55–79.

Atencio, Matthew, Becky Beal, and Charlene Wilson. 2009. "The Distinction of Risk: Urban Skateboarding, Street Habitus and the Construction of Hierarchical Gender Relations." *Qualitative Research in Sport and Exercise* 1 (1): 3–20.

Beal, Becky. 1996. "Alternative Masculinity and Its Effects on Gender Relations in the Subculture of Skateboarding." *Journal of Sport Behavior* 19 (3): 204–220.

Beal, Becky, and Charlene Wilson. 2004. "'Chicks Dig Scars': Commercialisation and the Transformations of Skateboarders' Identities." *Understanding Lifestyle Sports: Consumption, Identity and Difference*: 31–54.

Berg, Bruce L. 2007. *Qualitative Research Methods for the Social Sciences*. 7th ed. Boston, MA: Allyn and Bacon.

Birrell, S., and N. Theberge. 1994. "Feminist Resistance and Transformation in Sport." In *Women and Sport*, edited by D. M. Costa and S. R. Guthrie, 361–376. Champaign, IL: Human Kinetics.

Booth, Douglas. 2001. "From Bikinis to Boardshorts: Wahines and the Paradoxes of Surfing Culture." *Journal of Sport History* 28 (10): 3–22.

Carrington, Ben. 1998. "Sport, Masculinity, and Black Cultural Resistance." *Journal of Sport & Social Issues* 22 (3): 275–298.

Finley, Nancy. 2010. "Skating Femininity: Gender Maneuvering in Women's Roller Derby." *Journal of Contemporary Ethnography* 39: 359–387.

Fletcher, Thomas. 2014. "'Does He Look like a Paki?' an Exploration of 'Whiteness', Positionality and Reflexivity in Inter-Racial Sports Research." *Qualitative Research in Sport, Exercise and Health* 6 (2): 44–260.

Ford, Nick, and David Brown. 2006. *Surfing and Social Theory*. London: Routledge.

Hargreaves, Jennifer. 1994. *Sporting Females Critical Issues in the History and Sociology of Women's Sport*. Hoboken, NJ: Taylor & Francis.

Henderson, Margaret. 2001. "A Shifting Line Up: Men, Women, and Tracks Surfing Magazine." *Continuum: Journal of Media & Cultural Studies* 15: 319–332.

Johnson, M. John. 2002. "In-Depth Interviewing." In *Handbook of Interview Research: Context and Method*, edited by Jaber F Gubrium and James A. Holstein, 103–119. Thousand Oaks California: Sage.

Kay, Joanne, and Suzanne Laberge. 2004. "'Mandatory Equipment': Women in Adventure Racing." In *Understanding Lifestyle Sports: Consumption, Identity and Difference*, edited by Belinda Wheaton, 154–174. New York: Routledge.

Knijnik, Jorge Dorfman, Peter Horton, and Lívia Oliveira Cruz. 2010. "Rhizomatic Bodies, Gendered Waves: Transitional Femininities in Brazilian Surf." *Sport in Society* 13: 1170–1185.

Laurendeau, Jason. 2004. "The 'Crack Choir' and the 'Cock Chorus': The Intersection of Gender and Sexuality in Skydiving Texts." *Sociology of Sport Journal* 21 (4): 397–417.

Laurendeau, Jason, and Nancy Sharara. 2008. "'Women Could Be Every Bit as Good as Guys' Reproductive and Resistant Agency in Two 'Action' Sports." *Journal of Sport & Social Issues* 32 (1): 24–47.

McGinnis, Lee, Julia McQuillan, and Constance L. Chapple. 2005. "I Just Want to Play Women, Sexism, and Persistence in Golf." *Journal of Sport & Social Issues* 29 (3): 313–337.

Olive, Rebecca, Louise McCuaig, and Murray G. Phillips. 2015. "Women's Recreational Surfing: A Patronising Experience." *Sport, Education and Society* 20 (2): 258–276.

Olive, Rebecca, and Holly Thorpe. 2011. "Negotiating the 'F-Word' in the Field: Doing Feminist Ethnography in Action Sport Cultures." *Sociology of Sport Journal* 28 (4): 421–440.

Roy, Georgina, and Jayne Caudwell. 2014. "Women and Surfing Spaces in Newquay, UK." In *Routledge Handbook of Sport, Gender and Sexuality. Routledge International Handbooks*, edited by J. Hargreaves and E. Anderson, 235–245. Abingdon: Routledge.

Sisjord, Mari Kristin. 2009. "Fast-Girls, Babes and the Invisible Girls. Gender Relations in Snowboarding." *Sport in Society* 12 (10): 1299–1316.

Spowart, Lucy, Lisette Burrows, and Sally Shaw. 2010. "'I Just Eat, Sleep and Dream of Surfing': When Surfing Meets Motherhood." *Sport in Society* 13 (7–8): 1186–1203.

Stedman, Leanne. 1997. "From Gidget to Gonad Man: surfers, feminists and postmodernisation." *Journal of Sociology* 33 (1): 75–90.

Stoddart, Mark. 2011. "Constructing Masculinized Sportscapes: Skiing, Gender and Nature in British Columbia, Canada." *International Review for the Sociology of Sport* 46: 108–124.

Thorpe, Holly. 2005. "Jibbing the Gender Order: Females in the Snowboarding Culture [1]." *Sport in Society* 8 (1):76–100.

Thorpe, Holly. 2008. "Foucault, Technologies of Self, and the Media Discourses of Femininity in Snowboarding Culture." *Journal of Sport & Social Issues* 32 (2): 199–229.

Thorpe, Holly. 2009. "Bourdieu, Feminism and Women Physical Culture: Gender Reflexivity and the Habitus-Field Complex." *Sociology of Sport* 26: 491–516.

Waitt, Gordon. 2008. "'Killing Waves': Surfing, Space and Gender." *Social and Cultural Geography* 9: 75–94.

Waitt, Gordon, and Andrew Warren. 2008. "'Talking Shit over a Brew after a Good Session with Your Mates': Surfing, Space and Masculinity." *Australian Geographer* 39 (3): 353–365.

Wheaton, Belinda, and Alan Tomlinson. 1998. "The Changing Gender Order in Sport? The Case of Wind Surfing Cultures." *Journal of Sport & Social Issues* 22 (3): 252–274.

Challenging the gender binary: the fictive and real world of quidditch

Jeffrey O. Segrave

Department of Health and Exercise Sciences, Skidmore College, Saratoga Springs, NY, USA

ABSTRACT

Despite the recent emergence of women and gay men, lesbians, bisexuals, intersexuals and transsexuals (GLBITs) in sport, gender equity has been far from realized. Dominant forms of sport are bimodal in gender classification, a construction that creates an ideology of male superiority and marginalizes women and GLBITs. One recent example of a sport that confronts traditional gendering is quidditch. In its fictional form, the competitive sport featured in the fantasy world of J. K. Rowling's Harry Potter series and its real-world form, muggle quidditch, the sport is gender inclusive. The purpose of this study was to consider the ways in which both quidditch and muggle quidditch challenge the dominant forms of institutionalized sport and present an alternative structure for gender participation and identification. I draw upon a literary analysis of Rowling's portrayal of quidditch, relying in particular on Wolfgang Iser's literary anthropology, as well as a qualitative analysis of the personal testimonies of muggle quidditch players.

Introduction

It all began on 12 July 2014. The family called it a 'black day', the day Indian sprinter Dutee Chand was tersely informed that, despite just a month earlier having won two gold medals at the 16th Asian Junior Athletics Championships in Taipei City, she would not be considered for selection for the Commonwealth Games in Glasgow, Scotland. The reason, she was told by a doctor at the Sports Authority of India center in Kengeri, was that she had a condition called hyperandrogenism, the presence of excess androgen, specifically testosterone, in samples collected from her contravened guidelines put in place in 2011 by the International Association of Athletics Federation. On August 29, she was officially barred from all national and international sporting events. Rather than submit to hormone treatment or surgery, Chand instead filed an appeal with the Court of Arbitration for Sport in Switzerland (Macur 2014).

Chand's case is not the first to confront traditional notions about identity and fairness in sport. Gender testing has been a controversial element of competitive athletics since 1950, when Dutch sprinter Foekje Dillema became the first woman disqualified as a result of

189

testing positive for a Y-chromosome. Since then numerous cases have arisen to challenge the traditionally gendered organization of sport, including the well-publicized cases of Russian track and field athletes Irena and Tamara Press, US tennis player Reneé Richards, and Canadian mountain biker Michelle Dumaresq. In 2009, South African runner Caster Semenya was banned and reinstated after she was compelled to undergo gender testing. By refusing to 'change' her 'body for participation' – 'I'm not changing for anyone', she recently declared (Macur 2014) – Chand is directly confronting and contesting the gendered foundation of sport, and the culturally constructed edifice upon which sport is based, the hegemonic gender binary.

Envisioning arenas of organized sport that do not rely on the rigidly defined and policy defended gender binary remains a challenge in the sex segregated world of western society. Despite recent policy changes at the highest levels (Griffin and Carroll 2012), sport is still an inhospitable place for GLBIT athletes, especially transsexuals and intersexed athletes. And even though queer feminist writing and the transgender liberation movement have contested the naturalness of male and female categories, sex segregated sport remains the hegemonic mode of sport presentation and organization. Gay and lesbian athletes may have found some freedom of gender expression in gay and lesbian sport leagues and competitions that are anti-homophobic, but questions still remain about the extent to which any of these cultural spaces confound the entrenched gender binary and about how sports that are consciously gender blind ameliorate or perpetuate gender hierarchies and inequalities.

Quidditch, the fantasy sport depicted in J. K. Rowling's Harry Potter series[1], as well as muggle[2] quidditch, the real-world sport derivative of Rowling's imaginary sport, embrace a world of gender equality. In fact, in Rowling's fictive imagination, there is a simple assumption of gender equality, of equal access and participation between males and females, an assumption that is expanded in the real world of muggle quidditch to include the notion of all genders. Muggle quidditch actively embraces full gender equality and inclusiveness and challenges in form, constitution and culture the dominant forms of gendered sport. As Coakley (2009) argues, gender equity involves more than new ways to define and portray gender; it also entails changes in the ways that sports are organized and played, in the new vocabularies and images associated with sports and in the ways that success and enjoyment are evaluated. One possible new strategy for advancing gender equity, Coakley posits, is to develop programmes that 'bring together boys and girls, men and women, and heterosexual and GLBITs in shared sport experiences that promote new ideas about gender and sports in society' (270). Quidditch and muggle quidditch do.

The purpose of this study was to consider the ways in which both quidditch and muggle quidditch challenge the dominant gender binary of modern institutionalized sport and present an alternative structure for gender participation, experience and identification. Ultimately, I wish to argue that quidditch, in both its fictive and real forms, offers a powerful alternative to the biocentric gender model of contemporary sport and suggests a gender paradigm that empowers athletes and furthers the cause of gender equity in sport.

Sport and the gender binary

In his discussion of gender regimes, Connell (2002) contends that social institutions have 'regular sets of arrangements about gender', including such practices as who is recruited to play particular roles, 'what kinds of social divisions are recognized … how emotional relations are conducted … and how these institutions are related to others' (53). In other words, gender regimes form the 'structure of relations' within which we all make decisions about how we conduct ourselves as gendered individuals, how we do gender, how we confront 'the possibilities and consequences of action' (55). Gender regimes create the gender order of society and serve as the foundation for enduring social relations.

Despite contestation, current gender regimes remain dominated by the gender binary, a classification model that stipulates gender in terms of opposition and difference and naturalizes a hierarchical ordering of gender. As Risman and Schwartz (2002) succinctly put it: 'the very creation of difference is the foundation on which inequality rests' (25). Males who have historically had greater access to positions of privilege, power and influence than females have protected their culturally vaulted status. Furthermore, as Coakley (2009) recognizes, 'a two-category model provides no legitimate social space or recognition for gender non-conformists' (260). Consequently, within a binary classification, GLBITs are socially positioned and stigmatized as inferior, invariably fostering homophobic responses.

Ideas and beliefs about gender are both reflected and constructed within the world of sport. As Coakley (2015) notes, sports serve as significant social sites for affirming and re-affirming conceptions of male–female differences, valorizing heterosexual masculinity and legitimizing male power and privilege. Sport, in short, serves as a crucial site in the construction and preservation of orthodox gender ideology. The meaning of gender, how gender is enacted and expressed, and how men and women do gender are symbolized and played out in the arenas of sport. Hartman (2003) argues that sport 'makes male advantages and masculine values appear so normal and so "natural" that they can hardly be questioned' (20). The traditional binary classification of sport results in what Messner (2002) calls 'an almost uncontested institutionalized "center"'.

> The center is a position occupied by the biggest, wealthiest, and most visible sports programs and athletes. It is the site of domination and privilege. It is the major focal point of the gaze of millions of fans and spectators. We find sport's center as the core of athletic departments in schools and universities, at the locus of peer status systems among young people, and at the major nodes of sports media. And sport's center is still, by and large, a space that is actually constructed by and for men. (xviii)

The 'center' marginalizes and disempowers not only women, but also GLBITs whose participation in the world of sport has typically been deemed invasive or intrusive rather than innovative. As a result, GLBIT athletes have been discriminated against, harassed and victimized by homophobic attitudes and behaviours. In response to the International Olympic Committee's recent policy on gender in sport, known as the Stockholm Consensus, Cavanagh and Sykes (2006) note that

> The policy functions to manage a categorical gender binary in the face of social, medical, and legal uncertainty; gender identifications, anatomical, genital and chromosomal variations that aren't intelligible to those committed to a bio-centric two sex model; so called gender 'purity' in women's sport; and to mask fetischistic engagement with athletic bodies – as media spectacles – that are hyper-muscular, sculpted, highly toned, enervated, streamlined, and appear to be death-defying. (78)

In short, the gender binary serves as the entrenched blueprint of gender relations and the gender order in American society, and the traditional binary classification in sport serves as one of the most powerful cultural practices that affirm the inferiorization and marginalization of both women and GLBITs.

While sport may well have been, and, to a great extent, still is, a core patriarchal and masculinist institution, it operates within a contested gender order and it no longer plays a purely reactionary and regressive role in the fortification of binary gender relations. Just as postmodern theories of subjectivity and identity have sought to destabilize the bipolar notion of gender by insisting upon a spectrum of fluid identities, so also has the postmodern queer and feminist deconstruction of essential gender internally contested the world of gendered sport. The radically shifting opportunity structure and cultural imagery of the post-Title IX sports have ushered in developing forms of sports and emerging demographics of participation and spectatorship that have challenged the once normalized beliefs about male superiority, female inferiority and the marginalization of other gendered populations. The dramatic rise in women's sports, extreme sports, lifestyle sports, gay and lesbian community sports, and a wide variety of other recreational and alternative sports has created more space for the development of an array of meanings, identities, interactions and relationships, around the contested issues of gender and sexuality (Rinehart 2005; Thorpe 2005). Often subversive in both nature and intent, and certainly less integrated into or dominated by what Messner (2002) calls 'the sport-media-commercial complex' (xx), these sports have challenged the 'apartheid of sex' (Rothblatt 1995) and the related heteronormative model of gender as normal and given expression to a more equitably redistributive politics of engagement. Among these sports is the newly emergent sport of quidditch, a sport in its fictive form that abolishes the gender binary by unpretentiously assuming gender equity and in its real-world form that proactively rejects the gender binary by acknowledging the multiplicity of genders that constitute the lived experience of many athletes.

In order to make my case, I will draw upon a literary analysis of Rowling's portrayal of quidditch in the Harry Potter series, relying in particular on Wolfgang Iser's (1993) literary anthropology, as well as a qualitative analysis of the personal testimonies of a small, targeted group of club muggle quidditch players. In other words, I adopt a multidisciplinary and multimethodological approach in order to interrogate the ways in which both the fictive and real-world versions of quidditch further gender equity in sport.

Theoretical and methodological considerations

From a broad theoretical perspective, I rely heavily on a transdisciplinary approach (see Bandy, Gori, and Jinxia 2012) and include the perspectives of sociology, ethnography, literature and sport to interrogate experiential and gendered ways of being in the world. Transdisciplinarity acknowledges that knowledge exists on different levels of reality and is revealed in multiple ways of existential and disciplinary knowing. It is for these reasons that in his study of boxing, the sociologist Löic Wacquant (2004) uses 'three texts of deliberately disparate statuses and styles, which juxtapose sociological analysis, ethnographic description, and literary evocations in order to convey at once percept and concept, the hidden determinations and the lived experiences, the external factors and the internal sensations that intermingle' to constitute the lived world of the athlete (7). I also rely on intersectionality, what Nash (2008) calls the 'gold standard multi-disciplinary approach for analyzing subjects' experiences of both identity and oppression' (2). Intersectionality embraces the notion that 'subjectivity is constituted by mutually reinforcing vectors of race, gender, class, and sexuality' (Nash 2). Intersectionality highlights the 'multidimensionality of marginalized subjects' lived experiences' (2) and subverts race and gender binaries in the service of theorizing the complexity of identity.

In terms of methodological considerations, in order to increase our understanding of the ways in which athletes experience gender within the sport of muggle quidditch, data were collected informally from questionnaires completed by 18 active quidditch players ranging in ages from 18 to 24. Following appropriate institutional review approval, participants were recruited from club teams located in the environs of a large east coast city in the US. Participants were contacted by a 'cultural informant' (McCurdy, Spradley, and Shandy 2005), someone already familiar with the environment and the personnel. The clubs included a wide range of self-identified genders including heteronormative men and women, but also gay men, lesbians, bisexuals, intersexuals and transexuals. Data collection took place via email in the fall of 2014. Respondents self-identified by race, gender and sexual preference.[3] The questions invoked what Plummer (1995) identifies as 'sexual stories', 'narratives of intimate life, focused especially around the erotic, the gendered and the relational' which offer fascinating sociological insights into 'the late modern world' (6). The primary rationale for employing this type of research is, as Connell (1990) explains, that 'the theorized life history can be a powerful tool for the study of social structures and their dynamics as they impinge upon (and are reconstituted in) personal life' (84).

The quidditch club teams studied constitute what McCurdy, Spradley, and Shandy (2005) define as a microculture. Microcultures are similar to subcultures in that they exist within a larger, complex society but different in that they do not define an entire way of life. Microcultures are 'the cultures associated with groups that form for a variety of reasons but do not consume every hour of their members' time' (14–15). All of us participate in multiple microcultures at any one time and each group is characterized by unique, 'inside' cultural knowledge which facilitates social interaction (15–16).

Quidditch

Quidditch is the competitive sport featured in J. K. Rowling's Harry Potter series played throughout the wizard world, quidditch is a rough and tumble, semi-contact game played by two teams riding flying broomsticks. Each team is constituted of seven players (three Chasers, two Beaters, one Keeper and the Seeker) and there are four balls (the Quaffle, two Bludgers and the infamous Golden Snitch). The main goal of Quidditch is to score points by throwing the ball – the Quaffle – through hoops placed at either end of a large grassy pitch. Quidditch is played by kids on broomsticks in the backyard, by the students at Hogwarts School of Witchcraft and Wizardry and by professional athletes whose exploits attract a worldwide audience. At heart, quidditch indulges preadolescent flights of fancy. It is fast-paced, dangerous and exciting, and it presumes the ability to fly and chase. Because the sport is played in the near-contemporary world of the present, rather than in the imaginary and mediaeval flavoured netherworlds of Middle Earth or Earthsea or Narnia, it offers Rowling an inventive way to explore and interrogate significant issues in contemporary sport and culture, including the issue of gender in sport.

One of the most enduring critiques of Rowling's epic series, however, is that it is grounded in a conventional morality – 'conservative tomes for conservative times', as *The Guardian's* Claire Armistead (1999) puts it – and, because it is neither overtly didactic nor consciously idealistic, it inverts the subversive potential of fantasy by failing to challenge accepted norms, interrupting critical inquiry and affirming the hierarchical status quo. With regard to gender, the columnist Christine Schofer (2000) asserts that 'Harry's fictional realm of magic and wizardry perfectly mirrors the conventional assumption that men do and should run the world', and Gallardo C. and Smith (2003) more recently argue that 'Harry Potter is not particularly progressive in its gender representations' (194). Yet, there is one dimension of the Harry Potter story that seriously challenges these last claims, namely the fact that quidditch is not segregated on the basis of gender. Even if Rowling is not evangelical or overtly political in her literary treatment of gender, the sport of quidditch models full gender equality and Rowling gives voice to a world where equal opportunity among the sexes is a given.

In the wonderful world of Harry Potter, quidditch is a legitimately co-educational sport. The three Chasers for the Gryffindor house team are girls – Angelina Johnson, Alicia Spinnet and Katie Bell – and, when Harry is prevented from playing Seeker on his house team, Ginny Weasley takes his place. Even the umpire in this game is a woman – Madam Hooch. Girls serve as house team captains and assume all the risks associated with playing what is a physical and life-threatening sport. Girls and boys are treated equally in match commentaries: there are no references to gender differences, no differential descriptors, no particular language invoked or employed and no hint of irony or mockery. On the only occasion it occurs, sexist commentary is immediately censored at Hogwarts:

> And the Quaffle is taken immediately by Angelina Johnson of Gryffindor – what an excellent Chaser that girl is, and rather attractive too –
>
> JORDAN!
>
> Sorry, Professor. (Rowling 1997)

Women also play at the highest level of the sport. Of the three Irish Chasers in the quidditch World Cup, two, Mullett and Moran, are women. In the sport's fictitious history, Kennilworthy Whisp (2001), a.k.a. J. K. Rowling, also records, without commentary, that an all witch team, the Holyhead Harpies, founded in Wales in 1203, defeated the Heidelberg Harriers in 1953 in what was 'widely agreed to have been one of the finest quidditch matches ever seen' (34). In other words, as Gladstein (2004) points out, Rowling depicts a world where equal opportunity is as natural 'as flying broomsticks and nearly headless ghosts' (49). In fact, Rowling's inclusion of women on quidditch teams is given without any hint of self-consciousness, or without editorial. There is no suggestion that the women who play quidditch are unfeminine, or, as Starrs (2007) writes, 'butch' in their appearance (83); the Gryffindor team share a changing room; the participation of women is never subject to comment by their teammates; and there is no suggestion that women wear protective clothing or are protected or privileged in any other way during a game. We are not even told if the girls and boys have separate showers. The fact that women play quidditch on an equal basis as men is, according to Gladstein, 'a major statement about equality' (56). According to Starrs, the fact that the inclusion of women is decidedly un-noteworthy 'reflects the feminist stance of the Harry Potter author' (83).

None of this is to say, however, that Rowling's narrative is without sexism. Even though they score, girls rarely win games. Catching the Snitch wins the game, and the Seekers who do this are invariably male. Female quidditch players are not involved in the signature moments of games and they never seem to play dirty or rough, or suffer serious injury. Committed to winning, the thuggish Slytherin team summarily excludes female players. At Hogwarts, girls are also prone to fits of giggling, including when the girls on the Gryffindor team realize the possibility of playing with handsome new captain and Seeker, Cedric Diggory:

'He's that tall good looking one isn't he?' asked Angelina

'Strong and silent,' said Katie and they started to giggle again. (Rowling 1999a, 169)

But, the overt gender equality depicted on the quidditch pitch, and the covert presumption of equal access and treatment for both genders, clearly challenges the sweeping generalization that the Harry Potter series simply reaffirms a culturally hegemonic gender hierarchy, an invented world in which women are, as Heilman and Donaldson (2003) conclude, 'marginalized, stereotyped, and even mocked' (140). Contrary to Mendlesohn's perspective that Rowling is not 'seeking to create a society or world that can, through its mere depiction, inspire us to change' (2002, 152) or, Kern's (2003) opinion that the books fail to offer 'children a utopian vision of the way things should be' (209), Rowling's depiction of quidditch suggests the opposite that the Harry Potter series does, in one important aspect, bring us closer to the forward looking and Utopian-minded world described long ago by the English philosopher John Stuart Mill ([1869] 1996) in which the subordination of women should be replaced by a principle of 'perfect equality, admitting no power or privilege on one side, nor disability on the other' (117). Rowling may not be a trenchant political activist, or an evangelical idealist or even a feminist zealot – she once admitted, 'I didn't set out to preach to anyone' (1999b) – but, at least in the case of quidditch, she exudes an openness unburdened by orthodoxy, and assumes, rare in the world of contemporary sport, equal status among boys and girls and men and women.

A magical sport played in a magical world with its own fictitious history, quidditch operates as a powerful mythology, an ersatz reflection of our own modern institution of competitive sport, riddled, as it is, with unresolved ideological, cultural and gender issues. In most respects, quidditch does not offer us a utopian version of sport: Hogwarts is only a parallel universe, not necessarily a better one, but, in one aspect at least, namely gender, the magical sport of quidditch offers a new model of gender inclusion. Rowling's depiction of quidditch may not constitute a clarion call to social activism, but in its dispassionate presumption of gender equality Rowling's fantasy sport offers us a way to realize that we are not necessarily what we naturally think ourselves to be and that, as a consequence, we may become something we may never have imagined ourselves to be.

In his literary anthropology, Iser (1993) argues that the literature is 'a panorama of what is possible, because it is not hedged in either by limitations or by the considerations that determine the institutionalized organizations within which human life otherwise takes its course' (297). Consequently, to argue that in Rowling's allegorical universe 'the gender hierarchy is never challenged' (Kern 2003) is to miss the point that literature operates as what Iser (1993) calls a 'staging' (296), an 'indefatigable way to confront ourselves with ourselves' which allows us to 'lure into shape the fleetingness of the possible and to monitor the continual unfolding of ourselves into otherness' (303). In other words, Rowling's fantasy world of quidditch suggests, in fact assumes, a possible alternative to the hegemonic binary opposition upon which the edifice of modern sport is erected. 'What', Trites (1997) asks, 'is a feminist children's novel?' 'Defined simply', she responds, 'it is a novel in which the main character(s) is empowered regardless of gender' (4). In the fictive sport of quidditch, women are indeed empowered.

While the fictive quidditch may well offer a progressive model of gender inclusion, it does not contest or dismantle the bipolar presentation of gender as male and female or challenge gender relations as heteronormative. Quidditch acknowledges a world that embraces gender inclusion; it does not embrace a world that acknowledges the inclusion of genders. Muggle quidditch, on the other hand, does.

Muggle quidditch

A full-contact sport, muggle quidditch is a creative amalgam of rugby, dodgeball and tag, with more than a hint of wrestling and lacrosse. A muggle quidditch team is comprised of seven athletes (three chasers, two beaters, one keeper and one seeker) who play with brooms between their legs at all times. The game is played on a field comparable in size to a hockey rink. Three circular goals atop pipes are placed at either end of the pitch. The chasers score goals, worth 10 points, by throwing a volleyball, called the quaffle, through the goal. They advance the ball down the field by running with it, passing it to teammates or kicking it. The beaters use dodgeballs called bludgers to disrupt the flow of the game by 'knocking out' other players. Players hit by a bludger are out of play until they touch their own goal. Each team also has a seeker who attempts to catch the snitch, a ball attached to the waist band of the snitch runner, a neutral player who uses any means to avoid capture. The snitch is worth 30 points and its capture ends the game. If the score is tied after the snitch catch, the game goes into overtime (International Quidditch Association 2013). The sport was first adapted at Middlebury College, in Vermont, in 2005 and is now played at over 300 universities and high schools throughout North America, Australia and Europe. It is also played in South America, Asia and Africa. The International Quidditch Association (IQA) was founded in 2010, and annually hosts or sanctions approximately 25 events, including nine regional championships, the World Cup, the International Open, the Global Games and the QuidCon.

Since its inception, muggle quidditch has striven for gender equality. One of the IQA's stated core values, in fact, is 'to be a leader in gender inclusivity for all age groups' (IQA 2013). Consequently, muggle quidditch adheres to the foundational 'two-minimum rule' which dictates that 'each team must have at least two players in play who identify with a different gender than at least two other players. The gender that a player identifies with is considered to be that player's gender' (12). The 'two-minimum rule' ensures diversity and is written in such a way that it does not exclude players who do not identify with the gender binary. Because of the wording, muggle quidditch is considered by many to be the gold standard for breaching traditional gender stereotyping and attaining equality in sport among men, women and the LGBIT community. To bolster the sport's gender inclusive goals, in 2013, the IQA created Title 9 3/4[4] which actively promotes advocacy and awareness as well as gender equality and inclusiveness ('Title 9 3/4'). The culture of quidditch is grounded in the establishment of an ever-expanding international community based on mutual respect and quidditch love.

While the fictive quidditch assumes male/female gender equity, muggle quidditch determines genders on the basis of self-determination, what Travers identifies as the most enlightened and open-ended way to determine gender in sport (2006, 440). Or, as the *Huffington Post* reporter Sean Pagoda (2014) writes, when it comes to gender equity in sport, 'quidditch wins'. Grounded in a process that relies on self-identification, quidditch directly and profoundly challenges the biocentric two model of gender that still dominates institutionalized sport, a model that, in particular, problematizes the participation of transsexuals and intersexed athletes, the groups most commonly subject to discrimination and disqualification, and their gendered subjectivities ignored or erased (Namaste 2000). While the International

Olympic Committee's so-called Stockholm Consensus has sought to address the complicated issue of transsexuals in sport – and the policy has been acknowledged by many as a progressive access policy specifically designed to embrace transsexual athletes – its criteria have been criticized on the grounds that legal recognition is not always possible and that surgery is often unnecessary, not to mention prohibitively expensive. Furthermore, no provisions for non-surgical transgender athletes or intersexed athletes, who have commonly competed as their assigned sex, have been made. According to Cavanagh and Sykes (2006), the IOC's policy is in reality 'more consistent with the original sex-tests used to police gender' and as such constitutes 'a disciplinary regime only appearing to be based on a spirit of inclusion' (77–78). Cavanagh (2003) has further argued that 'bearing witness to the transsexual body threatens the mechanisms of repression used to consolidate the fantasmatic presumption of binary sexual difference' (380). In fact, safeguarding inclusion only of medically transitioned male and female athletes leaves the fundamental power relations underlying male/female and heterosexual/homosexual binaries virtually untouched (Travers 2006).

Because of the IOC's hegemonic power within the panoply of sport, the global sport community has widely accepted the Stockholm Consensus as the best available guide for determining the eligibility of transitioned athletes or athletes who have undertaken sex or gender reassignment. As a result, national and regional sporting bodies are invariably held captive to regressive and dated notions about gender in sport. British Olympic Ambassador, Delia Johnston states: 'The Commonwealth Games have no option but to follow the Stockholm Consensus, even though it's chronically out of date. It needs urgent review, but there's no realistic stomach for that. In the UK, the agreement has filtered down to local and regional competition, but the Sports Council principles, are far better. At the international level, the IOC has to lead, but I don't see that happening for some time' (Quoted in Jacques 2014).

There are some anomalies and some sport organizations have stipulated participation on the basis of self-determination. The 2003 Constitution of the North American Gay Amateur Athletic Alliance, for example, included the transinclusive policy statement that 'Any player shall be eligible for play in the Women's Division who self-identifies as female' (Quoted in Travers 2006), and in 2004, Women's Golf Australia amended its policy on transsexual golfers to read that 'members must assume that a person is of the sex they assert themselves to be' (Quoted in Cavanagh and Sykes 2006, 91). More recently, several US states, as well as the NCAA, have established rules supportive of transgender participation (Griffin and Carroll 2012). But despite these advances, the Stockholm Consensus remains symptomatic of institutionalized sport's inability, or refusal, to recognize the changeability of human bodies and embrace self-identification with respect to gender. However, if, as Cavanagh and Sykes (2006) maintain, there 'is in the western, Olympic, imperial white imagination a desire for corporeal homogeneity, bio-centric gender demarcation and stable corporeal body boundaries' (97), then quidditch with its broad gender inclusive dimensions and philosophy clearly stands on the cutting edge of challenging assumptions about the normalcy of a rigid male/female gender binary and policed mechanisms to ensure conformity and opens up for GLBIT athletes meaningful social spaces that are anti-homophobic and offer greater freedom for gender expression and comfort.

It is within this environment, one grounded in an identified ideology, regulated by the two-minimum rule, fostered and advanced by Title 9 3/4 and operationalized by gender self-determination, that quidditch athletes experience numerous benefits associated with their participation in the sport. As player testimonies show, virtually every player acknowledges that they benefit from the opportunity to meet and interact with a diverse array of gendered peers, that practicing and competing with and against athletes from a diverse array of sexualities enriches their personal, social and athletic experience. As one heterosexual female athlete simply put it: 'I like *being* in an environment of all genders'. Max, a heterosexual male, more expansively explains

> I have deeply enjoyed the gender integrated and gender inclusive aspect of quidditch because I believe it brings the community together … Participating in intercollegiate quidditch has allowed me to come in contact with many different people that identify themselves outside of the gender binary and sexual orientation system, and act as a sort of hub for all kinds of people.

For Ron, a gay African American, it was quidditch's gender inclusivity that drew him to the sport in the first place: 'I have really enjoyed that Quidditch is a sport w[h]ere literally everyone and anyone is welcome and players are viewed almost entirely based on their skill as opposed to gender, race, or any other uncontrollable and honestly irrelevant quality'.

Another powerful theme that emerges from player testimonies is that the environment of quidditch fosters tolerance and understanding to differently gendered individuals. Evan, a transsexual, who identifies as 'genderqueer', writes, 'It's fantastic how gender identity or sexual orientation really doesn't matter in Quidditch, other than maintaining some sort of balance through the gender rule'. Marnie, a gay woman, expounds upon the ways in which her experience with quidditch destabilizes gender stereotypes; with regard to 'sexual orientation/gender identities', she writes, 'there really isn't a problem with any sort of discrimination at all. In a lot of sports that I've seen or heard about, you get the hazing[5] for "being too gay" or "man, that's gay" or "don't be a faggot/pussy/etc" but I have never seen this in quidditch'. Herschel, a heterosexual male, celebrates the way in which quidditch normalizes relationships among all genders:

> I feel that playing Quidditch has definitely caused me to interact with a lot more non-cis[6] gender individuals than in all prior 18 years of my life combined. And seeing the way they are accepted and not treated as anomalies in our sport is spectacular. Playing Quidditch has definitely mad me more open-minded.

Caitlin, an international heterosexual female, likewise reports that 'playing among more sexually and gender fluid individuals, or at least, those who are more likely to talk about their fluidity … has facilitated many a conversation on sex and gender'. And Mario, a male heterosexual, admits on the basis of playing on quidditch that 'now I think I can confidently say that I assume a lot less and wait to get to know people, no matter their gender identity, before I make any opinions'. As Sean Pagoda notes, sports that include GLBIT-identified players challenge individual athletes to rethink any preconceived notions about gender and sexual orientation (2014).

Testimonies also suggest that the environment of quidditch fosters personal empowerment. Quidditch offers an environment in which athletes of all genders can enjoy, sometimes for the first time, the 'cultural kudos' (Wedgewood 2004) that typically accrue from participation in competitive sport but that are not always extended or made available to women or non-cis individuals. The physical nature of quidditch, in particular the fact that athletes of all genders can compete together in this rough and tumble contact sport, energizes participants and serves as a salient source of physical empowerment. While not all athletes in this study identified the physicality of quidditch as a positive dimension of the game, many did. For one female athlete, quidditch 'androgenizes everyone slightly'. She continues: 'I like tackling a big guy on the ground or standing up unscathed from being hit by a big, male player and having his team realize I can't be pushed around ... I like when I hear players say, you have to watch out for *HER*'. Or as another female proudly declares: 'A girl in quidditch is just as dangerous as a boy'. Another female athlete, who clearly enjoyed the physical nature of quidditch, noted that 'I never feel uncomfortable tackling a guy on the basis that he is a guy, or a girl on the basis that she is a girl ... I don't want to hurt anyone'. Theberge (2000) noted similar sentiments among female hockey players who found enjoyment in hitting as long as it did not break the rules or injure an opponent. Channon (2014) and Channon and Jennings (2013), on the other hand, reported among mixed martial artists differential levels of comfort when it came to hurting an opponent.

As in McGaughey's (1997) study of female martial artists and Mennesson's (2000) study of women boxers, many of the quidditch athletes we canvassed suggested that they appreciated the different skill sets required by different positions and that the variation of body sizes and types offered athletes the opportunity to find athletic success in ways that they had not encountered previously. Like Miggliaccio's and Berg's (2007) female football players, quidditch players 'found an arena in which they not only could compete but were desired' (283). 'I've learned no matter what the body type', one female quidditch player writes, 'there is always an advantage that could be played that is unique to that person'. Another female notes, 'I never feel like I am outdone in Quidditch simply because of their gender. We all have our own strengths that can be used to the advantage of the team'.

The opportunity to engage in a traditionally male endeavour, an aggressive physical contact sport, would also appear to physically empower GLBIT athletes. As one gay woman states, 'My body is a powerhouse. Everyone who plays Quidditch, male, female, non-identified, gay, straight, black, white, Asian, Jewish, atheist, trans, honour student, vegetarian it does not matter who you are, because you are powerful for deciding to play this extremely difficult sport'. Another GLBIT athlete reports that she took up quidditch precisely because she could be 'a beast' and exercise her penchant for physicality.

The testimonies reported in this study are consistent with the findings from several other studies that have found that participation in contact sports enhances women's sense of physical empowerment. Hargreaves (1997), for example, notes that female boxers 'enjoy the physicality of fighting, the excitement, the roughness, and the risk' (42), and, even without checking, Theberge (2000) states that female hockey players 'relish the challenge of physical play and the sense of empowerment it provides' (115). Female martial artists (Lawler 2002), boxers (Mennesson 2000) and football players (Miggliaccio and Berg 2007) alike report feelings of bodily empowerment and liberation as a result of the opportunity to engage in physically aggressive contact in activities that have traditionally been reserved for men. The testimonies from this study suggest that the same may well obtain for LGBIT-identified athletes. In other words, just as McGaughey (1997) draws upon a physical feminist perspective, framing engagement in physically aggressive activities for women as empowering, so also does this approach appear to work for GLBIT athletes, in all instances potentially destabilizing the contemporary bifurcation between masculinity and femininity.

As sport sociologists have long acknowledged, physical empowerment also leads to personal empowerment (see Coakley 2015), and of particular interest in this study is the way in which participation in quidditch strengthens and empowers GLBIT athletes particularly in reference to furthering feelings of gender security and confidence. Julia, a self-identified intersexed female, details her journey from anxiety to confidence:

> I was nervous to experience a team dynamic with people of mixed gender … People trusted me on and off the pitch, and that respect uplifted me as a player and as a person. I wasn't treated any differently because of my gender … I honestly think that being on the Quidditch team made me more comfortable having cis and non-cis friends because it was the first time I really felt an equal connection.

This testimony corresponds with the reports of other athletes from a variety of sports (Ravel and Rail 2008) which suggest that athletes of all gender identities, especially female athletes, find that an inclusive and respectful gender inclusive sport environment enhances self-confidence and feelings of safety and comfort and offers safe spaces where individuals are freed to express and explore all facets of their nonconventional sexualities. One lesbian female athlete marries the athletic and gender advantages of quidditch: 'As a coed sport quidditch fosters both a martial, chess playing objectivity, and a sexually-charged dialogue'.

The general theme of gender empowerment translates in several instances among the present sample into a more proactive disposition towards coming out and even towards adopting a more committed socially activist stance. Melanie, for example, who identifies as a transgender woman, writes that she considers her quidditch team 'her family' and that 'being accepted and loved by her teammates gave her the courage to come out to others'. Miggliaccio and Berg (2007) document a similar sense of empowerment among female football players, one athlete reporting that her participation in football, as well as her mother's interaction with many of her daughter's lesbian friends, 'eased things somewhat' in her own experience of coming out (277). Both instances demonstrate how interactions with a broad cross section of genders can impact the lives of non-cis individuals and reinforces what Ravel and Rail (2008) identify as 'the importance of openness toward nonconventional sexualities in sport and feelings of being at ease in the sport space for facilitating the coming out process and the expression of one's sexual identity' (7).

Other quidditch players indicate that playing quidditch not only enables coming out, but also heightens social activism. Sophia states that playing quidditch has made her more 'passionate' about the sport and its non-binary posture. Michael, a transsexual male, shows how passion can turn into action:

> Being in a welcoming environment, and the only non-binary individual on my team (at least the only one that's out), has allowed me to open myself up to the opportunity of mild activism. I don't have to March. I don't have to riot. I don't have to give speeches or run preaches. All I have to do is kindly remind members of my team that individuals like myself exist and that we need to be treated with as much consideration as anyone else. My sensitivities towards the 'issues' have not changed, but my willingness to be forward and active have.

Although the GLBIT community has made great strides over the past few decades, there is still a lot to be done to ensure full inclusiveness, representation and safety, particularly for trans- and non-binary individuals, but the two-minimum gender rule would appear to have encouraged quidditch players to become more confident with their identities and provided them with a safe social space where they can even come out for the first time and where, of even more social significance, they can develop a sense of social activism, perhaps even an action agenda, if only on a team level, that can challenge gender biocentricity and enhance diversity and inclusiveness in sport.

Finally, it is important to recognize that many of the claims I have made on behalf of quidditch rest on assumptions that are subject to a poststructuralist critique, including the notions that coming out leads to the development of a positive sexual/gender identity, which may not always be the case (Iannotta and Kane 2002), that there is not a complicated cultural politics associated with coming out, where there is (Chawansky and Francombe 2011), and also that sexual identities are fixed, stable and unchanging, which poststructuralists would argue they are not. Poststructuralism favours the idea of decentring the subject and posits the fluidity and fragmentation of subjectivity (Weedon 1999). Queer theory also questions the essentialist nature of concepts such as sex, gender and sexuality (Butler 1993), and likewise aims at destabilizing gender categories and advocates that stipulated genders, especially the two poles of the binary, be replaced by 'a proliferation of the differences that queer theory and politics refuse to hierarchize' (Weedon 1999). Broad (2001), for example, has shown how women rugby players challenge the idea of fixed categories of sexuality by exposing the existence of multiple and fluid sexualities. Likewise, in their study of Francophone sportswomen, Ravel and Rail (2008) found that 'sexuality was not fixed because subjects positioned themselves differently depending on sociocultural and discursive circumstances' (21). In each case, the multiplicity and fluidity of sexualities challenges the entrenched heterosexual/homosexual binary.

While my preliminary data may not have allowed me to investigate and hence validate or refute the nuances in these perspectives, they do suggest that the development of a complex plurality of conventional and nonconventional sexualities in the culture of muggle quidditch points to the attenuation of what Duncan and Messner (1998) call 'asymmetrical gender markers' (180) at the same time as it signifies the development of progressive gender relations that might be symbolic of an impending new gender order. Precisely because of its dedicated gender inclusive stance, muggle quidditch challenges the 'normalness' and 'naturalness' of the masculine/feminine and heterosexual/homosexual divide, and instead, offers in practice what the fictive quidditch offers in the imagination, the opportunity to envision and promote a gender order in sport that does not rely on traditional gender hegemonic conceptions and practices.

Conclusion

Quidditch, in both its fictive and real forms, offers an increasingly popular alternative to the traditional oppositional sport binary. If, as Coakley (2015) remarks, gender equity 'requires erasing normative boundaries so that sports are fully inclusive–for LGBITs *and* heterosexual males and females' (220), then quidditch clearly attempts to advance gender equity. While Rowling may well not be an authoritarian ideologue with a message to be promulgated through a trenchant morality tale (Mendlesohn 2002), her portrait of quidditch champions the capacity of the imagination to envision a world in which human bodies can experience a sport at the school and international level irrespective of gender or sexual orientation. Just because it is fantasy does not mean that it does not have social impact and that it is socially benign or politically inefficacious; rather, as Iser (1993) contends, it is through literature and the meaning-making process of literature that we can stage our values and ethics and test our human plasticity to determine what we might be capable of becoming. In this sense, Rowling's fantasy sport of quidditch operates on the imagination and posits the assumption of gender equity in sport to a whole generation of boys and girls and men and women.

From the very beginning, muggle quidditch has sought to 'build a safe, inclusive, and respectful community' (IQA 2013) and extends Rowling's premise of inclusiveness to all genders. In muggle quidditch, women and GLBITs, in particular, are less likely than in other sports, especially those that have been traditionally male defined and dominated, to have to confront assumptions about gender inferiority or have to deal with male scepticism about ability, embodied experiences of being 'othered' in a homogenous sport, limited and limiting representations of gender, positive and negative images of gendered bodies and status as symbolic invaders into the sport culture (Pflugfelder 2009). The limited data presented in this study confirm that quidditch, like other community-based programmes (Atencio and Beal 2011; Beaver 2012; Crocket 2012; MacKay and Dallaire 2012), offers a progressive sport environment that seeks to eradicate the constraining heteronormative limitations imposed by the dominant gender binary.

While sport and its various disciplinary practices may well be inherently 'fascist' (Pronger 1994), a powerful force in the 'oppressive territorialization of the body' (Messner 2007), especially the nonconventionally gendered body, numerous collective initiatives, such as quidditch, operate as incidents of resistance and emancipatory moments that demonstrate that sport, like all institutions, is not a 'seamless totalitarian system' (81). In fact, sport is a 'political terrain characterized by internal contradiction and paradox that leave room for the play of oppositional meanings, and potentially for the organization of collective resistance and institutional change' (82). At the very least, the success of quidditch and the new model of full gender inclusiveness that the sport champions suggests that we should continue to strive for an alliance politics that continues to promote gender equity and not capitulate to the forces of greed, violence and oppression that disavow gender equity as a worthwhile project of human liberation.

In the meantime, Dutee Chand awaits the deliberation of the Court of Arbitration at the same time as her performances are scrutinized with suspicion and distrust. Her appeal provokes accusations of gender manipulation, unfair advantage, economic avarice and performance enhancement. Furthermore, the future of sport is construed as under threat by a post-Chand, biomedically engineered assault on sport that obscures the distinction between male and female and therapy and performance. On face value, it may appear obvious that Dutee Chand violated the IOC's regulations on hyperandrogenism, but the case also illustrates the ways in which the cultural meanings and messages associated with gendered sporting embodiment are continually contested and negotiated. The case of Dutee Chand demonstrates how challenges to gender constructions, designations and determinations augment – primarily through the rationale of fairness and equality – pre-existing conceptions of what the gendered body should be and how eligibility currently relies on the processes of normalization and naturalization to define and defend the biocentricity of sport. Chand's case remains one of a number of recent cases that expose the failure of the modern gendered sport paradigm (Baird 2014). As Cole (2009) notes, such cases 'draw attention to the instability of all bodies and, by extension, the inadequate conceptualizations of the sporting body that constitute sport's sacred ground' (4). Both quidditch and muggle quidditch serve as important moments of resistance and attempt to address the problematic issues that surround matters of selves, identities, genders and participation in sport.

Notes

1. Authored by J. K. Rowling, the Harry Potter books are a series of seven fantasy novels which chronicle the adventures of a young wizard, Harry Potter, the titular character, and his friends Ronald Weasley and Hermione Granger, all of whom are students at Hogwarts School of Witchcraft and Wizardry. The main story line revolves around Harry's quest to overcome the evil wizard Lord Voldemort, who seeks to obtain immortality, conquer the wizard world, subjugate all non-magical people, and destroy all those who would stand in his way, especially

Harry Potter. In order as published, the series includes Harry Potter and the Sorcerer's Stone (1997), Harry Potter and the Chamber of Secrets (1998), Harry Potter and the Prisoner of Azkaban (1999), Harry Potter and the Goblet of Fire (2000), Harry Potter and the Order of the Phoenix (2003), Harry Potter and the Half-Blood Prince (2005), and Harry Potter and the Deathly Hallows (2007). The books were published in the UK in London by Bloomsbury Press and in the U.S. in New York by Scholastic Books.

2.   In the Harry Potter series, a muggle refers to someone who has no magical ability, was not born into the magical world, and has no magical blood. Simply put, muggles are ordinary humans, rather than witches or wizards. Muggle quidditch is, then, the real world version of Rowling's fictional sport. Although the sport is usually simply referred to as quidditch, I will use the term muggle quidditch throughout this paper in order to distinguish the fictional game from the real world one.

3.   All names used in the presentation of data are purely fictitious.

4.   Title 9 3/4 derives its name from both the fictional platform at Kings Cross station in London that students use to access the Hogwarts' Express and the US law Title IX passed in 1972 to prevent gender discrimination in sports.

5.   While hazing usually refers to often humiliating, and sometimes dangerous, initiation rituals, in this case, it simply means ragging, taunting or mocking.

6.   Sociologists Kristen Schilt and Laurel Westbrook (2009) define cisgender, often abbreviated to simply cis or non-cis, as a label for 'individuals who have a match between the gender they were assigned at birth, their bodies, and their personal identity' (461).

References

Armistead, Claire. 1999. "Wizard, but with a Touch of Tom Brown." *The Guardian*, July 8. Accessed February 19, 2003. http://guardian.co.uk/print/0,3858,3881430,00.html

Atencio, Mathew, and Becky Beal. 2011. "Beautiful Losers: The Symbolic Exhibition and Legitimization of Outsider Masculinity." *Sport in Society* 14 (1): 1–16.

Baird, Julia. 2014. "Neither Female nor Male." *New York Times*, April 7, A18.

Bandy, Susan, Gigliola Gori, and Dong Jinxia. 2012. "From Women and Sport to Gender and Sport: Transnational, Transdisciplinary, and Intersectional Perspectives." *The International Journal of the History of Sport* 29 (5): 667–674.

Beaver, Travis. 2012. "'By the Skaters, for the Skaters' The DIY Ethos of the Roller Derby Revival." *Journal of Sport and Social Issues* 36 (1): 25–49.

Broad, K. L. 2001. "The Gendered Unapologetic: Queer Resistance in Women's Sport." *Sociology of Sport Journal* 18: 181–204.

Butler, Judith. 1993. *Bodies that Matter: On the Discursive Limits of Sex*. New York: Routledge.

Cavanagh, Sheila. 2003. "Teacher Transsexuality: The Illusion of Sexual Difference and the Idea of Adolescent Trauma in the Dana Rivers Case." *Sexualities: Studies in Culture and Society* 6 (3): 361–383.

Cavanagh, Sheila, and Heather Sykes. 2006. "Transsexual Bodies at the Olympics: The International Olympic Committee's Policy on Transsexual Athletes at the 2004 Athens Summer Games." *Body & Society* 12 (3): 75–102.

Channon, Alex. 2014. "Towards the 'Undoing' of Gender in Mixed-Sex Martial Arts and Combat Sports." *Societies* 4 (4): 587–605.

Channon, Alex, and George Jennings. 2013. "The Rules of Engagement: Negotiating Painful and 'Intimate' Touch in Mixed-Sex Martial Arts." *Sociology of Sport Journal* 30 (4): 487–503.

Chawansky, M., and J. Francombe. 2011. "Cruising for Olivia: Lesbian Celebrity and the Cultural Politics of Coming Out in Sport." *Sociology of Sport Journal* 28 (4): 461–477.

Coakley, Jay. 2009. *Sports in Society: Issues and Controversies*. 10th ed. New York: McGraw Hill.

Coakley, Jay. 2015. *Sports in Society: Issues and Controversies*. 11th ed. New York: McGraw Hill.

Cole, Cheryl. 2009. "Oscar Pistorius's Aftermath." *Journal of Sport and Social Issues* 33 (1): 3–4.

Connell, R. W. 1990. "An Iron Man: The Body and Some Contradictions of Hegemonic Masculinity." In *Sport, Men and the Gender Order: Critical Feminist Perspectives*, edited by Michael Messner, and Don Sabo, 83–96. Champaign, IL: Human Kinetics Press.

Connell, R. W. 2002. *Gender*. Cambridge: Polity Press.

Crocket, Hamish. 2012. "'This is Men's Ultimate': (Re)creating Multiple Masculinities in Elite Open Ultimate Frisbee." *International Review for the Sociology of Sport* 48 (3): 318–333.

Duncan, Margaret, and Michael Messner. 1998. "The Media Image of Sport and Gender." In *MediaSport*, edited by Lawrence Wenner, 170–185. London: Routledge.

Gallardo C, Ximena, and Jason Smith. 2003. "Cinderella: J. K. Rowling's Wily Web of Gender." In *Reading Harry Potter: Critical Essays*, edited by Giselle Liza Anatol, 91–105. Westport, CT: Praeger Press.

Gladstein, Mimi. 2004. "Feminism and Equal Opportunity: Hermione and the Women of Hogwarts." In *Harry Potter and Philosophy*, edited by David Baggett, and Shawn Klein, 49–59. Chicago and LaSalle: Open Court.

Griffin, Pat, and Helen Carroll. 2012. *On the Team: Equal Opportunity for Transgender Student Athletes*. National Center for Lesbian Rights and the Women's Sports Foundation. http://www.transyouthequality.org/documents/TransgenderStudentAthleteReport.pdf.

Hargreaves, Jennifer. 1997. "Women's Boxing and Related Activities: Introducing Images and meanings." *Body & Society* 3 (4): 33–49.

Hartmann, Douglas. 2003. "Theorizing Sport as Social Intervention: A View from the Grassroots." *Quest* 55 (2): 118–140.

Heilman, Elizabeth, and Trevor Donaldson. 2003. "From Sexist to (Sort-of) Feminist: Representations of Gender in the Harry Potter Series." In *Harry Potter's World: Multidisciplinary Critical Perspectives*, edited by Elizabeth Heilman, 139–161. New York: Routledge Falmer.

Iannotta, J. G., and M. Kane. 2002. "Sexual Stories and Resistance Narratives in Women's Sports: Reconceptualizing Identity Performance." *Sociology of Sport Journal* 19: 347–369.

International Quidditch Association. 2013. *International Quidditch Association Rulebook*. Radford, VA: Impressed Books.

Iser, Wolfgang. 1993. *The Fictive and the Imaginary: Charting Literary Anthropology*. Baltimore, MD: Johns Hopkins University Press.

Jacques, Juliet. 2014. "Trans People and Sport: The Stockholm Consensus, Ten Years On." May 30. Accessed January 10, 2015. http://leapsports.org/blog/trans-people-and-sport-the-stockhom-consensus-ten-years-on

Kern, Edmund. 2003. *The Wisdom of Harry Potter: What our Favorite Hero Teaches us about Moral Choice*. Amherst, NY: Prometheus Books.

Lawler, J. 2002. *Punch! Why Women Participate in Violent Sports*. Terre Haute, IN: Wish.

MacKay, Steph, and Christine Dallaire. 2012. "Skirtboard Net-a-Narratives Young Women Creating their own Skateboarding (Re)presentations." *International Review for the Sociology of Sport* 44 (1): 25–40.

Macur, Juliet. 2014. "Fighting for the Body She was Born with." *New York Times*, October 7, B11, B14.

McCaughey, M. 1997. *Real Knockouts: The Physical Feminism of Women's Self-Defense*. New York: New York University Press.

McCurdy, David, James Spradley, and Dianna Shandy. 2005. *The Cultural Experience: Ethnography in Complex Society*. Long Grove, IL: Waveland Press.

Mendlesohn, Farah. 2002. "Crowning the King: Harry Potter and the Construction of Authority." In *The Ivory Tower and Harry Potter: Perspectives on a Literary Phenomenon*, edited by Lana A. Whited, 159–181. Columbia, SC: University of Missouri Press.

Mennesson, C. 2000. "'Hard' Women and 'Soft' Women: The Social Construction of Identities among Female Boxers." *International Review for the Sociology of Sport* 35: 21–33.

Messner, Michael. 2002. *Taking the Field: Women, Men, and Sports*. Minneapolis, MN: University of Minnesota Press.

Messner, Michael. 2007. *Out of Bounds: Critical Essays on Gender and Sport*. Albany, NY: State University of New York Press.

Migliaccio, Todd, and Ellen Berg. 2007. "Women's Participation in Tackle Football: An Exploration of Benefits and Constraints." *International Review for the Sociology of Sport* 42 (3): 271–287.

Mill, John Stuart. [1869] 1996. *On Liberty and on the Subjection of Women*. Ware: Wordsworth Classics.

Namaste, Vivian. 2000. *Invisible Lives: The Erasure of Transsexual and Transgendered People*. Chicago, IL: University of Chicago Press.

Nash, Jennifer. 2008. "Re-thinking Intersectionality." *Feminist Review* 89 (1): 1–15.

Pagoda, Sean. 2014. "Gender Equity in Sports – Quidditch Wins." *Huffington Post*, August 16 , 18–19.

Pflugfelder, Ehren Helmut. 2009. "Something Less than a Driver: Toward an Understanding of Gendered Bodies in Motorsport." *Journal of Sport and Social Issues* 33 (4): 411–426.

Plummer, Kenneth. 1995. *Telling Sexual Stories: Power, Change and Social Worlds*. London: Routledge.

Pronger, Brian. 1994. "Body, Territory: Sport and the Art of Non-Fascist Living." Paper Presented at the Annual Meeting of the North American Society for the Sociology of Sport, Savannah, Georgia, November 11–14.

Ravel, Barbara, and Geneviève Rail. 2008. "From Straight to *Gaie*? Quebec's Sportswomen's Discursive Constructions of Sexuality and Destabilization of the Linear Coming out Process." *Journal of Sport and Social Issues* 32 (1): 4–23.

Rinehart, Robert. 2005. "'Babes' & Boards: Opportunities in New Millennium Sport?" *Journal of Sport and Social Issues* 29 (3): 232–255.

Risman, Barbara, and Pepper Schwartz. 2002. "After the Sexual Revolution: Gender Politics in Teen Dating." *Contexts* 1 (1): 16–24.

Rothblatt, Martine. 1995. *The Apartheid of Sex: A Manifesto on the Freedom of Gender*. New York: Crown.

Rowling, J. K. 1997. *Harry Potter and the Sorcerer's Stone*. New York: Scholastic Books.

Rowling, J. K. 1999a. *Harry Potter and the Prisoner of Azkaban*. New York: Scholastic Books.

Rowling, J. K. 1999b. "Interviews and Essays." March 19. Accessed September 10, 2014. www.search.barnesandnobles.com/bppksearch.ubninquiry.esp?btab=Y&isbn=059035340&displayonly=authorinterview

Schilt, Kristen, and Laurel Westbrook. 2009. "Doing Gender, Doing Heteronormativity: 'Gender Normals', Transgender People, and the Social Maintenance of Heterosexuality." *Gender & Society* 23 (4): 440–464.

Schofer, Christine. 2000. "Harry Potter's Girl Trouble." Salon.com [online], January 13. Accessed September 10, 2002. www.dir.salon.com/books/feature/2000/01/13/potter/index.html

Starrs, D. Bruno. 2007. "Quidditch: J. K. Rowling's Leveler." In *Playing the Universe: Games and Gaming in Science Fiction*, edited by David Mead and Pawel Frelik, 77–85. Lubin: Maria Curie-Sklodowska University.

Theberge, Nancy. 2000. *Higher Goals: Women's Ice Hockey and the Politics of Gender*. Albany, NY: State University of New York Press.

Thing, L. F. 2001. "The Female Warrior: Meanings of Play-Aggressive Emotions in Sport." *International Review for the Sociology of Sport* 36: 275–288.

Thorpe, Holly. 2005. "Jibbing the Gender Order: Females in the Snowboarding Culture." *Sport in Society* 8 (1): 76–100.

Title 9 3/4. Accessed January 4, 2015. http://www.usquidditch.org/about/title-9-3-4

Travers, Ann. 2006. "Queering Sport: Lesbian Softball Leagues and the Transgender Challenge." *International Review for the Sociology of Sport* 41 (3–4): 431–446.

Trites, Roberta Selinger. 1997. *Working Sleeping Beauty: Feminist Views in Children's Novels*. Iowa City: University of Iowa Press.

Two Minimum Rule: International Quidditch Association. Accessed January 12, 2015. http://iqaquidditch.com/about/title-9-3-4/

Wacquant, Löic. 2004. *Body and Soul: Notebooks of an Apprentice Boxer*. Oxford: Oxford University Press.

Wedgewood, N. 2004. "Kicking Like a Boy: Schoolgirl Australian Rules Football and Bi-Gendered Female Embodiment." *Sociology of Sport Journal* 21: 140–162.

Weedon, Chris. 1999. *Feminism and the Politics of Difference*. Malden, MA: Blackwell.

Whisp, Kennilworthy. 2001. *Quidditch through the Ages*. London: Arthur A. Levine Books.

Challenging the gender binary? Male basketball practice players' views of female athletes and women's sports

Janet S. Fink[a], Nicole M. LaVoi[b] and Kristine E. Newhall[c]

[a]Mark H. McCormack Department of Sport Management, University of Massachusetts Amherst, Amherst, MA, USA; [b]Department of Kinesiology, University of Minnesota, Minneapolis, MN USA; [c]Exercise and Sport Studies, Smith College, Northampton, MA USA

ABSTRACT

Kane's 'sport as a continuum' theory posits many women can outperform many men in a variety of athletic endeavors. However, because sports are typically sex-segregated, this athletic continuum is rarely seen but provides a potentially powerful mechanism of transformation relative to views of female athletes and women's sport. In women's intercollegiate basketball, it is common for teams to practice against a male scout team. We used Kane's continuum theory to examine the effects of integrated playing experiences on male practice players' attitudes towards female athletes and women's sports. Data from interviews revealed divergent first-order themes ('Acknowledgement of the Sport Continuum' and 'Maintenance of Traditional Gender Stereotypes') and several related second-order themes. The divergent themes reflect the complexity of gender relations in sport as the men simultaneously experienced and articulated a gender continuum while reinforcing a gender binary, which kept their own power and privilege in sport intact.

Advances made relative to women's participation opportunities in sport in the United States since the implementation of Title IX are evident (Acosta and Carpenter 2012), yet sport continues to thrive as an institution that creates and fortifies hegemonic masculinity in the US and beyond (Messner 1988; Fink 2008). Sport participation opportunities and presentations of sport by most media outlets provide 'daily commonsense, apparent, physical proof that men are naturally superior to women' (Kane 1995). Thus, men's dominant status is continually reinforced while women's sports and female athletes are regarded as (naturally) inferior and less exciting (Bryson 1994; Hargreaves 1994). Two decades ago, Kane (1995) made a case against this 'binary gender logic' in which sport is viewed as a gendered hierarchy where men are always superior to women relative to performance. She argued sport should be regarded as a *continuum* because, in reality, many women can (and do) outperform many men in a variety of athletic endeavors, and not merely in those endeavors that require 'naturally feminine' traits like grace and flexibility. That is, there are men and women with varying levels of athletic ability – ability on a continuum from low to high that transcends gender. However, because sports are typically sex-segregated – even starting at the youth sport level where prepubescent athletes are developmentally similar – proof of an athletic continuum is rarely seen or experienced. If the production and construction of sport more often allowed for evidence of an athletic ability continuum to be seen or experienced, Kane argued, it would serve as a powerful means of transformation relative to beliefs about female athletes, female athleticism and women's sport. In this research, we use Kane's continuum theory to examine the effects of extended sex-integrated playing experiences on male practice players' attitudes towards female athletes, female athleticism and women's sports. In particular, we use the theoretical framework to explore the ways in which one group of men's experiences challenged or reinforced dominant gender ideologies.

Literature review

> But if Geno wants to continue the charade of breaking the men's record, he's going to have to start playing some men's teams. I think he knows how ugly that would get. There are probably 10 high school teams in the city that could beat the Connecticut women. (Potash 2010, para 15)

The preceding quote was part of a long derisive commentary in the *Chicago Sun Times* written during the 2008–2010 University of Connecticut's women's basketball team's record-breaking winning streak in which they surpassed the mark (88 wins) held by the UCLA men's team, since 1974. Derogatory, marginalizing reactions were quite common; many comments to positive media reports of the women's record-breaking streak derided the record as meaningless because it happened in the context of women's basketball. Most of those (male) writers and commentators automatically assumed the intercollegiate female athletes on the University of Connecticut basketball team were much less skillful than even average high-school basketball players (Fink 2015).

The attitudes surrounding the University of Connecticut's women's basketball historic streak reflect the incredible power of sport to produce and reinforce hegemonic masculinity and maintain gendered power relations that favor men (Messner 1988). For years, critical feminist sport scholars have decried sport's role in establishing a *biologically* based gender binary in which individuals are assumed to fall into 'natural' and mutually exclusive categories of men and women (Birrell and Cole 1990; Travers 2008). Feminist scholars contend gender is shaped by cultural, social and political forces, while scholars who adopt a biological determinism worldview assert gender differences are natural and inherent, and use biological differences as 'proof' that men are superior (i.e. bigger, faster, stronger). Sport provides an especially powerful reinforcement of this gendered hierarchy as it offers a context in which visible 'evidence' of male supremacy is constantly emphasized. Because objective measures are used to evaluate performance in sport (e.g. times, heights, records, etc.), it presents an unparalleled realm in which the abilities of men are frequently highlighted as superior in comparison to those possessed by women (Bryson 1994). This superiority becomes embedded as societal 'common sense' because differences can be *seen*. Indeed, Kane (1995) quoted cultural studies' scholar Paul Willis on this very issue:

> Sport and biological beliefs about gender difference combine into one of the few privileged areas where we seem to be dealing with unmediated 'reality', where we know 'what's what'

without [listening] to the self-serving analyses of theorists, analysts, political groups. Running faster, jumping higher, throwing farther can be seen – not interpreted. (1982, 117, as cited by Kane 1995).

While feminist sport scholars denounced the idea of an oppositional gender binary, Kane (1995) noted that some aspects of their arguments actually unwittingly reinforced the notion of a binary. For example, some scholars suggested elevating certain sports (Whitson 1990) and skills (Bryson 1990) more typically associated with women to higher prominence in order to combat sport's hegemonic methods. Kane (1995) noted, however, these suggestions *upheld* the idea that certain sports are *male* and others *female*. Further, she noted that the muscle gap literature (e.g. Messner 1988), which suggests that men's strength/athletic superiority is exacerbated by social and cultural forces, is actually grounded in a binary view of athletic ability (i.e. men's over women's).

Instead, she argued, we should envision sport as a continuum 'in which many women outperform many men' in a variety of athletic endeavors because 'the acknowledgement of such a continuum could provide a direct assault on traditional beliefs about sport – and gender itself – as an inherent, oppositional binary that is grounded in biological differences' (Kane 1995). Conceptualizing sport as a continuum in which men and women compete in various activities with fluctuating and overlapping performances would provide actual visible deconstruction of male hegemony in sport. Kane used a marathon race as an example. Women and men compete on the same course at the same time. If attending the event, one can clearly see that top female runners perform better than many of the male participants. Witnessing these women finishing the race prior to most men dispels the myth that all men are *naturally* faster than women. Further, it highlights strength and fortitude not typically associated with the female gender. Thus, a sport continuum would not only circumvent stereotypes of women's athletic abilities as inferior to men's, but would help dispel notions of women's inadequacy in other social, economic and political arenas (McDonagh and Pappano 2008).

Unfortunately, sport is rarely presented or constructed as a continuum. *Of course*, many female athletes can outperform many male athletes in a variety of activities, and yet evidence of this is often suppressed (Kane 1995). One of the strongest methods of sport continuum concealment is the sex segregation of sport. If boys and girls, or men and women, never compete with or against one another, fluctuating and overlapping performances are never witnessed. A talented female athlete might be considered quite skilled *for a girl*, but if she never competes against boys, the assumption will remain that she is naturally inferior to her male counterparts. In the documentary film, *Kick Like a Girl* (MacKenzie 2008), an undefeated third-grade girls' recreational soccer team (the Mighty Cheetahs) moves to the boys' division in order to experience greater competition. The common initial response to the pending move from the parents and players in the boys' division was that the boys' teams would 'crush' the girls' team. Such notions were quickly dispelled as the Mighty Cheetahs won most of their games. The film documents a variety of reactions and responses, but one undeniable outcome of the season was the boys experienced a transformed understanding of the girls' athletic abilities. For the boys in the film, it was probably the first time they saw and experienced direct evidence of the sport continuum, that is, that some of the girls were more skilled than the boys. And yet, had the girls been prohibited from competing in the boys' league, the opportunity for ideological transformation and a meaningful opportunity for challenging the boys' stereotypical gender ideologies would have remained unrealized.

Sex integration in sport

While some anecdotal evidence of the effects of sex integration in sport exists, such as that described in *Kick Like a Girl*, academic analysis of the effects of sex integration is scarce. Little is known about whether such sex-integrated sport experiences challenge or reinforce gender ideologies of the dominant sex (i.e. males). Henry and Comeaux's (1999) study of co-educational soccer revealed it was dominated by men and did very little to change perspectives of female athleticism amongst participants. Snyder and Ammons (1993) studied co-recreational softball and found similar findings in the most competitive (A level) leagues, but noted that there was much more respect for the playing abilities of women at the less competitive levels.

More recently, Anderson (2008) interviewed 68 former high school football players who became university cheerleaders, a sex-integrated sport. As a result of their participation with the female cheerleaders, nearly 70% of the men indicated an enhanced appreciation for women's athletic and coaching abilities, perhaps suggesting an acknowledgement of a sport continuum in this activity. Additionally, the men indicated their misogynistic attitudes toward women decreased as a result of their experiences. Dashper (2012a) found that within the sex-integrated sport of equestrian a culture of inclusive masculinity and decreased homophobia was evidenced, such that gay men felt comfortable and accepted in the sport; however, even in such an inclusive atmosphere she argued, 'those masculinities are still constructed in opposition to a devalued femininity, and this will have consequences for the relative value and status of women within the sport' (1121). Indeed, Dashper (2012b) found that while women competed with men in all levels of equestrian, many forces beyond the configuration of the sport (i.e. integration) were present that limited women's success at the highest ranks. Based on the data, the gender binary appears to be firmly embedded in the sport of equestrian in spite of its sex-integrated structure.

Notably, the above examples come from (mostly) noncontact sport. Kane (1995) contended that evidence of a sport continuum in confrontational, team sports (i.e. those more traditionally thought of as 'masculine' sports) would be especially transformational. Theberge (1998) echoed this sentiment and noted that women outperforming men in sports typically constructed as 'masculine' would be further proof of 'leaky hegemony' (Birrell and Theberge 1994) and provide a site for feminist resistance. Cohen, Melton, and Welty Peachey (2014) examined the sex-integrated, contact, alternative sport of quidditch (a sport based on the Harry Potter book series). Quidditch features a physical mix of dodgeball, rugby and tag in which tackling occurs regularly. Based on the data, many positive benefits occurred as a result of playing the sex-integrated sport of quidditch. Both male and female participants reported they enjoyed the coed structure and would not want integration to change (i.e. construct male only or female only teams). Female participants experienced increased confidence in their athletic abilities as a result of 'proving themselves' against men in a contact sport. Similarly, most of the male participants indicated their respect for female athletes increased substantially. Although limited in scope, existing data point to acknowledgement and existence of a sport continuum where transformative experiences occur. While the limited results are encouraging, Cohen, Melton, and Welty Peachey (2014) noted a sample bias might have influenced the results. Indeed, those choosing to play the sport of quidditch may have decidedly more progressive views relative to women in sport – one core value of quidditch is 'to be a leader in gender inclusivity for all age groups' (US Quidditch 2010).

To date, Theberge's (1998) work is the only examination of the impact of sex integration in a traditionally 'masculine' contact sport. She interviewed female Canadian hockey players who had sex-integrated playing experiences. In discussing their experiences, the women consistently emphasized the natural physical differences between men and women and how these differences contributed to their inability to successfully compete against elite male players. However, the women also recognized that the physical differences operated in a continuum; they were not able to be competitive with elite male players, but in recreational situations they were quite competitive. Further, the women noted that playing with men made them better. Thus, while the women hockey players perceived men were naturally stronger and subsequently better hockey players, they also realized that 'the muscle gap is a social construction, conditioned by social experiences' (Theberge 1998).

To date, the scant academic analysis of the effects of sex-integrated sport – some of which is dated (i.e. Theberge 1998) – has produced equivocal results. While some research has shown that sex-integrated sport can transform views of female athletes, other research does not support this hypothesis. Thus, further examination of sex integration in sport types constructed as masculine is warranted. In this study, the perceptions of male practice players of an elite women's basketball team are examined.

Significance of the study

This study is an extension of the extant literature. We examined basketball – a traditional masculine contact team sport that, unlike ice hockey, does not have drastically different rules (e.g. there is checking in men's hockey but not women's) which automatically renders women's hockey as a significantly different game (i.e. 'lesser' or not the 'real' version) from men's hockey. Further, while the women interviewed in Theberge's (1998) work acknowledged the presence of a sport continuum as a result of their experiences, male participants' perceptions were not examined.

Women's Division I intercollegiate basketball provides a setting particularly well suited to examine this issue. Most, if not all, of women's basketball teams in Division I regularly play against male players during their formal practices. Many of the teams hold tryouts for the male players who, in essence, serve as scout teams for the women's team. They simulate different players and different teams in order to provide the women with the best preparation possible. The idea behind the use of male practice players is that practicing against the taller (and perhaps stronger, quicker) men will make the women better. Obviously that notion is rooted in a gender binary logic, and yet, it presents an opportunity for the sport continuum to be witnessed.

The use of male practice players is not without controversy; in 2006 the National Collegiate Athletic Administration's Committee on Women's Athletics called for a ban of their use claiming it took away opportunities for female members of the team. However, the NCAA took a non-legislative approach to the issue and instead released guidelines for the use of male practice players (Johnson 2007). As a result, men are regularly playing with and against women in this highly competitive, traditionally masculine sport (Metheny 1965; Hardin and Greer 2009). Given the exploratory nature of the research, the study was guided by two broad research questions:

(1) Does evidence of a sport continuum exist in this unique sex-integrated sport space?

(2) Do the ideologies of male practice players, as a result of their experiences playing with and against women, challenge or reinforce hegemonic notions of gender?

We cannot simply interpret the narrative results of the informants using a paradigm of whether they do or do not recognize the existence of a sport continuum. What these subjects provide is a unique variable: mixed gender sport participation. Their beliefs about sport and gender, however, were neither constructed nor deconstructed solely through this experience. The ideologies that the sport continuum can potentially challenge are multifaceted and have been constructed in the same culture that one, impedes people from viewing sport as a continuum of performance based on skill rather than gender and two, has served to bolster the belief that male practice players are required to improve the performance of female basketball players, even the most elite and talented players. As an example of the ways in which hegemonic thinking about gender and sport impedes the recognition of the sport continuum, we note that female coaches and players have continued to support the use of male practice players and engage in the same discourse about improvement coming through the perceived challenge of playing against men, rather than, for example, female teammates.

To interpret the ways in which our respondents understood women's athletic abilities both in contrast to their own and as distinct from those of an abstract male population, we discuss, in the results, the role of the media in reifying the dominant discourse of male vs. female athletic ability and the ways in which this corresponds to the maintenance of hegemonic masculinity in Western culture, especially in sport. Though these factors alone may not entirely impede the acknowledgement of a sport continuum, they can affect the ability to engage in analysis of sport as a continuum beyond one's individual experience.

Method

Setting and study participants

We interviewed 10 male practice players utilized by a very successful NCAA Division-I women's intercollegiate basketball team. During the time of data collection, the women's team experienced tremendous conference and NCAA tournament success and included five players that eventually were drafted to play in the Women's National Basketball Association. After receiving IRB approval, one of the authors contacted the manager for the women's basketball team, described the study, and presented him with the study's research questions. The manager first received approval from the coaching staff then verbally informed the male practice players about the study. The practice players were provided the author's email address and contacted the author directly to volunteer for the study. Participants ranged in age from 18 to 21. Eight of the participants were White, one was Hispanic and one African-American. All had served as practice players from 1 to 3 years and had previously started on their respective high school varsity basketball teams.

Data collection

Face-to-face semi-structured interviews were conducted with all 10 participants in a private space. Interviews were digitally recorded and conducted with the aid of a 14-item interview guide that listed the essential questions to ensure consistency across interviews. Questions were designed to elicit participants' perceptions regarding their playing experiences with the women's team and their views of women's sports and female athletes more generally. Interviews lasted between 20 and 40 min.

Data analysis

Participants were given pseudonyms, and the depersonalized interviews were transcribed and analyzed with a focus on recurring themes that emerged throughout the interviews regarding participants' feelings, beliefs, and values relative to the study's research questions (Strauss and Corbin 1990). Participants were sent a copy of the transcript to provide an opportunity to clarify statements and ensure they were depicted accurately. Following the member checks, each transcript was independently coded by the two authors. Transcripts were analyzed using an ongoing content coding process and method of agreement (Miles and Huberman 1994), until saturation occurred. This method seeks to find common themes and patterns amongst responses, yet incorporate critical exceptions if noted. To increase trustworthiness, peer debriefing, collaboration, prolonged engagement with the data and constant comparison were employed (Marshall and Rossman 2011). Additionally, one 'critical friend' familiar with the setting but not primarily associated with the study also independently coded the data and provided an additional confirmatory perspective on emergent themes. Points of agreement/disagreement were recorded and our analysis continued until consensus was reached regarding major themes.

Results

Results of the analysis revealed two overarching first-order themes and related second-order themes. The two divergent first-order themes 'Acknowledgement of a Sport Continuum' and 'Maintenance of Traditional Gender Stereotypes' reflect the complexity and presence of gender issues in sport. As a result of the male practice players' sex-integrated playing experience, participants acknowledged the existence of a sport continuum, yet simultaneously reinforced traditional gender stereotypes and a gender binary. The themes and sub-themes are described in detail below.

Acknowledgement of a sport continuum

Data from the interviews suggested the sex-integrated playing experience exposed the male practice players to the possibility and existence of a sport continuum where athletic ability of males and females was perceived as fluid, dynamic and overlapping, rather than a static binary. Participants acknowledged the sport continuum through two sub-themes, 'changed perspectives' and 'acknowledgement that women are better players'. Interestingly, as seen in the quotes below, even when they shared evidence of a sport continuum, many did so by consistently referring to the female players as 'girls' which is a mechanism of containment and a way through language to assert dominance, create a gender hierarchy (i.e. girls vs. men), and marginalize women by infantilization (Messner, Duncan, and Jenson 1993).[1] Conversely, they never referred to themselves or other male players as boys.

Changed perspectives

Participants willingly admitted to having uncertain and mixed expectations before their first practice with the women's team, but it was clear that some preconceived notions were immediately tested. As John said:

> So, yeah, I came in thinking, you know, I got to take it easy and I don't know how hard these girls … you know? But I mean like the first couple of plays you're getting hit around by these, you know, strong girls … really strong girls and then you know, once you get hit a couple times you realize all right this is no joke. These girls are serious.

While John was expecting that he had to take it easy on the women, he quickly learned that he needed to play with full effort in order to compete. Many of the participants noted hesitancy to play too aggressively, but quickly discovered this concern was unfounded, as Shawn said, 'I was surprised how much they (female players) body up against me and pushed me around'. Lucas talked about his hesitation to be too aggressive only to have the player he was guarding hit several shots in a row, 'So it definitely, I had to step up, I had to play more aggressively and I don't know … it was good'.

These changed perspectives went beyond how strong the female players were and how aggressive the practice players needed to play to compete with them. Participants also indicated their views of the women's basketball skills and athleticism changed as a result of this sex-integrated playing experience. Dan talked about how he used to view female athletes, and how his experience transformed his views:

> … just the absolutely exponentially increased respect for women athletes and especially women's basketball players. 'Cause I used to probably be in the group that I'm sort of now poking fun at and saying they're idiots. I would have been … I probably still would be if I was, you know, not playing with them (the women). I'd like to think that I'm not, you know, ignorant of that but I mean it's a real … there's a real bias out there towards women athletes in general, women athletes especially for men who sort of have this superiority complex in thinking 'well I'm a guy, I can beat them' but it's really, really been an eye opening experience.

Certainly all participants knew the women on the team were good players, but until these men played against the women, they did not realize *how* good the women were. As Shawn said, 'It's gotten so much more respect for them. Not that I didn't have respect for them as athletes before but now I know how amazing each one of them is, it's great'. As J.J. said, '… these are just some of the best basketball players I've ever played with or against. Not best *girls* basketball players I've ever played with or against'. This is a clear acknowledgement of the sport continuum and, coupled with previous quotes, reflects how playing with talented female athletes changed their views of the female players' athleticism. Their experiences as practice players challenged the notion of a distinct male and female athleticism. This is the non-binary thinking, as evidenced in an altered way of speaking about these female athletes that marks some acceptance of sport as a continuum and was evident in other sub-category responses.

Acknowledgement that women are better players

Not only did the practice players admit their experiences changed their perspectives about female athletes, they openly conceded that the women were better players. This new realization was a direct result of their unique sex-integrated first-hand playing experience. As J.J. said:

> Some days we have our days where we play really well and we beat them and it's really nice to see that we won on the scoreboard. But, most days we don't. And like we live with it because we know that they're better than we are, they're better basketball players than we are, but I think it's something that not all, like coming in, not all of us knew that.

Many of the practice players expressed similar sentiments. For example, when his friends asked him if he could beat certain players one-on-one, Joe replied, 'I don't personally think I could beat either [one of those players]. I could probably beat them once out of 10 times, but 95% of the time, they're going to beat me. I'll admit it'.

Interestingly, the practice players reported this was a common question asked of them. Practice players' male friends also often inquired whether *they* [the friend] could beat certain female players and were typically skeptical when told they could not. Even though many of practice player's male friends had seen the women play, because these men had not played directly with or against the women, each assumed their skills to be superior to the women. J.J. tells this story about one female player's boyfriend:

> One of the player's boyfriends came up and played with us in few games of pickup and he told a bunch of us practice guys that he can guard [female player], no problem. Her team won three games in a row, 7- 1. He didn't score at all and she scored all the points for her team.

Despite knowledge, proximal status (i.e. boyfriend), and multiple experiences watching the women's team play, without the direct experience of playing against his girlfriend and her teammates, he assumed he could easily guard one of the best players on the team. Lucas provides further evidence of this as he said, 'they [his friends] always ask could they beat a certain player and I'm always like "No". And they always get mad 'cause they think they can beat them. Until you've played them obviously you can't (understand)'. Most of the practice players found these over-inflated male sentiments laughable because they had first-hand experience of the women's skill levels, but also realized that they, too, had harbored such views before becoming practice players. Dan spoke directly about how the sex-integrated playing experience has the power to challenge stereotypes:

> Girls on the team are way stronger than I am, most of 'em are faster than I am and it's not, you know, it sort of breaks down the sort of stereotype of well men are going to be faster, stronger, better at the sport.

The 'it' Dan is talking about is the experience of playing against the women. Clearly it positively impacted perceptions and beliefs about female athletes and illuminated the possibility of a sport continuum (although they did not use that language to describe their experiences). While the aforementioned theme revealed transformative aspects of sex-integrated sport experiences, alternatively and simultaneously, these same experiences reinforced traditional, albeit outdated, gender stereotypes along with notions of maintaining the gender binary.

Reinforcement of traditional gender stereotypes

While the male practice players acknowledged the existence of a sport continuum, they simultaneously held firm to traditional gender stereotypes. The sub-themes comprising the first-order theme included, 'biology as destiny'; 'don't play like women'; 'women's game is different'; 'women's game is naturally less exciting, athleticism redefined'; 'we helped get them here'. All sub-themes are indicative of traditional gender stereotypes, represent aspects of a constructed gender binary, and reveal how such concepts are deeply embedded in the fabric of sport, and basketball in particular.

Biology is destiny

Despite this unique context in which the practice players acknowledged the existence of a sport continuum, many made sweeping generalizations about men's athletic abilities that clearly positioned men as inherently and naturally superior to women. When asked about the difference between men's basketball and women's basketball, J.J. said, 'You know, they're men. They're bigger, they're stronger, it's like it's biology'. Michael noted that he didn't watch any other women's basketball games because 'They're just not as athletic, or strong, or physical, or tall (as men's teams)'. Notably, men who early in the interview clearly admitted the women they played against were stronger and more athletic than them, later generalized other female intercollegiate basketball players as inherently less athletic and believed men were *naturally* superior. As Alex noted, 'I think if you put our team of guys up against like an average women's team, I think we would beat them'.

Don't play like women

Kane (1995) noted one way women's athleticism and the gender binary is maintained and reinforced is to 'regender' her by describing outstanding female athletic performances as 'playing like men'. Through regendering, two important goals of the binary are accomplished: (1) reinforcement that superior athleticism is a male domain and (2) erasure of evidence that females can possess such skills (Kane 1995).

Many of the men, when trying to compliment the women's skill level and athleticism, made it a point to say that they did 'not play like women/girls'. J.J. said: '… they don't play like girls, like you think a girl would play'. Or, as Alex said:

> They're so much better than every other women's team I've ever seen. It's just amazing. I wouldn't even really consider them women's basketball. They're kind of like a step above. They're like in between women's and men's. Several indicated they played like men. For example, John said, '… they're kind of playing more of a man's game now'.

As they regendered the women they played against and respected, it became clear the male practice players saw this team as a special (i.e. not normal) case of women's basketball. As Lucas said: 'Because I mean everyone still looks at them as superwomen, you know? Like, because they're one of the best teams ever'. In fact, when asked how he thought he would fare as a practice player for a different women's team, Alex replied, 'I don't even know if I would be a practice player for (another team). I think it's this circumstance that makes it so, like, special'.

The 'special' description of this particular team is a form of what Kane (1995) argued is another mechanism of containment for female athletes – the deviant mutant. The deviant mutant so diverges from the feminine norm and exhibits such a high degree of athletic competence that she becomes suspicious. While the men in this study were certainly not casting suspicion on the women, they did see them as different than other female athletes. Similar to Messner's (2009) findings in youth sport, the women's athleticism failed to challenge the assumption of natural difference between the sexes, and instead the women became 'honorary' men. This was just another way in which the men reinforced traditional gender hierarchies that privilege men and male athleticism – and thereby themselves.

Women's game is different

Though the practice players made it a point to note that their women's team did not play like women, they also referenced the difference between men's and women's basketball – in short, they perceived the women's team to be 'special' but very different from a men's team. Most players' views can be summed up best by Shawn who said, 'Men's is more of a physical athleticism game and women's is more fundamental'. John echoed this sentiment, 'Men's basketball is so much more flashy. And women's basketball is so much more fundamental'. In fact, every practice player noted that women's basketball was more fundamental. This sentiment was not necessarily a disparagement, as many of the players truly appreciated the women's mastery of the essential elements of the game of basketball. As John said,

> The thing about the women's basketball game is that they're way more fundamentally prepared than any other men that I've seen. I played with the men here and I played with the women here and that's one thing I've definitely seen is the fundamental, technical, you know, perfect moves that they make in order to execute.

Like John, many of the practice players noted that most men's teams did not have the same mastery of the fundamental elements of the game. Several indicated that for true basketball aficionados, the women's game should be more enjoyable. As Jay said, 'I think women's basketball is definitely better basketball, though. If you just look at the game as a whole'. This group of male practice players constructed men's and women's basketball as dichotomous and oppositional games, rather than as the same game it is in reality. This imposed binary on the same game reproduces gender hierarchy and stereotypic notions of gender (Kane 1995), and is another mechanism of containment of female athleticism.

The 'fundamentals' or purity of the game discourse invoked in these interviews is one that continues to allow these athletes to ignore the existence of a sport continuum, while appearing to be appreciative of the women's game and maintaining a liberal discourse espousing gender equity in college sport in the post-Title IX era. The women's game as both the purer form of the sport and focused on fundamentals frames the discussion in a positive manner (Banet-Weiser 1999). This is one way in which hegemonic masculinity is maintained via sport and, in this case, media because it is a practice respondents likely learned from sports media. To maintain its role in the legitimization of male superiority sport, as a cultural institution, needs the media (Messner, Duncan, and Jenson 1993). It is not surprising, therefore, to hear male practice players echo some of the dominant discourses about women's sports generally and women's basketball specifically.

The discursive strategy also creates a separate space for the women's game that does not – on its surface – devalue it. This is a more subtle form of gendered othering that has manifested in sports media (Messner, Duncan, and Jenson 1993). It is similar to the distinctions made when discussing women's ice hockey and women's lacrosse. Both sports have historically been considered lesser versions of the men's game because of the altered rules, many of which seek to limit contact. Small changes in discussions of these sports, however, have revealed a liberal, equity-minded shift to suggest that these versions are purer, more skill based, or even entirely different sports (Theberge 2000; Wiser 2014). When placed against the space that the men's games occupy, however, the fundamentally sound women's game cannot compare to the entertaining and exciting men's game (Banet-Weiser 1999).

Women's game is naturally less exciting, athleticism redefined

Although the practice players appreciated the women's game, they consistently claimed it was (naturally) less exciting and maintained that the women's game, and female athletes, were not as athletic. These men seemed to have no realization that excitement and athleticism could be socially constructed. When asked why he didn't watch women's basketball, M.J. simply said: 'I don't know, it's not as exciting as men's basketball'. Alex explained a bit further:

> I guess it gets kind of boring if you want to say that just to watch the technical, you know the perfect hook shot or, you know, of a nicely run play to get a wide open jump shot. Comparing men's and women's, I mean it's clearly faster with the men I think just due to athletic ability. And can be more exciting in terms of, you know, big plays and stuff like that, you know, big blocks, big dunks, big fast breaks … but what's always been, you know, the calling card for the women has been great team play.

When describing the excitement of the men's game, most of the practice players claimed that it was just more *athletic*. When pushed to describe exactly what that meant, most players indicated this meant jumping ability. As Lucas said, 'I think just when you think of athleticism with the men's game, you think of how high can they jump'. When asked what he meant by athletic, Michael simply replied, 'Tall, jump high, dunk'. In fact, dunking was synonymous with excitement and athleticism for many of the practice players. As Joe said, 'Obviously with men's basketball, you're going to get the more exciting play. You're going to get the dunk'. When the researcher pushed further and asked whether shaking defenders with ball-handling skills and then pulling up and hitting a 20-foot jump shot was athletic, many players replied that those were fundamental skills. As Shawn said, 'Shooting? That's fundamentals'.

In general, in the minds of these practice players, excitement and athleticism were equated with playing above the rim. Without knowing it, the men were engaging in another mechanism of containment 'selective gender comparisons' where only the differences that construct men to be (naturally) superior (i.e. faster, dunking, jumping high, 'big'ness) are discussed (Kane 1995). While the skills women have mastered like 'fundamentals' and long-range shooting are complimented, they are constructed and viewed as less exciting, which together sets up men's basketball as the norm, in addition to the more valued version of the game (Banet-Weiser 1999).

We helped get them here

Though not formally recognized members of the team, many of the practice players felt like they were part of the team and, in turn, contributed to its success. For example, Jay said, 'I just love being there every day, it makes me feel like a part of the team'. And as J.J. said:

> it's really rewarding to know that we helped make them that much better, that playing against men obviously because we're stronger than most women that they play against, and quicker that, you know, when they get into March and April it's rewarding to know that you had a hand in that experience.

Similarly, when talking about the continued success of the women's basketball program during the post-season tournament that was taking place, Alex commented, 'I've heard Coach (women's head coach) say that our practice squad is the second best team in the country'. Alex was very proud of that designation and felt it showed the practice team had a major role in the women's success. In this regard, several practice players intimated the women's team would have been less successful without their involvement. These players who had earlier acknowledged many of the women on the team were stronger and faster than them conversely suggested the natural biological differences between men and women rendered their participation *necessary* for the success of the women's team. Such attitudes reflect aspects of benevolent sexism. Glick and Fiske (1996) described benevolent sexism:

> … as a set of interrelated attitudes toward women that are sexist in terms of viewing women stereotypically and in restricted roles but that are subjectively positive in feeling tone (for the perceiver) and also tend to elicit behaviors typically categorized as prosocial (e.g. helping) … (491).

Indeed, the practice players were complimentary of the women's team's success, but implied that the women would not have achieved such accomplishments without their help.

Discussion and conclusions

There is no doubt a sport continuum exists; however, due to how sport is structured and produced, including by sports media, most individuals never see or experience a continuum. Evidence of the continuum is masked in a variety of ways such as different sports for boys and girls (e.g. baseball vs. softball), sex-segregated teams/leagues from youth through adulthood, different rules for the same game (e.g. no checking in women's ice hockey) and media productions that artificially separate men's and women's performances (e.g. presenting a marathon as two separate races for men and women, thus failing to show that many of the female runners finish ahead of many male participants). As such, sport is constructed and individuals are socialized to believe sport is a naturally occurring gender hierarchy in which males are superior. The data in this study indicate the male practice players became aware of the sport continuum as a result of their integrated playing experiences, but obviously this is a highly selective group. Few boys and men (or girls and women) are provided sex-integrated sport opportunities, thus unfortunately, the opportunity to experience the sport continuum is a rare occurrence. Further, a limitation of this study is the fact that we did not examine the woman players' perspectives of playing against the men. It would be interesting to know if they, too, experienced the sport continuum as a result of playing against the men.

Our results show the gender binary was simultaneously challenged and reinforced by the male practice players. This highlights the incredibly complex nature of gender in sport. Similar to others' findings relative to sex-integrated experiences (e.g. Anderson 2008; Cohen, Melton, and Welty Peachey 2014), the men in this study noted the playing experience enhanced their perceptions of female athletes and women's sport. The women on this team provided evidence, through the perspectives of the male practice players, that redefined what it means to be a female athlete and transformed beliefs about the possibilities of female athleticism. Thus, this particular sex-integrated sport experience acted as a mechanism for feminist resistance (Kane 1995). However, it should be noted that the interviewer for the study was a female and thus, the male practice players may have been influenced to provide socially desirable answers. While this is a limitation of the study, the practice players did not hesitate to reinforce the gender binary.

This group of men who played with and against some of the best female intercollegiate basketball players in the nation (perhaps) inadvertently marginalized the very women they claimed to admire and respect. They accomplished this in the following ways: regendering, viewing this team as a 'special case', imposing a false binary on the game of basketball, engaging in selective gender comparisons and exhibiting benevolent sexism. It did not appear these strategies were employed *consciously* as a reactive counterweight to their acknowledgement of the sport continuum and subsequent loss of power. Instead, these reactions seemed almost instinctive, instructed by an engrained position of power and superiority in sport, reinforced by dominant discourses found in sports media and consequently more difficult to neutralize. Thus, while sex-integrated sport has the potential to challenge gender ideologies, it appears the strong and pervasive patriarchy of male-centered, male-run, and male-dominated sport culture makes it difficult for its full positive potential to be realized, even with one of the best women's basketball teams in the country. However, perhaps if sex-integrated experiences were more common in youth sport, they could provide early and consistent interruptions of the gender binary that might render future sex-integrated experiences stronger mechanisms for feminist resistance.

Ironically, the practice of using male practice players for women's basketball is an example whereby social change can occur for the young men who participate, but it is also another way women's sport is co-opted by men. The NCAA Committee on women's athletics argued this in 2007, when they stated that the use of male practice players 'sends a message to female student-athletes they "are not good enough to make our starters better …"'. It reinforces the notion that men are naturally superior, and delays progress toward gender equity (Patrick 2007). Given our results, we see the opportunity for the positive transformative nature of sex-integrated sport, but caution that its effects are not a simple matter. The outcomes of such experiences are quite complex and nuanced. For this reason, we agree with Love and Kelly (2011) who encouraged policy makers and scholars to examine how *certain* sex-integrated playing experiences can advance gender equity, rather than mandate comprehensive integration of all sports. While men clearly benefit from sex segregation in sport in a variety of ways, these benefits would certainly remain (or be exacerbated) with mandatory desegregation of all sporting opportunities. As Griffin (2011) has argued, 'What makes us believe that eliminating sex segregated sports would benefit anyone other than those who are already privileged in sport: Men (especially bio, heterosexual, white, traditionally masculine men)?' (51). Indeed, the men in our study played with some of the best female intercollegiate basketball players in the country and yet still spontaneously reinforced traditional gender stereotypes and kept notions of a gender binary securely in place. Clearly there is much more to this transformation equation than sex-integrated sport experiences. A move toward uncharted sex-integrated waters must be made with caution and thoughtfulness.

Relatedly, while this study examined the individual and interpersonal levels of social change, we realize such analysis does little to challenge or change structural- or societal-level gender ideologies where real and lasting transformation occurs. In fact, our results show that men playing in sex-integrated situations protect their current status by engaging in strategies to uphold traditional gendered hierarchies. While select sex-integrated sporting opportunities can lead to positive transformation, such experiences alone cannot mitigate the firmly embedded structural and societal barriers that lead to continued inequalities in sport. As shown in this research, male practice players simultaneously experienced and articulated what Kane (1995) argued is a gender continuum while also reinforcing a gender binary which kept their own power and privilege in sport intact.

Note

1. Though some female athletes will report that they do not mind and/or prefer to be referred to as girls, we must recognize the tension in such situations between individual agency and

structures of power and oppression, structures, for example, that have engendered a male-dominated and male-centric sports media complex. In this space, the agency of female athletes is severely limited and thus the choices are few: stay silent, embrace the label, or protest and face potential repercussions from media, fans and management.

Disclosure statement

No potential conflict of interest was reported by the authors.

References

Acosta, R. Vivian, and Jean Carpenter. 2012. "Women in Intercollegiate Sport. A Longitudinal, National Study. Thirty-five Year Update." http://www.acostacarpenter.org.

Anderson, Eric. 2008. "'I Used to Think Women Were Weak': Orthodox Masculinity, Gender Segregation and Sport." *Sociological Forum* 23: 257–280. doi:10.1111/j.1573-7861.2008.00058.x.

Banet-Weiser, Sarah. 1999. "Hoop Dreams: Professional Basketball and the Politics of Race and Gender." *Journal of Sport and Social Issues* 23: 403–420.

Birrell, Susan, and C. L. Cole. 1990. "Double Fault: Renee Richards and the Construction and Naturalization of Difference." *Sociology of Sport Journal* 7: 1–21.

Birrell, Susan, and Nancy Theberge. 1994. "Feminist Resistance and Transformation in Sport." In *Women and Sport: Interdisciplinary Perspectives*, edited by D. M. Costa and S. R. Guthrie, 361–376. Champaign, IL: Human Kinetics.

Bryson, Lois. 1990. "Challenges to Male Hegemony in Sport." In *Sport, Men and the Gender Order: Critical Feminist Perspectives*, edited by M. A. Messner and D. F. Sabo, 19–30. Champaign, IL: Human Kinetics Books.

Bryson, Lois. 1994. "Sport and the Maintenance of Masculine Hegemony." In *Women, Sport and Culture*, edited by C. Cole, 31–46. Champaign, IL: Human Kinetics.

Cohen, Adam, Elizabeth Nicole Melton, and Jon Welty Peachey. 2014. "Investigating a Coed Sport's Ability to Encourage Inclusion and Equality." *Journal of Sport Management* 28: 220–235.

Dashper, Katherine. 2012a. "'Dressage is Full of Queens!' Masculinity, Sexuality and Equestrian Sport." *Sociology* 46: 1109–1124.

Dashper, Katherine. 2012b. "Together, Yet Still Not Equal? Sex Integration in Equestrian Sport." *Asia-Pacific Journal of Health, Sport and Physical Education* 3: 213–225.

Fink, Janet S. 2008. "Gender and Sex Diversity in Sport Organizations: Concluding Comments." *Sex Roles* 58: 146–147.

Fink, Janet S. 2015. "Female Athletes, Women's Sport, and the Sport Media Commercial Complex: Have We Really 'Come a Long Way Baby'?" *Sport Management Review* 18: 321–486. doi:10.1016/j.smr.2014.05.001.

Glick, Peter, and Susan T. Fiske. 1996. "The Ambivalent Sexism Inventory: Differentiating Hostile and Benevolent Sexism." *Journal of Personality and Social Psychology* 70: 491–512.

Griffin, Pat. 2011. "The Paradox of Being a Sport Feminist. A Response to Cahn's "Testing Sex Attributing Gender: What Caster Semenya Means to Women's Sports." *Journal of Intercollegiate Sport* 4: 49–53.

Hardin, Marie, and Jennifer D. Greer. 2009. "The Influence of Gender-role Socialization, Media Use and Sports Participation on Perceptions of Gender-appropriate Sports." *Journal of Sport Behavior* 32: 207–226.

Hargreaves, Jennifer. 1994. *Sporting Women*. London: Routledge.

Henry, Jacques M., and Howard P. Comeaux. 1999. "Gender Egalitarianism in Coed Sport: A Case Study of American Soccer." *International Review for the Sociology of Sport* 34: 277–290.

Johnson, Gus. 2007. "Division I Sets Expectations for Practice Player Use". *NCAA News Archive – 2007*. http://fs.ncaa.org.

Kane, Mary Jo. 1995. "Resistance/Transformation of the Oppositional Binary: Exposing Sport as a Continuum." *Journal of Sport and Social Issues* 19: 191–218.

Love, Adam, and Kimberly Kelly. 2011. "Equity or Essentialism? U.S. Courts and the Legitimation of Girls' Teams in High School Sport." *Gender and Society* 25: 227–249.

MacKenzie, Jennie. 2008. *Kick like a Girl*. Salt Lake City, UT: Jenny Mackenzie Films.

Marshall, Catherine, and Gretchen B. Rossman. 2011. *Designing Qualitative Research*. 5th ed. Washington, DC: Sage.

McDonagh, Eileen, and Laura Pappano. 2008. *Playing with the Boys: Why Separate is Not Equal in Sports*. New York: Oxford University Press.

Messner, Michael A. 1988. "Sports and Male Domination. The Female Athlete as Contested Ideological Terrain." *Sociology of Sport Journal* 5: 197–211.

Messner, Michael A. 2009. *It's All about the Kids. Gender, Families, and Youth Sports*. Berkley: University of California Press.

Messner, Michael A., Margaret Carlisle Duncan, and Kerry Jenson. 1993. "Separating the Men from the Girls: The Gendered Language of Televised Sports." *Gender & Society* 7: 121–137.

Metheny, Eleanor. 1965. "Symbolic Forms of Movement: The Feminine Image in Sports." In *Connotations of Movement in Sport and Dance*, edited by E. Metheny, 43–56. Dubuque, IA: Brown.

Miles, Matthew B., and A. Michael Huberman. 1994. *Qualitative Data Analysis: An Expanded Sourcebook*. Thousand Oaks, CA: Sage.

Patrick, Dick. 2007. "Women Practicing versus Men: Yea or Nay?" http://www.usatoday.com.

Potash, Mark. 2010. "Sorry Folks, but UCONN Women Can't Break UCLA's Men's Streak." http://www.chicagosuntimes.com.

Snyder, Eldon E., and Ronald Ammons. 1993. "Adult Participation in Co-ed Softball: Relations in a Gender-integrated Sport." *Journal of Sport Behavior* 16: 3–16.

Strauss, Anselm, and Juliet Corbin. 1990. *Basics of Qualitative Research: Grounded Theory Procedures and Techniques*. Newbury Park, CA: Sage.

Theberge, Nancy. 1998. "Same Sport Different Gender: A Consideration of Binary Gender Logic and the Sport Continuum in the Case of Ice Hockey." *Journal of Sport and Social Issues* 22 (183): 198.

Theberge, Nancy. 2000. *Higher Goals*. New York: SUNY Press.

Travers, Ann. 2008. "The Sport Nexus and Gender Injustice." *Studies in Social Justice* 2 (79): 101.

US Quidditch. 2010. "About US Quidditch". https://www.usquidditch.org/.

Whitson, David. 1990. "Sport in the Social Construction of Masculinity". In *Sport, Men, and the Gender Order: Critical Feminist Perspectives*, edited by M. A. Messner and D. F. Sabo, 19–30. Indiana, IN: Human Kinetics Books.

Willis, Paul. 1982. "Women in Sport and Ideology." In *Sport, Culture, and Ideology*, edited by J. Hargreaves, 117–135. London: Routledge & Keagan Paul.

Wiser, Melissa. 2014. "Lacrosse History, a History of One Sport or Two? A Comparative Analysis of Men's Lacrosse and Women's Lacrosse in the United States." *The International Journal of the History of Sport* 31: 1656–1676.

'They kick you because they are not able to kick the ball': normative conceptions of sex difference and the politics of exclusion in mixed-sex football

Aleksandra Winiarska[a], Lucy Jackson[b,§], Lucy Mayblin[b,§] and Gill Valentine[b]

[a]Institute of Applied Social Sciences, University of Warsaw, Warsaw, Poland; [b]Department of Geography, University of Sheffield, Sheffield, UK

ABSTRACT

This study explores the role of normative conceptions of sex difference through a case study of an anti-discrimination football tournament in Warsaw, Poland. The tournament has a variety of anti-discriminatory aims, including anti-racism, anti-homophobia and anti-sexism, where sport is a way to overcome difference and stereotypes. We found that especially efforts to realize anti-sexism through football encountered barriers and normative conceptions of gender in this traditionally segregated sport were in many cases reaffirmed. Male participant's reactions to the presence of female players often contained surprise and concern, and sex difference was seen as an unavoidable, biological fact which hindered play. We explore participants' reactions to the gender-mixing rule, as well as the existence of normative conceptions of sex difference that lead to exclusionary practices concerning females in the context of mixed-sex football. We analyse these practices and explore whether participants declare a change of attitude over time.

Introduction

This study explores the role of normative conceptions of sex difference through a case study of an anti-discrimination football tournament in Warsaw, Poland, which takes the form of a league organized twice a year (spring and autumn), over a period of around 12 weeks each. The tournament has a variety of anti-discriminatory goals, including anti-racism, anti-homophobia and anti-sexism, as well as having the overriding aim of bringing together immigrants and Poles with a view to integration. The project is run by an NGO, whose mission is focused on promoting equality, integration of marginalized groups as well as cultural and ideological diversity. In accordance with the mission and ideals of the organizers, the rules of the tournament imply that teams should be mixed in terms of nationality and gender. Our focus in this study is on this last aspect, in relation to the anti-sexist goals of the project. It should be stressed that both women's sport and gender issues in the context of sport remain substantially under-researched in the Polish setting, where physical

---

[§]Lucy Jackson is currently moving to the Department of Geography and Planning, University of Liverpool, UK; Lucy Mayblin is now at the Department of Politics, University of Sheffield, UK.

activity is most often perceived as a masculine domain, often in contradiction to feminine attributes (Włoch 2013).

Although Poland has national women's football representation with a national women's cup as well as local female leagues (and some unique amateur mixed leagues), surveys indicate that football is a sport played exclusively by men, according to respondents' declarations (see, e.g. Public Opinion Research Centre in Poland, report number CBOS BS/129/2013[1].). Moreover, there is practically no data concerning the situation of women in Polish sport as well as the actual extent of female participation in different disciplines (as players and activists) (see: Włoch 2013). This relates to traditional perceptions of gender grounded in Polish society. Poland is in the process of introducing equality legislation, where the Government's Plenipotentiary for Equal Treatment plays an important role; however, public debate on these issues is heated. In February 2015, the Polish parliament passed an act ratifying the Council of Europe Convention on Preventing and Combating Violence Against Women and Domestic Violence, which caused much discussion and opposition arising especially from anxiety concerning the critique of 'traditional' gender roles and the promoting of 'non-stereotypical' ones, which is perceived as an attack on national culture and religion.

Historically and cross-culturally women have been regarded as subordinate to men and perceived as less intelligent, strong, competent or competitive (Longhurst 1995; Rose 1993; Valentine, Jackson, and Mayblin 2014). However, Valentine, Jackson, and Mayblin (2014) argue that 'this representation of women as weak, in need of protection, and caring is a benevolent form of prejudice'. Their research focuses on sexism shaping particular attitudes and assumptions regarding women's bodies and women's place in society. Discussions regarding the differences between man/woman/ and masculine/feminine have been identified in terms of both social constructions of gender and the anatomical categories of sex. Following this, there have been particular ideas of what women's bodies can, or indeed 'should' do/not do in particular spaces, contexts and situations (Longhurst 1995; Mills 2011; Women in Geography Study Group, hereafter WGSG 1997; Young 1980) and some practices are seen as acceptable for men and not women (c.f. Mills 2011).

For example, the WGSG (1997) argue that,

> girls and women are expected to exhibit feminine characteristics … There are sanctions for boys and girls, men and women, who don't conform to masculine and feminine characteristics attributed to them, for those who don't perform the correct gender for their sex.

As Butler's (1990) seminal work on gender argues, gender differences are socially conditioned (Lloyd 2007) and vary across contexts. However, as Harraway (1991 in Lloyd 2007, 28) argues, the concept of gender was developed specifically to rebut the assumption that a woman's biology determined not only her psychological make-up but also her role in life (Butler 1990). The deployment of the concept of gender by feminists was therefore a way of rejecting the idea of biological determinism, however, as Valentine, Jackson, and Mayblin (2014) research shows, existing perceptions of gender lead to 'common-sense' arguments regarding the embodied differences between men and women – such as those that women are worse than men at playing sports and 'they kick you because they are not able to kick the ball' (interview with male, 28, Polish/Serbian).

Whilst traditionally regarded as primarily a male territory (Dunning 1986; Koivula 1999b), there have been numerous discussions of gender and gender relations in sport (Birrell 1988; Bryson 1983; Csizma, Wittig, and Schurr 1988; Klomsten, Marsh, and Skaalvik 2005). These literatures include discussions of sport as a political site for the resistance and transformation of gender relations (Hall 1996), the categorization of sports as gender-neutral, feminine and masculine (Koivula 1999b), masculinity and violence in sport (Messner 1990), gender, competitive level and sport type as factors in observed aggression and aggression in sport as a learned behaviour (Coulumb-Cabagno and Rascle 2006; Tucker and Parks 2001), media cover photographs and constructions of gender (Buysse and Embser-Herbert 2004), the naturalization of (gender) difference in sports coaching (Theberge 1993), gender stereotyping in televised sports media coverage (Koivula 1999a), and on the motivations for exercise in different genders (Kilpatrick, Herbert, and Bartholomew 2005).

Sport activity is traditionally divided in terms of gender due to two opposing values: equality of chances on the one hand and an acknowledgement of difference in physical capacities on the other. These are linked to the assumption that women and men – due to their sex – have inherently different sport abilities (Jakubowska 2014). Authors also point to social processes taking place in the context of existing relations of power that transform specific difference into inequality defining some sports as 'masculine' (and others as 'feminine'), concurrently excluding women (or sometimes men) from certain contexts.[2] The existing gender order can thus be both reproduced as well as contested through sport (Caudwell 2006; Jakubowska 2013a).

In these discussions, it has been suggested that sport is a representation of the sociocultural system in which it occurs and that sports reflect, as well as reproduce, the attitudes, beliefs, rituals and values of the societies in which they are developed (Koivula 1999b; Tucker 2011). More specifically, women's involvement in football has also been researched in various ways (Bromberger 2010; Foley 1990; Lapchick et al. 2014; Macbeth 2004; Muller-Myrdahl 2010; Rubin 2009), including aspects of race and gender (Scraton, Caudwell, and Holland 2005), referee's decisions and associated gender relations (Mean, 2001), the image of women in football and associated stereotypes (Harris 2005), and women's football and the sexed body (Caudwell 2002, 2003, 2006). Feminist sport sociologists have begun to look more critically at the game and have looked at the social expectations and norms that govern the construction of heterosexual femininity (Caudwell 1999, 2002, 2003, 2006; Cox and Thompson 2000, 2001; Scraton, Caudwell, and Holland 2005). However, whilst a number of these literatures focus on the innate gender assumptions and learned behaviours in sports, and in football in particular, these literatures do not research football as a way to overcome difference and stereotypes (and their associated exclusionary practices)[3], nor have they looked at football as a way to facilitate meaningful contact (Valentine 2008). How, then, might sport, here football, be used as a way of creating encounters across difference? We suggest here that difference must be conceptualized as *experiential* diversity within our everyday lives.

We therefore do not focus on women's place in football per se but on the resulting experiential encounters of both male and female football players who have been purposely bought together in order to address issues of inequality through contact in an engineered encounter. In so doing, we develop further the findings of Tucker's (2011) research into Sunday league football in the UK. We look at how sporting activity, as a performative and bodily activity, may be used as both tactic and tool in promoting meaningful contact across difference. Here, we discuss how gender norms and expectations are bought to the encounter, how these are experienced by individuals, and how the encounter both challenged and, in some situations, reinforced these gendered assumptions in different ways. There has been a dearth of work on encounters across difference more broadly (e.g. Valentine 2008;

Wilson 2013) and encounters across difference have been studied in various contexts such as buses (Wilson 2011), markets (Watson 2009), schools (Wilson 2013) and cafes (Laurier and Philo 2006). However, whilst some of these studies have focused on the less fleeting forms of encounter (Hemming 2012; Laurier and Philo 2006; Wilson 2013), these have yet to identify how sport may be used as a way of negotiating sex integration.

Our research was conducted as part of a larger project on attitudes towards, and living with, difference in the UK and in Poland, funded by the European Research Council. For this discussion, we focus specifically on the case of a football league in Warsaw which attempted to bring different groups together in order to promote and facilitate positive ideals with a view to the creation of meaningful contact, that is, contact that 'actually changes values and translates beyond the specifics of the individual moment into a more general positive respect for – rather than merely tolerance of – others' (Valentine 2008). The presented case study is aimed at sex integration in the context of a strictly 'masculine' sport, where gender mixing is exceptionally rare, especially within teams (see e.g. Jakubowska 2014). We explore participants' reactions to gender-mixing rules, as well as the existence of normative conceptions of sex difference that lead to exclusionary practices concerning females in the context of mixed-sex football. We analyse these practices and explore whether participants declared a change of attitude over time. The study therefore contributes to and compliments current literature concerning gender differences and divisions in the context of sport by presenting a case study where men and women actually enter into direct contact across difference as football players in one team. The focus is thus on the contact situation and resulting perceptions and experiences of both male and female participants that may lead to breaking stereotypes and sex integration through sport.

Method

The research that we present here took place in Warsaw, Poland, between April and July 2013. Warsaw is a capital city with a population of almost 1.8 million people, where immigrants are most likely to settle; however, foreigners still constitute only about 2% of residents. The case study is a multicultural and anti-sexist football tournament, where registered teams must be mixed in terms of ethnicity (at least three different nationalities) and gender (each team should consist of at least two women and two men). Additionally, one woman in every team should be present on the field during the match otherwise the team plays with a limited line-up (one player less). The requirement that particular teams be mixed in terms of gender is a result of evolving views both in terms of ideology concerning integration between sexes, as well as the need to create equal conditions for competition between women and men.

Our research took place in the spring edition 2013 of the tournament, where 20 teams registered. One of the authors conducted a total of 22 individual interviews and 2 focus groups with participants and organizers of the project. None of the authors were involved in the tournament itself, nor in the work of the respective NGO. Our interviewees were a total of 10 women and 20 men, aged between 19 and 45 years. The majority of interviews were conducted in Polish, then transcribed and translated into English.

Findings

Football is a traditionally 'masculine' sport (Jakubowska 2014) and mixed-sex football leagues are a highly unusual event in general, where Poland is no exception. In this aspect, the researched tournament does not serve as a 'normal' context for encounter, within which people perform their typical roles and standard behaviours. It should be stressed that most of the participants entered the project due to pragmatic motivations – the occasion to play football in an organized league for free – and not necessarily its anti-discrimination ideals. The specific aims of the tournament therefore create a new context in which gender roles are not clear for many people (especially men), which they find unsettling, and thus try to normalize (Young 1980). The sex difference rule imposed by the tournament was seen by many as an unavoidable biological fact which hindered equal play. This observation corresponds with existing research concerning gender differences more broadly (Cooper 2004; Valentine, Jackson, and Mayblin 2014), and in particular with regards to sport (Jakubowska 2012b). In our case study, various discursive practices can be distinguished where interviewees made assumptions around gender and specific gender capacities as well as justifications as to why the gender-mixing rule was controversial.

Assumptions around gender and normative conceptions of sex difference

One large group of normative concepts used by the participants to emphasize differences between men and women in football – present also in other sport contexts (see, e.g. Brzuszkiewicz 2013; Jakubowska 2006; Jucewicz 2013; Valentine, Jackson, and Mayblin 2014) referred to arguments concerning biology and physical disparities such as physical strength and temperament. It was largely assumed that women were weaker, calmer, less aggressive and less skilled than men and that these characteristics were innately related to gender (see also Scraton, Caudwell, and Holland 2005):

> In my opinion they [men] are stronger in the first place, secondly often, but not always, but this girl is often considered a half-player, some of them try less, (…) it does make a difference and also in terms of endurance, speed. (Female, 28, Polish)

> Anyway a good guy will be better in terms of playing football, it's just the way it is. (Male, 32, Polish)

In this context, physical strength was perceived as a natural characteristic and used to differentiate between men and women and at the same time create a hierarchical relation in which the dominant position was accorded to men (see also: Jakubowska 2013a). It has been acknowledged that socially constituted notions of what are appropriate activities for both sexes are manifested through the concept of gender roles. 'Some of the most widely used invocations of gender roles in everyday language refer to modes of behaviour labelled "masculine" and "feminine", for example strong/weak, assertive/compliant' (WGSG, 1997). Male bodies are represented as hard and aggressive, as an 'over-phallusised picture of man' (Morgan 2002, 407) and associated with force, hardness, toughness and physical competence. This positions women's bodies as opposite, therefore, seen as weaker, physically incapable and thus unable to carry out particular (masculine) tasks (Hall et al. 2007, 536; see also Johannson 1996; Scraton, Caudwell, and Holland 2005). 'Biological facts' are used here as the basis for discrimination and exclusion that is reinforced through social norms. Such divisions between women and men are clearly visible at football stadiums, where both formal and informal norms of conduct lead to the reproduction of gender inequalities and power imbalances (Jakubowska 2013b), especially through segregation and the marginalization of women (Jakubowska 2006, 2014).

In our interviews, football was often, more or less overtly, conceptualized as a 'masculine sport' which is in line with existing research (Scraton, Caudwell, and Holland 2005), where it was specifically interlinked with masculine values and characteristics such as direct contact, team play, speed, aggression, strength and endurance. Authors point to the existence of a specific masculine type of relationship conceptualized as *homosociality*, built often around sport, where both women and non-masculine men (e.g. homosexuals) are excluded (Czubaj, Drozda, and Myszkorowski 2012; Jakubowska 2013b). Difference is constructed around representation, micro-interaction and social structure (Glenn 1999, In Scraton, Caudwell, and Holland 2005, 76–77) and is thereby legitimized. In our research, interviewees cited arguments that referred to an implicitly understood 'nature of the game', linked to the presumption that strength and aggression constitute a fundamental element of football (attributed stereotypically to men) and mixing genders in teams negatively changed these natural 'masculine' characteristics.

Do you think that this idea of having obligatory women is good?

Honestly? No.

Why?

Because they have a different physical strength. And mixing sexes in one team is not a good idea because it changes the nature of the game. I think that when compared to male play they are physically weaker and they play differently. I cannot see any point in mixing people within one team.

So it'd be better if teams were either male or female, and these competitions were separate?

I think so. It results from disproportions, the same is about mixed hockey ... basketball, male-female. And it is a matter of our physical strength and that's it. And I dislike promoting people by force, what I disagree with in this tournament is promoting, by force, certain ideas which in this case are ineffective. In fact, the truth will finally come out. (Male, 32, Polish)

... there are sometimes matches during which we want to play with men only. We have to be careful, with them [women] you need to play slower and less aggressive than with men. (Male, Togolese, age not disclosed)

A second group of normative explanations that were used to underline gender discrepancies concerned differences in socialization between girls and boys and resulting disparities in football skills, where many of the men presumed that these skills were lower among female players. Some women seemed to confirm this discrepancy and at the same time notice the underlying social mechanisms.

I am sometimes, I don't know, in better shape than various men, but I cannot find myself on the pitch, I need to be more comfortable and something like this, I need to have better skills, this is a result of frequent contact with football, rather than skills, because I am in a good shape, but still, even though I've been playing for a long time, I know I wouldn't stand chances to an average man. (Female, 28, Polish)

The existing patterns of 'feminine' and 'masculine' activity discourage women from active play but also watching football games which they – according to existing social norms – perceive as boring or violent and sometimes also as a manifestation of male dominance in relationships (Jakubowska 2006). Differences in socialization between boys and girls lead to different physical ability, frailty and different ways of 'using the body' (Young 2005 after: Jakubowska 2012b). In this context, several authors indicate that 'natural' biological differences between sexes are actually a result of social and cultural gender constructs with the additional influence of economic and political factors (Dowling 2000 after: Jakubowska 2012b, see also Jakubowska 2014). For example, Young (1980, 152) suggests that for the most part, girls and women are not given the opportunity to use their full bodily capacities in free and open engagement with the world, nor are they encouraged as much as boys to develop specific bodily skills. Girl play is often more sedentary and enclosing than the play of boys.

Indeed, some of our female interviewees confirmed that they faced social barriers against playing football, which enhanced gender differences:

> … the fact is there are a lot of barriers against women, and cultural barriers because football is considered a men's sport and women, girls, face ostracism, even if they're not forbidden, women rarely get approval. (Female, 41, Italian)

> A girl playing football it's interesting, but on the other, oh Jesus, a girl plays football, she must be a tomboy, I don't know, and they immediately say that she must be weird, and it's good in [this tournament] that nobody is surprised, that girls play football, better or worse, whatever, but they are not afraid of kicking a ball, it's also nice. (Female, 28, Polish)

This corresponds with Caudwell's (2002, 2003, 2006) research on the image of women footballers, with questions asked regarding women's sexuality as they are not conforming to gendered expectations nor 'norms' of femininity. The same female participant also suggests that women play differently in mixed-gender contexts than in homogenous settings because in the former their behaviour is automatically adapted to conform to existing social norms:

Do you think that girls change the style of playing?

> They make it milder, but it's weird because I played for a few years in a female league and girls were a way more aggressive, but here it's because these teams are mixed, women are more delicate after all, and women go up and level with men, this aggressiveness, anyway boys are aggressive and when girls get irritated they don't show it because they are embarrassed, we should be ladies on this pitch, I think that it is rooted in our consciousness. (Female, 28, Polish)

In this quote, we see that female participants themselves reinforce particular assumptions regarding women as Valentine, Jackson, and Mayblin (2014) also discovered. This can legitimize traditional gender prejudice (Valentine, Jackson, and Mayblin 2014) based on assumed biological and gendered differences. Other interviewees sometimes constructed multilevel justifications to underline the differences between sexes in the context of football:

> I understand equality of rights, but you cannot cheat on biology, and backyard. They don't have any opportunity to play in the backyard. If a girl wants to play at least so-so, then she must practice. I am not able to imagine many girls who want to get engaged into football. (Male, 28, Serbian/Polish)

This interviewee refers to the changing cultural norms where on the one hand, equality legislation is being formally introduced, but equal rights and opportunities actually do not exist in specific sport settings due to fixed patterns of behaviour and gender roles that pose implicit barriers and discourage women from engaging into football activity.

Politics of exclusion

Various authors identify different kinds of practices aimed at enhancing and reinforcing divisions between women and men in the context of sport. These practices reproduce power relations through different forms of excluding female participants from spheres perceived as masculine (Jakubowska 2012a; Valentine, Jackson, and Mayblin 2014). Whilst associated with sex, gender and bodily difference leads to the formation of stigma around the expectations of a particular type of body, resulting in the exclusion of that body based on assumptions of what it cannot do. However, the notion of gender is performative (Lloyd

2007) rather than static, and thus, the performative dimensions of bodily exclusion are important to note. In our case study, many women felt that sexism is a problem within the tournament and recalled overt as well as more latent acts of exclusion (see also Tucker 2011; Valentine, Jackson, and Mayblin 2014). This, they felt, led to different forms of discrimination on the part of both players and referees (see also Mean 2001).

Interviewees observed that many men presuppose, based on existing beliefs and normative concepts analysed earlier, that women will be worse players. They spoke in this context about poor football skills, admitting at the same time that women's engagement in the game was often high. However, comments still related women's involvement in the league to their sex, with regard to their appearance and involvement as a 'decoration' (Koivula 1999b). In this context, the gender-mixing rule seemed essential in order to motivate men to include women on the pitch. On the other hand, however, this sometimes enhanced exclusion as women were treated unequally during the game. This most often took such indirect forms as ignoring them and not passing the ball to them on the field. Female players were thus formally included in the teams but in some cases actually disregarded during the game. Participants precisely described different strategies that lead to such exclusion.

> Boys play only between themselves, a girl is just a decoration or stands to disturb an opponent and her role is to stop and kick a ball out, and it has nothing to do with passing a ball to organise some good action and score a goal, in some teams she is totally neglected, she just stands there as a decoration. (Female, 35, Polish)

In some cases, men wouldn't want to actually let women play because of the presumed risk of losing points, showing the presumption that women would not 'be able' to play well enough (Johannson 1996). The participants spoke of these dilemmas:

> It's good that these rules are in force that two girls must play, because, the first thought is to take the best players, usually girls are poorer players than men, at least now, maybe it will change, but for the time being it's true. (Male, 30, Polish)

> I mean, it is bad because if they force us to take a girl, this year it is better, but I know that two years ago …, they simply didn't play with these girls, she was on a pitch, great, I mean, on the one hand I am not surprised, because in fact girls are much worse players, if they play at all, and I know that there were girls who didn't play at all but wanted to engage into the project and so on, but they never played football before so I am not surprised that they didn't want to play with them. (Female, 28, Polish)

This again relates to the type of women that are involved in football (Caudwell 2002, 2003, 2006) with presumptions based upon women's bodily abilities and capabilities. Another explicit dilemma present in the opinions of both women and men taking part in the tournament referred to the lack of clear norms as to how to behave in inter-sex relations on the football pitch. Many male players recalled feeling anxious and uncertain in contact with female players during the game. On the one hand, they were afraid of using their full physical strength – as with male players – because that could hurt the women perceived as more delicate (Young 1980). The existence of social norms implying 'gentlemanly' and paternalistic (Jakubowska 2014) treatment of females, related to more care and interest concerning their comfort, reinforces this approach. This again related to presumed capabilities of the gendered body.

> I mean, when there are girls on the pitch, you know girls are more delicate, well, like, looking at it with a sound mind, and as a gentleman, then you know you kind of have to go easy in this fight with them, right? So, not at all costs, not trampling over everyone, but reasonably, no? (Male, 31, Polish)

Some women also seemed to expect such attitudes, and in many cases, incidents of direct bodily contact between male and female players during the game caused uncertainty as to how to behave. This tension could be relieved by referring to joking and humoristic comments:

> Women are physically weaker, that's the major difference. (…) It doesn't affect the level of the game, because 90% of girls who play also do some other sports and are good at football, so it's all right. Nobody has any problems with that. It enriches the game, it causes some funny situations, when you accelerate and bump into a girl, she is poor, battered, you need to apologise to her for that. They also answer back regarding these funny situations. (Male, 32, Polish)

On the other hand, interviewees observed that some women behaved similarly to male players and, presuming that they would be more delicate, could actually cause men to get hurt. Some men found this unpredictability of female players' behaviour, and hence uncertainty how to behave towards them, disturbing. Interviewees elaborated on this difficulty:

> But girls are more unpredictable and I reckon that some find is difficult because they don't know what to do. They don't know if they should be aggressive towards them or not. (Male, 24, Polish)

> There are girls who play so well that they treat them like a guy, because you can't do otherwise. Once I played against a team, well I decided that I wouldn't attack at full force, because I don't want anything to happen. But when she knocked me over, when she attacked me with her body, I understood that I was wrong. [laughter] And I shouldn't treat her like that. There are women who are simply excellent and they come to play for fun. And to practice. (Male, 23, Polish)

Whilst men may expect women to adopt gender appropriate behaviours (Coulumb-Cabagno and Rascle 2006), here we see the reverse – that the male player is surprised to find that the female player is just as aggressive. This subsequently led to a change in his perception and treatment of female players more broadly – that they are able to 'play like a man'. These excerpts illustrate the major dilemma described earlier in this study, concerning the accommodation of the value of equality in the context of sport and relating it to actual as well as perceived differences between genders. In the researched tournament, the gender-mixing rule created conditions for the inclusion of female players on equal rights; however, many male players were uncertain how to refer to existing physical differences and established gender roles in their behaviour towards these women during the game. In other words, male players faced the dilemma whether to treat women 'like girls' or rather 'like guys' in the sense constructed by existing social norms. This situation also proved ambiguous for many women. On the one hand, those men who treated females in a more delicate manner were sometimes judged as too indulgent and cautious not to enter into direct bodily contact. On the other hand, those men who treated female players equally as themselves were sometimes regarded as too aggressive towards women. Equal treatment in terms of physical capacities was sometimes perceived as discriminatory and aimed at proving male superiority (Coulumb-Cabagno and Rascle 2006) on the football pitch:

> (…) they didn't try to prove something like – listen, girl, get off because you stand no chances. Some teams showed off like that, you know, when you treat your opponent equally like shoulder to shoulder, girls stand no chances, I don't know, they may even hurt a girl. (Female, 45, Polish)

Participants also pointed to unequal (in this case better) treatment of women by referees in the tournament (see Mean 2001). This may confirm the presumption analysed earlier that football is a 'masculine' sport where women have less capacities and skills and are less familiar with the rules of the game and thus need to be treated more indulgently. Such attitude caused discontent on the part of both women and men who stressed another discrepancy – between formal equality manifesting itself in the inclusion of women in teams and actual inequality manifesting itself in different treatment of women on the pitch.

> Referees don't treat girls and boys equally as well. They treat girls better, they turn a blind eye on a situation when a girl touches a ball with her hand and so on, I don't think it's good because we all play the same football, rules are the same for everybody. (Female, 32, Polish)

Another very subtle form of excluding women in the tournament was a discursive practice aimed at trivializing the game as less serious than in a strictly male league. This can be perceived as a strategy to normalize the unusual context of encounter between men and women in a traditionally strictly male setting. The presence of women was perceived to change the 'nature' of the game, which in result lost its 'natural' masculine characteristics and subsequently became treated less seriously.

As the previous paragraphs have shown, the existence of the gender-mixing rule in the football tournament caused tensions between formal gender equality and actual inequalities where sometimes women were perceived to be treated worse, whilst at other times better than men. This is closely connected with existing relations of dominance between genders where women are accorded a marginal and decorative role in settings dominated by men (see e.g. Czubaj, Drozda, and Myszkorowski 2012). These attitudes are visible in some interview excerpts where men focused on women's physical attributes, which was sometimes linked to overtly sexist behaviour. This supports Caudwell's (2003) sex–gender–desire triad. In response, women at times intentionally hid their feminine attributes (e.g. by wearing long trousers) in order not to evoke too much interest.

> Maybe because there is too much testosterone, everything that is female is attractive. (Male, 28, Polish/Serbian)

> Actually there were some idiotic comments addressed to some girl who didn't have a bra on the pitch and we could see her breast. And there were stupid comments. (Male, 28, Polish/Serbian)

> These boys from Chechen, they are a bit, a bit … let's say highly enthusiastic when they see girls playing. [laughter] You can tell it's …, it's unhealthy arousal or some enthusiasm when, I don't know, you can receive a ball on your chest and one girl can do it and she did it during a match, and it caused a terrible animation. (Male, 32, Polish)

This last interview excerpt illustrates an additional observation that participants made where approaches to gender differences were closely linked to cultural (e.g. Chechen, Afghan, Latin American) and religious standards of behaviour, so disparities in this case were especially evident in a multicultural tournament. Some interviewees made assumptions that sexism can be linked to nationality and that sexist standards are embedded in culture (see Phillips 2012). This thinking sometimes turned out to be stereotypical, and our case study showed that different anti-discrimination goals can at times actually evoke different – for example national – stereotypes, as in the case of Chechen players:

> Being aware of Chechen hooliganism, regarding people who live there, we expected them playing aggressively, but it was totally different. (Female, 45, Polish)

Another interviewee recalls an ambiguous incident between a Chechen team and a team of female feminist players. What might have been perceived as discriminatory and lead to misunderstanding actually turned into an integrative contact.

> We thought we would win by walkover because their faith forbids playing with women, we thought we would win by walkover, that they wouldn't come. But they came, everyone brought

a flower, it was a rose, I guess, they approached us and gave it to each girl, and that's how our first match against [that team] started, it was very nice and they didn't play aggressively. (Female, 25, Polish)

The same incident is described from the point of view of one of the organizers who observes multilevel relationships and expectations concerning tradition, religion and ideology in the context of gender relations. He also suggests that integration may require compromise and giving up some values in order to achieve others:

> The girls went out, waited, and the Chechen boys didn't come out. And we wondered what it meant, is it a boycott, we're not playing with women, although they previously played with teams where there were individual women. (But) these were feminists. (…) And what happened? They came, they were just running late because they bought flowers and everyone rushed to give these women flowers.

And how did they react (the women)?

> It was interesting, they were also, because everything is complicated and there are many levels, sometimes you don't know what to expect. They reacted positively. And in the next round they brought a banner and yelled: 'Support the Chechens!' and so on, so it was very positive, although they probably had some kind of internal conflict. (Male, 34, Polish)

The interview excerpts indicate that sex integration in the context of sport is a complex process taking place both on the level of formal regulations as well as various actual behaviours and their perceptions as inclusionary or exclusionary. It is also embedded in culture and social norms as well as existing power relations and furthermore involves values, sometimes conflicting (Caudwell 2003).

Attitude change

The previous paragraphs have indicated that one of the tournament's aims to realize anti-sexism through football encountered barriers. Whilst the aims of the tournament are in facilitating meaningful contact (Valentine 2008), the encounters created in the league resulted in normative conceptions of sex difference being consequently reaffirmed despite the efforts of organizers. Within this specific context, the influence of cultural ideas of sex difference amongst male players, who were of diverse national backgrounds, as well as quite firmly established ideas about male and female roles and abilities within Polish society, and football culture more broadly, in many cases lead to adopting various politics of exclusion in the mixed-sex context of sport.

Interview excerpts illustrate that many participants entered the tournament holding stereotypical views about female players and acted according to these views. In some cases, male participants had difficulty expressing a clear-cut view of the mixing rule. What is visible in their opinions is the ambiguity between existing social presumptions (that women are weaker and less skilled in the context of football), their expressions of surprise and admiration when these presumptions proved false and the dilemmas of actual equal/unequal treatment during the game described earlier. The following interview expert is indicative of this mental balancing act:

Is it a good idea that you play with girls?

> (…) no, because they have different rights on the pitch and it sometimes disturbs, on the one hand people automatically ignore them, but on the other – they kick you because they are not able to kick the ball, because they cannot, and the referee doesn't stop the game, but it hurts equally strong, it disturbs when we play football … But it's nice when girls are gifted, for

example these two, they are really good. It's a good idea. I cannot express any clear opinion. (Male, 28, Polish/Serbian)

It should be stressed, however, that many participants expressed a change of attitude over time due to personal experience. Some specific phases of this change can be distinguished. The first step involved mere acceptance of, or 'getting used to', the fact that women play football on an equal basis as men and are thus included in mixed-gender teams (see Johannson 1996 on acceptance of breaking traditional gender boundaries in sport). At first, simply finding a female player for the team proved problematic but over time became a natural element of completing a line-up.

> You know, I've never played football with girls, even as a teenager. And here is the requirement … and I had to switch something in my mind. The fact that a girl is in the team. I started passing a ball to them, or even fix the line-up. (Male, 28, Polish)

The presence of female players on the football pitch could thus lead to a further step regarding respect and the appreciation of women's sport skills. Whilst initially, women players may have been seen as 'deviants' in not acting 'appropriately' for their gender, in getting to know female players and their abilities, the strange(r) became familiar which could lead to positive reinforcement (Johannson 1996). For example, many male players discovered that playing in mixed-gender teams did not necessarily cause distress and difficulty but could actually lead to important support during the game and equal competition. These observations were often related to feelings of surprise, amazement and even also admiration on the part of men, who were impressed when they discovered that many women did not comply with the existing stereotypes (Butler 1990; Johannson 1996; Johnston 1996; Young 1980). The interviewees elaborated on these changes of perception and attitude:

> Really, we never expected it would be so fun playing with girls … Well and really they play well. … Well, and also my attitude to girls on opposing teams changed, too. Take the ball off a girl? Nonsense. But like the first time when I felt that one blocked, and so what, I didn't use any force, because I thought it would be easy and then I changed the way I looked at girls. (Male, 19, Polish)

> I will put it this way, girls play well too. I didn't even think they would play like this, but it seems that they play just like boys. (Male, Ukrainian, 22)

This shift in perception was, in some cases, transferred outside of the tournament to wider social circles of participants' family and friends. This constitutes a further step of attitude change and could be interpreted as the creation of meaningful contact (Valentine 2008). This phase has the potential of generalizing new attitudes and questioning existing stereotypes.

> It's also a nice learning experience. Because I admit. I was aware that women could play and could play well, but I thought there were really very few of these women. Although women's football is different from men's football. But I saw how many there really are, who can play and play great. … They've definitely cut down on some sexist comments that I let go when I'm with my friends. (Male, 23, Polish)

> I must admit that playing with girls is really nice. Most people were surprised when I told them about it, they were surprised that you can play with girls, but to me it was something nice. Especially that some girls really impressed me with their skills, they were better than many boys who played there. (Male, 22, Polish)

Female players also observed that positive attitude change. Interviewees stressed that this required creating opportunities for women to play on *equal rights* as men, allowing them to demonstrate their football skills and capacities. Participants also noticed that where male and female players varied in physical strength, men came up with tactics to 'make the most use' of women, allowing them to score goals. Female players defined these changes of attitude as a shift from being treated like 'a girl' to being treated like 'a boy'. Though a number of stereotypes were broken this discourse does, however, point to the masculine nature and domination of football. Thus, whilst Lloyd (2007) argues that individuals can endeavour to take on the identity of another gender and indeed the women here felt that they were being treated 'like boys' after getting to know people in the league, questions may be raised as to the intentionality of this.

Conclusion

The case study presented is an example of a multicultural, anti-discriminatory and anti-sexist football league which aimed to bring people who are different from each other together in order to facilitate contact and understanding. We have demonstrated that the tournament rule that proved most controversial for interviewees was that concerning mixed-gender teams. Socially grounded perceptions of gender difference were in many cases reinforced through normative assumptions expressed by participants, which often lead to the confirmation of divisions – and also inequalities – between men and women.

Different arguments were made for opposing the gender rule. First, football was perceived as a masculine sport and many people pointed to differences in physical strength and aggression on the football field; others recalled anxiety on the part of many men as to how to behave in close contact with women during the game – for example when tackling. One of the major arguments made to justify the division of men and women in football referred thus to arguments concerning differences in physical characteristics as well as football skills perceived as inherently distinct between genders. Some male players expressed concern that treating women equally on the field might lead to harming them. On the other hand, many female players also seemed to expect more delicate treatment than in the case of strictly male football.

Interviewees pointed additionally to cultural norms and traditions of some groups of migrants of different nationalities that prevented them from complying with the mixing rule, often ignoring the fact that perceptions of gender abilities are related to social patterns of conduct in general. Gender relations are nevertheless closely interrelated to issues of religion, tradition or ideology and aiming to achieve equality goals might require compromising conflicting cultural values. Thus, as Bryson argued (1983), whilst it 'is implicit that equal participation will mean equality in the future... This ignores a whole set of issues and assumes that sport is somehow homogenous and that all people experience such social activity in the same way'. We therefore need to think carefully about how sport might bring groups of different people together in different contexts with the intention of creating meaningful contact and integration. Such dilemmas around gender equality and cultural difference, as well as the intersections of these issues in the context of sport, constitute significant questions for further research.

In our case study, many participants recalled that in the previous editions of the tournament, the introduction of the gender-mixing rule did not lead to actual equality and integration in teams. Whilst women were formally playing in the tournament, they were actually excluded from the game. This was done by ignoring them on the field and not passing the ball to them. Many interviewees stated that the presence of women on the field changed the character of the game; it decreased aggression and violent rivalry and improved the atmosphere. This was sometimes related to comments concerning a change in 'the nature of the game' based on a more or less implicit assumption that football is a 'masculine' sport characterized by aggression and direct contact (see Jakubowska 2014). Participants also pointed to instances of unequal treatment, when referees treated women less restrictively and ignored fouls and other behaviours that were against strict football rules but were perceived as resulting from difference in football skills. This sometimes caused ambiguity in the participant's evaluations of the specific gender-mixing rule.

The change of attitude towards sex integration on the football pitch required time and positive experience. Although at first the existence of a rule that forced men and women to mix in teams seemed to lead to negative effects. Over time this turned into appreciation and sometimes also admiration. Indeed, some men admitted to being both impressed and surprised by the women's football skills. Many male participants recalled a change in their own mentality, though this was usually a gradual process. Playing with women at first seemed something unusual or even unthinkable but eventually their presence became a natural and obvious fact. Women also observed these changes and appreciated the atmosphere of normality that was being created in regard to female football players, which for them was a positive experience in comparison with other social milieus, where they experienced surprise, suspicion or rejection. In this aspect, we might state that sex integration through sport was to some extent successful in the specific case study; however, assumptions around gender made by the participants, as well as behaviours that resulted from these assumptions, in many cases seemed to reaffirm existing power relations between men and women. Although projects such as the researched tournament lack enough potential to disrupt existing gender imbalances in sport in general, they might nevertheless constitute sites of meaningful encounter at a microscale, and taking that into account, they seem worth developing.

Notes

1. The Public Opinion Research Centre in Poland/Centrum Badania Opinii Społecznej (CBOS) reports are available online http://www.cbos.pl/PL/publikacje/publikacje.php
2. See, for example, Koivula's (1999b) research where a sport in which aggressiveness is not only approved but even regarded as an essential part of the sport and considered as part of an athlete's sporting skills (such as ice hockey and football) is qualified as especially masculine.
3. However, for an example of this type of research in a British context, see Tucker (2011).

Disclosure statement

No potential conflict of interest was reported by the authors.

Funding

We are grateful to the European Research Council which funded this research through an Advanced Investigator Award to Prof Gill Valentine [grant agreement no. 249658] entitled Living with Difference in Europe: making communities out of strangers in an era of supermobility and superdiversity.

References

Birrell, S. J. 1988. "Discourses on the Gender/Sport Relationship: From Women in Sport to Gender Relations." *Exercise Sport Science Review* 16: 459–502.
Bryson, L. 1983. "Sport and the Oppression of Women." *ANZJS* 19 (3): 413–426.
Brzuszkiewicz, A. 2013. "To nie jest sport dla kobiet – analiza dyskursu wykluczającego na przykładzie wyścigów formuły I ["It's not a Sport for Women" – An Analysis of the Discourse of Exclusion Based on the Example of Formula One Racing]." In *Sport kobiet i mężczyzn: uwarunkowania, różnice,*

granice, [Women's and Men's Sport: Determinants, ifferences, Boundaries] edited by H. Jakubowska, Człowiek i Społeczeństwo, vol. XXXVI (1): 129–144. Poznań: Wydawnictwo Naukowe UAM.

Bromberger, C. 2010. "Sport, Football and Masculine Identity." In *Stadium Worlds: Football, Space and the Built Environment*, edited by S. Frank and S. Steets, 181–194. Abingdon: Routledge.

Butler, J. 1990. *Gender Trouble: Feminism and the Subversion of Identity*. Abingdon: Routledge.

Buysse, J. M., and M. S. Embser-Herbert. 2004. "Constructions of Gender in Sport: An Analysis of Intercollegiate Media Guide Cover Photographs." *Gender & Society* 18 (1): 66–81.

Caudwell, J. 1999. "Women's Football in the United Kingdom: Theorizing Gender and Unpacking the Butch Lesbian Image." *Journal of Sport & Social Issues* 23 (4): 390–402.

Caudwell, J. 2002. "Women's Experiences of Sexuality within Football Contexts: A Particular and Located Footballing Epistemology." *Football Studies* 5 (1): 24–45.

Caudwell, J. 2003. "Sporting Gender: Women's Footballing Bodies as Sites/Sights for the (Re) Articulation of Sex, Gender and Desire." *Sociology of Sport Journal* 20: 371–386.

Caudwell, J. 2006. "Women Playing Football at Clubs in England with Socio-political Associations." *Soccer and Society* 7 (4): 423–438.

CBOS BS/129/2013. *Aktywność Fizyczna Polaków* [Poles Physical Activity]. Warszawa: Komunikat z badań Centrum Badania Opinii Społecznej. http://www.cbos.pl/SPISKOM.POL/2013/K_129_13.PDF.

Cooper, D. 2004. *Challenging Diversity – Rethinking Equality and the Value of Difference*. Cambridge: University of Cambridge Press.

Coulomb-Cabagno, G., and O. Rascle. 2006. "Team Sports Players' Observed Aggresion as a Function of Gender, Competitive Level, and Sport Type." *Journal of Applied Social Psychology* 36 (8): 1980–2000.

Cox, B., and S. Thompson. 2000. "Multiple Bodies: Sportswomen, Soccer and Sexuality." *International Review for the Sociology of Sport* 35: 5–20.

Cox, B., and S. Thompson. 2001. "Facing the Bogey: Women, Football and Sexuality." *Football Studies* 4: 7–24.

Csizma, K. A., A. F. Wittig, and K. T. Schurr. 1988. "Sport, Stereotypes and Gender." *Journal of Sport & Exercise Psychology* 10: 62–74.

Czubaj, M., J. Drozda, and J. Myszkorowski. 2012. *Postfutbol. Antropologia piłki nożnej* [Post-football. Anthropology of Football]. Gdańsk: Wydawnictwo Naukowe Katedra.

Dowling, C. 2000. *The Frailty Myth*. New York: Random House.

Dunning, E. 1986. "Sport as a Male Preserve: Notes on the Social Sources of Masculine Identity and Its Transformations." *Theory, Culture & Society* 3 (1): 79–90.

Foley, D. E. 1990. "The Great American Football Ritual: Reproducing Race, Class, and Gender Inequality." *Sociology of Sport Journal* 7: 111–135.

Glenn, E. N. 1999. "The Social Construction and Institutionalization of Gender and Race." In *Revisioning Gender*, edited by M. M. Ferree, J. Lorber and B. B. Hess, 3–43. London: Alatmira Press.

Hall, M. A. 1996. *Feminism and Sporting Bodies: Essays on Theory and Practice*. Ann Arbor, MI: Human Kinetics, The University of Michigan.

Hall, A., J. Hockey, and V. Robinson. 2007. "Occupational Cultures and the Embodiment of Masculinity: Hairdressing, Estate Agency and Firefighting." *Gender, Work & Organization* 14 (6): 534–551.

Harraway, D. 1991. *Simians, Cyborgs and Women: The Reinvention of Nature*. London: Free Association Books.

Harris, J. 2005. "The Image Problem in Women's Football." *Journal of Sport & Social Issues* 29 (2): 184–197.

Hemming, P. J. 2012. "Meaningful Encounters? Religion and Social Cohesion in the English Primary School." *Social and Cultural Geography* 12 (1): 63–81.

Jakubowska, H. 2006. "Kobiety i piłka nożna [Women and Football]." *Czas Kultury* 2: 28–38.

Jakubowska, H. 2012a. "Od wykluczonych do outsiderek wewnątrz sportowego świata, czyli o (nie) zmienności statusu kobiet w profesjonalnym sporcie [From Excluded to Outsiders within the Sports World, or about the (non) Variability of the Status of Women in Professional Sport]." In *Oblicza męskości i kobiecości* [Aspects of Masculinity and Femininity], edited by A. Wachowiak, 34–46. Szczecin: Wydawnictwo OR TWT.

Jakubowska, H. 2012b. "Trzymanie kobiet na dystans. Wykorzystywanie kategorii płci, rasy i różnicy w profesjonalnym sporcie [Keeping Women at a Distance. The Use of Gender, Race and Difference Categories in Professional Sport]." *Kultura i Społeczeństwo* 3: 75–94.

Jakubowska, H. 2013a. "Płciowe porządki - granice płci w sporcie według koncepcji Mary Douglas [The gender order: gender boundaries in sport according to Mary Douglas's theory]." In *Sport kobiet i mężczyzn: uwarunkowania, różnice, granice* [Women's and Men's Sport: Determinants, Differences, Boundaries], edited by H. Jakubowska, Człowiek i Społeczeństwo, vol. XXXVI (1): 113–127. Poznań: Wydawnictwo Naukowe UAM.

Jakubowska, H. 2013b. "Stadion z perspektywy płci [The Stadium from Gender Perspective]." In *Futbol i cała reszta. Sport w perspektywie nauk społecznych* [Football and Everything Else. Sport in the Perspective of the Social Sciences], edited by R. Kossakowski, 56–69. Pszczółki: Wydawnictwo Orbis Exterior.

Jakubowska, H. 2014. *Gra ciałem. Praktyki i dyskursy różnicowania płci w sporcie* [A Game of the Body. Practices and Discourses of Gender Differentiation in Sport]. Warszawa: Wydawnictwo Naukowe PWN.

Johannson, T. 1996. "Gendered Spaces: The Gym Culture and the Construction of Gender." *Young* 4 (3): 32–47.

Johnston, L. 1996. "Flexing Femininity: Female Body-builders Refiguring 'the Body'." *Gender, Place & Culture* 3 (3): 327–340.

Jucewicz, M. 2013. "Praktyki performatywne a dyskurs wykluczający na przykładzie pływania synchronicznego oraz gimnastyki uprawianej przez mężczyzn [Performative Practices and the Discourse of Exclusion Based on the Examples of Men Practicing Synchronized Swimming and Gymnastics]." In *Sport kobiet i mężczyzn: uwarunkowania, różnice, granice* [Women's and Men's Sport: Determinants, Differences, Boundaries], edited by H. Jakubowska, Człowiek i Społeczeństwo, vol. XXXVI (1): 145–158. Poznań: Wydawnictwo Naukowe UAM.

Kilpatrick, M., E. Herbert, and J. Bartholomew. 2005. "College Student's Motivation for Physical Activity: Differentiating Men's and Women's Motives for Sport Participation and Exercise." *Journal of American College Health* 54 (2): 87–94.

Klomsten, A. T., H. W. Marsh, and E. M. Skaalvik. 2005. "Adolescents' Perceptions of Masculine and Feminine Values in Sport and Physical Education: A Study of Gender Differences." *Sex Roles* 52 (9–10): 625–636.

Koivula, N. 1999a. "Gender Stereotyping in Televised Media Sport Coverage." *Sex Roles* 41 (7/8): 589–604.

Koivula, N. 1999b. "Sport Participation: Differences in Motivation and Actual Participation due to Gender Typing." *Journal of Sport Behaviour* 22 (3): 360–373.

Lapchick, R., D. Donovan, S. Rogers, and A. Johnson. 2014. *The 2014 Racial and Gender Report Card: National Football League*. The Institute for Diversity and Ethics in Sport (September 10 2014).

Laurier, E., and C. Philo. 2006. "Cold Shoulders and Napkins Handed: Gestures of Responsibility." *Transactions of the Institute of British Geographers* 31: 193–207.

Lloyd, M. 2007. *Key Contemporary Thinkers: Judith Butler*. Cambridge: Polity Press.

Longhurst, R. 1995. "Viewpoint the Body and Geography." *Gender, Place & Culture* 2 (1): 97–106.

Macbeth, J. L. 2004. "*Women's Football in Scotland: An Interpretive Analysis.*" Unpublished PhD manuscript, Department of sports studies, University of Stirling. Submitted January 2004.

Mean, L. 2001. "Identity and Discursive Practice: Doing Gender on the Football Pitch." *Discourse & Society* 12 (6): 789–815.

Messner, M. A. 1990. "When Bodies Are Weapons: Masculinity and Violence in Sport." *International Review for the Sociology of Sport* 25 (3): 203–220.

Mills, S. 2011. "Scouting for Girls? Gender and the Scout Movement in Britain." *Gender, Place & Culture* 18 (4): 537–556.

Morgan, D. 2002. "You Too Can Have a Body like Mine." In *Gender: A Sociological Reader*, edited by S. Jackson and S. Scott, 406–422. London: Routledge.

Muller-Myrdahl, T. 2010. "Producing Gender-normative Spaces in US Women's Professional Soccer." In *Stadium Worlds: Football, Space and the Built Environment*, edited by S. Frank and S. Steets, 195–212. Abingdon: Routledge.

Phillips, R. 2012. "Interventions against Forced Marriage: Contesting Hegemonic Narratives and Minority Practices in Europe." *Gender, Place and Culture: A Journal of Feminist Geography* 19: 21–41.

Rose, G. 1993. *Feminism and Geography: The Limits of Geographical Knowledge.* Cambridge: Polity Press.

Rubin, M. 2009. "The Offside Rule: Women's Bodies in Masculinised Spaces." In *Development and Dreams: The Urban Legacy of the 2010 Football World Cup,* edited by U. Pillay, R. Tomlinson and O. Bass, 266–280, Capetown: HSRC Press.

Scraton, S., J. Caudwell, and S. Holland. 2005. "'Bend it Like Patel': Centring 'Race', Ethnicity and Gender in Feminist Analysis of Women's Football in England." *International Review for the Sociology of Sport* 40 (1): 71–88.

Theberge, N. 1993. "The Construction of Gender in Sport: Women, Coaching, and the Naturalization of Difference." *Social Problems* 40 (3): 301–313.

Tucker, L. 2011. "Forza, Forza Republica: A Case-Study of Politics in a Sunday League Football Club." In *Community and Inclusion in Leisure Research and Sport Development,* edited by A. Ratna and B. Lashua, 143–154. Eastbourne: LSA.

Tucker, L. W., and J. B. Parks. 2001. "Effects of Gender and Sport Type on Intercollegiate Athletes' Perceptions of the Legitimacy of Aggressive Behaviours in Sport." *Sociology of Sport Journal* 18: 403–413.

Valentine, G. 2008. "Living with Difference: Reflections on Geographies of Encounter." *Progress in Human Geography* 32: 321–335.

Valentine, G., L. Jackson, and L. Mayblin. 2014. "Ways of Seeing: Sexism the Forgotten Prejudice?" *Gender, Place & Culture* 21 (4): 401–414.

WGSG (Women in Geography Study Group). 1997. *Feminist Geographies: Explorations in Diversity and Difference.* Harlow: Addison Wesley Longman.

Watson, S. 2009. "Brief Encounters of an Unpredictable Kind: Everyday Multiculturalism in Three London Street Markets." In *Everyday Multiculturalism,* edited by A. Wise and S. Velayutham, 125–139. London: Palgrave Macmillan.

Wilson, H. F. 2013. "Learning to Think Differently: Diversity Training and the 'Good Encounter.'" *Geoforum* 45: 73–82.

Wilson, H. F. 2011. "Passing Propinquities in the Multicultural City: The Everyday Encounters of Bus Passengering." *Environment and Planning A* 43: 634–649.

Włoch, R. 2013. "Sport kobiet w polsce: zaproszenie do diagnozy [Women's Sport in Poland: An Invitation to Diagnosis]". In *sport kobiet i mężczyzn: uwarunkowania, różnice, granice* [Women's and Men's Sport: Determinants, ifferences, Boundaries], edited by H. Jakubowska, Człowiek i społeczeństwo, vol. XXXVI (1), 56–77. Poznań: Wydawnictwo Naukowe UAM.

Young, I. M. 1980. "Throwing like a Girl: A Phenomenology of Feminine Body Comportment Motility and Spatiality." *Human Studies* 3 (1): 137–156.

Young, I. M. 2005. *On Female Body Experience.* Oxford: University Press.

Men in a 'women only' sport? Contesting gender relations and sex integration in roller derby

Adele Pavlidis[a] and James Connor[b]

[a]School of Humanities, Griffith University, Gold Coast, Australia; [b]University of New South Wales, c/o School of Business, Canberra, Australia

ABSTRACT

Roller derby is a growing, popular sport, where teams compete on roller skates, and where rules allow 'blocking' and full body contact. Roller derby is primarily played by women, with men restricted to support roles during its revival stage in the early 2000s. However, men and gender diverse skaters are increasingly playing the sport, in mixed/co-ed leagues and Men's teams. This has created deep divisions within the derby community regarding the role of men in a women's space and the playing of a full-contact sport with men against women on the track. The tensions within derby highlight the wider gendered problems in sport regarding perceptions of athletic ability, strength and capability. Drawing on an ethnographic methodology, we present a range of perspectives from derby players and counter-point their lived experiences with the structural constraints on gender enforced by the governing bodies with the sport Women's Flat Track Derby Association and Men's Roller Derby Association. We explicitly engage from a radically inclusive position inspired by Hargreaves' call for sport to challenge gendered notions of capability.

Introduction

> I'm not doing full game practice if there are men involved … I'm scared of it. (Female participant from a mixed league)

The above quote was from a female derby player who was part of our research. As a member of a mixed league, she was clearly against mixed practice and this quote illustrates some of the key tensions we address via a qualitative methodology. The place of men in roller derby is a deeply contentious issue. Men's role in the sport, as teammates, as support and officials, and as members of their own men's leagues has not been interrogated in detail, despite the growing body of work written on women and roller derby. As with netball in the 1920s and 1930s, many roller derby leagues have adhered to 'majority women' governance policies to ensure men do not 'take over' (see Tagg (2014) for a history of men in netball). Women in roller derby are passionate about the sport and feel a strong sense of belonging and ownership (Pavlidis and Fullagar 2014), and this sometimes translates into a sense of gender exclusivity and a feeling that men are 'invading' or 'encroaching' on women's space.

Yet men are involved. They play, coach, referee and provide input into all areas of the sport. Pretending they don't will not work – as one contributor noted 'men are here to stay' (female participant, women only league).

Since the early 2000s, a revived flat track version of roller derby has gained popularity, after the spectacularized banked track version fell out of fashion in the 1980s. This revival of roller derby was led by women and the sport has since become known as a 'women-only' space (Donnelly 2012). Often espoused as a 'feminist' sport, researchers such as Finley (2010) in the United States, argue that the sport is empowering and enables the disruption of conventional definitions of femininity. However, there tends to be an uncritical hagiography of roller derby in both academic and populist publications, often espoused via the derby mantra of 'derby saved my life' (Leon 2007). Most research on the topic of roller derby is hopeful about the sport's potential, particularly in relation to supporting alternative femininities and opportunities for women (as noted by Beave 2012; Breeze 2013; Carlson 2010; Pavlidis and Fullagar 2014; Peluso 2011; Storms 2008). There are only limited critiques of derby as a feminist endeavour and whether it actually can be a space of liberation and challenge to gender norms remains unclear (for example, Cohen 2008).

One means of critically re-dressing the analysis of derby is to incorporate an account of men in the sport. Although both Donnelly (2012) and Pavlidis and Fullagar (2014) do make some forays into the position of men, it is not the core of their work. This, increasingly large, gap in the literature is what this current article aims to address. It does so through incorporating both textual information found mainly online (news outlets, official roller derby websites, social media sites and popular blogs), as well as ethnographic material and interviews with key stakeholders. Because the academic literature has not yet provided an account of men in roller derby, this article illustrates both the macro- and micro-level issues that have unfolded as men's participation in roller derby has developed through the years. This article is written with the critiques of sport sociology of Zirin (2008) and Eckstein, Moss, and Delaney (2010) in mind, in that we aim for it to 'be more relevant, more accessible, and more public' (Zirin 2008, 2). Zirin (2008, 2) quotes Rich King, the former president of the North American Society for the Sociology of Sport, who states, 'many sociologists of sport want to do more than simply make observations or apply esoteric theories. They direct their work to have an impact on sport. They hope to challenge and change sport and society'. In that vein, we connect our experiences, with those of research subjects further enhanced via secondary sources to take a micro–macro approach to the vexed question of sport, woman, men and derby. We propose that the rigid conceptualizations of gender as a binary are deeply problematic yet consistently reproduced with derby. This is exemplified via the imaginary construction of men in derby as 'big', 'strong' and 'tough' which is not (often) the reality, with all types of body shapes represented across the gender spectrum. Indeed, projects such as The Rollergirl Project specifically seek to show the range of bodies/genders within the derby community to demonstrate diversity (Erbentraut 2015; Layman 2015).

After the background and methods section which follows, empirical material from Australia and the United States from key governing bodies is presented that outlines some of the 'official' views in relation to men and gender more broadly in roller derby. This is followed by some of the polarized views that were found through our research and go to the core of issues of gender and inclusion in sport. This leads to our concluding discussion and points towards areas of future research.

SEX INTEGRATION IN SPORT AND PHYSICAL CULTURE

Background

In her 2014 article on mixed sport competition, Pam Sailors begins with a quote from John Stuart Mill taken from *The Subjection of Women*:

> What women by nature cannot do, it is quite superfluous to forbid them from doing. What they can do, but not so well as the men who are their competitors, competition suffices to exclude them from; since nobody asks for protective duties and bounties in favor of women; it is only asked that the present bounties and protective duties in favor of men should be recalled. (Mill, 1869 in Sailors 2014, 65)

This view, invoked in the 1800s, persists today. As Lorber noted in 1993, in sport 'physiological differences are invoked to justify women's secondary status, despite the clear evidence that gender status overrides physiological capabilities' (571). Women's sport has always (and largely continues to be) classified as 'less than' – less hard, strong, tough, fast and crucially in the increasingly commercialized sporting world, less watchable and therefore profit making. The Legends Football League, previously the Lingerie Football League, is a women's sport that has gained considerable commercial success. Yet despite the opportunities it presents for women to engage in tough and skilful competition, there are some major issues in the ways it represents women in very narrow terms: white, slim, heterosexual and with little variation in terms of facial features and hair (Khomutova and Channon 2015).

Even as 'new' sports have become more accessible and culturally sensitive to women's participation (such as roller derby, triathlon and crossfit), there remains a constant comparison to 'men's sport'. Coupled to this over-arching conception of 'less' are a panoply of constraints to women's and girls' participation in sport and physical activities, including specific issues around body image (Johns and Johns 2000), sexism (Fink 2014), income (McKay 1991), capacity (Young 2005), and most importantly, cultural and ideological norms pertaining to the abilities of and possibilities for women (for example, Chase 2006; Clasen 2001; Cronan and Scott 2008).

In her seminal paper on some of the responses to these 'problems' for women in sport, Hargreaves (1990) pointed towards the potential of mixed sport, that is, sport played by both women and men (girls and boys) in the same team as well as competing against each other. By examining some of the theoretical positions characteristic of sports feminist writing at the time, she extrapolates an explicitly revolutionist argument for a focus on gender *relations*, rather than simply gender differences. She writes,

> As in other areas of life, in sport there are numerous, different male/female relationships and situations where sex and sexuality, as well as, for example, ethnicity, class and age are unimportant. In some contexts women are unequivocally subordinated in their relationships with men, in other situations women collude in apparently subordinate roles, in some spheres women share power with men and have greater autonomy than in the past, and in a limited number of situations women wield power over men. (Hargreaves 1990, 294)

Her argument is that a radically different model of sport is needed where women participate in 'a co-operative venture with men for qualitative new models in which differences [between] the sexes are unimportant' (302). At the same time, she notes that this idea

> tends to remain at the level of theoretical discourse and is seldom put into practice … it is an idea which has never been treated seriously by those who are in entrenched positions of power in sport and resistant to fundamental change. (301)

This comment, made in 1990, maintains its relevancy, as sports still struggle to address the ongoing issues of sexism, discrimination and unnecessary violence and

241

corruption (on and off the field). There has been some critical literature written about 'new' sports that might provide a space for more inclusive and productive gender relations (Channon 2012; Channon and Jennings 2013; Cohen, Brown, and Peachey 2012; Pavlidis and Fullagar 2014). And also limited research has been undertaken on more 'traditional' sports such as equestrian (Dashper 2012) and mixed-doubles tennis (Lake 2012) where gender relations are visible and ongoing. Yet so far, Hargreaves' call for a fundamentally different model of sport where sexual difference is unimportant has not been fulfilled. The current debates around gender identity and hormonal/physical differences in terms of who can compete in 'male' and 'female' sport indicate that we have made little progress on the equality project (Henne 2014). This potential, however, for a 'new' model of sport, remains.

Roller derby

Over the past decade, roller derby has emerged on the sport landscape and has been sometimes been put forward as 'revolutionary' – with the mantra of 'by the skaters – for the skaters' evoking political revolutionary tropes. Indeed, the Women's Flat Track Derby Association's (WFTDA) stated values are 'Real, Strong, Athletic, Revolutionary' (WFTDA 2015), almost the opposite to the popular conception of women in sport. Roller derby is a contact sport and has some affinities with music subcultures such as punk, rockabilly, rock and burlesque. Its history is connected with rock n wrestling as a professional, televized and staged sport, yet its future seems much different.

Donnelly's (2012) work in derby and other spaces, such as home improvement work-shops, focuses on the construction of 'women only' spaces as relational and in opposition to men and male spaces. These spaces are construed via essentialist ideal types of gender, where femininity is defined against masculinity in a binary set. Donnelly identifies two women structured discourses, one of 'sisterhood' and 'one of mean girls' – either the inter-actions are nice, emotional and supportive; or they are nasty, competitive and sexually charged. She found that it was often essentialist notions of gender that were used to justify the women only spaces. Men are constrained in Donnelly's derby analysis by being limited to support roles, thus allowing women to define the space by limiting the involvement of men to the role of adjunct. Thus, men can never challenge the assumed gendered authority of women skaters. Donnelly rightly notes that the 'women only' nature of derby is merely a reproduction of essential binaries and the assumed need to gender segregate in sport. Her research, conducted between 2008 and 2012, enabled a particular type of analysis; roller derby was just gaining momentum around the globe and the role of men was still marginal. For us, writing and researching roller derby in 2015, we are able to look back on the rapid development of the sport and document some of the challenges and positive outcomes of the changing gender relations and dynamics of the sport.

Pavlidis and Fullagar (2014), too, noted the complexity of mixed gender leagues, despite the focus of their research being on women's experiences. Their research, based in Australia, found sex-integrated leagues and teams to espouse more open and inclusive gender percep-tions (both at micro- and macro-levels), including the acceptance of trans and non-gender identified skaters in their leagues. They also found a suspicious and fixed position expressed by many women, particularly in the more competitive leagues, as they felt threatened and protective of roller derby – a sport they had come to love and find a strong sense of belong-ing within. The love and belonging experienced by many women in Pavlidis and Fullagar's research is important to note in our current research into sex-integrated leagues/teams.

Ensuring roller derby puts the bodies of women at its centre is part of what Pavlidis and Fullagar (2014) argue needs to be part of a new derby ethos as the sport continues to grow, become more competitive and professional, and as men's role in the sport increases. The question of *how* to keep women's bodies central – while being an inclusive space for all genders – is one that this article contributes towards.

Methodology

As researchers we have come together because of our differing subject positions in an attempt to address the failure of the literature to interrogate mixed derby. The first author identifies as female and is an ex-roller derby player and has been engaged in research about roller derby for several years. Her theoretical perspective draws on a post-structural feminist trajectory and is explicitly interdisciplinary – with insights from cultural studies, sociology and leisure studies forming the basis of her work. With a focus on the sensual, affective aspects of roller derby, the first author views the sport as a complex terrain where women can experiment with their selves and indeed the notion of femininity.

The second author identifies as male and currently plays roller derby in a mixed gender league. He started skating to avoid the 'derby widow' phenomenon and support his partner in the sport – a very common trajectory for men in derby. His background is as an emotions researcher (Connor 2007) who looked at sporting fandom and has branched out into sport issues more generally but with a focus on doping and regulation. He theoretically tends to mix a Marxist and symbolic interactionalist perspectives to be deeply critical of the structures of sporting activity while acknowledging its experienced purpose (and perceived value) for those involved.

It is beyond the scope of this article to attempt to resolve our different theoretical perspectives and understandings of gender, sex and sexuality. Indeed, this is a wider project that sport sociology is making some forays into each year and is one in which sociology more broadly attempts to address. Instead, what we provide is a collaborative ethnography, illuminating important perspectives on mixed gender roller derby in an Australian context, partly informed by that difference. We have come together to gain a fuller understanding of the challenges the sport is facing as it grows and gains popularity. In doing so, we hope to illuminate some areas that might be improved, or at the least made more transparent as the sport grows. This also provides insight to sport sociologists, as nowhere else is a women's sport rapidly growing into a mixed sport with the concomitant issues – providing a rich field of data on gender and sport. Some of the material presented below is controversial, however, we must give voice to these views and only by examining them we might find a way through for people of all genders to continue to enjoy roller derby. We are not 'preaching to the converted', but instead we are entering into a conversation, suspending judgment and participating in an act of openness.

This methodical approach requires a suspension of judgment and a rejection of any fixed position or 'truth', while accounting for particular assumptions about gender and sport. Both researchers assume that most participants in roller derby, regardless of gender, would like to continue their participation. We both assume that the violence of a full-contact sport (on eight wheels) is an attraction for people of all genders who choose to participate. And we both assume that gender is socially constructed and that not all aspects of gender are constraining or limiting and that both femininity and masculinity has both damaging and liberating aspects that can be negotiated and influenced in a range of ways (Butler 1990).

Drawing on the methodological traditions of ethnography, our particular methods for collecting research material included participant observation, interviews (with representatives from the Men's Roller Derby Association, Roller Derby Australia and a number of skaters of varied gender/sexual preferences), and what is sometimes called 'virtual ethnography', observing blogs and social media sites that are in the public domain. The first author used her field notes from participating in roller derby 2010–2013, and the second author recorded his field notes through 2014–2015.

The authors undertook both purposive sampling to target specific people in high profile or leadership positions within leagues as well as random/emergent sampling of skaters who they came into contact with. This ensured a representative sampling of the views of skaters. The issues discussed in the article were discussed with 30 people across a range of leagues at numerous events/games in Australia. Secondary source material was sourced via key word internet searches and by cascade link following. All material, including interviews and relevant text found online, was read through by both authors and key areas of discussion are provided below. As very little has been written about mixed gender roller derby, the article does provide substantial description to set the scenes and engage the debates in sufficient detail to allow theoretical contributions in future research.

Gender policies and trends

Roller derby is currently confronting a number of tensions as it attempts to expand and professionalize. Some of these tensions are common to all sports, and some are specific to derby because of its unique position within the sporting landscape. The tensions that are all too common in marginal/alternative sport are funding (Turner 2013), publicity/media coverage (Messner 2002), facility access (Rafoss and Troelsen 2010) and maintaining a critical mass to support suppliers and maintain enough competition. More peculiar to derby is the negotiation of gender and its development as a 'women's only' space (Donnelly 2012). As a women's sport, roller derby has, since its reinvention in the early 2000s, privileged the sensual and visual aspects of sport, alongside competition, skill and strength (Kearney 2011; Pavlidis and Fullagar 2014). As a sport that proudly presents its radical, punk, alternative, queer friendly and female-controlled position as a great advantage, roller derby is certainly not a utopian space for women. As Pavlidis and Fullagar (2014) note, there is a dark side to belonging and the relationships between women cannot be assumed to be always positive as they have different needs, desires and skills. And also, importantly to this article, men have always been and remain key elements to the sport (initially as support people) and their participation is continuing to grow.

As men's participation in the sport grows, with men's and sex-integrated leagues developing around the globe, gender policies are being highlighted as important artefacts for understanding. The WFTDA, despite professing to be a radically inclusive organization, maintains the same deeply problematic biological distinctions of male and female 'sex' as defined by a person's body as most organized sports. As of June 2015, the WFTDA gender policy as listed on its website requires that all skaters be living as a female, clarifying this with the requirement that an: 'athlete's sex hormones are within the medically acceptable range for a female'. This must be verified by a medical practitioner. This sort of sex testing/ verification has been discredited by the medical and socio-medical literature as absolutist, binary manufacturing and all-encompassing. Most damning is that it assumes that hormones define gender and do not take into account the myriad of variations in the expression of human gender and sex (Koh, Adair, and Sonksen 2014).

> In a public blog post-titled 'time for the Bleeding Heartland Roller Girls to protest the WFTDA gender policy', Jacob, a skater who self-identifies as queer, outlines her views on the problems with WFTDA's gender policies. Jake writes,I would be ineligible according to the WFTDA policies. This is because I am not living as a female – I identify as genderqueer, and many of my friends refer to me as 'Jake' and use male pronouns to refer to me. Additionally, several of my friends – many of whom skate for various roller derby teams – have hormone levels that are outside of the 'normal' female range. They are cisgendered females, living as women, but would be disqualified to skate under WFTDA policies. (Mcwilliams 2012)

This example is an important one as it illustrates a range of issues, including self-identification, and biologically determinate markers of gender exclusion. It should also be noted that there is opposition from within Women's teams to this particular policy, for example, in response to 'Jake' above:

> I love roller derby and I love skating with one of the top-ranked WFTDA leagues in the entire world, but WFTDA's gender policy needs to be changed. In particular, because we gain nothing from following the Olympic policy on eligibility and just make everyone angry (myself included). (Tremaine 2015)

This comment, made by a blogger and transgender skater, who identifies as female and *does* meet WFTDAs gender policy requirement, speaks to the need for work in this area. What is striking is that such a queer/alternative friendly sport would be so deterministic about what constitutes a 'woman'.

There are some derby groups that explicitly celebrate their diversity, for example the Vagine Regime, a group of skaters that expressly celebrate all aspects of sex/gender and self-expression (Berrick 2015). However, these groupings are becoming more marginalized as the formal control of the game solidifies with the governing body WFTDA – closing down grass roots play options.

Conversely, and in a very different stance to most sporting organizations dealing with 'men's' sport, the MRDA Non-Discrimination Policy as outlined on their website in June 2015 allows anyone to play:

> MRDA, pursuant to its mission of promoting men's roller derby, does not and will not discriminate on the basis of race, color, religion (creed), gender, gender expression, age, national origin (ancestry), disability, marital status, sexual orientation, or military status, in any of its activities or operations. MRDA does not and will not differentiate between members who identify male and those who identify as a nonbinary gender (including but not limited to genderqueer, transmasculine, transfeminine, and agender) and does not and will not set minimum standards of masculinity for its membership or interfere with the privacy of its members for the purposes of charter eligibility. These activities include, but are not limited to, membership eligibility, disbursement of resources, and eligibility for office. MRDA is committed to providing an inclusive and welcoming environment for all skaters, officials, volunteers, and fans.

In our interview with the President of MRDA, we asked about this gender policy and how the Association decided on its content. He stated,

> The essence of what it was designed to achieve was to give skaters who don't identify with a binary gender a place to compete in roller derby as long as they are committed to playing what we call men's roller derby.

This quite radical view of gender in sport (a 'men's' sport allowing anyone) came about via the intervention of skaters, as the President notes:We never intended to exempt a trans or non-binary gendered skater who wasn't skating or couldn't skate on a women's league – we had just never thought of it. As our membership grew, we were thankfully able to get more eyes on this wording and more suggestions. One of our league representatives (there are 3 from each league) is a founding member of the 'trans, gender non-conforming, and intersex athlete network', and offered us some much needed perspective on how this language was affecting/could affect a person with a non-binary gender identification.

As a result of this, the MRDA has an inclusive and fluid conception of gender that focuses on a person's self-identification instead of biological markers of sex and receives significant support from the derby community for their view: 'Yay for MRDA, but fuck WFTDA. That entire page [WFTDA rules] pissed me the fuck off'. (Dragon Age Thoughts, n.d.).

In the Australian context, the body tasked to support the growth of the sport, Roller Derby Australia (RDA), also takes an open view:

> RDA work with all aspects of derby regardless of gender. With the steady rise in men's roller derby leagues, RDA will work with these leagues to ensure their needs are met. All of RDA's initiatives are non-gender specific and encourage engagement from all members

(Interview with official representative of RDA). Yet, despite this broad acceptance of men's roller derby, RDA does not have a firm position or direction for the sport in this regards. They explicitly work with WFTDA, which means that WFTDA's rigid gender policy is still in effect.

On the surface, WFTDA's gender policy 'makes sense'. In a world where biological determinism is often the norm, having a policy that relies on biological markers of gender becomes acceptable to some. Even feminist researchers working throughout the twentieth century and twenty-first century still struggle with biology and gender. As Birke (2003) notes,

> feminists tend to object strongly (and with good reason) to claims that, say, women's hormones predispose them to like ironing. Yes few of us, I assume, would want to contest that oestrogens affect the uterus, or that evolutionary processes have helped to shape our opposable thumbs. (41)

In efforts to reject crude determinism – necessary efforts though they were – some feminists ended up relying on dualistic notions of gender and sex. And even as poststructural accounts emerged which prioritized flux and fluidity, the problems of biological/social dualism remain. Birke notes how 'tricky it is to talk about biology without falling into the abyss of determinism (just as it's tricky to speak of social processes without falling into the abyss of relativism)!' (48).

It is beyond the scope of this current article to more fully engage with interdisciplinary notions of sex and gender. However, what is important to note is the difficulty of accounting for sexual difference. Scholars, such as Irigaray (1993) and Grosz (1994) have come some way in challenging us to think about bodies as *process(es)* rather than as fixed. And poststructuralist thinkers, such as Deleuze and Guattari (1987) have helped to reconsider humanness. Yet, for the majority of our research participants, these ideas are unknown, and many of our participants experienced an ongoing struggle with questions of gender in roller derby.

The position (and related policy above) posited by WFTDA does a range of troubling things. First, it delimits 'women' via biological markers (hormone levels) and therefore excludes a whole range of people who might identify as 'women'. In making this distinction, WFTDA is making a range of assumptions about gender, femininity, masculinity and specifically 'sport'. WFTDA's gender policy is connected closely with a conception of sport as competitive and serious (Breeze 2013). Our interview with RDA also acknowledged this competitive and serious aspect of the sport, with the representative stating:

> Currently there seems to be a strong trend towards making the sport more athletic and focusing on the competitive aspects. While there are still many recreational leagues, more and more seem to be pushing roller derby as a legitimate sport.

In wanting to be taken seriously, the WFTDA has taken a firm stance on who can and who cannot participate and dictate whom a women is. This is sometimes expected, though not accepted, by more conservative types of organizations. However, for an organization such as WFTDA, who are leading the charge on what is being discussed as the fastest growing sport in the world and one of the few contact sports women can enter into at any age or ability, these exclusions are not supportive of the kinds of transformations in sport such as those Hargreaves (1990) argued for.

Gendered perspectives: fixed and fluid

In roller derby, there exists a deep, ongoing and troubled discourse within the members of the sport regarding the position and role of men in the sport. This ranges across all aspects of the sport, from playing together, co-ed/mixed leagues, and the role of men in coaching, administration and leadership positions. Illustrative of the deep divide in derby are these comments made by a globally famous female identifying skater/coach was asked what she thought of men in derby in 2015. During an ethnographic interview she stated: 'We should treat Men's derby like how we'd wish the mainstream would treat Women's sport in general. We can't close the door now, it is too late for that. The MRDA and WFTDA should merge'. Through our ethnographic work, we were able to interview many people about this issue. One queer/femme identifying skater disclosed her opposition towards men in derby: 'Look I know it's not politically correct to say it and people will hate me for it, but I'd just wish the men would fuck off from derby, it's our sport and I just want the female energy'. Conversely, Swirko, a female skater and blogger (2015, emphasis in original) comments:

> I've read all the blogs. I've scrolled through the comments. I thought it would have all petered out by now, but still the occasional post pops up on some corner of the web about how men shouldn't be allowed to play roller derby because they don't deserve it. I'm sorry, guys: I wish these women would *stop misusing feminism* and hurry up and drop out of this sport which is quickly outgrowing them.

The ongoing debates around gender indicate its performative, contested nature, with many people we observed struggling to reconcile 'traditional' gendered stereotypes with their lived experiences in the sport.

This is most apparent in the arguments around whether men should play with/against women. The trope of sport is that men are bigger, stronger faster and 'better' then women, this is reinforced constantly across all sporting domains, and thus is carried over into derby. Men and women playing together is seen as both problematic and liberating, dependant on the persons perception, their athletic level and their view of the future of the sport. However, what came through most strongly in our research was the ongoing and persistent view that men were stronger, more able and ultimately hesitant to engage in sex-integrated derby into the future. Particularly as the sport grows and as players' skills and strength improves, sex integration is viewed as less and less the ideal. For example, this blog post captures that tension:

(I'm about to say something I know some people disagree with, but for what it's worth I do believe to be true.)

Why do we split sports into sexes? Because men are on average faster and stronger than women. So we split them for the same reason we split intermediate and professional level play- to get closer, fairer, competitive games. From that pov [Point of View], the female game has to create rules to keep out male athletes who would push out females; whereas in the male game, females are out competed and removed naturally from top level play. See – the NFL. This explains why the rules are probably always going to look different.

It doesn't even begin to touch on trans* players- apart from that we will always be fitting people in to the m/f binary where they don't necessarily want to be, unless a whole new ground up structure is built. (Her Ain Sel 2015)

These kinds of sentiments were expressed by some of our participants and demonstrate the need for a more consultative approach towards the development of sex-integrated derby.

At the elite level of men's derby, there is a strong resistance to playing women's teams – this is despite their inclusive gender policy for their own leagues. Speaking to a senior American skater who identified as male about his experiences playing women we noted the following interaction:

Interviewer: Are you looking forward to playing [a particular women's league]?
Participant: Nope, we don't usually skate against Women
Interviewer: Really?
Participant: Yep, it's a lose/lose situation
Interviewer: Why?
Participant: If we lose that is bad for the team as women have beaten us and if we win everyone just complains about guys hitting girls. No one likes a 200 lb guy smashing a 100 lb girl. Ya know, you can't hit girls. We just look bad.

Conversely, women can be encouraging of what is offered in co-ed training and bouts. In both our ethnographic interviews and in the material found online in publicly accessible blogs, women would sometimes express a very open, excited and inclusive view of men in derby. One Australian blogger wrote,

Watching the co-ed [roller derby] bout you could be forgiven for wincing as the men charged through blockers, some of them female, and knocking them over. But it is not harsh … they all know each other and are all friends, with a passion for Roller Derby.

Varsity Derby League DHR Sophomores player, *Maleficent Mara* says the men and women train together so it was nice to play against the men.

It makes you tougher and you learn to deal with the harder hits and the bigger skaters, you do get some bigger and taller girls when you line up against them it makes it a lot easier because you are used to playing with the boys. (Lorenz 2014)

One of our participants a (now former) president of what she called a 'co-ed' league reflected thoughtfully on sex integration in roller derby and gave the following extended response.

We had instituted segregated training as well so they didn't even train with us. I must admit I did really push that. Again, not because I had a problem with training with the boys and in fact I didn't even mind doing contact with them but it had previously been a problem for us so it was just easier just to split it. However, having these sorts of issues that came up and realising that we were developing a bit of a them and us kind of culture, I've now switched my thinking to realize, okay, if we're a coed league, we've got to be a coed league. Which doesn't mean again, I'm still not for coed contact but training together in non-contact drills, in that sort of way and having the guys part of the organisational process of the league I think is really important. We had a training meeting the other night and interestingly enough one of the members of that committee was clearly quite emotional about the idea and not in a positive way.

This response, taken from an interview conducted in 2011, is illustrative of the large pro-portion of derby players, both male and female, who are hopeful and positive about sex-integrated leagues, including training and governance. Secondly, it also points towards the ongoing and consistent concern about gendered differences in body strength.

Among referees, the majority of whom identify as male (often partners of female skaters), we found a constant debate as to whether they should penalize differently based on size of skater – with the implicit undertone being – should bigger, larger *men* be more penalized for 'hits' on skaters? The WFTDA rules are very clear on penalties and do not take into account skater size/weight/height or strength. But this does not deter ongoing discussion. For example, a male acknowledged that at one game he saw a male legally block a female player ('sending her flying') on the track and thought it excessive. He then admitted that he witnessed exactly the same hit and effect next day, but from a women – and he admitted he had to re-assess the first event. The refrain that men are 'too big' and hit 'too hard' also deeply troubles some woman skaters – comments such as 'bullshit, don't you dare pull your hits on me' and 'c'mon, women can hit just as hard/well – not all men are big and not all women are small'. Tough and strong female play is lauded as good derby, whereas the same from men is often interpreted differently. As one of our male participants noted during a discussion regarding the percep-tion that men play too hard: 'Look we just have to accept that men hitting hard and well will just look dangerous and likely get people penalized, whereas women hitting hard and well will get a pat on the back for strong derby' (male skater). Despite the ongoing biological and sociological challenges to the deeply rooted binary gender ideals, they persist and influence popular understandings of gender in sport (Matthews 2014). Even in roller derby, which might perhaps be described as a type of socially 'safe' female enclave (Matthews 2014, 115), pseudoscientific narratives of gender and sexuality are used to justify and understand prac-tices. Rather than entertaining the possibility of weight categorization, or alternative modes of play that pits those at the same skill level against each other, instead the problem is reduced to gender. Some women are 'scared of them [men]', while men are scared of 'looking like a douche' ('douche' being the common derby term regarding unfair/mean play).

Conclusions

We cannot successfully integrate the gender spectrum and reduce/eliminate discrimination until one of the most obvious, visible, valourized and re-produced binaries of gender is broken – that of *sport* and *women's sport*. That very qualifier (women's) attached to nearly all sport is a perpetual marker of inferiority. Integrated sport should be the goal of all. As Louisey Rider (2014), a female skater, argues in a blog post on men, derby and feminism: 'to have a chance of achieving its goals feminism as a movement needs to redefine itself as sexless, and position itself in a way that is more relevant to modern society – people as people, not men and women'. Derby offers an opportunity to enact a genderless sporting landscape in the shape that Hargreaves called for so long ago.

Wearing (1998) argues that

in the area of leisure, feminists need to move beyond the continuous documentation of women's oppression to see the many and varied ways that women and men can challenge and change male domination and also to suggest ways that both genders may work together to bring about change. (160)

Demonstrations of integration are crucial to re-fashioning gendered views in society and sport offers an obvious site for challenge. What we have shown, however, is the deeply challenging ideas that come from trying to combine traditional conceptions of men, women and their sporting prowess to a sport that is full contact, on roller skates. Derby, as a 'first-mover' in the space of integration, management by players for players and an overt alternative view offers an avenue for gender emancipation, if players can resolve their own troubled feelings on gender and only if WFTDA ceases its regressive restrictions on what a women is.

> Even as we finish writing this article, blog posts and discussions about sex integration in roller derby continue. Despite the authoritative position of WFTDA, players are creatively attempting to envision a sex-integrated future for the sport. One of our participants, a member of a sex-integrated league that is struggling to find ways forward, stated:Perhaps one idea could be for women to play against each other and then every third jam is all male. Rather than having males and females on the track at the same time. So if we had the capacity to do that, then I'll be interested in looking. (female participant, Interview)

These kinds of creative responses are needed if the sport is to continue to be a space of inclusion and empowerment for people of all genders. The opportunities for leagues around the world to trial alternative formats of play, including suggestions such as the one above, would be one way forward.

Disclosure statement
No potential conflict of interest was reported by the authors.

References

Beaver, T. D. 2012. "By the Skaters, for the Skaters: The DIY Ethos of the Roller Derby Revival." *Journal of Sport & Social Issues* 36 (1): 25–49. doi:10.1177/0193723511433862.

Berrick, G. 2015. "What Exactly is the Vagine Regime?" *Daily Life*, February 27. http://www.dailylife.com.au/news-and-views/dl-culture/what-exactly-is-the-vagine-regime-20150226-13pntk.html.

Birke, L. 2003. "Chapter 3. Shaping Biology. Feminism and the Idea of 'the Biological'." In *Debating Biology: Sociological Reflection on Health, Medicine and Society*, edited by S. Williams, L. Birke, and G. Bendelow, 39–52. London: Routledge.

Breeze, M. 2013. "Analysing 'Seriousness' in Roller Derby: Speaking Critically with the Serious Leisure Perspective." *Sociological Research Online*, 18 (4): 23. http://www.socresonline.org.uk/18/4/23.html.

Butler, J. 1990. *Gender Trouble: Feminism and the Subversion of Identity*. New York: Routledge.

Carlson, J. 2010. "The Female Significant in All-women's Amateur Roller Derby." *Sociology of Sport Journal* 27 (4): 428–440.

Channon, A. 2012. "Way of the Discourse: Mixed-sex Martial Arts and the Subversion of Gender." PhD diss., Loughborough University.

Channon, A., and G. Jennings. 2013. "The Rules of Engagement: Negotiating Painful and 'Intimate' Touch in Mixed-sex Martial Arts." *Sociology of Sport Journal* 30 (4): 487–503.

Chase, L. 2006. "(Un) Disciplined Bodies: A Foucauldian Analysis of Women's Rugby." *Sociology of Sport Journal* 23 (3): 229–247.

Clasen, P. R. W. 2001. "The Female Athlete: Dualisms and Paradox in Practice." *Women and Language* 24 (2): 36–41.

Cohen, J. H. 2008. "Sporting-self or Selling Sex: All-girl Roller Derby in the 21st Century." *Women in Sport and Physical Activity Journal* 17 (2): 24–33. http://vc.bridgew.edu/sociology_fac/11.

Cohen, A., B. Brown, and J. Peachey. 2012. "The Intersection of Pop Culture and Non-traditional Sports: An Examination of the Niche Market of Quidditch." *International Journal of Sport Management and Marketing* 12 (3/4): 180–197.

Connor, J. 2007. *The Sociology of Loyalty*. New York: Springer Science & Business Media.

Cronan, M., and D. Scott. 2008. "Triathlon and Women's Narratives of Bodies and Sport." *Leisure Sciences* 30 (1): 17–34. doi:10.1080/01490400701544675.

Dashper, K. 2012. "Together, Yet Still Not Equal? Sex Integration in Equestrian Sport." *Asia-Pacific Journal of Health, Sport and Physical Education* 3 (3): 213–225.

Deleuze, G., and F. Guattari. 1987. *A Thousand Plateaus: Capitalism and Schizophrenia*. Minneapolis: University of Minnesota Press.

Donnelly, M. K. 2012. *The Production of Women Onlyness: Women's Flat Track Roller Derby and Women-only Home Improvement Workshops*. PhD diss., McMaster University.

Dragon Age Thoughts, n.d. "Tumblr Post." *Sneople Mage Trash*. http://kremdelafuckyou.tumblr.com/post/109669408660/mens-roller-derby-association-does-not-and-will.

Eckstein, R. D. Moss, and K. Delaney. 2010. "Sports Sociology's Still Untapped Potential." *Sociological Forum* 25 (3): 500–518. http://www.jstor.org/stable/40783513.

Erbentraut, J. 2015. "Gorgeous Roller Derby Photos Redefine Beauty and Strength." *Huffington Post Women*, October 3. http://www.huffingtonpost.com/2015/03/10/body-by-derby-photo-series_n_6833316.html.

Fink, J. S. 2014. "Female Athletes, Women's Sport, and the Sport Media Commercial Complex: Have We Really 'Come a Long Way, Baby'?" *Sport Management Review*. Advance Online Publication. doi:10.1016/j.smr.2014.05.001.

Finley, N. J. 2010. "Skating Femininity: Gender Maneuvering in Women's Roller Derby." *Journal of Contemporary Ethnography* 39 (4): 359–387. doi: 10.1177/0891241610364230.

Grosz, E. A. 1994. *Volatile Bodies: Toward a Corporeal Feminism*. Indianapolis: Indiana University Press.

Hargreaves, J. A. 1990. "Gender on the Sports Agenda." *International Review for the Sociology of Sport* 25 (4): 287–307. doi: 10.1177/101269029002500403.

Henne, K. 2014. "The "Science" of Fair Play in Sport: Gender and the Politics of Testing." *Signs* 39 (3): 787–812. doi: 10.1086/674208.

Her Ain Sel. 2015. "Tumblr Post." *Her Ain Sel*, January 27. http://myainsel.tumblr.com/post/109305984038/mens-roller-derby-association-does-not-and-will.

Irigaray, L. 1993. *This Sex Which is Not One*. New York: Cornell University Press.

Johns, D. P., and J. Johns. 2000. "Surveillance, Subjectivism and Technologies of Power: An Analysis of the Discursive Practice of High-performance Sport." *International Review for the Sociology of Sport* 35 (2): 219–234. doi: 10.1177/101269000035002006.

Kearney, M. C. 2011. "Tough Girls in a Rough Game." *Feminist Media Studies* 11 (3): 283–301. doi: 10.1080/14680777.2010.535309.

Khomutova, A., and A. Channon. 2015. "Legends' in 'Lingerie': Sexuality and Athleticism in the 2013." *Sociology of Sport Journal*. Advance Online Publication. doi: 10.1123/ssj.2014-0054.

Koh, B., D. Adair, and P. Sonksen. 2014. "Testosterone, Sex and Gender Differentiation in Sport – Where Science and Sports Law Meet." *Law in Sport*, Online Article, 14 October. http://www.lawinsport.com/articles/item/testosterone-sex-and-gender-differentiation-in-sport-where-science-and-sports-law-meet.

Lake, R. J. 2012. "Gender and Etiquette in British Lawn Tennis 1870–1939: A Case Study of 'Mixed Doubles'." *The International Journal of the History of Sport* 29 (5): 691–710. doi:10.1080/09523367.2012.675203.

Layman, C. 2015. "About the Rollergirl Project." *The Rollergirl Project*. Accessed March 17, 2015. http://therollergirlproject.blogspot.com.au/p/about-rollergirl-project.html

Leon, C. 2007. "Roller Derby Saved My Soul." *On Roller Derby Saved My Soul* [song lyrics].

Lorber, J. 1993. "Believing is Seeing: Biology as Ideology." *Gender & Society* 7 (4): 568–581. doi:10.1177/089124393007004006.

Lorenz, N. 2014. "All's Fair in Love and Derby." *Her Canberra*, July 28. http://hercanberra.com.au/cplife/alls-fair-in-love-and-derby/.

Louisey Rider. 2014. "Feminism, Roller Derby, and Why Men Are Not the Devil." *Nottingham Roller Girls*, April 29. http://nottinghamrollergirls.com/feminism-roller-derby-and-why-men-are-not-the-devil/.

Matthews, C. R. 2014. "Biology Ideology and Pastiche Hegemony." *Men and Masculinities* 17 (2): 99–119. doi: 10.1177/1097184x14526699.

McKay, J. 1991. *No Pain, No Gain? Sport and Australian Culture*. New York: Prentice Hall.

McWilliams, J. 2012. "Time for the Bleeding Heartland Roller Girls to Protest the WFTDA Gender Policy." *Making Edible Playdough is Hegemonic*, March 9. http://www.jennamcwilliams.com/2012/03/09/time-for-the-bleeding-heartland-roller-girls-to-protest-the-wftda-gender-policy/.

Messner, M. 2002. *Taking the Field: Women, Men and Sports*. Minneapolis: University of Minnesota Press.

Pavlidis, A., and S. Fullagar. 2014. *Sport, Gender and Power: The Rise of Roller Derby*. Surrey: Ashgate.

Peluso, N. M. 2011. "Cruisin' for a Bruisin: Women's Flat Track Roller Derby." In *Embodied Resistance: Challenging the Norms, Breaking the Rules*, edited by C. Bobel and S. Kwan, 37–77. Nashville: Vanderbilt University Press.

Rafoss, K., and J. Troelsen. 2010. "Sports Facilities for All? The Financing, Distribution and Use of Sports Facilities in Scandinavian Countries." *Sport in Society* 13 (4): 643–656. doi: 10.1080/17430431003616399.

Sailors, P. R. 2014. "Mixed Competition and Mixed Messages." *Journal of the Philosophy of Sport* 41 (1): 65–77. doi:10.1080/00948705.2013.858398.

Storms, C. E. 2008. "There's No Sorry in Roller Derby: A Feminist Examination of the Collective Identity Formation of Women in the Full Contact Sport of Roller Derby." *New York Sociologist* 3: 68–147. http://newyorksociologist.org/08/Storms-08.pdf.

Swirko, K. 2015. "An Open Letter to All My Derby Brothers." *Derby Central*, January 23. http://www.derbycentral.net/2015/01/open-letter-derby-brothers/.

Tagg, B. 2014. "Men's Netball or Gender-neutral Netball?" *International Review for the Sociology of Sport*. Advance Online Publication. doi: 10.1177/1012690214524757.

Tremaine, K. L. 2015. "Tumblr Post." *A Widdershins Girl*, Accessed March 17, 2015. http://baeddelshinsgirl.tumblr.com/post/109670683577/mens-roller-derby-association-does-not-and-will

Turner, D. 2013. "The Civilized Skateboarder and the Sports Funding Hegemony: A Case Study of Alternative Sport." *Sport in Society* 16 (10): 1248–1262. doi: 10.1080/17430437.2013.821256.

Wearing, B. 1998. *Leisure and Feminist Theory*. London: Sage.

Women's Flat Track Derby Association. 2015. *WFTDA Mission Statement*. Women's Flat Track Derby Association. Accessed February 17, 2015. http://wftda.com/mission

Young, I. M. 2005. *On Female Body Experience*. Oxford: Oxford University Press.

Zirin, D. 2008. "Calling Sports Sociology off the Bench." *Contexts* 7 (3): 28–31. doi:10.1525/ctx.2008.7.3.28.

Playing like a girl? The negotiation of gender and sexual identity among female ice hockey athletes on male teams

Danielle DiCarlo[‡]

Department of Exercise Sciences, University of Toronto, Toronto, Canada

ABSTRACT

While no one can deny the rich history of girls and women in sport, they continue to face obstacles to their full participation and representation in mixed-sex sport environments. Sex integration in sport is often contentious for those female athletes who participate in sports traditionally played by men, such as ice hockey. We do not know enough about the lived experiences of girls and women who navigate these gendered sport spaces. With this in mind, this study qualitatively explored how seven female ice hockey athletes negotiate their identities as female athletes, in such a way that focuses on the social constructions of gender and sexuality. Findings of this study highlight the tensions and contradictions of being a female athlete in a traditionally male sport and the rigid categories used by the women interviewed in negotiating their gendered and sexual identities while playing on male ice hockey teams.

While no one can deny the rich history of girls and women in sport, they continue to face obstacles to their full participation and representation, specifically in the Canadian ice hockey system. For example, in March 2009, the Hockey Hall of Fame announced they would be re-writing their by-laws to allow female athletes to be considered for induction separately from their male counterparts (Cox 2009). The separation of male and female ice hockey inductees highlights the cultural ambivalence and ideological struggle around women's sport generally, and the legitimacy of women's ice hockey specifically. To that end, with the inclusion of female athletes in the Hockey Hall of Fame, almost 50 years after its conception, it remains evident that the world of sport continues to be identified and associated primarily as a male terrain such that the presence of women is, at times, seen as unusual and problematic (Daniels 2009; Hoffman 1995).

Indeed, the gendering of ice hockey space is not new; there have been numerous well-known cases of women playing on, or attempting to play on, male ice hockey teams.[1] Women have migrated into these sport spaces through the development of female teams and leagues, but also through their participation on male teams and leagues. Sport is often contentious for those female athletes who participate in sports traditionally played exclusively by men

---

[‡]Research was conducted at York University, School of Kinesiology and Health Science, Toronto, Ontario, Canada.

and, arguably, even more so for those women who participate on male teams (Theberge 1995, 2000). Apart from media portrayal of female athletes, our knowledge of the lived experience of non-celebrity girls and women is under-researched in the study of sex, gender and sexuality, especially in and around the subculture of ice hockey. The lived experiences of female ice hockey athletes playing on male teams is important in revealing details about how females come to negotiate binaries of gender created through sport and how these negotiations shape their thoughts regarding the female athlete. To that end, we simply do not know enough about the lived experiences of girls and women who navigate these gendered sport spaces. With this in mind, the purpose of this Research Insight is to explore the ways in which seven young women, who play or have played on male ice hockey teams before transitioning to female ice hockey teams, negotiate their identities as female athletes, in such a way that focuses on the social constructions of sex, gender and sexuality. In the following brief engagement with the literature, I begin with an attempt to frame the participants' experiences within the context of previous academic work around sport, gender and sexuality, connecting this work to current broader perspectives regarding women's ice hockey. Next, I discuss the results of this study paying attention to how these female athletes experience and negotiate their female sporting identities, with particular emphasis on the tensions and contradictions around gender and sexual identity.

Sport and the construction of sex, gender and sexuality

Sex, gender and sexuality are socially constructed phenomena (Coakley and Donnelly 2009). Sex has been constructed as a binary where all people are classified into one of two sex categories, male or female. These expectations, defined by the sex binary, outline a basis for how individuals identify and define gender or what is considered masculine and what is considered feminine. While competitive sport is an arena where the production and expression of gender continues to be challenged, sport is a social institution where this gender logic is perhaps most apparent (Burke 2004). Historically speaking, in contrast to the empowerment of men through sport, women were often excluded from sport or admitted on restricted teams where events were changed in order to coincide to a view of women as fragile and weak (Kidd 1996). The long-standing perception that women are the 'weaker sex' who cannot handle the same level of physical activity as their male counterparts was borne out of the Victorian era (Vertinsky 1990). In order to prove his fitness and physical capabilities, males had to exercise mind and body more than females, and females were incessantly advised to accept arranged limits upon their actions, including athletic limitations, as the ultimate price for having a female body (Balsamo 1996). This historical influence and the assumption that females are inherently fragile, and, thus, incapable of taking part in athletic endeavours, has proven to be quite problematic for female athletes. The naturalization of women being 'less able' than men has become status quo and remains, although at times subtle, evident today (Anderson 2005; Burke 2004; Ezzell 2009).

What Theberge (1997) has called the 'myth of female frailty' has had a long-lasting effect on the history of women's restriction to sport and has perpetuated problematic gender binaries concerning athletic participation. Too often, sport has been used to reify differences between men and women in order to justify male domination on the basis of natural difference and to legitimize unequal power relations between the sexes (Messner 1988). In fact, cultural conceptions of femininity and female beauty make women's sport participation quite problematic. As such, female athletes who participate in traditional male sports, considered outside the female domain, are reminded that they are challenging the outer ranges of 'acceptable' feminine behaviour (Daniels 1992). Thus, sport has functioned as a male preserve, or an all-male domain, in which men not only play games together, but also demonstrate and affirm their manhood by dictating the gender appropriate behaviours of men and women (Sartore and Cunningham 2009).

In addition to sport being identified as an institution organized by hegemonic masculinity (Connell and Messerschmidt 2005) reinforcing a distinction between two genders, sport has also been organized around the notion of 'compulsory heterosexuality' (Anderson 2008; Theberge 2000). The gender binary classification model followed today is based on the notion that heterosexuality is natural and normal and those who express feelings, actions and thoughts outside of the socially constructed categories of masculine and feminine are considered 'deviant' or 'out of bounds' when it comes to gender (Coakley and Donnelly 2009). A two-category model does not recognize nor provide space for those individuals who are neither heterosexual males nor heterosexual females. In the realm of sport, where heterosexuality is considered by most compulsory, this may have dire consequences for individuals who push the boundaries of what constitutes traditional masculinity and femininity. Given this, the historical social constructions of gender and sexuality has influenced and, at times, has resulted in problematic consequences concerning the development and organization of sport in Canada, in general, and in ice hockey in particular.

The case of women's ice hockey: sporting identities and broader perspectives

As noted above, traditionally male sports, such as ice hockey, are archetypal in their strong association of the sport to the male identity and differentiation between female and male athletes. Thus, female athletes who play traditionally male dominated sports, in particular, may not be free to construct any version of identity they desire; identity construction is thus influenced by a number of micro- and macro-social processes (Anderson 2005).

That said, broader social tensions still exist in the sport of ice hockey and these tensions are rooted in the gender binary. For example, a common question within ice hockey culture is whether female athletes should play solely within female leagues to enhance their development or if this development should essentially transfer over into male ice hockey (Schneider 2000). There is a strong cultural and societal element which favours the argument for separate development. Individuals opposed to female athletes participating on male teams argue that girls and women should not imitate male sport, but instead should build different models of sport which are fundamentally more humane (or less violent than male ice hockey) and empowering for female athletes (Lenskyj 2003).

Despite the significance of all female ice hockey teams providing empowering group association for female athletes, as argued by Lenskyj, proponents of women participating on male ice hockey teams diverge from this claim. Supporters of women playing on male ice hockey teams have argued that women's presence in what is known as 'male ice hockey culture' challenges the oppositional binary of what constitutes femininity (e.g. the female athlete as weak and less capable) and masculinity (e.g. the male athlete as aggressive and disciplined) in sport (McDonagh and Pappano 2009). Given these diverging perspectives, how might sex integration in the sport of ice hockey challenge and/or reaffirm hegemonic constructions of gender and sexuality in this unique sport space?

Methodology

The decision to use qualitative methods for this study arose because of the very nature of the research questions; more specifically, I was interested in the detailed accounts of female ice hockey athletes' lived experiences within the production and reproduction of hegemonic discourses surrounding contemporary sport. I aimed to recruit participants willing to discuss their lived experiences as female ice hockey athletes who have played on male ice hockey teams in order to learn how participants made sense and meaning of themselves as female athletes in a traditionally male sport.[2]

Initially, participants for this study were recruited via the distribution of flyers posted in ice hockey arenas and university gyms and through snowball sampling. The decision where to distribute recruitment flyers was made based on insider familiarity of the female ice hockey community and knowledge of particular female teams' home arenas. In terms of snowball sampling, potential participants were initially approached through friends who knew of women who play(ed) ice hockey on male and female teams as well as through my own contacts. Further contacts were recruited based on referral from those initial participants. No explicit attempts were made to target groups on the basis of race, ethnicity, (dis)ability and/or sexual orientation. While participants were not asked about their sexual orientation, one participant did identify herself as homosexual. It is important to note, the sample population used for this study is limited to white, middle-class, (majority) heterosexual and able-bodied female ice hockey athletes. While a methodological goal of this research was to gather a more diverse group of participants by enlisting a broad range of female ice hockey athletes that crossed racial, ethnic, sexual, cultural, educational and class lines, the final participants for this study did not adequately reflect this intent. As such, the experiences of minority (individuals of colour, multiple sexualities) female ice hockey athletes who have played on both male and female teams remains understudied. The goal of future research should take into account the above social demographics in order to get a broader picture and deeper understanding of the experiences of Canadian female ice hockey athletes.

To that end, seven female ice hockey athletes who have experience participating on male and female teams in the past were recruited to participate in in-depth, semi-structured interviews. Participants, all of whom resided in the Greater Toronto Area of Ontario, Canada, ranged from 18 to 25 years of age. The majority of the women interviewed joined male house league teams at a young age (between six and eight years of age) and identified wanting to begin playing ice hockey with the boys due to male family members already playing. Many of the participants made the decision to transition to female leagues to play on REP[3] teams (between 12 and 14 years of age) because of not 'being able to keep up' with the physicality of male teammates while playing on a male team. Despite this, many of the women interviewed discussed transitioning back to male ice hockey teams.

Interviews were transcribed verbatim and analysed using a grounded theory approach (Charmaz 2005) to produce themes from participants' descriptions of their own experiences and feelings. Ultimately, three interconnected thematic categories emerged, which are discussed in the subsequent results section.

It is important to note, while I have not explicitly and purposefully employed an auto-ethnographic analysis, I have most certainly drawn on my own experiences as a female ice hockey athlete immersed in ice hockey culture. My status as a female athlete and an insider in this particular culture helped a great deal in the preparation of this research since the topic of study pertains to female ice hockey athletes, a group to which I belong. As a female athlete who has played on female ice hockey teams, I share similar experiences with my participants which, at times, influenced the interview process and the co-construction of data between interviewer and interviewee. Having intimate knowledge of the game and being a female ice hockey player there were many instances in the interviews where I understood the participants' experiences. Juxtaposed to this is the position of 'outsider'. Despite, being a female athlete who has played competitive ice hockey for a number of years, I do not have the experience of playing on male teams. Given this, and as Fletcher (2014) suggests, the subjectivity of researcher positionality during the research process is never certain but rather is a fluid and ongoing performance. With this in mind, and as both an insider *and* outsider, I recognize how contingent these identities are and how my role as a researcher during the interview process was constantly being negotiated.

Results

Gender identity: the conceptualization of female athletes as weak

The view that female athletes are fragile was particularly problematic for the women interviewed in this study. Although none of the women in this study explicitly stated there was a belief among male players that the female athlete is inherently weaker than the male athlete, they expressed that not being treated the same as male athletes in terms of physical contact and aggression was a contentious issue. As such, a common question the participants found themselves asking while playing on male teams was: 'Why am I treated differently?' According to the participants, these women were involved in situations where it was assumed by others (particularly by male coaches and male teammates) that they would get hurt and, as female athletes, they did not completely understand the reasoning behind this belief. As female athletes involved in a traditionally male sport and playing on all male teams, this view of female frailty had a lasting influence on these athletes' experiences. Despite the women discussing feeling angry by the fact that many of their male teammates would 'hold back' from hitting them or as one participant says, 'they'd be afraid to hit me', these women never voiced their opinion to their teammates regarding this volume while playing on male teams. In this way, they consented to the view of the female athlete as fragile by their male teammates. The social construction of being weak and, in some cases, infantilized, is part and parcel of the construction of idealized femininity (see Channon 2013). For example, some of the participants spoke of the treatment they received from their coaches and male teammates as childlike in nature:

> They [coaches] I don't know. They treated us like … I wouldn't say a baby, but if the guys made a mistake they'd get yelled at. But, if I made a mistake it was, 'It's okay, you'll do fine next time'. The coaches would always … kind of talk to us like we're stupid, explaining plays and stuff like we wouldn't understand it. I didn't really think of it at the time because I was still learning, but now it would be kind of insulting.

When asked how she was treated as a female athlete playing on a male team by her (male) coaches, another participant added, 'They [male teammates and coaches] always stuck up for me. My coaches always stuck up for me. The coaches, they were sometimes a little easier on me than the guys'. As these narratives illustrate, an essential part of the social construction of idealized femininity, particularly for the women interviewed for this study, centred on infantilization of the female athlete. Dominant gender meanings – in particular, the ideology that female athletes are inferior to male athletes especially with regard to strength – are somewhat reaffirmed by the women studied as these athletes did not challenge nor reject this 'hierarchical' difference. Although the participants, by very nature of being involved as female athletes in a traditionally male sport, challenged hegemonic constructions of femininity, they still embodied normative gender expectations. Furthermore, these women failed to connect their experiences as female athletes on male teams to greater struggles around equity in sport. In not politicizing their experiences/actions, these women consented, to a degree, to the social construction of women as weak, fragile and needing protection in spite of the fact that they are strong, active female athletes playing ice hockey with boys and men.

A possible reason why these female athletes did not challenge the cultural contradiction between femininity and athleticism and, instead, seemed to consent to the presumption of gender difference on the ice may be explained by the consistent and traditional (re)production of the rhetoric in and around female athletes and female sport in general (Étue and Williams 1996; Theberge 2006).[4] It is plausible that the rhetoric regarding female athletes not only helped in framing these women's thoughts, ideas and behaviours, but have also framed the way in which these women may have come to negotiate their role as female athletes participating on male ice hockey teams.

The female athlete and aggression

If female athletes playing on male teams are thought of and, at times, construct themselves as inherently fragile, what specifically does this mean for female athletes and their displays of aggressiveness in sport? Even though participants all possessed varying levels of aggressive on-ice behaviour themselves, they were particularly consistent in their descriptions of themselves as tomboys. One said:

> I'm the exception to the rule. I never fit inside this very traditional little square cube of what you would define a girl so I feel like a lot of my life things have been okay for me because that's always just been me. I think I was fortunate enough to come across a lot of my friends who accepted me for being that tomboy.

It is interesting to note that even though this participant recognized the problematic way in which gender is socially constructed, she still feels the need to classify herself. Although she spoke about not classifying herself as a 'typical' female, she does, nonetheless, place herself in a category belonging to tomboys. By categorizing herself as a tomboy, she is reifying exactly what she argued against; not fitting the idealized and socially acceptable role of what being a female means. For these participants, they used the notion of being a tomboy to help with their negotiations in and around aggressiveness. By classifying themselves as tomboys, these women believed that although they are women and understood by coaches and male teammates as inherently weaker than or not naturally as tough as male athletes, because they grew up as tomboys they can be or are 'allowed' to be aggressive. Also, identifying female athletes who play on male teams as tomboys, these women are reaffirming that they belong to the male sporting community (Helstein 2005). In a sense, being a tomboy provides these participants with an excuse to be aggressive.

This paradox between femininity and aggressiveness is clear regarding the discourse these women used when they spoke of body contact and aggression on the ice. It is interesting to note that the participants considered themselves aggressive because they had experience playing on all male teams, however, were conflicted in their discussions around aggressiveness and female athletes who do not have the experience of playing in a male dominant environment. As one participant explained:

> I wish I played still. Sometimes I miss it. But girls' hockey ruined it for me. Girls are *so* [emphasis in original] timid and they can't take criticism at all. In guy's (ice) hockey, you learn because your coaches they yell at you, they yell at guys. They're so much harder on guys. But the girls … I think it's female's nature to be that way and also (ice) hockey's more of a manly sport, you know? So maybe they [female athletes] feel they can't compete to that level in a way.

For this participant, there is a deeply embedded contradiction or tension surrounding the notion of female athletes and aggressiveness. Her reasoning behind female athletes not being aggressive on the ice, once again, reinforces the ideology that females are weak and thus not naturally aggressive. While playing ice hockey, these athletes were continuously involved in, at times consciously and at others subconsciously, a gendered performance (Butler 1990). Rather than putting on a gendered performance where they engaged in feminizing behaviours on the ice, they engaged in masculinized behaviour(s) (such as identifying themselves as tomboys) in order to legitimate their involvement in sport and a traditionally aggressive sport. In fact, this gendered behaviour was so influential for these participants that, throughout the interview, the discourse used was one describing female athletes on all female teams in highly feminized ways (e.g. catty, emotional, timid, etc.) when it came to aggression and physical contact on the ice. Their discourses closely parallel the reification of the ice hockey rink as male domain and questions women's ability to compete with men as well as one another powerfully, aggressively and successfully in ice hockey (Migliaccio and Berg 2007).

Identity and sexuality

There seemed to be a common discourse used by participants throughout the interviews which compared their body ideal with non-heterosexual athletes. The female athletes interviewed constructed their identities as heterosexual ice hockey players in order to distinguish themselves from their homosexual female teammates. Some of the participants suggested that homosexual athletes were the 'butch' or 'manly' athletes who they described as the better players on an all female team:

> Well within girls' (ice) hockey I found that the better players were the ones who were more butch. They're more … they look like men. Their body image is more manly. I also found that there was more gay girls. A lot of female players who are good are gay. That's just something I found. And, when I think of a female athlete I just think built, like broad shoulders. I don't think very thin or skinny or feminine body. I see a more manly body with muscle. I see muscle.

Based on the response by this particular athlete, it is impossible to ignore the connection between the view of the female sporting body, masculine hegemony and the gender binary. The notion of the female sporting body, for this participant, does not challenge masculine hegemony nor the gender binary as female athletes who are considered the highly skilled players 'look like men' and engage their bodies in socially constructed masculine ways. The female athlete, as representative of westernized femininity, is read against the 'gender deviant other' sporting body as embodied by the homosexual female athlete (Davis-Delano, Pollock, and Ellsworth Vose 2009).

While women acknowledged the promotion of heteronormative sexuality within ice hockey culture, none of the women explicitly recognized that within their narratives around sexuality there was clearly a sexualized image of the female athlete. For example, as one participant described her experience playing on a male team:

> There'd always be flirting. I was okay. This was okay. I was a huge flirt, like, huge, ridiculous. Whether it was at high school or whether it was on the bench playing ice hockey with them it didn't really matter. I was flirting with them. So, yes, there was a lot of sexual tension on the bench because I created it by being there, by flirting and stuff. There was a lot of tension too because I'd flirt with the Refs.

This sexualized image of the female athlete was, at times, (re)produced by the female athletes themselves. In this sense, women collude with being sexy and attractive at the same time as being sportswomen. As the above narratives illustrate, these women's experiences assist in the maintenance of heterosexuality and heteronormativity. It is also interesting to acknowledge the silence around the negation of heterosexuality. The women interviewed spoke very little to sexual relations with teammates (male or female) and, at times, seemed to resist or struggle with questions relating to sexuality and sexual relations. Silence around the negation of heterosexuality was quite unexpected since the women interviewed were playing on female ice hockey teams at a time/age when sexual experimentation is perhaps most evident (Sharpe 2003).

Conclusion

Some of the women in this study accepted normative constructions of femininity and the female body. Despite engaging in new terrain through their participation on male ice hockey teams, many of these women (re)produced hegemonic ideas about sex, gender and sexuality.

Female athletes in this study exhibited neither a complete adherence to nor rejection of ideal femininity within their constructions of gender. Their definitions of femininity tended to fall within the traditional and reinforced gender differences as natural and inherent, which was evident in their discourse around gender identity. Contradiction and tension marked these women's experiences as the women in this study negotiated a path of both acceptance of and resistance to the assumption of female frailty and lack of aggression and struggled over hegemonic masculinity and idealized femininity. For example, many of the participants were quite consistent in linking together female athlete and tomboy to help with their negotiations in and around aggression. Yet, none of the participants critiqued or explored the implications of assuming this gendered role – that is, no one questioned why a woman had to rationalize her athleticism via the use of the concept of tomboy (a pseudo-boy). It is important to add that none of the participants connected to or problematized the fact that if men ventured into traditionally feminine sports, they would be called 'sissies' – a term with far more negative connotation than the more positive term of 'tomboy'. Furthermore, participants constructed their (heterosexual) identities through comparison of self with homosexual female teammates and their narratives around heteronormativity. Female athletes within this sample also spoke openly about the promotion of heteronormative sexuality within the sporting community and how this translated into an overt sexualized image of the female athlete. Narratives of their experiences assist in the maintenance of heterosexuality and heteronormativity in and around the sporting realm.

Although these women are engaging their bodies in practices that challenge the presumed stable relationship between sex, gender and sexuality, they struggled to connect their experiences as female athletes in a traditionally male sport to greater struggles around equity in sport. By not politicizing their experiences, these women consented, to a degree, to the social constructions of the feminine ideal and heteronormativity. These women are still dealing with hegemonic notions of sex, gender and sexuality that often, but not always, conflict with their experiences as active and vibrant women in sport. Identity is a fluid and dynamic concept that struggles against seemingly rigid binaries of sex, gender and sexuality such that the participants – even though their actions resist hegemonic notions of idealized femininity – offer numerous examples of their adoption of cues, symbols and practices of idealized femininity and their acceptance (i.e. consent) of a gender binary. The women interviewed demonstrated that the sporting culture of ice hockey is a site – where these women were, at times, complicit in following – for reaffirming beliefs not only regarding the sex binary and gender logic, but also concerning the promotion of a hierarchical ranking of the sexes and the maintenance of heterosexuality. The ambiguous nature of the participants' responses on matters of gender identity and sexuality mirrors conceptions of binary categories and the contradictory nature of constructing gender and the sporting body.[5] Indeed, the reflections of these seven women raise important questions regarding the argument for separate development leagues and different sporting cultures. Nonetheless, issues pertaining to biology, social construction and comparative performance of male and female athletes are beyond the scope of this Research Insight. I would argue that the players' reflections in this study demonstrate uncertainty by these particular female athletes around redefining the meanings of sport as empowering and liberating for the female athlete. Among the competing arguments for mixed/single sex sport spaces, it may be argued that the dominant interpretation, at least by the female athletes interviewed for this study, demonstrate the cultural precariousness and ideological struggle around women's sport generally, and the female athlete more specifically. These women's narratives demonstrate how difficult it is to challenge the technologies of femininity and the reification of the above-mentioned themes while at the same time illustrating critical issues in the social construction of sport (Theberge 1995).

Future research should consider how the institutional space of ice hockey, parents, coaches and fans contribute to the discourses surrounding sport and female athletes, and the ways in which these discourses affect how we conceptualize various sporting practices (Butryn and Masucci 2009), and the role of the athletic body.

Notes

1. Such female athletes include, but are not limited to, Abigail Hoffman, Justine Blainey, Manon Rhéaume and Hayley Wickenheiser.
2. The research was carried out in 2010.
3. REP hockey refers to a level in youth hockey considered more competitive than recreational 'house' league teams (Staff Writer 2014).
4. While the Ontario Women's Hockey Association (OWHA) is the largest governing body of women's hockey, the structure of this organization has somewhat encouraged an impasse attitude towards female hockey.

5. Despite the contradictions and tensions lived by the participants, it would be inappropriate to suggest that there was no transformative potential in their experiences (see Young and White 1995).

Acknowledgements

This research insight is based on findings from the author's master's thesis and was presented at the 31st Annual North American Society for the Sociology of Sport conference. I would like to thank Dr Parissa Safai for her guidance and support in completing this research as well as the two anonymous reviewers for their helpful feedback.

Disclosure statement

No potential conflict of interest was reported by the author.

References

Anderson, E. 2005. "Orthodox and Inclusive Masculinity: Competing Masculinities among Heterosexual Men in a Feminized Terrain." *Sociological Perspectives* 48 (3): 337–355.

Anderson, E. 2008. "'I Used to Think Women Were Weak': Orthodox Masculinity, Gender Segregation, and Sport." *Sociological Forum* 23 (2): 257–280. doi:10.1111/j.1573-7861.2008.00058.x.

Balsamo, A. M. 1996. *Technologies of the Gendered Body: Reading Cyborg Women*. Durham, NC: Duke University Press.

Burke, M. 2004. "Radicalising Liberal Feminism by Playing the Games That Men Play." *Australian Feminist Studies* 19 (44): 169–184.

Butler, J. 1990. *Gender Trouble: Feminism and the Subversion of Identity*. New York: Routledge.

Butryn, T., and M. Masucci. 2009. "Traversing the Matrix: Cyborg Athletes, Technology, and the Environment." *Journal of Sport and Social Issues* 33 (3): 285–307.

Channon, A. G. 2013. "Enter the Discourse: Exploring the Discursive Roots of Inclusivity in Mixed-sex Martial Arts." *Sport in Society* 16 (10): 1293–1308. doi:10.1080/17430437.2013.790896.

Charmaz, K, ed. 2005. "Grounded Theory in the 21st Century: Applications for Advancing Social Justice Studies". In *The Sage Handbook of Qualitative Research*, edited by N. Denzin and Y. Lincoln, 507–537. Thousand Oaks, CA: Sage.

Coakley, J., and P. Donnelly. 2009. *Sport and Society: Issues and Controversies*. McGraw-Hill Ryerson. http://www.primisonline.com.

Connell, R., and J. Messerschmidt. 2005. "Hegemonic Masculinity: Rethinking the Concept." *Gender and Society* 19 (6): 829–859. doi:10.1177/0891243205278639.

Cox, Damien. 2009. "Women to Be Admitted to Hockey Hall of Fame." *Toronto Star*, April 1.

Daniels, D. B. 1992. "Gender (Body) Verification (Building)." *Play and Culture* 5: 370–377.

Daniels, D. B. 2009. *Polygendered and Ponytailed: The Dilemma of Femininity and the Female Athlete*. Toronto, ON: Canadian Scholars Press.

Davis-Delano, L., A. Pollock, and J. Ellsworth Vose. 2009. "Apologetic Behavior among Female Athletes: A New Questionnaire and Initial Results." *International Review for the Sociology of Sport* 44: 131–150. doi:10.1177/1012690209335524.

Étue, E., and M. Williams. 1996. *On the Edge: Women Making Hockey History*. Toronto, ON: Second Story Press.

Ezzell, M. 2009. "'Barbie Dolls' on the Pitch: Identity Work, Defensive Othering, and Inequality in Women's Rugby." *Social Problems* 56 (1): 111–131.

Fletcher, T. 2014. "'Does He Look like a Paki?' An Exploration of 'Whiteness', Positionality and Reflexivity in Inter-racial Sports Research." *Qualitative Research in Sport, Exercise and Health* 6 (2): 244–260. http://dx.doi.org/10/1080/2159676X.2013.796487.

Helstein, M. T. 2005. "Rethinking Community: Introducing the Whatever Female Athlete." *Sociology of Sport Journal* 22 (1): 1–18.

Hoffman, A. 1995. "Women's Access to Sport and Physical Activity." *Avante* 1 (1): 77–92.

Kidd, B. 1996. *The Struggle for Canadian Sport*. Toronto, ON: University of Toronto Press.

Lenskyj, H. 2003. "Good Sports? Feminists Organizing on Sport Issues." Chap. 4 in Out on the Field: Gender, Sport and Sexualities. Toronto, ON: Canadian Scholars' Press.

McDonagh, E., and L. Pappano. 2009. *Playing with the Boys: Why Separate is Not Always Equal in Sports*. New York: Oxford University Press.

Messner, M. 1988. "Sports and Male Domination: The Female Athlete as Contested Ideological Terrain." In *Women, Sport and Culture*, edited by S. Birrell and C. L. Cole, 65–81. Champaign, IL: Human Kinetics.

Migliaccio, T., and E. Berg. 2007. "Women's Participation in Tackle Football: An Exploration of Benefits and Constraints." *International Review for the Sociology of Sport* 42 (3): 271–287.

Sartore, M., and G. Cunningham. 2009. "Gender, Sexual Prejudice and Sport Participation: Implications for Sexual Minorities." *Sex Roles* 60: 100–113.

Schneider, A. 2000. "On the Definition of Woman in the 'Sport' Context." In *In Philosophical Perspectives on Gender in Sport and Physical Activity*, edited by P. Davis and C. Weaving, 40–55. New York: Routledge.

Sharpe, T. 2003. "Adolescent Sexuality." *The Family Journal: Counseling and Therapy for Couples and Families* 11 (2): 210–215.

Staff Writer. 2014. "New to Hockey? A Quick Rundown of the Different Minor Hockey Levels." *Inside Edge*, October 13. http://insideedge.onemillionskates.com/inside-edge/new-to-hockey-a-quick-rundown-of-the-different-minor-hockey-levels/.

Theberge, N. 1995. "Playing with the Boys: Manon Rheaume, Women's Hockey and the Struggle for Legitimacy." *Canadian Woman Studies* 15 (4): 37–41.

Theberge, N. 1997. "It's Part of the Game: Physicality and the Production of Gender in Women's Hockey." *Gender and Society* 11 (1): 69–87.

Theberge, N. 2000. *Higher Goals: Women's Ice Hockey and the Politics of Gender*. New York: State University of New York Press.

Theberge, N. 2006. "The Gendering of Sports Injury: A Look at 'Progress' in Women's Sport through a Case Study of the Biomedical Discourse on the Injured Athletic Body." *Sport in Society* 9 (4): 634–648.

Vertinsky, P. 1990. *The Eternally Wounded Woman*. Chicago, IL: Manchester University Press.

Young, K., and P. White. 1995. "Sport, Physical Danger, and Injury: The Experiences of Elite Women Athletes." *Journal of Sport and Social Issues* 19: 45–61.

Friendships worth fighting for: bonds between women and men karate practitioners as sites for deconstructing gender inequality

Chloe Maclean

Sociology Department, University of Edinburgh, Edinburgh, Scotland

ABSTRACT

Sport is argued to be one of the few remaining domains for constructing masculine identity and reproducing ideas of men's (hierarchical) distinction from women. As a shared emotional (yet 'masculine') experience, sport lays the grounds for building close, intimate, friendships which, in men's single-sex sport, are suggested to be underpinned by sharing sexist ideology. This paper argues that sex-integrated karate practice not only challenges the expectations/ interpretations of women's bodies, but can also situate women and men within mutually respectful, cherished relationships which diverge from conventional sexualized and unequal ways of 'doing gender' in mixed-sex relationships.

Introduction

Sport is argued to be a key arena for constructing masculine identity and reproducing ideas of men's (hierarchical) distinction from women, and the ensuing subordination of women and femininity (Burstyn 1999; Connell 1990, 2012; Hargreaves 1994). It is also recognized and enjoyed as a field founded on generating, encouraging and amplifying emotions (Elias and Dunning 1986). As a shared physical and emotional (yet 'masculine') experience, participation in sport lays the grounds for building intimate friendships. Yet there remains little sociological investigation into friendships in sport: how they are crafted, who they are crafted between, how gender is constructed/performed within these sporting relations, their role in recreating or challenging ideas of women's subordination to men.

Ways of doing our relationships are embedded with ways of 'doing gender' (Jamieson 1997; West and Zimmerman 1987). Doing gender is a social, interactive, act, done relationally to the specific setting and people present, and embedded with ways of performing differences that re/create the distinct categories of man and woman (West and Zimmerman 1987). The perceived differences between what it is to 'be a man' and what it is to 'be a woman' not only entail distinct expectations of what women and men should *do* and how they should *present themselves* in social situations, but are also used to legitimize a gender hierarchy that subordinates women, and what women do (Connell 2009). As a woman doing gender thus entails doing/being subjected to subordination. The extent to which our relationships reflect traditional, hierarchically distinct, ways of doing gender vary – some relationships may strongly recreate notions of difference that subordinate women, whilst others might render certain notions of difference unviable, and in the process, begin to 'undo' gender (Deutsch 2007). As such, how we 'do' our relationships can impact the extent to which we recreate a gender hierarchy that subordinates women.

In comparison to family, work or couple relationships, friendships are argued to be freer in form, with greater emphasis on mutual negotiation of terms and interactions of the relationship (Budgeon 2006). Friendships are deemed to be freely chosen (or terminated), less bound by social norms, expectations and hierarchical power relations than our family or couple relationships (Allan 2005), and characterized by fun, trust, mutual respect and reciprocal 'work' or 'giving' to the relationship (Budgeon 2006). As a relationship privileging mutual negotiation over hierarchically structured (and gendered) expectations, friendships theoretically offer space where gendered scripts of interaction can be renegotiated (Jamieson 1997). Friendships between women and men particularly hold potential to challenge notions of hierarchical difference between women and men through challenging conventional (hierarchical) ways of doing gender in woman-man relationships. Yet despite friendship's more negotiable form, current literature points towards the tendency to befriend people similar to ourselves, with a strongly sex-segregated pattern that predominates most friendships (Belot 2009; Davies 2011; Jamieson 1997). If our friendships – the relationship of choice, equality and negotiation – are held predominantly with people of the same sex as us, then our ability to challenge hierarchically distinct notions embedded in ways of doing gender relationally with members of the opposite sex is limited.

Sport is an amplified arena for constructing ideas of gender difference: it plays a central role in attaching meanings of triumph, strength, weakness and fragility to the sexed body, thus aligning bodies more or less to masculinity or femininity (Connell 1990); It is predominantly practised sex-segregated, reiterating ideas that men and women require separated practice due to differences in ability/desires in sport (McDonagh and Pappano 2008); and is disproportionately dominated by men – from club practice to coaching/managerial roles to ownership/investment – constructing sport as a male domain and something *intrinsic* to masculine identity (Burstyn 1999), but not feminine identity. However, precisely because of sports association to masculinity, as growing numbers of women enter the field it is an arena oozing challenges to conventional ideas of women's bodies and the exclusivity of characteristics previous deemed masculine to men's bodies (e.g. see: Anderson 2008; Dworkin and Messner 2002; McNaughton 2012).

As the majority of sports are practised sex-segregated, the ability to generate cross-sex friendships in sport remains limited, and with this, opportunities to renegotiate ways of doing gender interactively with members of the opposite sex are also limited. In men's team sport, the sex-segregated set up is argued to not only take away the opportunity for men and women to generate sporting friendships, but actively places sharing sexist attitudes towards women at the foundations of building and performing friendships with male teammates (Anderson 2008; Curry 1991; Pratt 2000). If friendships are characterized by potential to mould more equal relationships, but remain relatively uncommon between men and women (Belot 2009; Davies 2011; Jamieson 1997), and friendships between men in sport are actively founded in sexism, then spaces where friendships between men and women in sport do develop, and *how* these develop, are of great value in pointing to mechanisms of bridging more equal relations between women and men, and challenging the societal subordination of women.[1]

Mixed-sex combat sports have been highlighted as key arenas challenging ideas of gender difference by placing women and men in direct bodily combat with one another where they must negotiate their interactions. In this space women and men reconceptualize ideas about women's bodies and bodily capabilities (McCaughey 1997; McNaughton 2012), and ability to fight *with men* (Channon and Jennings 2013; Guerandel and Mennesson 2007; Maclean 2015). As such, the ways in which men and women 'do' gender in mixed-sex martial arts diverge from conventional notions of gendered interactions, and as such, disrupt the expected gendered power dynamic embedded in men and women's interactions.

Karate is a sex-integrated combat sport utilizing kicks punches and throws, with intensified emotional excitement due to its close-spaced, fast-paced, sweaty body-to-body practice. Although men and women compete separately, and men do still dominate coaching and organizing roles, training is integrated, with an embedded philosophy of respect for ones level in the sport reflected by belt colour. Currently, there is debate about the implications of sex-segregated competition upon the value given to women in sport, and their (hierarchical) relations with men (Space does not allow for a thorough discussion of this to take place here, please see Maclean 2015; McDonagh and Pappano 2008; Guerandel and Mennesson 2007; Henry and Comeaux 1999), however, in karate's mixed sex training the embedded respect for higher level practitioners allows for women to be seen, accepted and respected as better than some men (Channon 2013; Maclean 2015). Within this arena men and women train together, spar together, hurt together, laugh together, contend directly with one-another for sporting capital (Maclean 2015), and in doing so, do indeed build close emotional friendships. This article seeks to add insight to the matrix of ways in which mixed-sex sports training can challenge ideas of gender by illuminating some key ways in which mixed-sex friendships are made in karate training, and how these in turn pull into question conventional ideas of hierarchically 'doing gender'.

Methodology

Data presented and discussed in this article are drawn from a six-month ethnographic emersion into three karate clubs (two in Scotland, one in the north of England), alongside 17 years of participation in the sport. The ethnographic study involved 'observant participation' (Wacquant 2004) of club training at least once per week at each club, alongside 15 photo-elicitation interviews (6 men, 9 women) spread evenly across the three clubs.

The photographs discussed in the individual photo-elicitation interviews were taken by the participants with the aim of reflecting their experiences of karate – what I had termed in the studies information leaflet 'photographing "the good, the bad, and the ugly" of karate'. These photographs were then discussed in one-to-one interviews allowing the participant and their photographs to lead the conversation (Wang 1999), and room for myself to intersperse discussion of the photos with questions to further illuminate how gender was (or was not) entwined with each photographed topic. Friendship emerged as a theme photographed and brought to discussion by almost all interview participants. Observant participation of the different clubs post-interviews allowed for exploration of how the ideas of friendships in karate discussed in the interviews were actively done in practice. Observations gathered in field notes previous to the interviews were reviewed and coded for friendship. The theme of friendship was then coded into smaller subsections.

Drawn from the map of data gathered on friendship, this article draws on three ways in which mixed-sex friendships are developed and 'done' through karate club training – through sharing an activity together; mutually offering guidance, tips and support to aid each other's development in karate; and sharing joking 'banter' – and suggests that such friendships hold potential to deconstruct conventional ideas of gender that subordinate, and objectify, women.

Sharing space, activity and passion together

In the dojo[2] a blend of people from different social classes, religions, ages and genders come together to learn, practise and improve their karate. All these people spar, sprint, sweat, hit, hurt, learn and laugh together within the same karate class. Within this mix of karate practitioners, many individuals are placed in a situation where they meet and physically interact with others they would not usually come into contact with. In this space, boundaries and hierarchies that usually divide people's social life by class, race and gender (Jamieson 1997), melt away (at least temporarily):

> Karate is great because it's something everybody can do, and when you go into the dojo everyone's the same. You might have a Doctor in there who you know is very high up – wealthy, highly educated. And then you might have someone else in there, in the same dojo, who's unemployed, or a tradesman, or a student. There are so many variations of people within the dojo on an equal level, I think it brings together people that otherwise wouldn't mix. (Josh)

The tendency to interact, socialize and befriend others who are similar to ourselves (Davies 2011) is stirred by bringing all sorts of people together where, inevitably, they will have to train with one-another at some point – be it in sparring, practicing technique examining each other's technique, or holding punch bags for one-another. Sharing the experience of doing karate together was seen by karateka[3] to bridge a privileged understanding of each other:

> 'They know everything about you because I think karate builds you so much as a person that unless someone knows you in that environment, then they don't really know you. And unless you're in it then I don't think you can really understand it.' (Rosie)

This privileged understanding was seen to build a unified karateka identity that overrode notions of differences between them:

> It's like the 'Casa Rosa' – the mafia. It means 'our thing' and with karate it's 'our thing' – we all understand each other because it's 'our thing'. So its like, my friends in karate are closer than my friends at work because it's 'our thing', we are training towards the same thing. You're trying to help each other that special bit more. (Keith)

Through sharing the exact same physical activity, the same passion, in the same dojo, in the same gender neutral outfit, within intimate interactive proximity, focus shifts from class, race or gender as central sites of homogeny that enable bonding, to that of being karateka. The shared unisex sports practice provides a counter framework to 'doing gender' (Guerandel and Mennesson 2007) allowing ideas of differences between women and men to take a secondary position to their similarities as karateka. It is this idea of sharing a karateka identity – of being 'cut from the same cloth' – that sets the foundations for cross-sex friendships to be built:

> I haveny got any female friends outside of karate, I think it's just something programmed into you: Your friends should be men. There's women I was at school with that I'd say hi to and speak to, but I wouldn't class them as friends. But in karate I do. Emma's a friend, Sally's a friend – the women you train with you get close to. You know, you socialize with these folk in class and you get the giggles and the laughs with them. (Keith)

Indeed, the unifying ground of sharing an activity, passion and understanding with members of the opposite sex creates an environment where mixed-sex friendships are viable, and embraced. As Rachel and Scott highlight, for those who have practised the sport since a young age the idea that there would be a social division between men and women in training seemed particularly obscure and undesirable:

> I think growing up doing karate with guys makes you more comfortable and confident around guys. You don't really think 'oh, I'm training with guys' – you just are. We have a good laugh, we train … I wouldn't have a second thought about it. It's normal for me. I'm comfortable with these guys. (Rachel)

> There's nothing at any point where I think 'oh I should stick with the lads'. Its more relaxed, we all chat as you would. I don't see any segregation. I can go up to a woman and just start chatting away, just as a friend – not thinking 'oh your good looking' – ken, nothing like that. It's just an 'Awright, what's the crack?' because at training that's what it is: everyone goes in and mixes – doesn't matter if you're a girl or a guy.' (Scott)

As notions of gender difference are dissolved in recognition of, and doing of, a shared karateka identity, a gendered segregation of friendship based on ideas of difference between women and men is challenged, and along with it, a primary understanding of men and women's relationship as a sexual relationship (Jamieson 1997). Sharing a karateka identity and understanding provides the base for friendships between women and men in karate to be generated.

Helping, supporting and learning: building practical intimacy

As a martial art, a large part of training involves close bodily work with others: to execute techniques, understand how the moves are effective, tweak the positioning of body parts in order to hit the opponent correctly, and in sparring, to playfully use the techniques learnt in creative, fluid, interaction with a sparring partner. The reciprocal intercorporeal helping, supporting, and learning from one-another to aid each other's development as a karateka forms a type of practical intimacy (Jamieson 1997)[4] which layers greater depth to the initial mixed-sex friendship-relations of similarity found in karate.

As women and men train together within the club, higher level karateka intermittently provide advice on technique, tips on movement and suggestions of training drills to lower or equal graded partners. Karate has a deeply embedded hierarchy of respect (Maclean 2015) which entails that such advice trickles from highest grade downwards. But equally lower grades can, and do, utilize other ways of offering help in the dojo such as: being a target for another; holding pads; sharing equipment; providing words of encouragement. These offerings of help not only aid the training partner's karate development *practically*, but also build a bond of being there *with another* through their emotional journey of a sport they both love:

> Some people will say to me 'try this or try that' and I say 'oh thanks, and you should try this or that' And we all try to help each other get better at what we love. It's just such a great thing that all these people go out of their way to help *you* – where else do you get that? (Sarah)

The more two karateka choose to mutually share these aspects of practical help with one another, the deeper feelings of closeness and affection are created. Karateka tend to pair most frequently with those of the same coloured belt as themselves, and as such, women and men frequently choose to pair with each other in karate due to being placed on the same skill level, where women and men can develop such feelings of closeness. Through interchanges of advice, help and inspiration developed *with* training partners, men and women come to learn each other's bodies and capabilities quite intimately, and in ways which challenge conventional ideas of women as passive, fragile and weak (Maclean 2015; McNaughton 2012), and of men as distinctly physically superior and emotionally silent. Women's potential as *good* training partners who can physically help, share and support the development of another's karate is drawn into light, appreciated and respected:

> I was training with Emma on Saturday and she just let rip on me, and it was brilliant – she can move so quick. So what I focused on was, not hitting hard, but trying to get out of the way quickly with a sweep. So she's coming in full pelt and I'm saying to her brilliant and having a wee shot at sweeping when she's coming in. That helps me because it pushes me, and hopefully the sweeping pushes her. (Alex)

Here women and men are placed on an equal footing as givers and receivers of help, support and advice. As equal training partners, and equal intimacy providers, a mutual respect for the training partner of the opposite sex is built, as well as an appreciation of the other's support. Part of this supportive role is reading, and being mindful of, the training partner's emotions in order to gauge *how* to train with them: to fight intensely with them when they are in good spirits; allowing them to score a couple of hits when they need to build confidence; to shout in words of support when they look like they are tiring or need encouragement; or to be prepared to fight hard when they need a break from whatever else is going on in the outside world. These supportive elements were highlighted by all karateka interviewed, but appeared to be particularly appreciated by women when the support was coming from men:

> When you're fighting someone you have to give your best, particularly if you're with someone that's good, they … push you, but not in a bad way – like they help you push yourself. And the guys, are like 'come on Alice! Come on Alice!' They always encourage you so much. There's not many places you're with guys together and you're all giving that level of support. (Alice)

Friendships between women and men in karate create a space where women and men can, and do, feel and express mutual levels of care. With such mutual levels of respect and care are often found missing in women's couple relations with men (Duncombe and Marsden 1993; Jamieson 1997), the meaningfulness of men's support of women is amplified. Women's appreciation of men's support reflects feelings of being embraced within caring, *respectful* and supportive relations with men, where women are treated equally to the men around them – as fellow karateka.

Together, the physically and emotionally intimate practice of karate challenges conventional ideas of gender difference and ways of doing gender. Through frequent and chosen interchanges of physical help, support and learning together, women and men karateka form friendships grounded in mutual respect for one another.

Inclusive banter

Alongside the elements of practical intimacy characteristic of doing mixed-sex friendships in karate clubs, banter amongst karateka is used to further solidify friendships between men and women in the sport. Joking 'banter' bounces backwards and forwards throughout karate classes, leavening the serious atmosphere of technique work and intense atmosphere of competitive sparring, encouraging an inclusive atmosphere. Such banter is characterized by light-hearted mocking of either self or others, often in regard to: lack of control of techniques; hitting or being hit hard; ability in comparison to a training partner.

Although the idea of mocking each other might sound at first to represent an emotionally closed off and competitive friendship, it is actually quite the opposite – individuals will usually share more banter with those that they feel particularly close to or comfortable with (Plester and Sayers 2007). Banter in karate works as a mechanism to forge lighthearted unifying bonds by (1) Sharing an *equal and privileged* position with everyone else in the club as someone *close enough* to be playfully mocked; (2) The desire to make others, especially those the banter is directed at, laugh; and (3) Carefully avoiding any sentiments that might actually be hurtful (although this line is sometimes walked very closely).

Banter is often seen to be something characteristic and fundamental to men's friendships with one another – a 'masculine form' of affection expressed through humour – and far less recognized as something embodied in women's friendships (Hay 2000). Due to its prominence in men's close friendships with men (Hay 2000), lack of recognition of women's ability to engage in banter places a barrier between women and men developing feelings of affinity and friendship. Yet in the karate hall, it is something women too are included in, and contribute to:

> There's a lot of banter at karate. I don't know if its just karate or just how I am, but I do have a lot of guy friends, and I like the banter there is with that. I don't know why but some girls (who don't do karate) are afraid to be friends with guys because of the banter they have, but I've never found that. (Alice)

Women's participation in the banter of the karate hall also shapes the type of banter produced, and in the process, temporarily displacing sexualized discussion *of* women as a form of banter and a way of bonding:

> When I done football it was always lads vs. lads, and it had that, like boyish banter. Ken, talking about girls sometimes, and just stupidness. In karate we still have funny chats, but at football lads would talk about lassies, which, obviously at karate wouldn't happen because lassies are there. But I wouldn't say it's completely different… In football we done sport, had a laugh, got on. In karate, even if its with girls, we talk and have a laugh, and we get to know people quite closely, and like nobody holds back with each other – its the same sort of banter and openness' (Scott).

In engaging in cross-sex banter together, women and men are placed on a level (and privileged) playing field to mock, make laugh and build friendships with. It is an area where women can be publicly funny, silly and make other's laugh, and in doing so challenge the perception of banter as an exclusively male behaviour (Hay 2000), whilst forging feelings of similarity and solidarity between women and men (Plester and Sayers 2007). Here, the nature of the banter shifts away from being based on sexist ideas of women. Rather, banter between men and women within the karate club karate often emerges from, or draws upon, the lived *contradictory* nature of gendered stereotypes:

Keith was fighting with Sarah – a woman feared as a fighter by most in the club due to her intense determination, merciless stamina, and thundering body round kick. I could see out the corner of my eye kick after punch darting at Keith, whilst he tried to find a space to hit Sarah. Coach Alan shouts in 'stop going easy on him Sarah' with a cheeky smile across his face. Sarah laughs and continues to work away whilst Keith jokes back 'Aye, I'm just *letting* her get all those kicks and punches in! Its not at all that I cant actually see her move because she's so fast!' Stuart joins in laughing at poor Keith, and Sarah shouts 'You're the next victim Stuart!' (Field notes)

We were both trying to knock off the other's timing, waiting for the right moment to catch the other out of step and pounce with a face punch. Unfortunately we both chose that moment at the exact same time, and as 6 ft 2″ Blair's arms are a good bit longer than mine, my movement forward was met with his punch. Luckily my nose broke the fall of his punch. Blair stopped for a moment, wide-eyed, unsure how to react, until I burst into fits of giggles. It was like something out of a slapstick comedy – a disaster waiting to happen. 'I am the champion!' Blair announces in his laughter. We stayed crunched over giggling, trying to build composure to continue fighting, until the coach shouted for us to change partners. I was, of course, completely fine physically – a bit of a stinging nose, yes, but I wasn't hurt. As we moved onto the next partner we tapped gloves and Blair said 'Where else could me, hitting a woman in the face, cause so much laughter?' (Field notes)

Both excerpts above challenge conventional ideas of women as: (1) fragile and weak (2) unsuitable for fighting (3) less skilled than men at fighting. The jokes and laughs which surround these events laugh at the contradictions of such gender stereotypes in relation to the women karateka in the excerpts, and act to reinforce an appreciation of the women as skilled fighters who can hit and *be* hit (Channon and Jennings 2013), and as friends close enough to 'take a laugh' and make other's laugh.

Conclusion

Mixed-sex friendships in karate training offer a unique site for exploring the subversion of gender norms, ideals and hierarchies. The sex-integrated practice of karate elevates the respect given to women by simultaneously disrupting both ideas of women's bodies as primarily sexual objects subordinate in ability to men (Maclean 2015), and of men and women as having, offering and wanting distinctly different qualities in their intimate relations. In focusing on *how* friendships between women and men are forged in mixed-sex karate practice, this article has suggested that sharing the experience of, and passion for, karate in club training, the gender homogeny characteristic of much sports practice, and many friendships (Belot 2009; Davies 2011; Jamieson 1997), is broken down, allowing for the development of mixed-sex friendships founded on mutual understanding of the other.

These mixed-sex relationships are turned into friendships through sharing a mutually respectful and respected practical intimacy, and a lighthearted inclusive banter. Such intimacy challenges the idea that men's friendships in sports are purely competitive, lack emotional disclosure and refrain from showing it (Anderson 2008; Curry 1991; Pratt 2000), notions of women as primary intimacy providers in relationships (Duncombe and Marsden 1993; Jamieson 1997), and also of men as exclusive 'expert knowers' in sport (Theberge 1993). Whilst the inclusive banter thrown between and amongst karateka equally addresses conventional ideas of women's friendships and men's friendships: the former by allowing women a space to be publicly funny, and the latter by (1) sharing laughs *with* women and (2) inadvertently laughing at, rather than laughing because of, sexism towards women. Here, mixed-friendships are built on mutually supportive grounds, with an embedded mutual respect for one-another as athletes and friends.

This is not to suggest that all ideas of gender difference and inequality are washed away in the practice of karate, that all men and women that do karate become best friends with members of the opposite sex, or that there are not gendered elements to the ways in which some of these friendships are made and performed. Indeed, women karateka do lean towards having other women as their strongest friends in the dojo, at times there are elements of men protecting their female karate friends, and of course not everyone who seeks to learn karate wants to make friends. Rather, the purpose of this research insight has been to point to the ways in which, despite sport being a male domain often used to subordinate women (Burstyn 1999; Connell 1990, 2012; Hargreaves 1994), and friendships predominantly being sex-segregated (Belot 2009; Davies 2011; Jamieson 1997), friendships between women and men in karate *are* forged, and to illuminate *how* these relationships can and do debunk notions of hierarchical gender distinction.

In karate club training women and men not only generate close, meaningful and enjoyable friendships, they create friendships which draw into question many conventional notions of (hierarchically) doing gender (West and Zimmerman 1987), and gendered ways of doing friendship. They choose to form relationships that disembark from expectations of (exclusively) sexual relations between men and women, that avoid jokes or talk that objectifies women, that laugh *at* such stereotypes of women, that appreciate women's expert advice and encourage men to be mutually supportive, that are grounded in mutual respect, and that are underlined by an understanding each other based on notions of similarity – of being karateka. Men and women's friendship in karate isn't bound by sexism (Curry 1991), but rather is a friendship that begins to unravel it.

Notes

1. This is not to argue that mixed-sex friendships, or mixed-sex sports practice, completely eradicate gender hierarchies, rather that they pose challenges to gender stereotypes, and under certain circumstances, challenge such hierarchies (for more on this debate see: Channon and Jennings 2013; Hay 2000; Henry and Comeaux 1999; Lynch 2010; Guerandel and Mennesson 2007).
2. Japanese Term for Karate Hall.
3. Term for karate practitioner.
4. The term 'practical intimacy' is not used to suggest that such intimacy involves no emotional elements. Rather it is used in comparison to 'disclosing intimacy' (Jamieson 1997) – that of reflexively talking about feelings, experiences and emotions with others.

Acknowledgements

I would like to thank Angus Bancroft and John MacInnes for their comments, suggestions, questions and moments of inspiration in helping me prepare this article. I would also like to thank the karate practitioners I have trained with, those I continue to train with and those who kindly gave up their time to tell me their karate stories – all have helped contribute to the ideas expressed in this article, so thank you kindly.

Disclosure statement

No potential conflict of interest was reported by the author.

Funding

This work was supported by the Economic Social Research Council.

References

Allan, Graham. 2005. "Boundaries of Friendship." In *Families in Society: Boundaries and Relationships*, edited by Linda McKie and Sarah Cunningham-Burley, 227–240. University of Bristol: Policy Press.

Anderson, Eric. 2008. "'I Used to Think Women Were Weak': Orthodox Masculinity, Gender Segregation, and Sport." *Sociological Forum* 23 (2): 257–280.

Belot, Michelle. 2009. "Gender Differences in Close Friendship Networks over the Life Cycle." In *Changing Relationships*, edited by M. Brynin and J. Ermisch, 44–58. London: Routledge.

Budgeon, Shelley. 2006. "Friendship and Formations of Sociality in Late Modernity: The Challenge of Post Traditional Intimacy." *Sociological Research Online*, 11 (3). http://www.socresonline.org.uk/11/3/budgeon.html.

Burstyn, Varda. 1999. *The Rites of Men: Manhood, Politics, and the Culture of Sport*. Toronto: University of Toronto Press.

Channon, Alex. 2013. "Enter the Discourse: Exploring the Discursive Roots of Inclusivity in Mixed-sex Martial Arts." *Sport in Society* 16 (10): 1293–1308.

Channon, Alex, and George Jennings. 2013. "The Rules of Engagement: Negotiating Painful and 'Intimate' Touch in Mixed-sex Martial Arts." *Sociology of Sport Journal* 30: 487–503.

Connell, Raewyn W. 1990. "An Iron Man: The Body and Some Contradictions of Hegemonic Masculinity." In *Sport, Men and the Gender Order: Critical Feminist Perspectives*, edited by Michael Messner and Donald Sabo, 83–96. Champaign, IL: Human Kinetics.

Connell, Raewyn W. 2009. *Gender*. Cambridge: Polity Press.

Connell, Raewyn W. 2012. "Supremacy and Subversion – Gender Struggles in Sport." *Asia-Pacific Journal of Health, Sport and Physical Education* 3 (3): 177–179.

Curry, Timothy J. 1991. "Fraternal Bonding in the Locker Room: A Profeminist Analysis of Talk about Competition and Women." *Sociology of Sport Journal* 8: 119–135.

Davies, Katherine. 2011. "Friendship and Personal Life." In *Sociology of Personal Life*, edited by Vanessa May, 72–84. Basingstoke: Palgrave Macmillan.

Deutsch, Francine M. 2007. "Undoing Gender." *Gender and Society* 21 (1): 106–127.

Duncombe, Jean, and Dennis Marsden. 1993. "Love and Intimacy: The Gender Division of Emotion and 'Emotion Work': A Neglected Aspect of Sociological Discussion of Heterosexual Relationships." *Sociology* 27 (2): 221–241.

Dworkin, Steven I., and Michael A. Messner. 2002. "Gender Relations in Sport." *Sociological Perspectives* 45 (4): 347–352.

Elias, Norbert, and Eric Dunning. 1986. *Quest for Excitement: Sport and Leisure in the Civilizing Process*. Oxford: Blackwell.

Guerandel, Carine, and Christine Mennesson. 2007. "Gender Construction in Judo Interactions." *International Review for the Sociology of Sport* 42 (2): 167–186.

Hargreaves, Jennifer. 1994. *Sporting Females: Critical Issues in the History and Sociology of Women's Sports*. London: Routledge.

Hay, Jennifer. 2000. "Functions of Humor in the Conversations of Men and Women." *Journal of Pragmatics* 32: 709–742.

Henry, Jacques M., and Howard P. Comeaux. 1999. "Gender Egalitarianism in Coed Sport: A Case Study of American Soccer." *International Review for the Sociology of Sport* 34 (3): 277–290.

Jamieson, Lynn. 1997. *Intimacy: Personal Relationships in Modern Societies*. Cambridge: Polity Press.

273

Lynch, Owen. 2010. "Cooking with Humor: In-group Humor as Social Organisation." *International Journal of Humor Research* 23 (2): 127–159.

Maclean, Chloe. 2015. "Beautifully Violent: The Gender Dynamic of Scottish Karate." In *Global Perspectives on Women in Combat Sports: Women Warriors around the World*, edited by Alex Channon and Christopher Matthews, 155–171. London: Routledge.

McCaughey, Martha. 1997. *Real Knockouts: The Physical Feminism of Women's Self-defence*. London: New York University Press.

McDonagh, Eileen, and Laura Pappano. 2008. *Playing with the Boys: Why Separate is Not Equal in Sports*. New York: Oxford University Press.

McNaughton, Melanie. 2012. "Insurrectionary Womanliness: Gender and the (Boxing) Ring." *The Qualitative Report* 17. *Article 33*: 1–13.

Plester, Barbara, and Janet Sayers. 2007. "'Taking the Piss': Functions of Banter in the IT Industry." *Humor* 20 (2): 157–187.

Pratt, Simon. 2000. "Teenage Kicks: A Study of the Construction and Development of Adolescent Masculine Identities in Organised Team Sport." In *Masculinities: Leisure Cultures, Identities and Consumption*, edited by John Horne and Scott Fleming, 23–38. Britain: Leisure Studies Association.

Theberge, Nancy. 1993. "The Construction of Gender in Sport: Women, Coaching and the Naturalisation of Gender Difference." *Social Problems* 40 (3): 201–313.

Wacquant, Louis. 2004. *Body and Soul: Notebooks of an Apprentice Boxer*. Oxford: Oxford University Press.

Wang, Caroline. 1999. "Photovoice: A Participatory Action Research Strategy Applied to Women's Health." *Journal of Women's Health* 8 (2): 185–192.

West, Candice, and Don Zimmerman. 1987. "Doing Gender." *Gender and Society* 1 (2): 125–151.

Index

Note: Boldface page numbers refer to figures and tables, n denote endnotes

'acceptable' feminine behaviour 255
'Age of the Gonads' 32
aggressiveness, femininity and 258–9
AIS *see* Androgen Insensitivity Syndrome
Albertville Winter Games (1992) 38
alpha femininities 64
Amsterdam Games (1928) 33
anatomical investigations 31–4
Androgen Insensitivity Syndrome (AIS) 35
anti-sexism 3
Asian Games (2006) 34, 39
athletic ability continuum 207
athletic identity 145–7
Atlanta Olympics (1996) 39

banter in karate works 270–1
Barr body test 35
Becker, Boris 116
BEF *see* British Equestrian Federation
benevolent sexism 108, 218
binary classification model 77, 191, 225
binary gender logic: concept of 206; feminist
    scholars' views on 207–8; in sex-integrated
    structure 209
Birrell, Susan 20
Black, Wayne 112, 113, 115, 117
British Empire & Commonwealth
    Games (1966) 34
British Equestrian Federation (BEF) 147, 148
buccal smear test 29, 35
Bullen, Jane 141

Canadian Hockey Association 23
Canadian hockey players 210
Carlson, Alison 37, 38
CDA *see* critical discourse analysis
Chand, Dutee 189
Chechen players 231

chromosomal testing: Androgen Insensitivity
    Syndrome 35; Barr body test 35; Patino, María
    José Martínez 36–7
Chuirazzi, Sara 108
coaching guides 109, 114
co-ed leagues, roller derby 242–3, 247–9
co-ed soccer project 83–8, 209
coercive segregation 5
Comley, Cassie 8
Conseil de l'Ordre des Médecins 38
continuum theory of sport: *Kick Like a Girl*
    analysis 208; oppositional gender binary
    208; overview of 206–7; research study
    of *see* women basketball team, research
    study on; sex-integrated structure and
    209–10; University of Connecticut
    basketball team 207
Cory, Matthew 112
Coubertin, Pierre de 32
crisis of masculinity 116–19
critical discourse analysis (CDA) 77–8
Cronbach's alpha 51
cultural imperialism 160, 170

Daubney, Martin 108
Derby, Roller 19
'DeSTrOY' (TWA forum) 112, 118
DiCarlo, Danielle 10
disclosing intimacy 272n4
disorders of sex development (DSD) 42n3
DNA replication study 38
'doing gender' 264–5
dojo, karate training 267
Dressage riding 143, 151–2
DSD *see* disorders of sex development

embodied masculinity 63
English, Jane 17, 18
Epstein, David 29
Equestrian Olympics (1956) 142
Erhardt, Anke 37

European Association of Single-Sex Education (2012) 46–7
Evert, Chris 116
exclusion politics 228–32

female hyperandrogenism 40–1
floorball, in Swedish school sport 7; boys' way of playing 98–100; exercise of power 100–1; gender as social institution 94; gender differences 96–7; marginalization effects 101; research participants 94–5; sex-integrated participation 97–8; Swedish Floorball Federation 92; tradition of masculinity 92; transcending gender hierarchies 7, 101–2
Foucauldian analysis of power 61–2, 64–5
Foucault, M. 64

gay men, lesbians, bisexuals, intersexuals and transsexuals (GLBITs) 190, 191, 199
gender as 'social institution' 94
gender competence 78
gender debate 61, 63
gender equality, sporting inclusion 5
gender identity 257–8
'gender injustice' in sport 4
gender-mixing rule 229–31, 234
gender stacking 113
gender stereotypes 214–18
gender testing see sex determination
GLBITs see gay men, lesbians, bisexuals, intersexuals and transsexuals
Government's Plenipotentiary for Equal Treatment 223
Grenoble Winter Olympics (1968) 36
Griner, Brittney 17

Harry Potter series (Rowling) 190, 193–5, 202n1, 203n1, 203n2
Hartel, Lis 141–2
Hay, Eduardo 36
hegemonic masculinity 63, 78, 107, 126
hercampus.com 108
heteronormativity: in ice hockey culture 259–60; in physical education 47–9, 56
heterosexist behaviour 50, 51, **52–4**, 55
hetero-sociality 3
Hockey Hall of Fame, induction ceremony 253
homohysteria 47, 56
homophobic behaviour 46–57
homosexuality 47–9, **54**, 55–6
homosexually-themed language 6, 49, 56–7
homosociality 227
Hopman Cup 120n1
hybrid masculinity 8, 107
hyperandrogenism 39–41, 189
hyperfemininity 48

ice hockey teams 10; conceptualization of female athletes as "weak" 257–8; female athletes' lived experiences 256–7; femininity and aggressiveness 258–9; heteronormative sexuality 259–60; REP hockey 261n3; sex integration in 255–6; 'tomboys' category 258, 260
inclusive behaviour 50
Inclusive Cheerleading Association 128
Independent Women's Forum 108
International Amateur Athletic Federation (IAAF): anatomical investigation 34; chromosomal testing 35–7; female hyperandrogenism, regulations on 40–1; 'health check' 37; Ljungqvist, Arne 34; privacy concerns 42n3; sex testing 34; Workshop on Approved Methods of Femininity 37
International Olympic Committee (IOC): anatomical investigation 32–3; chromosomal testing 36; Coubertin's view on womanhood 32; female hyperandrogenism, regulations on 40–1; Medical Commission 36, 37; notion of sex-segregation 32; polymerase chain reaction testing 38–9; privacy concerns 42n3; Stockholm Consensus 196–7
International Quidditch Association (IQA) 196
International Surfing Competitions 181
IOC see International Olympic Committee
IQA see International Quidditch Association
Isom, Mo 16, 17
Italian Football Federation 161

Johnston, Delia 197

Kane, Mary Jo 19
Kane's continuum theory see continuum theory of sport
karate club training: banter in 270–1; building practical intimacy 268–9, 272n4; dojo 267; Maclean's study of 3; mixed-sex friendships 265, 269, 271–2, 272n1; notion of 'doing gender' 264–5; photo-elicitation interviews 266; shared karateka identity 267–8
Kick Like a Girl, MacKenzie's documentary film 208
King, Rich 240
Kinue, Hitomi 33
knowledge system, critical discourse analysis 77
Kłobukowska, Ewa 35–6
korfball, sporting equality and gender neutrality: being vocal 63; concept of 'playing together' 62–3; definition of 62; development of 62; ethnographic fieldwork 65–6; Foucauldian analysis 61–2, 64–5; masculinity and femininity 68–70; participation issues 63–5; physical difference 70–2; rules of 71; skorts and shorts 67–8; 'whole package' of 65
Kornberg, Arthur 38

Lake, Rob 7
Larneby, Marie 7
Legends Football League, women's engagement in 241
lesbian sexuality 64
Ljungqvist, Arne 34, 37
London Games (2012) 40
'lose-lose' situation 4

Maclean, Chloe 10
MACS see martial arts and combat sports
male chivalry 108, 117
male dominance/superiority 4–5, 94
male homosexuality 56
Mangold, Holley 17
marginalization, surfing sport 179, 185–6
martial arts and combat sports (MACS) 79
Matthews, Norma 141
McDonagh, Eileen 17–18
MDT etiquette see mixed-doubles tennis etiquette
Meyers, Ann 16
microcultures, definition of 193
Migrants' Inclusion Model of Sport for All (MIMoSA) 161–2
misguided feminism 108
mixed-doubles tennis (MDT) etiquette: coaching guides 109, 114; crisis of masculinity 116–19; forums and blogs analysis 109–11; fun and sociable diversion 110–12; masculinity and femininity 107–8; mixed-sex participation, notion of 105–6; negotiation of court positioning 112–14; overview of 104–5; paternalistic chivalry 108; persistence of gender inequalities 119–20; shot selection and behavioural restraint 114–16
mixed-sex cheerleading 3, 8; feminist and queer frameworks 124; gender status of sport 126–7; hegemonic masculinity 126; implications 136–7; interview data 128–9; multiple discourses of 127–8; participant portraits 129–34; potential and pitfalls 134–6; sports elements 124–5; teamwork and complementary skills 125
mixed-sex friendships 265, 269, 271–2, 272n1
mixed sport, potential of 241
mocking, cross-sex friendships 270
modality, levels of 81–2
modern sport and gender 1
mosaicism, chromosomal 35
MRDA Non-Discrimination Policy 245
muggle quidditch: gender empowerment 200; gender stereotypes 198; International Olympic Committee 196–7; poststructuralism 200–1; testimonies 199; two-minimum rule 196

muscle gap literature 208
muscular Christianity 62
myth of female frailty 254

Nagano Winter Olympics (1998) 39
National Collegiate Athletic Administration (NCAA): Committee on Women's Athletics 210, 211, 219; transgender participation 197
National Organization for Women (NOW) 20
naturalization of women, being 'less able' 254
natural superiority of men 30
Non-Discrimination Policy 245
normative conceptions of sex difference: anti-discriminatory goals 222; assumptions 226–8; attitude change 232–4; exclusion politics 228–32; gender norms and expectations 224; methodology 225; opposing values 224; sociocultural system 224; Women in Geography Study Group 223

Old Boys Club 184–5
Olympic and Paralympic equestrian sport: athletic identity 145–7; Dressage competition 151–2; ethnographic approach 147, 150, 151; gay experiences with 3; gendered discourse in 141–2; history of 140; 'horsey' 150, 151, 153; interview experience 148, **149**; participatory parity in 142–5, **143**; sport-specific identities 148; women's participation in 2
one-sex model 31
Ontario Women's Hockey Association (OWHA) 23, 261n4
oppositional gender binary 208
orthodox masculinity 93, 107
OWHA see Ontario Women's Hockey Association

Pappano, Laura 17–18
Para-Equestrian Dressage 140–1, **149**, 152
Parks Pieper, Lindsay 6
paternalistic chivalry 108
Patino, María José Martínez 36–7, 40
PCR testing see polymerase chain reaction testing
PE see physical education
Pease, Kevin 111, 113, 115
photo-elicitation interviews 266
physical activity project 80, 81, 84–6, 88
physical education (PE) 6–7, 46
Piedra, Joaqium 6
play and competition, conceptualization of 99
polymerase chain reaction (PCR) testing 38–9
post-Title IX sports 192
practical intimacy 268–9, 272n4

quidditch 9, 209–10; description of 193–6; gender regimes 190–2; hyperandrogenism 189; muggle *see* muggle quidditch; theoretical and methodological considerations 192–3

RDA *see* Roller Derby Australia
Reczek, Wlodzimierz 36
refugee players, in women-only team: cultural and religious factors 165; in outdoor physical activity 164; pilot activities 163; training session 163; volunteers *vs.* 163
Reis, Elizabeth 32
REP hockey 261n3
resilient paternalism 4–5
roller derby: 'by the skaters–for the skaters' 242; 'derby saved my life' 240; Donnelly's analysis 242; as 'feminist' sport 240, 242; men's role in 239–40; mixed/'co-ed' leagues 242–3, 247–9; MRDA's Non-Discrimination Policy 245; revived flat track version 240; Rollergirl Project, The 240; trans and non-gender in 242, 245; virtual ethnography 244; WFTDA gender policies 244–7, 250; women's passion for 239, 242
Roller Derby Australia (RDA) 246
Roman touch rugby team *see* touch rugby team, Rome
Rowling, J. K. 9, 190, 193–5, 202n1

Sailors, Pamela 6
Schaeffer, Sabrina 108
Schneider, Angela 18
School of Tennis (SOT) blog 111
Segrave, Jeffrey 9
Semenya, Caster 40
sex determination: anatomical investigation and 32–4; chromosomal testing 35–7; Dreger's analysis 'Age of the Gonads' 32; female hyperandrogenism 40–1; one-sex model 31; polymerase chain reaction testing 38–9; two-sex model 31; Women in Geography Study Group gender policies 244–5
Sex Equality in Sports (English) 17
'sex/gender' ideology 42n1
sex-segregation: coercive and voluntary 5; creation of 30–1; culture of 2, 3, 32; elusiveness of 28–42; Olympic Games 32; in women competition against men 19–20, 23, 24
sexual orientation 51–2, **54**
shared karateka identity 267–8
social construction of sex 1, 254–5
social practices, critical discourse analysis 77–8
Spanish PE teachers' perceptions, homophobia and heterosexism: contact procedure 49; English translation technique 51; gays and lesbians 48, 56; gender-related analysis **53**;

heteronormativity in 47–9, 56; mixed-sex schools and 48; overview of 46–7; questionnaire, use of 50; relative frequencies about 51, **51**; sexual orientation 51–2, **54**; and student awareness 57; teachers' role 55
sport as continuum *see* continuum theory of sport
sport as 'male preserve' 1
sport ethic 114
sport-for-development program 158–9
sport-media-commercial complex 192
sport sociology 243
St Cyr, Henri 142
Stephens, Helen 33
Steve G Tennis (SGT) forum 117
Stockholm Consensus 191, 196–7
Subjection of Women, The (Mill) 241
surfing sport: definition of 180; exclusionary and marginalizing practices 181; marginalized status 179, 185–6; Old Boys Club 184–5; physical cultures and activities 180–1; in Polynesian Islands 179; subcultural barriers 182, 183
Swedish mixed-sex floorball group 92–103
Swedish Research Council, ethical guidelines of 82
Swedish Sports Confederation 76, 77
Swedish sports initiatives, in gender discourse: co-educational experiences 86–8; conception, reproduction and questioning of 84–6; fieldwork 80–1; leisure-time sports, children's experiences with 83–4; modality levels 81–2; overview 76–7; theoretical framework 77–80

Talk Tennis at Tennis Warehouse (TTTW) forum 112, 115, 116
The Tennis Space (TTS) blog 115
Tennis Western Australia (TWA) forum 110
Theberge, Nancy 23–4
third-wave feminism 105, 107
'tomboys' concept 258, 260
touch rugby team, Rome: competences 168; context and methods 160–2; male participants 166, 169; mixed-sex combat sports 166–9; overview of 157–8; principles and values 170, 171; range of sports 168; refugee players *see* refugee players, in women-only team; social-mixing potential of 171; sport-for-development programmes 158–60; sporting and social networks 169; sporting reputation 172; symbolic relevance 170; unintentional cultural imperialism 170
traditional gender stereotypes 214–18
transcending gender hierarchies 101–2
Trason, Ann 18
two-sex model 31

United States Professional Tennis Association Thoughts on Tennis (USPTATOT) blog 112
University of Connecticut basketball team 207

Vittoria, Maria 42n2
voluntary segregation 5

'weaker opponents' 120
Wellington, Chrissie 18
WFTDA *see* Women's Flat Track Derby Association
WGSG *see* Women in Geography Study Group
wider inclusivity, sex-integrated sport 3
Willis, Paul 207
windsurfing subcultures 181
womanhood, Coubertin's view on 32; *see also* sex determination
women basketball team, research study on 219n1; acknowledgement of sport continuum 212–14; analysis of transcripts 212; gender stereotypes, reinforcement of 214–18; interview process 211–12; recruitment of participants 211; use of male practice players 210, 218
women competition against men: amateur *vs.* professional/elite sport 22; 'attempt anyway' 17–18; contact *vs.* non-contact sports 21–2; difficulties 24–5; direct *vs.* indirect competition 21–3; excitement and athleticism 217; individual *vs.* team sports 21; mixed competition 18–19, 22–4; physical traits 16–17; sex segregation 19–20, 23, 24; uniqueness in 216
Women in Geography Study Group (WGSG) 223
Women's Flat Track Derby Association (WFTDA): gender policies and trends 244–7, 250; Real, Strong, Athletic, Revolutionary 242
Workshop on Approved Methods of Femininity 37
World University Games (1985) 36

Zirin, Dave 19